taste of home
comfort
FOOD diet
COOKBOOK

CHICKEN FETTUCCINE ALFREDO, PAGE 233

taste of home
comfort FOOD *diet*
COOKBOOK

It's here! A weight-loss plan from the people who know comfort food best! The editors of Taste of Home, the world's No. 1 cooking magazine, gathered 416 mouthwatering dishes and combined them with a sensible approach to healthy living. Now you can drop pounds, lose inches and feel your best…while enjoying your all-time family favorites.

154   285

A TASTE OF HOME/READER'S DIGEST BOOK

© 2010 Reiman Media Group, Inc.
5400 S. 60th St., Greendale WI 53129
All rights reserved.

Taste of Home and Reader's Digest are registered trademarks of The Reader's Digest Association, Inc.

Editor in Chief: Catherine Cassidy
Vice President, Executive Editor/Books: Heidi Reuter Lloyd
Creative Director: Howard Greenberg
North American Chief Marketing Officer: Lisa Karpinski
Food Director: Diane Werner RD
Food Editor: Peggy Woodward RD
Senior Editor/Books: Mark Hagen
Art Director: Rudy Krochalk
Content Production Supervisor: Julie Wagner
Layout Designer: Emma Acevedo
Proofreaders: Linne Bruskewitz, Victoria Soukup Jensen
Recipe Asset System Manager: Coleen Martin
Premedia Supervisor: Scott Berger
Recipe Testing & Editing: Taste of Home Test Kitchen
Food Photography: Taste of Home Photo Studio
Administrative Assistant: Barb Czysz
Project Assistant Editor: Danielle Calkins

THE READER'S DIGEST ASSOCIATION, INC.
President and Chief Executive Officer: Mary G. Berner
President, North American Affinities: Suzanne M. Grimes
President/Publisher Trade Publishing: Harold Clarke
Associate Publisher: Rosanne McManus
Vice President, Sales and Marketing: Stacey Ashton

For more Reader's Digest products and information, visit rd.com (in the United States) or see rd.ca (in Canada).

International Standard Book Number (10): 0-89821-863-2
International Standard Book Number (13): 978-0-89821-863-3
Library of Congress Control Number: 2010932464

COVER PHOTOGRAPHY
Photographer: Jim Wieland
Food Stylist: Diane Armstrong
Set Stylist: Stephanie Marchese

Pictured on front cover: Favorite Skillet Lasagna (p. 172).

Pictured on back cover from left to right: Grilled Pork Chops with Cilantro Salsa (p. 167), Chocolate Peanut Butter Parfaits (p. 282) and Bistro Turkey Sandwiches (p. 136).

Printed in China
1 3 5 7 9 10 8 6 4 2

163

269

108

203

table of contents

WELCOME to the Comfort Food Diet

What happens when you pair a weight-loss strategy with all of the hearty foods you crave? You get the Taste of Home Comfort Food Diet!

Based on the overwhelming success of our delicious diet plan, the Taste of Home editors couldn't wait to bring you this exciting new title—*Comfort Food Diet Cookbook: Family Classics Collection.*

If you're not familiar with the popular plan, let me fill you in. The Comfort Food Diet is a sensible approach to weight-loss that's easy, affordable and, most important, scrumptious. The plan is simple; eat three complete meals a day and two snacks for a total of 1,400 calories. Watch your portion sizes and go for regular walks, and the pounds will melt away.

The plan offers hundreds of lightened-up recipes for your all-time favorite foods. You'll never feel as though you're sacrificing when cheesy casseroles, juicy burgers and rich chocolate fudge are on the menu. We cut the calories from classic dishes, tested every recipe, calculated all of the Nutrition Facts and ran everything past a registered dietitian for approval. All you need to do is enjoy the satisfying meals, snacks and desserts that this book offers.

With *Comfort Food Diet Cookbook,* the key to healthy living—for you and your family—is at your fingertips! Ready to get started? The new you is just around the corner!

Diane Werner

—Diane Werner, RD
　Food Director, Taste of Home

more on the WEB

FAMILY CLASSICS
without the guilt!

It's hard to believe the words "comfort food" and "diet" actual work together. With *Taste of Home Comfort Food Diet Cookbook*, however, that's truly the case! It offers a healthy way to slim down without giving up the foods you adore.

Being a working mom, I'm so happy this new edition focuses on foods that are perfect for the whole family. Dishes such as Easy Chicken Alfredo (p. 192), Slow-Cooked Mac 'n' Cheese (p. 203), Favorite Skillet Lasagna (p. 172) and Weeknight Chicken Potpie (p. 213) not only satisfy, they fit into busy schedules, too.

Home cooks looking to eat healthy no longer have to rely on tasteless frozen dinners or prepare one meal for their family and a light dish for themselves. Now everyone at the table can enjoy luscious, stick-to-your-ribs foods…and cut calories at the same time.

Losing weight has never been easier…or tastier. Page through *Comfort Food Diet Cookbook: Family Classics Collection* and you'll find:

- *416 incredible recipes that pare down calories and fat.*

- *A 6-week meal guide that takes menu planning off your shoulders.*

- *Nutrition Facts with every recipe.*

In addition, we added a "Classic" icon **classic** to recipes that stood the test of time with families from coast to coast. You'll find it alongside items such as pot roast, lasagna, meat loaf, tuna casserole and dozens of other all-time favorites.

I hope you enjoy this new edition of *Comfort Food Diet Cookbook*, and I just know you and your entire family will discover how delicious losing weight can be!

Peggy Woodward

— Peggy Woodward, RD
   Food Editor, Taste of Home

FAVORITE SKILLET LASAGNA, PAGE 172

making it work
FOR YOU!

A No-Fuss Plan with Impressive Results

258 CALORIES
PAGE 107

212 CALORIES
PAGE 186

Whether you're looking to lose weight, control diabetes or feel and look your best, the Comfort Food Diet can help. The easy-to-follow plan pairs a commonsense approach to healthy eating with the tools you need to succeed. In addition, a series of success stories, tips from readers and access to the *Comfort Food Diet Cookbook* online community provide friendly motivation and support.

This is the food we love. My husband didn't even realize he was eating healthier! …Pamela Moffett, Johnson City, Tennessee

Each of the 416 recipes found here includes a complete set of Nutrition Facts, and many of the recipes include Diabetic Exchanges when applicable. But don't let those numbers fool you. We're sure that no matter how light the recipes are, your family will be too busy enjoying the delicious meals you serve to ever realize that they are eating healthy.

I lost 24 pounds on the diet! The plan allows anyone to lose weight while enjoying the foods they love.

…Vergel Voth, Stillman Valley, Illinois

That's because the recipes in the *Comfort Food Diet Cookbook* offer all of the hearty, satisfying goodness you'd expect from a classic home-cooked meal.

The recipes are already a hit with families because they were shared by cooks who submitted their favorite dishes to *Taste of Home* magazine or one of its sister publications. And now they're sharing those recipes with you!

The recipes are for the things my family craves, so I don't have to cook separate meals. The online forum offers great support. …Elza Reeves, Louisville, Kentucky

Each recipe in this book was evaluated by a registered dietitian and passed a review in the Taste of Home Test Kitchen. Every recipe is not only healthy and delicious, but you can be assured that each dish will turn out perfectly every time you make it.

In addition, the recipes come together easily with common, everyday ingredients you likely have on hand. No need to run to expensive specialty stores for items you'll use only once or twice. You'll also find no-fuss menu suggestions (with calorie counts) throughout the chapters to help you round out meals.

The diet focuses on down-home cooking with ingredients I have on hand. You can trust the recipes are going to be great because each is from Taste of Home. …Lori Herr, Springfield, Missouri

There are tips on exercise, hints for making the most out of grocery shopping and secrets to lightening up your own recipes. So what are you waiting for? Turn the page and get ready to discover how delicious eating right can be.

316 CALORIES
PAGE 218

143 CALORIES
PAGE 128

222 CALORIES
PAGE 290

IT'S TRUE! You can indulge in all of the family-favorite foods you love and still lose weight!

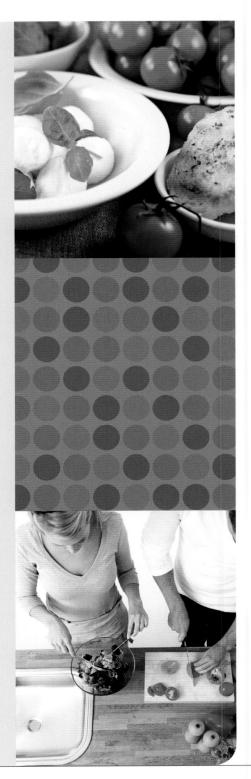

Many of today's weight-loss plans focus on the participant alone. This means that family cooks end up preparing multiple meals...traditional menus for their loved ones and low-calorie dishes for themselves. With the Taste of Home Comfort Food Diet, however, the whole gang can enjoy the flavor of classic foods while gaining the benefits of eating right!

The basics behind the Comfort Food Diet are easy—count your calories, watch your portion sizes and burn off more calories than you consume. But it's the family approach to preparing healthy meals and snacks that makes this plan different than most. Take a look through this book, and you'll see how easy the diet plan is, discover how to lighten up your own recipes and learn how others lost weight and made deliciously healthy foods a daily part of their family's lives.

COMFORT FOOD DIET BASICS—
so easy, anyone can do it!

It's a snap to get your entire family to eat healthy without depriving them of their most-loved foods. In fact, they likely won't realize they're eating healthy at all! You can follow the diet, and all they have to do is sit back and enjoy the incredible foods this book offers. Best of all, you'll slim down by simply following the three simple steps outlined here.

1 Eat three meals a day and two snacks for a total of 1,400 calories.

If you're a woman, shoot for a total calorie consumption of 1,400 calories per day. Men should consume 1,500 calories per day. Check with your doctor before you begin this plan to see if this calorie guideline is appropriate for you. Then, consider the Six-Week Meal Plan on pages 44-65. There you'll find detailed menus that total roughly 1,400 calories per day.

Use the following guide to distribute calories through the day:

- 350 calories for breakfast
- 450 calories for lunch
- 500 calories for dinner
- Two 50-calorie or two 100-calorie snacks, depending on the total calories you're shooting for per day. You can consume more or less calories in a snack or meal than what is suggested here, as long as your daily total is 1,400 or 1,500 calories.

2 Start a food diary, keeping track of everything you eat. See pages 294-295 for blank Do-It-Yourself Meal-Planning Worksheets.

Keeping a food diary is a key to success on the Comfort Food Diet. By jotting down everything you eat, you can easily identify eating habits you weren't previously aware of. You're also less likely to cheat if you know you'll have to write down that milk shake you had at lunch or that extra piece of cake you snuck in after dinner.

Use your food journal or the Meal-Planning Worksheets to help you plan menus in advance as well. Browse through this cookbook and decide which of the hearty dishes you plan to make. Map out menus and snacks for an entire day in advance, then go back and record what you actually ate.

Always remember to watch portion sizes, and review the Nutrition Facts at the end of each recipe to learn what a serving size is. If you increase the serving size, the amount of calories (and nutrients) will obviously increase as well.

It's also important to understand that you can mix and match foods however you'd like as long as you stay within the 1,400 or 1,500 daily calorie limit.

For instance, let's say you enjoy a California Pizza (p. 126) for lunch. Note that the recipe makes two individual pizzas, but the serving size and Nutrition Facts are based on one pizza. As such, you can enjoy one pizza and serve the other to a family member or refrigerate it for tomorrow's lunch.

The guideline for lunch is 450 calories, and one California Pizza weighs in at 245 calories. This means you can also enjoy a cup of Watermelon Cooler (82 calories) found on page 69 in addition to a medium kiwifruit (46 calories) for a lunch that totals only 373 calories. You can pat yourself on the back for saving 77 calories or you can spend those calories later in the day. It's up to you—as long as your daily caloric intake meets the 1,400 or 1,500 goal.

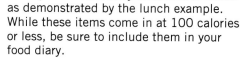

3

See the Smart Snacks List (p. 67), the Free Foods Chart (p. 43) and the calorie breakdowns before each chapter when pairing foods with entrees.

The lunch example covered in Step 2 noted that a medium kiwifruit was 46 calories. How would you know that? Simply turn to page 67 for the Smart Snacks list. There you'll find 45 ideas for low-calorie bites that don't require a recipe. These items are great for snacking, but they also make tasty additions to meals as demonstrated by the lunch example. While these items come in at 100 calories or less, be sure to include them in your food diary.

Similarly, the Free Foods Chart offers dozens of items that you can enjoy without guilt. In fact, these foods are so light, there's no need to worry about their calorie content as long as you follow any portion restrictions they might offer.

The chapters in the Comfort Food Diet Cookbook are broken down into Snacks, Breakfasts, Lunches, Dinners, Side Dishes and Desserts. Every chapter begins with lower-calorie staples and ends with higher-calorie specialties.

If you ate a lunch below the 450 calorie guideline, you may want to consider a higher-calorie dinner. If you enjoyed a high-calorie breakfast and morning snack, you may want to stick with a lunch that's a bit lighter.

Many of the chapters overlap a little, making meal planning easy! For example, some of the higher-calorie lunches make wonderful low-calorie dinners. You could also see the calorie breakdown at the beginning of the side dish chapter, and use one of those recipes for a meat-free lunch or substantial snack.

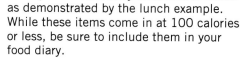
the basics | THE COMFORT FOOD DIET

THE COMFORT FOOD DIET **11**

My Comfort Food Diet
SUCCESS!

Thanks to the *Comfort Food Diet Cookbook*, I'm healthier, happier…and 30 pounds lighter! It worked for me!

By Beth Schuetz-Wilson

before

Like most women, I always put my family's needs ahead of my own…and like most women, I truly don't mind doing so. But it wasn't until I noticed a few extra pounds creeping up on me that I realized I needed to make a change.

Looking back, I was a petite, active child who didn't worry about weight. In fact, weight was never an issue–even in my 20s and 30s. But after having my daughter, Jordyn, I couldn't lose those extra pounds caused by pregnancy.

In addition to Jordyn, who is a special-needs child, my family also consists of my husband, Don, and three stepchildren ranging in age from 14 to 19. I was busy with my family and career, and I wasn't focused on taking care of myself.

To top it off, Don is a great cook, and I hadn't watched my portion sizes for years. I'm 5'4 and weighed 185 pounds. I was getting frustrated buying clothes in sizes ranging from 14/16 to 18/20. In addition, I was being treated for

high blood pressure. This made me worry about something happening to me. Who would be here for my family?

This all changed when I received the first edition of *Taste of Home Comfort Food Diet Cookbook*. That's when I realized I could make a few adjustments to my lifestyle and still easily care for my family.

I read the simple diet plan, followed the tips, started drinking more water and paid attention to portion sizes. Best of all, I began preparing family meals from the book. In fact, I started to plan meals more than ever before, making hearty entrees three to four times a week. I then packed up the leftovers for lunch at the office.

Since I don't eat lunch until 1 p.m. and don't get home

after

until almost 7 at night, tasty yet effortless snacks became a lifesaver. Light string cheese, rice cakes and fruit got me through the day without being tempted by vending machines or overindulging in snacks shared by coworkers. In addition, I found that eating a healthy breakfast before leaving for work really helped curb cravings throughout the day…and *Taste of Home Comfort Food Diet Cookbook* has so many delicious breakfast options to choose from!

As I prepared items from the cookbook, I became much more careful about what I bought at the grocery store, too. I learned about cooking with

healthy ingredients such as lean ground beef, whole grain pasta and brown rice. Being selective and checking nutrition labels makes grocery shopping take a little more time, but it's worth it.

Tracking how many calories I consumed each day really helped me stick to the Comfort Food Diet plan. Each day I wrote down the calories of everything I ate. Not only did this help me stay on track, but it was easier to resist a high-calorie treat because I didn't want to have to add that item to my daily journal.

I knew that to be successful, I needed to get moving, so I began walking 20 to 30 minutes at lunchtime every day. Once I got into a walking groove, I started to add other exercises to my routine at home twice a week. Taking the stairs at work as often as possible was also a calorie-burning boost. My office is on the third floor, so I had ample opportunities to skip the elevator and hit the stairs.

My biggest challenge was getting through holidays and attending gatherings without overeating. It was also hard to motivate myself in the winter to step outside for a walk. The trick was to not let a little setback get me down or make me fall back to my old ways.

To date I've lost 30 pounds, going from 185 pounds down to 155.

I've even been able to reduce the amount of blood pressure medication I take. I have more energy and feel healthier. I buy tops and pants in size 10/12, and I love shopping for clothes now!

Sometimes it's still hard to keep the focus on me and the new healthy elements of my lifestyle, but I try to keep a positive attitude. That helps me stay on track. I'm going to continue to make healthy food choices, work in a little bit more exercise and keep preparing family meals from the *Comfort Food Diet Cookbook*.

With this book, there's no need to miss out on any of my family-favorite foods. I can still enjoy them while losing weight. It worked for me!

Classic Casserole

chicken stuffing bake `classic`

There are several dishes my gang enjoys from the first edition of the *Comfort Food Diet Cookbook*, but this casserole is one I come back to time and again. Chicken Stuffing Bake was shared by Jena Coffey of Sunset Hills, Missouri, and it weighs in at just 247 calories per serving. Best of all, it comes together easily with ingredients I usually have on hand!

- 1 can (10-3/4 ounces) condensed reduced-fat reduced-sodium cream of mushroom soup, undiluted
- 1 cup fat-free milk
- 1 package (6 ounces) stuffing mix
- 2 cups cubed cooked chicken breast
- 2 cups fresh broccoli florets, cooked
- 2 celery ribs, finely chopped
- 1-1/2 cups (6 ounces) shredded reduced-fat Swiss cheese, divided

---

- In a large bowl, combine soup and milk until blended. Add the stuffing mix with contents of seasoning packet, chicken, broccoli, celery and 1 cup cheese. Transfer to a greased 13-in. x 9-in. baking dish.

- Bake, uncovered, at 375° for 20 minutes or until heated through. Sprinkle with remaining cheese; bake 5 minutes longer or until cheese is melted.

YIELD: 8 servings.

NUTRITION FACTS: 1 cup equals 247 calories, 7 g fat (4 g saturated fat), 42 mg cholesterol, 658 mg sodium, 24 g carbohydrate, 3 g fiber, 22 g protein. **DIABETIC EXCHANGES:** 2 lean meat, 1-1/2 starch.

BRING BALANCE
& variety to your diet

Watching calories is key to losing weight, but it's just as important (and easy) to hit nutrition goals with a balanced diet.

FIBER

Most Americans eat much less fiber than they should. Shoot for 20 to 30 grams of fiber each day, whether that fiber is soluble or insoluble. Insoluble fiber can be found in whole wheat and brown rice, while soluble fiber is a part of oatmeal, beans and barley. Soluble fiber helps to lower cholesterol and insoluble fiber keeps your digestive tract healthy. The best part—fiber helps keep you feeling full, which can help prevent you from overeating.

tips to help boost your fiber

- Making a soup? Add extra veggies.

- Add wheat germ or oat bran to yogurt and casseroles. You won't notice the difference.

- When eating fruits and vegetables, leave the skins on.

- Include garbanzo beans or kidney beans in your salads.

- Choose whole grain breads and crackers. Whole wheat or whole grain flour should be listed as the first ingredient on the food label.

CARBOHYDRATES

Most people who are dieting fear carbohydrates. Although moderation is key when consuming them, carbohydrates also energize your body—an important factor in a healthy eating plan.

There are two types of carbohydrates: sugar and starch. Sugars include fructose and lactose. Grains, pastas and potatoes make up starches. The body converts all sugars and starches to glucose—a source of energy. Diabetics need to keep careful watch on their carb intake because their bodies regulate glucose in the bloodstream differently than most.

Positive carbohydrate choices include whole grains, reduced-fat dairy products and a variety of fruits and vegetables. Want to eliminate empty calories? Cut out packaged cakes, pies and cookies. These choices are highly processed and don't contribute to a healthy diet. For example, 4-1/2 teaspoons of sugar may have about the same calories and carbohydrates as a medium apple, but the medium apple is a far healthier choice.

SODIUM

An advisory committee working on new U.S. Dietary Guidelines recently recommended that all adults restrict their intake of sodium to no more than 1,500 milligrams a day, equivalent to about two-thirds of a teaspoon of table salt, down from a current limit of 2,300 mgs. The dietary guidelines, which are updated every five years, currently suggest a limit of 1,500 mgs for people with hypertension, anyone over 40 years old and African-Americans, who are at greater risk for high blood pressure—a group that represents about 70% of all adults. The best way to reduce salt is to cut back on processed and restaurant foods, eat fresh produce, and reduce portion sizes. Generally, a food product that has been prepared for you to buy—such as frozen dinners, and convenience products—will contain a high amount of sodium.

CHOLESTEROL

Although saturated and trans fats have a larger effect on blood cholesterol than eating foods high in cholesterol, you should still limit your daily intake of cholesterol to 300 mg. Cholesterol is found in foods from animals, such as eggs, meat and dairy products.

FAT

Although fat seems like a dangerous word to incorporate into any diet, there are some healthy fats you can pick from. Monounsaturated and polyunsaturated fats, which are found in olive and canola oils and nuts and seeds, are all healthier options. Adults should limit fat to about 30% of their calories each day. This means you should be eating no more than 50 grams of fat per day if you are consuming 1,400 to 1,500 calories a day.

SATURATED FAT

While saturated fat is found mostly in high-fat meats and dairy foods, it is also found in coconut oil, palm kernel oil and some processed foods. Consume only 17 grams of saturated fat per day, which is 10% of calories following a 1,400 to 1,500 calorie-a-day diet.

TRANS FAT

LDL (bad) cholesterol increases with saturated fat and trans fat, increasing your risk of coronary artery disease. Trans fats can also decrease HDL (good) cholesterol. Limit trans fat as often as you can, and try to stay below 1.5 to 2.0 grams per day. Foods containing trans fat include vegetable shortening, stick margarine, fried foods, processed foods and store-bought baked goods.

PROTEIN

The body needs a constant supply of protein to repair and rebuild cells that are worn or damaged. About half of the protein we consume creates enzymes, which help cells carry out necessary chemical reactions. Proteins also bring oxygen to blood, help muscles contract and produce antibodies. As a general rule, men should consume about 55 grams of protein a day, while women should consume about 45 grams per day.

produce
POWER

As you're well aware, an essential factor in dieting is the addition of fruits and vegetables. They supply valuable antioxidants and phytonutrients, which can help prevent disease. They also provide your body with vitamins, minerals and fiber, and they're low in calories so you reap the rewards of high-nutrition items without breaking the calorie bank. To easily get a wide spectrum of vital nutrients, try eating fruits and vegetables in a mixture of colors.

SWEET
temptation

Let's take a second and talk about sugar. As you may know, sugar is a carbohydrate that produces energy for the body. The catch? Sugar is only a temporary energy fix. Consuming a sugary drink will give you the get-up-and-go you might crave, but the effects quickly fade. Before you know it, you will be yearning for another sugary substance, adding empty calories to your diet. Worse yet, when your body takes in more sugar than it needs for energy, it converts that sugar into body fat. In addition, sugar can truly complicate particular health issues such as diabetes.

Remember, sugar isn't just found in desserts; many of your daily staples contain excessive amounts of sugar, too. When in doubt, check the Nutrition Facts label. You'll find a listing for sugar under the "Total Carbohydrate" heading.

portion size
CHART

With super-sized fast food options and over-the-top restaurant portions, many of us forget what a decent serving truly is. Try to keep these visual clues in mind when estimating a proper portion size.

- **1 teaspoon butter,** a postage stamp or the tip of your thumb
- **1 cup beans,** a tennis ball or a cupped handful
- **2 tablespoons nuts,** a golf ball or a small cupped handful
- **1 small muffin,** the round part of a light bulb or half your fist
- **3 ounces meat,** a purse-pack of tissues or your outstretched palm
- **1 dinner roll,** a bar of soap or half your palm
- **1 pancake,** a music CD or your palm plus ½ to 1 inch
- **1 tablespoon salad dressing,** a silver dollar or the center of your cupped hand
- **1 cup chips,** a tea cup or a cupped handful
- **1 3x3-inch piece of cake,** a tennis ball or your palm

get your (nutrition)
FACTS STRAIGHT!

Nutrition Facts

Serving Size 1/4 Cup (30g)
Servings Per Container About 38

Amount Per Serving	
Calories 200 Calories from Fat 150	
	% Daily Value*
Total Fat 17g	**26%**
Saturated Fat 2.5g	**13%**
Trans Fat 0g	
Cholesterol 0mg	**0%**
Sodium 120mg	**5%**
Total Carbohydrate 7g	**2%**
Dietary Fiber 2g	**8%**
Sugars 1g	
Protein 5g	

Vitamin A 0%	•	Vitamin C 0%
Calcium 4%	•	Iron 8%

*Percent Daily Values are based on a 2,000 calorie diet.

Buying the best food for your gang is easy thanks to the nutrition information found on packaged foods.

Regulated by the Food Safety and Inspection Service and the Food and Drug Administration, Nutrition Facts panels are found on nearly every item in the grocery store. And while food labels can be a bit confusing, they're not impossible to translate once you understand them.

SERVING SIZE

The top of the Nutrition Facts panel (see example above) lists serving information. Food manufacturers follow guidelines that ensure the serving sizes of like products are comparable. This makes it a cinch for shoppers to determine which brand of orange juice offers the most vitamin C per serving, which spaghetti sauce has the least calories, and so on.

CALORIES. The panel lists the number of calories each serving contains…and how many of those calories come from fat. In the example above, there are 200 calories in one serving…and 150 of them come from fat. Remember, however, that if you ate 1/2 cup (or 2 servings), you'd take in 400 calories, of which 300 would be fat.

FATS. Also listed is the total number of fat grams per serving and how many of those grams come from saturated and trans fats (the "bad" fats).

CARBOHYDRATES. The "Total Carbohydrate" figure lists all of the carbs contained in the item. Since dietary fiber and sugars are of special interest to consumers, their amounts are highlighted individually as well as being included in the total carb number.

The "sugars" listed include those that occur naturally in foods, such as lactose in milk, as well as sugars that are added during processing.

PERCENT DAILY VALUE

The Percent Daily Value listed on the nutrition panel indicates how much each component in the product contributes to a 2,000-calorie-per-day eating plan. In the example at left, the total fat for a serving comprises 26% of the daily value, whereas the sodium comprises 5%.

Manufacturers must list the Percent Daily Value of vitamin A, vitamin C, calcium and iron on every food label so that consumers will know how the product fits into a well-balanced diet. Other vitamins and minerals may also be listed, depending on the space on the label and the manufacturer's preference.

If the Daily Value for calcium, iron, vitamin A, etc., is more than 10%, the product is generally considered to be a good source of that particular nutrient.

At the end of the nutrition label, you'll find an ingredients list—a requirement on all food products that contain more than one ingredient. Ingredients are listed in order, with the most major component (based on weight) of the product listed first and other ingredients following in decreasing order.

SHOPPING SMART
for family groceries

Saving calories, time and money is easier than you think!

You've been to the grocery store hundreds of times; so why when you're trying to eat healthier, does it suddenly feel like a foreign country?

Probably because you weren't paying much attention to things you didn't need to know. You could always find the soda, junk food and frozen pizzas, but you were not necessarily looking for the foods that could help you build a cornerstone of healthy eating.

In other words, you spent too much time in the middle of the store—looking through row upon row of processed foods—and not enough time in the outer aisles, where the gems like fresh fruits and vegetables hang out.

Yes, many of the foods that are the best choices for healthy eaters are at the perimeter, in a rectangle that sets the framework of the store. That includes produce, dairy and the butcher's section, with its array of fresh meat and fish. They naturally flow from one to the next by simply following the outer aisles.

Getting to know these parts of the store is beneficial because many of your meals can come from this formula: choose your protein, then add vegetables and fruit to make a meal. You'll still need to go to the middle of the store for pasta, rice, frozen foods and other items, but you can avoid the big sections of processed foods such as chips, meals in a box or can, and the cookie and candy aisles that beckoned to you in the past.

If you're busy (and who isn't?), it's probably tempting to say you don't have the time to shop for healthy foods. But it doesn't take any longer to shop for healthy foods than unhealthy ones. It's all about knowing what you need to buy. Taking a few minutes to plan your menus and write out family grocery lists will save you time at the store and even in the kitchen. You won't be standing in front of your refrigerator wondering what to make for dinner. You'll KNOW, because you have a plan.

Shopping healthy is about choosing the right foods for your meal plan: lean, unprocessed meat and fish, high-quality fruits and vegetables, whole grains and low-fat dairy. Eating healthy means taking these basic starters and preparing them for your family without adding unnecessary fat and calories.

ABOUT PRODUCE

When it comes to good-for-you staples, fresh produce is best, followed closely by frozen fruits or vegetables. Canned products are a distant third. So, head to the fresh produce department of the grocery store.

You're standing in the produce aisle, and what do you see? You recognize the carrots, celery, onions and potatoes but some of those bulky veggies and green leafy things…well, you're not quite sure about those. Your new favorite food could be right here, and you don't even know it!

That's OK. Trying new produce is one of the fun parts of healthy eating. Give yourself the goal of trying a new vegetable or fruit every week. Then stick with it.

The produce manager can explain individual produce items and how they're best cooked. Ask questions; these folks like to share their knowledge. (And you should share with them that you're looking for a healthy way to add new produce to your meals.)

Fresh produce is even fresher at a farmers market. If there's one near you, go early on the day it's open for the best selection. Talk to the farm families who produce the crops. They are used to eating what they grow, so they often have simple recipes and healthy preparation tips to share.

ABOUT MEAT & FISH

When you're at the meat counter, avoid processed meats like sausage and wieners. They're often made with high-fat ingredients and a number of additives. Instead, look for fresh chicken and turkey with the occasional lean cuts of beef and pork.

When buying chicken or turkey, watch for pockets of fat. Either buy skinless or take the skin and fat off at home so your pieces are lean. The breast is the leanest. When buying ground turkey, make sure it is ground breast, not turkey pieces, which can also include skin. Otherwise ground turkey can have as much fat as regular ground beef!

For red meat, cuts that have the word "round" or "loin" are generally leaner. Look for firm meat that smells and looks fresh, with no off-color areas. Read packages to make sure the meat wasn't injected with water, flavorings or preservatives.

For fish, choose fresh, firm fish that doesn't smell fishy. It's OK to ask when it was delivered to the store. If the fresh fish looks or smells iffy, go for frozen seafood instead.

KNOWING THE INS & OUTS

While sticking to the perimeter of the store can help you pick healthy items, you'll need to venture into the aisles as well. When considering packaged or canned goods, get into the habit of checking Nutrition Facts labels. (See the story on page 19.) Avoid convenience items with long lists of additives…and ingredients you can't pronounce.

Look for foods that don't get many of their calories from fat…and consider items that are low in saturated fat.

When the carbohydrate total on the label is more than twice the amount of sugar, the food is usually loaded with good-for-you complex carbohydrates. Consider making these items a part of your family's weekly menu plan.

Many items found in the deli or bakery are not required to provide nutritional facts. Luckily, many of today's supermarkets make this information available upon request. When in doubt, ask. You'd be surprised at how often nutrition information is available.

When hitting the dairy case, consider non-fat or low-fat options. If your family can't adapt to a lower-fat new milk, start mixing the low-fat option with the milk they're accustomed to. Over time, increase the amount of low-fat milk.

In addition, don't go shopping when you're hungry. And if your kids are looking for a snack, this may not be the best time to bring them to the supermarket either. You'll be tempted to give in to instant gratification (code words for junk food), and you won't stick to your healthy eating plan. Eat something substantial and satisfying before you leave the house.

And finally, here's the best shopping advice: If it's not good for you, simply don't put it in your cart. That way you can't take it home and eat it!

TRIM DOWN
your waistline & pocketbook

It IS possible to eat healthy and frugally all at the same time if you follow three simple rules:

1 Check It Out: Look what's in your fridge or freezer NOW that fits into your family meal plan. Make use of those items rather than buying something new. Wasted food is wasted money. And an unnecessary trip to the grocery store is wasted time. (Go for a walk, instead.)

2 Plan ahead: Knowing your menu plan and having a grocery list will save you time and money. Don't deviate from the list unless it's a super-sale you didn't know about, and the food fits into your plan. Those unplanned little extras add up quickly—in dollars and calories.

3 Be Informed: Look online, in newspapers or at in-store flyers to find out what's on sale and for coupons. If a food fits into your menu plan, buy it when it's cheapest.

Grocery List

- low-fat milk
- whole grain bread
- tomatoes
- green peppers
- carrots
- sweet potatoes
- walnuts
- ground turkey

more on the WEB

Visit www.ComfortFoodDietCookbook.com for additional ways to cut calories from your grocery list, save money and more.

supermarket SAVVY!

The next time you hit the grocery store, keep these slimmed-down substitutions in mind. Consider the foods pictured, and you'll cut back on calories and fat…and you might even trim a few dollars off your grocery bill.

BUY THIS **instead of this**

- How long has it been since you popped a big bowl of popcorn on the stove? Maybe you've forgotten just how easy it is or haven't noticed the cost of those microwave bags lately.

- Instead, with a heavy saucepan, a small amount of oil and a few minutes, you can have popcorn seasoned your way without all the salt, artificial flavor and coloring of some microwave versions.

BUY THIS **instead of this**

- Hot oatmeal can be a comforting start on a chilly morning, but the cost of those quick-and-easy "instant" packets adds up. They also contain additives and sugar.

- Instead, get the real thing. Add some fresh or dried fruit, honey or nuts to old-fashioned or quick-cooking oats for a more nutritious breakfast. Or try our Raisin Oatmeal Mix on page 94.

BUY THIS **instead of this**

- Not only are you paying more for a few berries, but you're also paying for added sugar, high fructose corn syrup and food coloring.

- Instead, pick up some plain yogurt and add your own fresh fruit for sweetness and additional nutrients. It will also cost you less in calories.

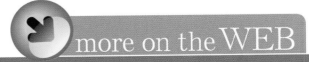
more on the WEB

For additional recipes that are easy on your waistline as well as your wallet, visit www.ComfortFoodDietCookbook.com. Use MyDiet as your private access code.

BUY THIS   **instead of this**

- When a crunchy craving hits, don't reach for a bag of salty chips and fatty dip.

- Instead, enjoy some salsa and baked chips. One ounce of chips and ¼ cup salsa contains fewer than 130 calories and has only 3 grams of fat. The same amounts of chips and dip packs on nearly 300 calories and a whopping 20 grams of fat.

BUY THIS   **instead of this**

- Think all leafy greens are the same? While spinach and iceberg offer about the same calories and fiber cup for cup, you don't have to settle for a lackluster salad.

- Instead, enjoy a spinach salad that's loaded with far more vitamins and minerals. Spinach is a good source of vitamins K, A, C and folate and magnesium.

BUY THIS   **instead of this**

- Pasta is an all-time dinner staple in most homes. Don't feel you have to forget pasta just because you're trying to lose weight.

- Instead, make a smarter pick with whole wheat pasta and work more fiber into your diet. It has three times as much fiber per serving as plain pasta. Be sure to read the ingredient list on the box to check for 100% durum whole wheat flour.

BUY THIS   **instead of this**

- Fish is high in protein, low in calories and can be a great source of heart-healthy omega-3 fatty acids. But those handy breaded or sauced frozen fish products can be high in calories and fat.

- Instead, buy fresh or plain frozen fish fillets and season them with your own breading or herbs.

BUY THIS   **instead of this**

- If you're watching your cholesterol and intake of saturated fats, you might have given up butter and switched to stick margarine. Think you've made a change for the better?

- Instead, make a real difference and switch to margarine in tubs. It has 1/3 the trans fat of stick margarine! Compare labels to find the brands lowest in trans fat.

supercharge your diet with
10 SUPER FOODS

Work these wonders into your day and get the biggest
nutritional bang for your caloric buck!

TOMATOES. On top of being an exceptional source of vitamin C, these plump favorites are a superb source of lycopene, an antioxidant that can boost your immune system. So toss some chopped tomato into a pot of simmering soup, set them over your eggs at breakfast or try these Comfort Food Diet recipes: Basil Cherry Tomatoes (p. 243) and Fettuccine with Mushrooms and Tomatoes (p. 158).

SALMON. Fish isn't just for Fridays anymore. The health benefits of salmon are simply too great to ignore. The omega 3s found in fish lower your risk for heart disease, help arthritis and have been linked as a possible aid regarding memory and Alzheimer's disease. The high levels of monounsaturated fat help lower cholesterol, just another reason why fish is the perfect meal for any day of the week. Need some salmon recipes? Try Salmon Chowder (p. 129) or Chipotle-Sparked Mustard Salmon (p. 188) tonight.

CHILI PEPPERS. When most people want their daily dose of vitamin C, they reach for an orange. But few know that chili peppers contain twice the amount of vitamin C than most citrus fruit. Chili peppers contain capsaicinoids, compounds that not only give each bite a fiery spark, but also create an anti-inflammatory and helps prevent certain cancers. Even adding a small amount of jalapeno, cayenne, anaheim, habanero, hungarian or serrano pepper to your dishes can help keep you healthy. Spice up menus with Jalapenos with Olive-Cream Cheese Filling (p. 71) and Jalapeno-Apricot Pork Tenderloin (p. 232).

SPINACH. Add spinach to your leafy green salad, and you'll pump up the health benefits enormously. In fact, spinach is tough to beat for the amount of protein and vitamin K it offers. It might be hard to get kids to eat spinach, but once you incorporate it into your family's diet, the health benefits are worth it. Give Creamy Spinach Casserole (p. 265) and Spinach-Tomato Phyllo Bake (p. 168) a try!

OATS. The pure goodness of oats make them a natural for this list; they're loaded with vitamin E and thiamine and healthy doses of magnesium, phosphorus and zinc. Also providing decent amounts of fiber and protein, oats help lower cholesterol as well as the risk of heart disease. In addition, enjoying oatmeal on a regular basis may decrease insulin resistance and help to stabilize blood sugar. Whip up some Applesauce Oatmeal Pancakes (p. 85) and Raisin Oatmeal Mix (p. 94) and experience the goodness oats have to offer.

BLUEBERRIES. Talk about a super food! This list wouldn't be complete without these tiny gems that pack a powerful punch. Blueberries are loaded with antioxidants, which can protect your cells against free radicals keeping cells healthy. A handful of blueberries also provides your body with phytoflavinoids, potassium and vitamin C, which helps lower cholesterol levels and act as an anti-inflammatory. When choosing your berries, remember, the deeper the color the more chock-full of antioxidants they are. Blueberry Oat Pancakes (p. 108) and Slow Cooker Berry Cobbler (p. 292) are great ways to start and end your day.

BEANS. Beans, especially the red, pinto and dark varieties, are a great way to add fiber to your diet. One cup of beans has an average of 16 g dietary fiber, which is more than half of the recommended 25 g you should be consuming daily. When combined with grains such as oats or barley, beans provide the necessary amino acids to make a complete protein. Black Bean Veggie Enchiladas (p. 208) and Spicy Three-Bean Chili (p. 135) are sure to become favorites with your gang.

BROCCOLI. Whether eaten cooked as a side dish or enjoyed raw for a snack, a cup of broccoli contains a substantial amount of calcium, folic acid and vitamin C. Along with a number of other super foods, broccoli is a leading food component associated with cancer prevention. The green veggie also helps boost the immune system, working toward keeping you healthy every day. Consider Broccoli with Lemon Sauce (p. 244) and Broccoli Cheddar Brunch Bake (p. 93) when adding this classic veggie to your menu plan.

WALNUTS. These crunchy all-stars make great snacks and wonderful additions to low-fat cakes and muffins. Walnuts offer solid amounts of vitamins A and E, as well as calcium, magnesium, phosphorus and potassium. Best of all, they provide decent amounts of fiber, omega-3s and protein. The flavorful nuts can also help lower the risk of heart disease and improve cholesterol. Best of all, walnuts are the only nut with a significant amount of ellagic acid, a cancer-fighting antioxidant. If you'd like to add walnuts to your weekly plan, Stir-Fried Walnut Chicken (p. 194) and Tomato Walnut Tilapia (p. 183) are ideal options.

TURKEY. Don't reserve this family classic for the holidays! Serve it all year. Having trouble sleeping? Try eating turkey on a regular basis. Tryptophan, the amino acid contained in turkey, has a major role in sleep cycles. People who experience insomnia can often find relief for this exact reason. At the same time, these amino acids can boost your immune system. Still not feeling your best? Eating turkey can also improve your mood. See for yourself by trying tasty Garlic-Ginger Turkey Tenderloins (p. 186) and Moist & Tender Turkey Breast (p. 194).

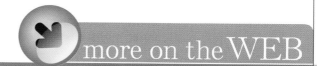

more on the WEB

Visit www.ComfortFoodDietCookbook.com for additional recipes that involve these super foods. Remember to use the code MyDiet for free access.

LIGHTEN UP
your family favorites!

With the Comfort Food Diet you can serve your gang their most-requested dishes and still keep calories at bay.

DINNER STANDBYS:

- When serving pasta and rice, pay attention to portion sizes. A serving of cooked rice is typically 1/2 or 2/3 cup, while pasta is usually 1-1/2 ounces, uncooked, per serving.

- A serving of meat is considered 4 ounces, uncooked.

- 10-inch tortillas have 213 calories before any fillings are even added. To go healthier, choose 8- or 6-inch flour tortillas instead.

- See the Portion Size Chart on page 18 for visual cues of common portion sizes.

- Until you get a feel for typical serving sizes, invest in a food scale. It will help you keep on track right from the start.

- Choose lean meat when cooking. Look for skinless poultry, white-meat poultry, pork with "loin" in the name and beef with "loin" or "round" in the name.

- Consider low-sodium/no-sodium alternatives when cooking with packaged foods, boxed mixes, olives, cheese and savory seasoning mixes. For example, instead of canned products, choose fresh or frozen (corn, sliced mushrooms, green beans, etc.).

- Cut back on adding high-calorie and fatty ingredients such as nuts, olives, cheese and avocado.

DESSERT FAVORITES:

- When adding chopped mix-ins such as nuts, chips, raisins or coconut to dessert, decrease the amount a bit. Try using mini chips.

- Toast nuts and coconut so smaller amounts have stronger flavor.

- Reduce the amount of frosting. You can usually cut that amount by 1/4 or 1/3 without missing it.

- When making frosting, confectioners' sugar can almost always be decreased without losing any of the sweetness. One tablespoon of confectioners' sugar equals 29 calories.

- Using reduced-fat butter and reduced-fat cream cheese works well in homemade frosting. Since these lighter products tend to be soft-set, the recipe may need less liquid.

- When baking, replace 1/4 or 1/2 of the butter or oil in a recipe with unsweetened applesauce. Keep in mind that applesauce is a better replacement for oil than it is for butter.

- If you're substituting a substantial amount (1/2 to 1 cup) of applesauce for fat, you can cut down on sugar a bit because of the natural sweetness of the applesauce.

- Instead of using all whole eggs in baked products, use some egg whites as a replacement. Do not use all egg whites (unless the recipe specifies to do so), as the resulting item can be spongy and tough.

- Often times, sugar can be decreased slightly without making a difference in the recipe. This is especially true for recipes that are over 40 years old since they tend to be disproportionately high in sugar.

- One tablespoon of sugar equals 48 calories—be careful when adding it to any of your baked goods.

- If your lightened-up cakes turn out tough with a dense texture, try substituting cake flour for all-purpose flour the next time you prepare it.

- It's rather difficult to lighten cookie recipes successfully in order to keep the original shape and texture. The best option is to prepare cookies as usual and savor a single serving.

I lost 110 pounds...and gained a
NEW ATTITUDE!

After changing my eating habits, counting calories and cooking my own meals, I'm feeling healthier than ever!

By Jeffrey Jacobs

before

Even at my heaviest, I never thought I looked overweight. I still pictured myself as a teenager with broad shoulders and a great jaw line. Unfortunately, that wasn't the case.

I have been obese since I began college. Most people gain the infamous "Freshman 15," but I think I gained the "Freshman 40." In fact, between the ages of 18 and 27, I think I gained almost 90 pounds.

I loved food. Eating made me happy in so many ways—the texture of the food, the satisfaction of being full and, of course, the flavor. If a plate of brownies was set before me, I shamelessly ate every last crumb. Give me a pie, and before the day was over, it was gone. Pizza? Hope you ordered your own because I alone could eat an entire one...effortlessly.

It wasn't until my body began shouting for help that I realized I had to do something about my weight. I was 27, yet I developed the problems of an unhealthy 55-year-old man. I was pre-diabetic and nearly hypertensive. I had both a high heart rate and high cholesterol, and I began experiencing sleep apnea. I realized that if I continued to gain weight, my health would be in serious trouble.

I didn't have much of a goal in mind, and I just thought I'd try to get healthy. I wanted to see my jaw-line again. I wanted to feel better. I wanted to lose weight.

My biggest challenge was cutting back the amount of unhealthy food I ate. Instead of eating excessively until I was uncomfortable, I began focusing on a few small meals and snacks until I was satisfied. Calorie counting and portion control were key. I looked at an

after

item's calorie count, noted the portion size and then determined if eating the item was worth the calories involved.

Best of all, I got cooking! I realized that opening a can of this and adding a jar of that doesn't constitute cooking...and those convenience products can pack on calories quickly. By staying away from processed foods, I instantly felt healthier.

Once I got the cooking bug, I quickly learned how to double, and sometimes even triple, recipes. This way I had plenty of leftovers, ensuring I'd eat right throughout the week.

I also began exercising. Since an expensive gym membership didn't fit my budget, I found ways to exercise for free. I ran outdoors and took advantage

of a weight set collecting dust in my basement. I also followed an exercise DVD.

By changing my habits and staying consistent, I began losing weight. When I lost 80 pounds, and saw how close I was to reaching the 100-pound mark, I found the motivation to keep going. Like everyone trying to lose weight, however, I eventually reached a plateau.

While it's a very discouraging feeling, I realized that I had to push through the plateau in order to start losing again. The best way I found to deal with the situation was to change my exercise habits and even my diet. I gave my metabolism a run for its money with a good offensive game plan.

I thought of this as a competition. If my opposing team, my metabolism, caught on to my tricks and tactics, I simply changed my strategy a little. I mixed up my workouts; I ate breakfast earlier or lunch later. I was surprised how well this worked!

I also allowed myself the chance to occasionally eat the foods I craved. When I convinced myself that I could no longer eat cookies, for instance, I ended up telling myself that I just "had to have those cookies one last time." I constantly found myself having a "one-last-time" experience.

Now I tell myself that I will, indeed, have those cookies…just not today, just not right now. I know that if I watch the calories I take in, then I'll be able to enjoy a cookie or two another day. Or, better yet, I can try to find a low-calorie recipe for those same cookies and work them into my menu plan. I'm able to enjoy my favorite comfort foods as long as I eat them in moderation, take portion size into consideration and account for their calories.

By pushing myself and making changes to the way I ate, I far surpassed my goal, changing my life for the better! I lost a total of 110 pounds, and I went from a size 40 waist to a size 30. Best of all, that jaw line I missed so much? It's back for good, and I couldn't be happier.

3 ways to make a world of difference

1. Shop locally. I purchase my meat from local butchers who don't use growth hormones, and I shop at public and farmers markets. I even go so far as to visit independent coffee shops and restaurants. These establishments are special because of the owner's capability to use fresh, organic and local foods. It is such a refreshing feeling to know where the flavor and the foundation of your cuisine stems from.

2. Drink up! Make water your new beverage of choice. Not only does drinking plenty of water help fill you up, but you'll be amazed at how it helps your skin, too. I've always had acne problems, and those issues decreased substantially once I started drinking more water. Best of all, water is an easy, healthy and economical choice.

3. Go lean. Health-conscious people tend to avoid meat as a protein source. While fat and cholesterol play a part in meat proteins, remember that meats aren't bad for you in moderation…and you need the protein. It's essential to think smart when choosing proteins. Fresh tuna, for instance, is a great way to work lean protein into your diet.

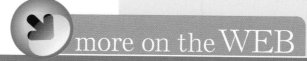

more on the WEB

Jeffrey discusses his incredible weight-loss and offers a few more tips at www.ComfortFoodDietCookbook.com. Remember to use MyDiet for your exclusive access code.

OUT OF THE KITCHEN
...not out of control

Being away from home doesn't mean giving up on your
diet goals. Be sure to make smart choices when you're at...

A RESTAURANT

Go fish! Most family restaurants have a number of fish and
seafood options to choose from. Resist the urge to order fried
shrimp or anything with a cream or butter sauce.

If seafood doesn't strike your fancy, there are usually plenty of
other smart choices on hand. Stir-fries, lean cuts of meat and
baked chicken dishes are healthier than other menu items.

Scan the entire menu, looking for items that are baked, roasted,
poached, broiled or steamed. Avoid those that are fried or come
with a heavy sauce.

Look over the appetizers and you might find something that
makes an ideal low-calorie entree (with a perfect portion size).
Grilled vegetable platters and side salads are great options.

THE VENDING MACHINE

Vending machines feel like your best friend when hunger comes calling.
Whether at work, volunteering with a neighborhood organization or
cheering the kids on during an after-school activity, vending machines
promise comforting nibbles...but deliver few rewards.

If you need to drop a few coins into a vending machine, spend them
on baked chips or pretzels. Similarly, small bags of snack mix and
plain animal crackers make decent snacks. Many machines offer an
assortment of mints and low-sugar gum. Give these options a try as the
strong flavor of peppermint will often curb any cravings.

A PARTY

Family celebrations mean good people, good times…and lots of good food. In fact, many families celebrate with bring-a-dish buffets that stretch out for what seems like miles. With the Taste of Home Comfort Food Diet, you can partake in these hearty meals, as long as you keep a few things in mind.

Before you grab a plate, scan the food first and pick the healthiest options. Look for items such as veggie and fruit platters, boiled shrimp and whole wheat crackers.

Next, decide which items you truly have to try and which you can do without. Be leery of thick dips and spreads (try a salsa or chutney instead), and stay clear of fried foods.

Lastly, try to eat something healthy before arriving at the get-together. You're less likely to overindulge if your stomach is full when you get to the party.

THE MOVIES

A night at the movies is a favorite outing for most families. Like many restaurants, however, movie theaters have created a new (and unhealthy) standard where portion sizes are concerned. If you need to nibble at a movie, skip the opportunity to super-size your order, and scan the candy counter for small boxes of sweets. Licorice and jellied fruit candies make decent choices.

While the aroma of movie-house popcorn is nearly iconic, try your best to resist it. The butter and oils involved can really pack on the pounds and detour all that you've worked toward. If you must give in to temptation, order the smallest size available and ask for no butter. Sharing popcorn with the family means you'll eat less and consume far fewer calories, so be sure to pass the bucket regularly.

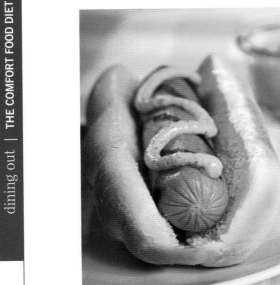

THE GAME

Taking the kids to the ballpark? While it's not always easy, you can munch your way through a game, feel full and not break the calorie bank.

Many stadiums offer high-end dining with healthy foods you won't likely find at the concession stands. While these hot spots offer great menus, they're not particularly family friendly. That said, do your research before leaving for the game. Many stadiums list healthy options on their Website, making it easier to find the stand that sells grilled chicken or locate the cart with the baked potato bar.

More sports venues are offering veggie or tofu dogs, California rolls and even fresh produce. You can also try a baked pretzel (avoid the salt if that's an option), but be sure to split it with a family member or two.

THE OFFICE

Family cooks are often so busy packing lunches for the kids, they forget to fill a brown bag for themselves. Bring your own lunch to work (as well a snack or two), and you can easily keep your caloric goals intact.

For many, the lure of high-calorie snacks is greatest at the workplace. Avoid high-calorie temptations by bringing your own munchies to work. Keep a container of granola or low-calorie snack mix in your office, or bake up a batch of bran muffins or light cookies specifically to keep on hand at the office.

THE SHOPPING MALL

Anyone trying to lose weight will tell you that the neon roundabouts known as food courts spell trouble. Try to avoid these fast-food havens when possible, but if you're stuck at a shopping mall with no other food choices, look for a spot that offers salads with low-fat dressing. Other smart options include baked chicken breast sandwiches (not breaded or fried) and turkey sub sandwiches (hold the cheese and mayo).

If your sweet tooth comes calling, pick up a refreshing fruit smoothie or low-fat frozen yogurt, and tell the cookies and cinnamon rolls to take a hike!

more on the WEB

Visit www.ComfortFoodDietCookbook.com and learn how to eat out and not fill out. Remember to use MyDiet for your exclusive access code to more tips on sticking to your goals when away from home.

MOVE IT
and lose it!

Jump-starting your weight loss is as easy as putting one foot in front of the other.

The Comfort Food Diet suggests adding exercise to your week for surefire, calorie-burning success. And while it might seem intimidating at first, it's easier than you think to take that first step...literally.

Whatever activity you choose should be easy, affordable and, most of all, fun! Try to find a form of exercise that you'd enjoy doing every day...or at least on a very regular basis. Consider options that fit into your schedule and meet with your doctor's approval. Look for opportunities to work out with a spouse, family member or friend. Then, grab your walking shoes and take that first step!

WALK IT OFF!

Walking is a perfect way to start an exercise routine. After all, you can burn roughly 100 calories by briskly walking a mile. In addition, walking lowers blood pressure and improves cholesterol.

If you're new to fitness walking, begin with a daily 10-minute stroll. Those 10 minutes will likely turn into 20 minutes or more in a matter of days. Set a goal for yourself to walk every day for one week. Get out there and enjoy a walk around the neighborhood!

During the next week, pay attention to the speed with which you move. The average walking speed is between 1-1/2 and 2-1/2 mph, but a good walking speed is 3 to 4 mph. Start using short strides with quick heel-to-toe movements. Long strides may cause your front foot to act like a brake, jarring your joints and slowing you down.

Using a pedometer, start increasing your steps by 10% to 20% per week. You are at a great level when you've reached 10,000 steps per day or 70,000 steps per week.

Your muscles need oxygen, so don't forget to inhale deeply and exhale fully, both to a count of three. When possible, walk on soft surfaces such as dirt, sand or grass—these areas are gentle on your joints. Always stretch before and after walking to prevent muscles from tightening or cramping.

One of the benefits of walking is that you can fit in a long walk once during the day, or you can walk for short bursts throughout the day…and still burn calories. In other words, if you can't fit in a 45-minute walk, you can take three 15-minute walks instead.

Walking with a buddy can make the time fly, motivate you to stick with it and push you to increase your pace. Better yet, grab your family and take a relaxing walk together.

- Enjoy a family walk before dinner to discuss the day's events.

- Make walking a special event by taking the gang to the zoo, a museum or a shopping mall.

- When the kids are frustrated, walk around the block with them. They'll burn off the stress, and you'll all burn calories.

Regardless of how you work this activity into your day, be sure to carve out walking time on your schedule. Remember, the ultimate goal is to lose weight, feel good and become the best you can be. Commit to walking regularly, and with a little dedication and perseverance, you'll take a step in the right direction.

get moving!

In a landmark Harvard study of some 40,000 women over the age of 45, those who walked as little as 1 hour a week—even at a stroll—were half as likely to have heart attacks or blocked coronary arteries as those who rarely walked for exercise. Walking is easier with good form, so follow these easy tips for proper posture to get started on your way to healthier tomorrows!

HEAD
Imagine a string attached to the top of your head, pulling it straight toward the sky. Keep your chin lifted and your ears in line with your shoulders.

SHOULDERS
Keep them relaxed, down and slightly back. If they start hunching up toward your ears, take a deep breath and drop them back again.

ARMS
Elbows should be bent at about 90-degree angles, hands slightly cupped. Relax your arms and pump them forward and back as you walk; they should not crisscross in front of you. Walking with light hand weights can help build muscle and burn calories, but too much weight will strain elbows and shoulders.

CHEST
Yoga practitioners sometimes refer to the breastbone area as your "heart light." Keep your heart light lifted and shining straight ahead.

ABDOMINALS
Pull your belly button toward your spine as if you were zipping up a snug pair of jeans. Keep those abs firm and tight as you walk.

FEET
With each step, plant your heel, roll onto the ball of your foot, and push off with your toes. Avoid rolling your foot inward or outward. To protect your feet and joints, wear good walking shoes. A proper fit means they feel great right out of the box. Make sure there's a finger-width between the end of your longest toe and the inside of the front of the shoe.

Source: 30 Minutes a Day to a Healthy Heart from Reader's Digest

move it | THE COMFORT FOOD DIET

ready, set, HIKE!

Head for the hills and sing 'Happy Trails' to excess body fat.

Looking for a new activity to get your family off the couch?

Hit the trails with a nature hike! If you've been walking for fitness, getting off the proverbial beaten path—or sidewalk—will bring a new level of excitement to your routine, not to mention some breathtaking scenery.

No matter where you live, chances are there's a lovely park within a short drive. Every state has more than a dozen state parks with hundreds of thousands of trails between them. Nature trails are a great way to enjoy the outdoors, see fascinating sights and learn a little bit about the earth. If wooded parks aren't your thing, consider a floral garden with walkways or visit military or historic parks with self-guided tours.

If you're new to hiking, choose a trail that is described as being easy or moderate and is only a few miles long. A short trail will teach you how well you and your family hike. This assessment will help you select ideal trails for future hikes.

Buy a trail map to prevent you from losing your way, but always stay on the trail or closely follow the marked pathway. Stick together, and don't let small children run too far ahead of the group.

When you begin the hike, let the least fit person—even if it's a child—set the pace. Remember that you don't just have to reach the trail's destination...you also have to hike back. If you need to stop early, go ahead. You can always try to finish the hike next time.

Ready to round up the troops and take a hike? Keep these ideas in mind before you head out.

- When hiking, carry about 1 quart of liquid per person for every two hours of hiking you plan to do.
- Dress in layers before hitting the trails. As you warm up, you can remove the extra layers.
- Snacks are a great addition to a hike, but pack light as to not weigh yourself down.

Like walking, hiking is a simple activity with many rewards. While a hike may involve more hills and rugged terrain, the benefits of enjoying the world around you make the extra effort well worth it!

EXERCISE
is a family affair

By changing our idea of 'working out,'
we made fitness fun.

By Jeff Nowak

A NEW APPROACH

"THERE ARE FOUR simple things you can do to increase your chances for a long healthy life," a wise friend once told me. "Eat right, don't smoke, wear a seat belt and exercise."

From his simplified assessment, I felt my wife, Jenny, and I were doing pretty well...until he mentioned the dreaded eight-letter "E" word... exercise!

Like many parents, we found that exercise didn't fit into our schedules. It's not that we didn't try. Each New Year's Day, for example, I'd renew my vow to regularly exercise. By February 1, though, my mind and body would barely recall the resolution.

One year, Jenny and I discovered a better way to exercise...we simply changed our approach. Instead of adjusting our lifestyle to include routine exercise, we made exercise fit our routine lifestyle. We found that exercising as a family is more fun and a great way to promote healthy living to our growing boys, Ben and Aaron.

We looked for things to do as a family. This included riding bikes, taking walks and playing games of street hockey. We realized that it was just as easy to get a good workout at home or in our neighborhood as it was at a health club.

The benefits have been tremendous. Jenny lost a few nagging pounds, and I found a way to chase our sons around the yard without becoming winded.

Here are a few things that helped us fit exercise into our schedule:

- **SLOW DOWN.** Jenny and I checked with our doctor before we began exercising (and you should, too!). Then we started slow but stuck to 20-minute bouts of activity.

  As our stamina and pace increased, we added light hand weights (1 to 3 pounds) to the routine. When we went for family walks, for instance, we did different lifting exercises with the weights. What a great cardiovascular workout!

- **BE FLEXIBLE.** We exercise together for about 20 minutes, 3 or 4 times each week. This gives us a chance to skip working out on those extremely busy days or when the boys have after-school activities to attend.

- **CREATE GOALS.** If you're like me, it's much easier to exercise if you have something to work toward. For instance, I began playing recreational hockey with an adult league, so I needed to keep exercising at home to stay in shape for the season. Signing the family up for a local charity walk or bike ride is a wonderful way to keep the whole gang motivated to exercise.

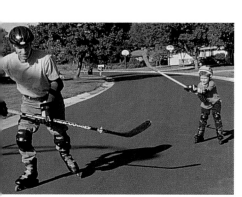

I was my own
BIGGEST LOSER

I shed 60 pounds and learned a lot about myself along the way.

By Christy Sprotte

before

Like most women on their wedding day, I felt as though I was the most beautiful bride...despite the fact that I didn't reach my weight-loss goal prior to the big day.

During the flurry of wedding planning, I visited bridal boutiques and was shocked to discover that based on my measurements, I had to try on gowns from the plus-sized department.

I quickly began a fad diet and a few months later became ill. My doctor told me that I had developed a kidney stone that could very likely have been caused by the diet I was following. I decided to forgo the diet and concentrate on wedding plans.

Even though my weight wasn't where I wanted it to be on the big day, it was a glorious summer wedding nonetheless, and I couldn't have been happier.

As autumn quickly approached, and I settled into marital bliss, I decided it was time to revisit my goals and take off those extra pounds. I wanted to do this not only for me, but also for the family my husband and I planned to have.

I work as a psychologist at a middle school, and when a coworker proposed a weight-loss competition for the staff, I jumped onboard. I knew the friendly wager was the exact shove I needed to start shedding pounds.

Like the TV show, "The Biggest Loser," each participant was matched with a friend. Everyone weighed in with his or her partner weekly, and after 3 months the pair who lost the most pounds and percentage of weight won a monetary award.

I was motivated to win that prize, but knew

after

the pounds weren't going to simply melt off. I recalled having some success in the past using food journals to track what I ate and count calories. By logging my food intake, I became much more aware of what I ate every day as well as the portion sizes.

I combined journaling with meal planning and drinking eight glasses of water daily. I also started walking 15 minutes a day, and it was much easier than I imagined. Eventually, I worked my way up to a minimum of 30 minutes of cardio activity every day in addition to strength-training exercises three times a week.

My attitude, however, was the most challenging obstacle I faced. You see, I am a perfectionist by nature, and because of this, I quickly became disappointed in myself when I overindulged or skipped a workout. Instead of pushing myself harder the next time, my self-criticism would set me back, and I would ignore my goals for days.

Eventually, I realized that one of the most important factors in weight loss is consistency. It dawned on me that when I strayed too far from the path, I undid several weeks of weight-loss success. I quickly learned that humans make mistakes, and that I needed to let them go in order to move forward.

I began following an 80-20 rule. By this I mean that I ate healthy 80% of the time and indulged the remaining 20% of the time. This truly helped me as I became less flustered and found it easier to stick to my goals. I found that maintaining an overall healthy lifestyle isn't as challenging when you treat yourself occasionally, hold yourself accountable and forgive yourself for any mishaps that might occur.

Since I work in a school where tempting snacks, such as birthday cakes, muffins and other sweets, make regular appearances, I began taking healthy snacks to work. Low-fat string cheese, light yogurt, apples and bananas helped me avoid all of those enticing treats found in the teachers lounge. I also began eating every 3 to 4 hours in order to control my hunger and curb any cravings.

Whenever I felt like giving up, I reminded myself of the reasons I wanted to trim down in the first place. Besides needing a healthy body to carry a child, I also wanted to be able to teach my family how to stay healthy.

I was determined to gain the skills and confidence I needed to maintain a healthy lifestyle before my husband and I had children and started our own family. And the best way to do that was to lose the weight and understand what it takes to eat right and live well.

Three months later the contest came to an end, and my partner and I were announced the winners...we lost the most weight! I was 50 pounds lighter and I was thrilled to win the award. I realized, however, that my greatest prize was gaining the skills I needed to maintain a healthy lifestyle for myself.

Currently, I am down 60 pounds, and I couldn't feel better. While my journey began as a plus-sized bride, today I am a happy, healthy wife, ready for anything that comes my way.

The secrets to my success

While on my weight-loss journey, I relied on a few secrets that helped me shed pounds and stay motivated.

- **PLAN, PLAN, PLAN.** Every weekend, my husband and I plan our meals for the upcoming week and then do our shopping. All of the recipes from the *Comfort Food Diet Cookbook* have been a huge help!

- **CHECK IN OR CHECKOUT.** Don't be afraid of the scale. Weekly weigh-ins are great. Losing 5 pounds gained over the holidays is significantly easier than losing 25 pounds gained carelessly by not keeping track of your weight.

- **DO SOME SURFING.** The Web is a great place for information and interactive tools on weight-loss. If you have plans to go out to dinner, you can even check the menu online and plan your order in advance.

- **DOWNSIZE DINNERWARE.** In order to keep myself from feeling deprived, I ate dinners off salad plates. This made me feel as though the portions were larger, and I felt fuller quickly.

- **TREAT YOURSELF.** I love desserts, so eliminating them from my diet was not realistic. Instead, I found low-calorie alternatives and allowed myself indulgences.

- **STIR IT UP.** Mixing up my exercise routine is motivating and keeps my body in fat-burning mode. My exercise routine includes hiking, biking, jogging, using an elliptical trainer and following a few exercise DVDs.

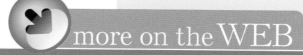

more on the WEB

For more tips from Christy and four of her favorite recipes, log on to www.ComfortFoodDietCookbook.com. Use the code MyDiet.

free foods
CHART

Add these foods to your menu plan without worry!

Listed at right are items considered "free foods" on the Taste of Home Comfort Food Diet. A free food is an item that has fewer than 20 calories and 5 or fewer grams of carbohydrate per serving. Whether you add these items to your meal plan, rely on them for snacks or simply use them to enhance the flavor of your favorite dishes, feel free to enjoy as many free foods as you'd like.

Free foods are an ideal way to fill you up because they are mostly non-starchy vegetables. When you make a low-calorie turkey sandwich, for instance, give it a bit of crunch with sliced cucumber, pickles or even radishes. Or, pump up the flavor with fresh herbs, horseradish or hot pepper sauce...and don't worry about adding up any calories these items might contain.

Note the chart also offers free foods that list specific portion sizes. Feel free to enjoy a serving of these items and not count the calories; but if you eat these foods in portion sizes larger than what's noted in the chart, the calories will have to be counted toward your daily goal.

EAT ALL YOU WANT

- Artichoke
- Artichoke hearts
- Asparagus
- Baby corn
- Bamboo shoots
- Bean sprouts
- Beans (green, wax, Italian)
- Beets
- Broccoli
- Broth or bouillon
- Brussels sprouts
- Cauliflower
- Carrots
- Celery
- Cucumber
- Eggplant
- Flavored sugar-free gelatin
- Garlic
- Green onions or scallions
- Greens (collard, kale, mustard, turnip)
- Hearts of palm
- Herbs (fresh or dried)
- Horseradish
- Hot pepper sauce
- Jicama
- Kohlrabi
- Leeks
- Lemon juice
- Mixed vegetables (without corn, peas or pasta)
- Mushrooms (fresh)
- Mustard
- Okra
- Onions
- Pea pods
- Pickles
- Radishes
- Rutabaga
- Salad greens (lettuce, romaine, chicory, endive, escarole, arugula, radicchio, watercress)
- Sauerkraut
- Spices
- Spinach
- Squash (summer, crookneck, zucchini)
- Sugar snap peas
- Swiss chard
- Tomato (fresh or canned)
- Turnips
- Vinegar
- Water chestnuts
- Worcestershire sauce

FREE FOOD AND BEVERAGES— DRINK AS MUCH AS YOU WANT

- Carbonated or mineral water
- Club soda
- Coffee (unsweetened or with sugar substitute)
- Diet soft drinks
- Drink mixes (sugar-free)
- Flavored water (20 calories or less)
- Tea (unsweetened or with sugar substitute)
- Tonic water (diet)
- Water

FREE FOODS WITH RESTRICTED PORTIONS

- Barbecue sauce, *2 teaspoons*
- Cream cheese (fat-free), *1 tablespoon (1/2 ounce)*
- Creamer:
  Nondairy, liquid, *1 tablespoon*
  Nondairy, powdered, *2 teaspoons*
- Honey mustard, *1 tablespoon*
- Jam or jelly (light or no-sugar added), *2 teaspoons*
- Ketchup, *1 tablespoon*
- Margarine spread:
  Fat-free, *1 tablespoon*
  Reduced-fat, *1 teaspoon*
- Mayonnaise:
  Fat-free, *1 tablespoon*
  Reduced-fat, *1 teaspoon*
- Parmesan cheese (freshly grated), *1 tablespoon*
- Pickle relish, *1 tablespoon*
- Salad dressing:
  Fat-free or low-fat, *1 tablespoon*
  Fat-free Italian, *2 tablespoons*
- Salsa, *1/4 cup*
- Sour cream: Fat-free or reduced-fat, *1 tablespoon*
- Sweet and sour sauce, *2 teaspoons*
- Soy sauce, *1 tablespoon*
- Sweet chili sauce, *1 tablespoon*
- Syrup (sugar-free), *2 tablespoons*
- Taco sauce, *1 tablespoon*
- Whipped topping:
  Light or fat-free, *2 tablespoons*
  Regular, *1 tablespoon*

six-week MEAL PLAN

The following pages take the work out of calorie counting by offering a complete six-week meal plan. Each day suggest three meals and two snacks, totaling roughly 1,400 calories. Feel free to substitute foods or mix and match the meals from various days. Be sure, however, to pay attention to calories. To plan future weeks, record what you're eating and track calories, using the blank Do-It-Yourself worksheets found on pages 294-295.

Comfort Food Diet Strategies:

- The great thing about the Comfort Food Diet is that you can serve incredible meals to your family members...who won't even realize they're eating healthy. Look through the recipes in this book, and immediately begin the meal plan by swapping in the dishes you know they'll enjoy most.

- The Comfort Food Diet tracks calories per day to make it easier to stay within the 1,400 calorie guideline. If you should exceed that limit one day, however, simply plan on consuming fewer calories the following day. Keeping a food/calorie journal will help you track such instances.

- Consider making extras and freezing the leftovers for busy days or work lunches. When preparing large-batch recipes, stash a few in the freezer for low-calorie snacks and desserts.

- Review the items on the Free Foods Chart (p. 43), and use them to satisfy hunger between meals. They're also tasty ways to round out a menu without adding too many calories.

- Try to get the most nutrients from calories. In other words, a couple tablespoons of chocolate-covered raisins have nearly the same amount of calories as four dates. The dates offer more health benefits than the chocolate treats, but feel free to enjoy the raisins if your sweet tooth is begging for a little attention.

day 1

BREAKFAST:

- Berry & Yogurt Phyllo Nest (p. 83)
  72 CALORIES
- 1 large scrambled egg
  101 CALORIES
- 1 slice whole wheat toast
  69 CALORIES
- with 1 teaspoon reduced-fat margarine spread
  FREE FOOD
- 1 cup fat-free milk
  86 CALORIES
- 1 cup hot tea (with sugar substitute if desired)
  FREE FOOD

  BREAKFAST TOTAL: 328 CALORIES

LUNCH:

- 1-1/2 cups Zesty Hamburger Soup (p. 125)
  222 CALORIES
- 1 whole wheat dinner roll
  76 CALORIES
- 1 medium banana
  100 CALORIES
- 1 can mineral water
  FREE FOOD

  LUNCH TOTAL: 398 CALORIES

DINNER & DESSERT:

- 1 fillet Baked Parmesan Roughy (p. 177)
  211 CALORIES
- 1 whole wheat dinner roll
  76 CALORIES
- with 1 teaspoon reduced-fat margarine spread
  FREE FOOD
- Shredded cabbage topped with 1 tablespoon reduced-fat salad dressing
  FREE FOOD
- 1 glass ice water
  FREE FOOD
- 1 piece Ice Cream Sandwich Dessert (p. 291)
  244 CALORIES

  DINNER TOTAL: 531 CALORIES

SNACKS:

- 3/4 cup air-popped popcorn
  24 CALORIES
- 1 cup whole strawberries
  45 CALORIES
- 1 piece string cheese
  80 CALORIES

  WEEK 1, DAY 1 TOTAL: 1,406 CALORIES

day 2

BREAKFAST:

- 1 slice Crustless Spinach Quiche (p. 95)
  197 CALORIES
- 1 slice whole wheat toast
  69 CALORIES
- with 1 tablespoon no-sugar-added jam
  FREE FOOD
- 1 cup hot tea (with sugar substitute if desired)
  FREE FOOD
- 1/2 cup orange juice
  55 CALORIES

  BREAKFAST TOTAL: 321 CALORIES

LUNCH:

- 1 cup Salmon Chowder (p. 129)
  198 CALORIES
- 4 saltine crackers
  52 CALORIES
- 2/3 cup red grapes
  86 CALORIES
- 1 cup fat-free milk
  86 CALORIES

  LUNCH TOTAL: 422 CALORIES

DINNER & DESSERT:

- 1 cup Zippy Spaghetti Sauce (p. 170)
  220 CALORIES
- served over 1 cup cooked spaghetti
  100 CALORIES
- 1 big green salad (see Free Foods Chart on p. 43) with 1 tablespoon reduced-fat salad dressing
  FREE FOOD
- 1 cup fat-free milk
  86 CALORIES
- 1 Chocolate Peanut Butter Parfait (p. 282)
  146 CALORIES
- 1 cup of coffee (with sugar substitute and 1 tablespoon liquid non-dairy creamer, if desired)
  FREE FOOD

  DINNER TOTAL: 552 CALORIES

SNACKS:

- 1 piece of string cheese
  80 CALORIES
- 1 medium peach or plum
  40 CALORIES

  WEEK 1, DAY 2 TOTAL: 1,415 CALORIES

meal plan | THE COMFORT FOOD DIET

day 3

BREAKFAST:

- 2 servings Vegetable Scrambled Eggs (p. 86)
  180 CALORIES
- 2 mini bagels (2-1/2 inch diameter)
  144 CALORIES
- with 1 tablespoon whipped cream cheese
  35 CALORIES
- 1 cup of coffee (with sugar substitute and 1 tablespoon liquid non-dairy creamer, if desired)
  FREE FOOD

BREAKFAST TOTAL: 359 CALORIES

LUNCH:

- 1 California Chicken Wrap (p. 142)
  300 CALORIES
- 1 medium banana
  100 CALORIES
- 1 diet soft drink
  FREE FOOD

LUNCH TOTAL: 400 CALORIES

DINNER & DESSERT:

- 1 serving Grilled Stuffed Pork Tenderloin (p. 190)
  296 CALORIES
- Steamed fresh or frozen green beans topped with 1 teaspoon reduced-fat margarine
  FREE FOOD
- 1 big green salad (see Free Foods Chart on p. 43) with 1 tablespoon reduced-fat salad dressing
  FREE FOOD
- 1 cup fat-free milk
  86 CALORIES
- 1 Mini Apple Strudel (p. 272)
  100 CALORIES
- 1 cup hot tea (with sugar substitute if desired)
  FREE FOOD

DINNER TOTAL: 482 CALORIES

SNACKS:

- 1/2 cup sugar-free chocolate pudding (prepared with fat-free milk) topped with a crushed chocolate wafer
  99 CALORIES
- 1/2 cup fresh blueberries
  41 CALORIES

WEEK 1, DAY 3 TOTAL: 1,381 CALORIES

> In order to best fit your schedule, feel free to move days around on this meal planner.

day 4

BREAKFAST:

- 2 Yogurt Pancakes (p. 118)
  242 CALORIES
- with 1 teaspoon reduced-fat margarine spread
  FREE FOOD
- drizzled with 1 tablespoon maple syrup
  52 CALORIES
- 1/2 cup orange juice
  55 CALORIES

BREAKFAST TOTAL: 349 CALORIES

LUNCH:

- 1 cup Southwestern Chicken Soup (p. 128)
  143 CALORIES
- 1 half-sandwich made with 1 piece whole-wheat bread and 2 slices deli smoked turkey breast spread with 1 teaspoon fat-free mayonnaise
  89 CALORIES
- 1 piece of string cheese
  80 CALORIES
- 1 medium banana
  100 CALORIES
- 1 bottle flavored water
  FREE FOOD

LUNCH TOTAL: 412 CALORIES

DINNER & DESSERT:

- 1 Makeover Li'l Cheddar Meat Loaf (p. 184)
  187 CALORIES
- 1 medium baked russet potato
  161 CALORIES
- Steamed fresh broccoli florets
  FREE FOOD
- 1 cup fat-free milk
  86 CALORIES
- 1 piece Chunky Fruit 'n' Nut Fudge (p. 270)
  92 CALORIES
- 1 cup of coffee (with sugar substitute and 1 tablespoon liquid non-dairy creamer, if desired)
  FREE FOOD

DINNER TOTAL: 526 CALORIES

SNACKS:

- 1 medium peach or plum
  40 CALORIES
- 1/3 cup 1% cottage cheese with 1/4 cup unsweetened pineapple tidbits
  81 CALORIES

WEEK 1, DAY 4 TOTAL: 1,408 CALORIES

day 5

BREAKFAST:

- 1/2 cup Raisin Oatmeal Mix (prepared) (p. 94)
  186 CALORIES
- 1 Turkey Breakfast Sausage Patty (p. 82)
  86 CALORIES
- 1/4 cup cubed fresh pineapple
  37 CALORIES
- 1/2 cup fat-free milk
  43 CALORIES

BREAKFAST TOTAL: 352 CALORIES

LUNCH:

- 1 Open-Faced Portobello Sandwich (p. 124)
  236 CALORIES
- 1 piece of string cheese
  80 CALORIES
- 1 medium pear
  96 CALORIES
- 2 medium celery ribs with 1 tablespoon fat-free ranch salad dressing
  40 CALORIES
- 1 can mineral water
  FREE FOOD

LUNCH TOTAL: 452 CALORIES

DINNER & DESSERT:

- 1 serving Smothered Chicken Italiano (p. 195)
  252 CALORIES
- 1 big green salad (see Free Foods Chart on p. 43) with 1 tablespoon reduced-fat salad dressing
  FREE FOOD
- 2 sesame bread sticks (5g each)
  40 CALORIES
- 1 serving Broccoli with Lemon Sauce (p. 244)
  76 CALORIES
- 1 diet soft drink
  FREE FOOD
- 1 piece Chunky Fruit 'n' Nut Fudge (p. 123)
  92 CALORIES
- 1 cup hot tea (with sugar substitute if desired)
  FREE FOOD

DINNER TOTAL: 460 CALORIES

SNACKS:

- 2/3 cup Cheerios with 1/4 cup fat-free milk
  93 CALORIES
- 1/2 cup sliced strawberries with 2 tablespoons reduced-fat frozen whipped topping
  47 CALORIES

WEEK 1, DAY 5 TOTAL: 1,404 CALORIES

day 6

BREAKFAST:

- 1 cup Cappuccino Smoothie (p. 101)
  166 CALORIES
- 1 Turkey Breakfast Sausage Patty (p. 82)
  86 CALORIES
- 1 mini bagel (2-1/2 inch diameter)
  72 CALORIES
- with 1 tablespoon whipped cream cheese
  35 CALORIES
- 1 cup hot tea (with sugar substitute if desired)
  FREE FOOD

BREAKFAST TOTAL: 359 CALORIES

LUNCH:

- 1 Simon's Famous Tuna Salad (p. 140)
  289 CALORIES
- 1/3 cup red grapes
  43 CALORIES
- 1 cup fat-free milk
  86 CALORIES

LUNCH TOTAL: 418 CALORIES

DINNER & DESSERT:

- 1 serving Grilled Pork Chops with Cilantro Salsa (p. 167)
  240 CALORIES
- 1 small baked sweet potato
  128 CALORIES
- with 1 teaspoon reduced-fat margarine spread
  FREE FOOD
- 1 cup Grilled Broccoli & Cauliflower (p. 242)
  47 CALORIES
- 1 glass ice water
  FREE FOOD
- 1 Chocolate Pudding Sandwich (p. 275)
  73 CALORIES
- 1 cup of coffee (with sugar substitute and 1 tablespoon liquid non-dairy creamer, if desired)
  FREE FOOD

DINNER TOTAL: 488 CALORIES

SNACKS:

- 1/2 small apple with 2 tablespoons fat-free caramel ice cream topping
  93 CALORIES
- 1 medium plum
  40 CALORIES

WEEK 1, DAY 6 TOTAL: 1,398 CALORIES

meal plan | THE COMFORT FOOD DIET

day 7

BREAKFAST:

- 2 Nutmeg Waffles (p. 94)
  196 CALORIES

- with 1 teaspoon reduced-fat margarine spread
  FREE FOOD

- drizzled with 1 tablespoon maple syrup
  52 CALORIES

- 1/4 cup cubed fresh pineapple
  37 CALORIES

- 1/2 cup orange juice
  55 CALORIES

BREAKFAST TOTAL: 340 CALORIES

LUNCH:

- 1 California Pizza (p. 126)
  245 CALORIES

- 1 big green salad (see Free Foods Chart on p. 43) with 1 tablespoon reduced-fat salad dressing
  FREE FOOD

- 3/4 cup fresh blueberries
  62 CALORIES

- 1 cup Watermelon Cooler (p. 69)
  82 CALORIES

LUNCH TOTAL: 389 CALORIES

DINNER & DESSERT:

- 1 serving Cornmeal Oven-Fried Chicken (p. 182)
  244 CALORIES

- 3/4 cup Potato Vegetable Medley (p. 241)
  59 CALORIES

- 1 slice whole wheat bread
  69 CALORIES

- with 1 teaspoon reduced-fat margarine spread
  FREE FOOD

- 1 cup fat-free milk
  86 CALORIES

- 1 Chocolate Pudding Sandwich (p. 275)
  73 CALORIES

DINNER TOTAL: 531 CALORIES

SNACKS:

- 1 cup Strawberry Mango Smoothie (p. 74)
  100 CALORIES

- 1/2 cup baby carrots
  25 CALORIES

- 1 cup prepared sugar-free gelatin
  8 CALORIES

WEEK 1, DAY 7 TOTAL: 1,393 CALORIES

day 1

BREAKFAST:

- 1 Brunch Enchilada (p. 110)
  258 CALORIES

- 1 small orange
  45 CALORIES

- 1 cup coffee (with sugar substitute and 1 tablespoon liquid non-dairy creamer, if desired)
  FREE FOOD

BREAKFAST TOTAL: 303 CALORIES

LUNCH:

- 1 Open-Faced Salmon Sandwich (p. 148)
  270 CALORIES

- 1 medium apple
  72 CALORIES

- 1 cup fat-free milk
  86 CALORIES

LUNCH TOTAL: 428 CALORIES

DINNER & DESSERT:

- 1 Crab-Stuffed Chicken Breast (p. 169)
  225 CALORIES

- served with 1/2 cup prepared egg noodles
  111 CALORIES

- 3/4 cup Zippy Green Beans (p. 242)
  98 CALORIES

- 1 big green salad (see Free Foods Chart on p. 43) with 1 tablespoon reduced-fat salad dressing
  FREE FOOD

- 1 glass ice water
  FREE FOOD

- 1 serving Broiled Pineapple Dessert (p. 274)
  98 CALORIES

- 1 glass iced tea (unsweetened or with sugar substitute)
  FREE FOOD

DINNER TOTAL: 532 CALORIES

SNACKS:

- 1/2 piece of string cheese
  40 CALORIES

- 9 tiny twist fat-free pretzels
  50 CALORIES

- served with 1 tablespoon honey mustard for dipping
  FREE FOOD

- 1 medium peach or plum
  40 CALORIES

WEEK 2, DAY 1 TOTAL: 1,393 CALORIES

day 2

BREAKFAST:

- 1 serving Vegetable Frittata (p. 101)
  141 CALORIES
- 1/2 of a Cinnamon Honey Grapefruit (p. 32)
  63 CALORIES
- 1 slice whole wheat toast
  69 CALORIES
- with 1 tablespoon no-sugar-added jam
  FREE FOOD
- 1/2 cup orange juice
  55 CALORIES
- 1 cup hot tea (with sugar substitute if desired)
  FREE FOOD

BREAKFAST TOTAL: 328 CALORIES

LUNCH:

- 1 piece Chicken Caesar Deluxe Pizza (p. 152)
  358 CALORIES
- 1 piece of string cheese
  80 CALORIES
- 1/4 cup cubed fresh pineapple
  37 CALORIES
- 1 bottle flavored water
  FREE FOOD

LUNCH TOTAL: 475 CALORIES

DINNER & DESSERT:

- 2 Sesame Beef 'n' Veggie Kabobs (p. 179)
  216 CALORIES
- 1/2 cup prepared long-grain white rice
  103 CALORIES
- 1 big green salad (see Free Foods Chart on p. 43)
  with 1 tablespoon reduced-fat salad dressing
  FREE FOOD
- 1 cup fat-free milk
  86 CALORIES
- 1 Chocolate Pudding Sandwich (p. 275)
  73 CALORIES
- 1 cup of coffee (with sugar substitute and
  1 tablespoon liquid non-dairy creamer, if desired)
  FREE FOOD

DINNER TOTAL: 478 CALORIES

SNACKS:

- 1 medium banana
  100 CALORIES
- 3/4 cup air-popped popcorn
  24 CALORIES

WEEK 2, DAY 2 TOTAL: 1,405 CALORIES

day 3

BREAKFAST:

- 1 Apple Yogurt Parfait (p. 89)
  170 CALORIES
- 1 medium grapefruit
  92 CALORIES
- 1/2 mini bagel
  36 CALORIES
- with 1 tablespoon fat-free cream cheese
  FREE FOOD
- 1/2 cup fat-free milk
  43 CALORIES
- 1 cup of coffee (with sugar substitute and
  1 tablespoon liquid non-dairy creamer, if desired)
  FREE FOOD

BREAKFAST TOTAL: 341 CALORIES

LUNCH:

- 1 cup Jamaican-Style Beef Stew (p. 147)
  312 CALORIES
- 1/2 cup prepared long-grain white rice
  103 CALORIES
- 1/3 cup red grapes
  43 CALORIES
- 1 glass ice water
  FREE FOOD

LUNCH TOTAL: 458 CALORIES

DINNER & DESSERT:

- 1 serving Skillet Pasta Florentine (p. 229)
  383 CALORIES
- 1 big green salad (see Free Foods Chart on p. 43)
  with 1 tablespoon reduced-fat salad dressing
  FREE FOOD
- 1 glass sparkling water
  FREE FOOD
- 1 Peanut Butter Granola Mini Bar (p. 272)
  93 CALORIES
- 1 cup hot tea (with sugar substitute if desired)
  FREE FOOD

DINNER TOTAL: 476 CALORIES

SNACKS:

- 3/4 cup skinny latte (made with fat-free milk)
  60 CALORIES
- 1/2 cup cubed fresh pineapple
  37 CALORIES
- 1 cup prepared sugar-free gelatin
  8 CALORIES

WEEK 2, DAY 3 TOTAL: 1,380 CALORIES

week 3

day 1

BREAKFAST:

- 2 Spiced Bacon Twists (p. 81)
  75 CALORIES
- 1 large scrambled egg
  101 CALORIES
- 1 slice whole wheat toast
  69 CALORIES

  with 1 teaspoon reduced-fat margarine spread
  FREE FOOD
- 1 cup orange juice
  110 CALORIES

BREAKFAST TOTAL: 355 CALORIES

LUNCH:

- 1 Taco Chicken Wrap (p. 124)
  211 CALORIES

  with ¼ cup salsa
  FREE FOOD
- 1/2 cup baby carrots
  25 CALORIES
- 1 cup fat-fre milk
  86 CALORIES
- 1/2 cup sugar-free chocolate pudding (prepared with fat-free milk) topped with a crushed chocolate wafer
  99 CALORIES

LUNCH TOTAL: 421 CALORIES

DINNER & DESSERT:

- 1 serving Honey-Glazed Ham (p. 164)
  166 CALORIES
- 1 serving Never-Fail Scalloped Potatoes (p. 256)
  196 CALORIES
- 1 cup baby corn
  FREE FOOD
- 1 glass iced tea (unsweetened or with sugar substitute)
  FREE FOOD
- 1 piece Frozen Chocolate Delight (p. 278)
  134 CALORIES

DINNER TOTAL: 496 CALORIES

SNACKS:

- 1 Shrimp Canape (p. 70)
  43 CALORIES
- 1 medium plum
  40 CALORIES
- 3/4 cup tomato juice
  31 CALORIES

WEEK 3, DAY 1, TOTAL: 1,386 CALORIES

day 2

BREAKFAST:

- 1 serving Vegetable Frittata (p. 101)
  141 CALORIES
- 1 slice whole wheat toast
  69 CALORIES
- with 1 teaspoon no-sugar-added jam
  FREE FOOD
- 1 medium banana
  100 CALORIES
- 3/4 cup tomato juice
  31 CALORIES

BREAKFAST TOTAL: 341 CALORIES

LUNCH:

- 1 cup Spicy Sausage and Penne (p. 127)
  228 CALORIES
- 1 whole wheat dinner roll
  76 CALORIES
- spread with 1 teaspoon reduced-fat margarine
  FREE FOOD
- 1 big green salad (see Free Food Chart on p. 43) with 1 tablespoon reduced-fat salad dressing
  FREE FOOD
- 1/3 cup red grapes
  43 CALORIES
- 1/2 cup 1% chocolate milk
  84 CALORIES

LUNCH TOTAL: 431 CALORIES

DINNER & DESSERT:

- 1 Pork Chop with Onion Gravy (p. 182)
  210 CALORIES
- 1 Herbed Twice-Baked Potato (p. 262)
  150 CALORIES
- Steamed fresh broccoli florets
  FREE FOOD
- 1 glass carbonated water
  FREE FOOD
- 1 Cinnamon Peach Enchilada (p. 285)
  143 CALORIES
- 1 cup hot tea (with sugar substitute if desired)
  FREE FOOD

DINNER TOTAL: 503 CALORIES

SNACKS:

- 2 Jalapenos with Olive-Cream Filling (p. 71)
  58 CALORIES
- 1/2 English muffin topped with 1 slice tomato and 1 tablespoon shredded part-skim mozzarella cheese, broiled
  87 CALORIES

WEEK 3, DAY 2, TOTAL: 1,420 CALORIES

day 3

BREAKFAST:

- 3/4 cup Baked Southern Grits (p. 104)
  158 CALORIES

- 1 mini bagel (2-1/2 inch diameter)
  72 CALORIES

- with 1 teaspoon no-sugar-added jam
  FREE FOOD

- 1 Turkey Breakfast Sausage Patty (p. 82)
  86 CALORIES

- 1 cup of coffee (with sugar substitute and 1 tablespoon liquid nondairy creamer, if desired)
  FREE FOOD

BREAKFAST TOTAL: 316 CALORIES

LUNCH:

- 1/2 Pulled Pork Sub (p. 156)
  417 CALORIES

- 1 dill pickle spear
  FREE FOOD

- 1/2 cup baby carrots
  25 CALORIES

- 1 can mineral water
  FREE FOOD

LUNCH TOTAL: 442 CALORIES

DINNER & DESSERT:

- 1 serving Italian Cabbage Casserole (p. 168)
  223 CALORIES

- 1 serving Basil Cherry Tomatoes (p. 243)
  42 CALORIES

- 1 big green salad (see Free Food Chart on p. 43) with 1 tablespoon reduced-fat salad dressing
  FREE FOOD

- 1 cup fat-free milk
  86 CALORIES

- 2 Coconut Macaroons (p. 284)
  108 CALORIES

- 1 cup hot tea (with sugar substitute if desired)
  FREE FOOD

DINNER TOTAL: 459 CALORIES

SNACKS:

- 1/2 cup Special Summer Berry Medley (p. 71)
  85 CALORIES

- 2 medium celery ribs with 1 tablespoon fat-free ranch salad dressing
  40 CALORIES

- 1/2 cup cheese popcorn
  40 CALORIES

WEEK 3, DAY 3, TOTAL: 1,382 CALORIES

day 4

BREAKFAST:

- 1 Black Forest Crepe (p. 107)
  256 CALORIES

- 1 cup cubed fresh pineapple
  74 CALORIES

- 1 cup hot tea (with sugar substitute if desired)
  FREE FOOD

BREAKFAST TOTAL: 330 CALORIES

LUNCH:

- 1 cup Chicken Chili (p. 133)
  201 CALORIES

- 4 saltine crackers
  52 CALORIES

- 1 medium apple
  72 CALORIES

- 1 cup fat-free milk
  6 CALORIES

LUNCH TOTAL: 411 CALORIES

DINNER & DESSERT:

- 1 Orange Roughy with Rice (p. 203)
  320 CALORIES

- 3/4 cup Savory Brussels Sprouts (p. 243)
  76 CALORIES

- 1 big green salad (see Free Food Chart on p. 43) with 1 tablespoon reduced-fat salad dressing
  FREE FOOD

- 1 cup brewed ice tea (with sugar substitute if desired)
  FREE FOOD

- 1/2 cup Jelled Champagne Dessert
  96 CALORIES

- 1 glass ice water
  FREE FOOD

DINNER TOTAL: 492 CALORIES

SNACKS:

- 1 slice Mexican Salsa Pizza (p. 77)
  64 CALORIES

- 1 serving Zucchini Fritters (p. 73)
  67 CALORIES

WEEK 3, DAY 4, TOTAL: 1,364 CALORIES

Top off slices of angel food cake with fresh fruit and a dollop of reduced-fat whipped topping or frozen yogurt for a no-fuss dessert that's light, too.

meal plan | THE COMFORT FOOD DIET

day 5

BREAKFAST:

- 1/2 Prosciutto Egg Panini (p. 114)
  228 CALORIES

- 1 cup Fruit Smoothie (p. 85)
  97 CALORIES

- 1 cup of coffee (with sugar substitute and 1 tablespoon liquid nondairy creamer, if desired)
  FREE FOOD

  BREAKFAST TOTAL: 325 CALORIES

LUNCH:

- 1 serving Seasoned Chicken Strips (p. 123)
  188 CALORIES

- 1 serving Cheese Fries (p. 261)
  129 CALORIES

- 1 medium pear
  96 CALORIES

- 1 can diet soda
  FREE FOOD

  LUNCH TOTAL: 413 CALORIES

DINNER & DESSERT:

- 1 serving Pot Roast with Vegetables (p. 235)
  417 CALORIES

- 1 big green salad (see Free Food Chart on p. 43) with 1 tablespoon reduced-fat salad dressing
  FREE FOOD

- 1 bottle flavored water
  FREE FOOD

- 1 Strawberry Banana Delight (p. 269)
  78 CALORIES

- 1 cup hot tea (with sugar substitute if desired)
  FREE FOOD

  DINNER TOTAL: 495 CALORIES

SNACKS:

- 1 Crispy Baked Wonton (p. 70)
  38 CALORIES

- 1 medium kiwifruit
  46 CALORIES

- 1 small cucumber, sliced with 2 tablespoons reduced-fat French onion dip
  49 CALORIES

  WEEK 3, DAY 5, TOTAL: 1,366 CALORIES

> Don't forget to clip out the calorie chart on the back flap of this book. Tape it to the inside of a kitchen cabinet to give your family ideas for low-calorie snacks.

day 6

BREAKFAST:

- 1 Pepper Cheese Omelet (p. 88)
  156 CALORIES

- 1 slice whole wheat bread, toasted
  69 CALORIES

- with 1 teaspoon reduced-fat margarine spread
  FREE FOOD

- 1 medium grapefruit
  92 CALORIES

- 1 glass ice water
  FREE FOOD

  BREAKFAST TOTAL: 317 CALORIES

LUNCH:

- 1 cup Creamy Pepperoni Ziti (p. 141)
  340 CALORIES

- 1 cup mixed greens with 1 tablespoon crumbled blue cheese and 1 tablespoon fat-free Italian salad dressing
  49 CALORIES

- 1 medium plum
  40 CALORIES

- 1 glass ice water
  FREE FOOD

  LUNCH TOTAL: 430 CALORIES

DINNER & DESSERT:

- 1 serving Pecan-Crusted Chicken (p. 167)
  214 CALORIES

- 1 serving Grilled Garden Veggies (p. 247)
  61 CALORIES

- 1 cup fat-free milk
  86 CALORIES

- 2 Coconut Macaroons (p. 284)
  108 CALORIES

- 1 cup of coffee (with sugar substitute and 1 tablespoon liquid nondairy creamer, if desired)
  FREE FOOD

  DINNER TOTAL: 469 CALORIES

SNACKS:

- 1/2 cup Cranberry Popcorn Deluxe (p. 68)
  96 CALORIES

- 1/2 cup broccoli florets with 2 tablespoons fat-free ranch salad dressing
  58 CALORIES

  WEEK 3, DAY 6, TOTAL: 1,370 CALORIES

day 7

BREAKFAST:

- 2 Makeover Multigrain Waffles (p. 91)
  187 CALORIES
- with 2 tablespoons sugar-free syrup
  FREE FOOD
- 1 cup Cappuccino Smoothie (p. 101)
  166 CALORIES
- 1 bottle flavored water
  FREE FOOD

BREAKFAST TOTAL: **353 CALORIES**

LUNCH:

- 1 serving Green Tea Teriyaki Chicken (p. 129)
  184 CALORIES
- 1/2 cup cooked long-grain white rice
  103 CALORIES
- 3/4 cup Zippy Green Beans (p. 242)
  98 CALORIES
- 1 small orange
  45 CALORIES
- 1 can diet soda
  FREE FOOD

LUNCH TOTAL: **430 CALORIES**

DINNER & DESSERT:

- 1 serving Gingered Pork Tenderloin (p. 180)
  214 CALORIES
- 3/4 cup Colorful Veggie Saute (p. 245)
  51 CALORIES
- 1 medium baked russet potato
  161 CALORIES
- 1 glass ice water
  FREE FOOD
- 1 Coconut Macaroon (p. 284)
  54 CALORIES
- 1 cup hot tea (with sugar substitute if desired)
  FREE FOOD

DINNER TOTAL: **480 CALORIES**

SNACKS:

- 2 Artichoke Rye Toasts (p. 75)
  78 CALORIES
- 1/2 cup baby carrots with 1 tablespoon hummus
  48 CALORIES

WEEK 3, DAY 7, TOTAL: 1,389 CALORIES

> Store leftover Coconut Macaroons in the freezer for lunch additions and snacking options for the following week.

day 1

BREAKFAST:

- 1 Apple Yogurt Parfait (p. 89)
  170 CALORIES
- 1 slice whole wheat toast
  69 CALORIES
- with 1 teaspoon reduced-fat margarine spread
  FREE FOOD
- 1/3 cup Cheerios with 1/4 cup fat-free milk
  93 CALORIES
- 1 cup coffee (with sugar substitute and 1 tablespoon liquid nondairy creamer, if desired)
  FREE FOOD

BREAKFAST TOTAL: **332 CALORIES**

LUNCH:

- 3/4 cup Makeover Hash Brown Soup (p. 123)
  206 CALORIES
- 4 Saltine crackers
  52 CALORIES
- 1 medium banana
  100 CALORIES
- 3 pieces snack rye bread topped with 1 tablespoon reduced-fat vegetable cream cheese and 6 cucumber slices
  89 CALORIES
- 1 can mineral water
  FREE FOOD

LUNCH TOTAL: **447 CALORIES**

DINNER & DESSERT:

- 1 cup Skillet Tacos (p. 205)
  267 CALORIES
- 1 cup Grilled Broccoli & Cauliflower (p. 242)
  47 CALORIES
- 8 white corn tortilla chips
  93 CALORIES
- 1 can of diet soft drink
  FREE FOOD
- 1 Cookie Fruit Basket (p. 276)
  100 CALORIES
- 1 cup hot tea (with sugar substitute if desired)
  FREE FOOD

DINNER TOTAL: **507 CALORIES**

SNACKS:

- 2 Cheese Puffs (p. 74)
  68 CALORIES
- 1/3 cup unsweetened applesauce sprinkled with cinnamon
  35 CALORIES

WEEK 4, DAY 1 TOTAL: 1,389 CALORIES

day 2

BREAKFAST:

- 1 wedge Anytime Frittata (p. 90)
  138 CALORIES

- 1 medium peach
  40 CALORIES

- 2 mini bagels (2-1/2 inch diameter)
  144 CALORIES

- with 1 tablespoon whipped cream cheese
  35 CALORIES

- 1 cup hot tea (with sugar substitute if desired)
  FREE FOOD

BREAKFAST TOTAL: 357 CALORIES

LUNCH:

- 1 Open-Faced Tuna Melt (p. 130)
  165 CALORIES

- 1 serving Tomato Corn Salad (p. 251)
  84 CALORIES

- 1 cup mixed greens with 1 tablespoon crumbled blue cheese and 1 tablespoon fat-free Italian salad dressing
  49 CALORIES

- 1 clementine
  35 CALORIES

- 1/2 cup sugar-free chocolate pudding (prepared with fat-free milk) topped with a crushed chocolate wafer
  99 CALORIES

- 1 can diet soft drink
  FREE FOOD

LUNCH TOTAL: 432 CALORIES

DINNER & DESSERT:

- 1 serving Maple-Glazed Chicken (p. 174)
  226 CALORIES

- 1 Seasoned Baked Potato (p. 258)
  167 CALORIES

- 3/4 cup Colorful Veggie Saute (p. 245)
  51 CALORIES

- 1 cup brewed ice tea (with sugar substitute if desired)
  FREE FOOD

- 1 Cocoa Mint Truffle (p. 269)
  58 CALORIES

- 1 cup hot tea (with sugar substitute if desired)
  FREE FOOD

DINNER TOTAL: 502 CALORIES

SNACKS:

- 1/4 cup Garlic Pumpkin Seeds (p. 79)
  87 CALORIES

- 1/2 cup grape tomatoes with 2 tablespoons fat-free Italian salad dressing
  36 CALORIES

WEEK 4, DAY 2, TOTAL: 1,414 CALORIES

day 3

BREAKFAST:

- 2 Flaxseed Oatmeal Pancakes (p. 120)
  273 CALORIES

- drizzled with 1 tablespoon maple syrup
  52 CALORIES

- 1/4 cup blueberries
  21 CALORIES

- 1 cup coffee (with sugar substitute and 1 tablespoon liquid nondairy creamer, if desired)
  FREE FOOD

BREAKFAST TOTAL: 346 CALORIES

LUNCH:

- 1 Grilled Pepper Jack Chicken Sandwich (p. 140)
  335 CALORIES

- 1 piece string cheese
  80 CALORIES

- 1 big green salad (see Free Food Chart on p. 43) with 1 tablespoon reduced-fat salad dressing
  FREE FOOD

- 1 cup prepared sugar-free flavored gelatin
  8 CALORIES

- 1 glass ice water
  FREE FOOD

LUNCH TOTAL: 423 CALORIES

DINNER & DESSERT:

- 1 Makeover Li'l Cheddar Meat Loaf (p. 184)
  187 CALORIES

- 1/2 Herbed Twice-Baked Potato (p. 262)
  150 CALORIES

- 1/2 cup fat-free milk
  43 CALORIES

- Shredded cabbage topped with 1 tablespoon reduced-fat salad dressing
  FREE FOOD

- 2 Cocoa Mint Truffles (p. 269)
  116 CALORIES

- 1 cup coffee (with sugar substitute and 1 tablespoon liquid nondairy creamer, if desired)
  FREE FOOD

DINNER TOTAL: 496 CALORIES

SNACKS:

- 1 cup Watermelon Cooler (p. 69)
  82 CALORIES

- 1 medium kiwifruit
  46 CALORIES

WEEK 4, DAY 3, TOTAL: 1,393 CALORIES

day 4

BREAKFAST:

- 1 Ham Potato Puff (p. 95)
  165 CALORIES
- 1 cup orange juice
  110 CALORIES
- 1 cup fresh raspberries
  60 CALORIES
- 1 cup coffee (with sugar substitute and 1 tablespoon liquid nondairy creamer, if desired)
  FREE FOOD

BREAKFAST TOTAL: 335 CALORIES

LUNCH:

- 1 cup Jamaican-Style Beef Stew (p. 147)
  285 CALORIES
- 4 Saltine crackers
  52 CALORIES
- 1/2 small baked potato with 3 tablespoons salsa
  81 CALORIES
- 1/2 cup baby carrots
  25 CALORIES
- 1 cup brewed ice tea (with sugar substitute if desired)
  FREE FOOD

LUNCH TOTAL: 443 CALORIES

DINNER & DESSERT:

- 1 serving Orange-Maple Glazed Chicken (p. 185)
  240 CALORIES
- 2/3 cup Bulgur Wheat Salad (p. 263)
  137 CALORIES
- Steamed fresh broccoli florets topped with 1 teaspoon reduced-fat margarine
  FREE FOOD
- 1 cup brewed ice tea (with sugar substitute if desired)
  FREE FOOD
- 1 Heavenly Surprise Mini Cupcake (p. 280)
  130 CALORIES
- 1 cup coffee (with sugar substitute and 1 tablespoon liquid nondairy creamer, if desired)
  FREE FOOD

DINNER TOTAL: 507 CALORIES

SNACKS:

- 2 Cheese Puffs (p. 74)
  68 CALORIES
- 1 whole cinnamon graham cracker
  35 CALORIES

WEEK 4, DAY 4, TOTAL: 1,388 CALORIES

day 5

BREAKFAST:

- 1 Breakfast Crepe with Berries (p. 92)
  182 CALORIES
- 1 cup Cappuccino Smoothie (p. 101)
  166 CALORIES
- 1 cup hot tea (with sugar substitute if desired)
  FREE FOOD

BREAKFAST TOTAL: 348 CALORIES

LUNCH:

- 1-1/2 cups Asian Chicken with Pasta (p. 137)
  320 CALORIES
- 1 whole wheat dinner roll
  76 CALORIES
- spread with 1 teaspoon reduced-fat margarine
  FREE FOOD
- 1/2 small grapefruit with 1 teaspoon sugar
  48 CALORIES
- 1 glass club water
  FREE FOOD

LUNCH TOTAL: 444 CALORIES

DINNER & DESSERT:

- 1 Grilled Pork Chop with Cilantro Salsa (p. 167)
  240 CALORIES
- 2/3 cup Roasted Potatoes with Thyme and Gorgonzola (p. 252)
  150 CALORIES
- Steamed fresh or frozen green beans topped with 1 teaspoon reduced-fat margarine spread
  FREE FOOD
- 1 big green salad (see Free Food Chart on p. 43) with 1 tablespoon reduced-fat salad dressing
  FREE FOOD
- I glass ice water
  FREE FOOD
- 1 Broiled Pineapple Dessert (p. 274)
  98 CALORIES
- 1 cup hot tea (with sugar substitute if desired)
  FREE FOOD

DINNER TOTAL: 488 CALORIES

SNACKS:

- 1 serving Cannellini Bean Hummus (p. 76)
  78 CALORIES
- 2 chocolate kisses
  49 CALORIES

WEEK 4, DAY 5, TOTAL: 1,407 CALORIES

day 6

BREAKFAST:

- 1/2 Very Veggie Omelet (p. 102)
  197 CALORIES

- 2 Spiced Bacon Twists (p. 81)
  75 CALORIES

- 1/2 mini bagel
  36 CALORIES

- with 1 tablespoon fat-free cream cheese
  FREE FOOD

- 1 small orange
  45 CALORIES

- 1 glass ice water
  FREE FOOD

BREAKFAST TOTAL: 353 CALORIES

LUNCH:

- 1 Turkey Sloppy Joe
  304 CALORIES

- 10 baked potato chips
  100 CALORIES

- 1/2 cup fat-free milk
  43 CALORIES

LUNCH TOTAL: 447 CALORIES

DINNER & DESSERT:

- 1-1/3 cups Southwestern Goulash (p. 166)
  224 CALORIES

- 1 whole wheat dinner roll
  76 CALORIES

- 1/2 cup fat-free milk
  43 CALORIES

- 1 big green salad (see Free Foods Chart on p. 43) with 1 tablespoon reduced-fat salad dressing
  FREE FOOD

- 1 cup brewed ice tea (with sugar substitute if desired)
  FREE FOOD

- 1 piece Fresh Raspberry Pie (p. 288)
  163 CALORIES

- 1 cup coffee (with sugar substitute and 1 tablespoon liquid nondairy creamer, if desired)
  FREE FOOD

DINNER TOTAL: 506 CALORIES

SNACKS:

- 2 Artichoke Rye Toasts (p. 75)
  78 CALORIES

- 1/2 cup sliced zucchini with 2 tablespoons salsa
  19 CALORIES

WEEK 4, DAY 6, TOTAL: 1,403 CALORIES

day 7

BREAKFAST:

- 1 piece Harvest Vegetable Tart (p. 109)
  256 CALORIES

- 1/2 cup cubed fresh pineapple
  74 CALORIES

- 1 cup coffee (with sugar substitute and 1 tablespoon liquid nondairy creamer, if desired)
  FREE FOOD

BREAKFAST TOTAL: 330 CALORIES

LUNCH:

- 1 Roasted Pepper Chicken Sandwich (p. 160)
  404 CALORIES

- 1 big green salad (see Free Food Chart on p. 43) with 1 tablespoon reduced-fat salad dressing
  FREE FOOD

- 1/2 medium banana
  50 CALORIES

- 1 can diet soft drink
  FREE FOOD

LUNCH TOTAL: 454 CALORIES

DINNER & DESSERT:

- 1-1/2 cups Veggie Cheese Ravioli (p. 189)
  322 CALORIES

- 2 sesame breadsticks (5g each)
  40 CALORIES

- 1 big green salad (see Free Food Chart on p. 43) with 1 tablespoon reduced-fat salad dressing
  FREE FOOD

- 1 can diet soft drink
  FREE FOOD

- 1 Heavenly Surprise Mini Cupcake (p. 280)
  130 CALORIES

- 1 cup hot tea (with sugar substitute if desired)
  FREE FOOD

DINNER TOTAL: 492 CALORIES

SNACKS:

- 1 cup Hot Buttered Coffee (p. 77)
  67 CALORIES

- 7 miniature caramel-flavored rice cakes
  60 CALORIES

WEEK 4, DAY 7, TOTAL: 1,403 CALORIES

Keep a bag of frozen peas on hand. Toss a handful of peas into soups, sauces, casseroles...even morning omelets. They add a nice burst of color and extra nutrition.

day 1

BREAKFAST:

- 1 piece Crustless Spinach Quiche (p. 95)
  197 CALORIES

  3/4 cup tomato juice
  31 CALORIES

- 2/3 cup red grapes
  86 CALORIES

- 1 glass ice water
  FREE FOOD

BREAKFAST TOTAL: 314 CALORIES

LUNCH:

- 1 California Pizza (p. 126)
  245 CALORIES

- 1 serving Basil Cherry Tomatoes (p. 243)
  42 CALORIES

- 3/4 cup minestrone soup
  90 CALORIES

- 1 cup fresh raspberries
  60 CALORIES

- 1 big green salad (see Free Food Chart on p. 43)
  with 1 tablespoon reduced-fat salad dressing
  FREE FOOD

- 1 can diet soft drink
  FREE FOOD

LUNCH TOTAL: 437 CALORIES

DINNER & DESSERT:

- 1 cup Jambalaya (p. 176)
  228 CALORIES

- 1 cup Garlic Oregano Zucchini (p. 251)
  90 CALORIES

- 1 big green salad (see Free Food Chart on p. 43)
  with 1 tablespoon reduced-fat salad dressing
  FREE FOOD

- 1 glass carbonated water
  FREE FOOD

- 3/4 cup Makeover Toffee Crunch Dessert (p. 289)
  177 CALORIES

- 1 cup coffee (with sugar substitute and 1
  tablespoon liquid nondairy creamer, if desired)
  FREE FOOD

DINNER TOTAL: 495 CALORIES

SNACKS:

- 1 Cordon Bleu Appetizer (p. 79)
  86 CALORIES

- 1/2 frozen waffle with 1 tablespoon sugar-free syrup
  58 CALORIES

WEEK 5, DAY 1, TOTAL: 1,390 CALORIES

day 2

BREAKFAST:

- 2 Blueberry Oat Pancakes (p. 108)
  221 CALORIES

- with 2 tablespoons sugar-free syrup
  FREE FOOD

- 1 medium banana
  100 CALORIES

- 1 cup coffee (with sugar substitute and 1
  tablespoon liquid nondairy creamer, if desired)
  FREE FOOD

BREAKFAST TOTAL: 321 CALORIES

LUNCH:

- 1 sandwich Simon's Famous Tuna Salad (p. 140)
  289 CALORIES

- 1 serving Cheese Fries (p. 261)
  129 CALORIES

- 1/2 cup baby carrots
  25 CALORIES

- 1 cup brewed ice tea (with sugar substitute if
  desired)
  FREE FOOD

LUNCH TOTAL: 443 CALORIES

DINNER & DESSERT:

- 1 Sizzling Beef Kabob (p. 163)
  227 CALORIES

- 3/4 cup Steamed Kale (p. 246)
  61 CALORIES

- 1 whole wheat dinner roll
  76 CALORIES

- 1 can mineral water
  FREE FOOD

- 1 Tortilla Dessert Cup (p. 281)
  130 CALORIES

- 1 cup hot tea (with sugar substitute if desired)
  FREE FOOD

DINNER TOTAL: 494 CALORIES

SNACKS:

- 7 miniature caramel-flavored rice cakes
  60 CALORIES

- 1/2 medium apple with 1/2 ounce sharp cheddar
  cheese
  93 CALORIES

WEEK 5, DAY 2, TOTAL: 1,411 CALORIES

day 3

BREAKFAST:

- 1 serving Too-Yummy-To-Share Scramble (p. 92)
  136 CALORIES
- 1 Turkey Breakfast Sausage Patties (p. 82)
  86 CALORIES
- 1 cup orange juice
  110 CALORIES

BREAKFAST TOTAL: 332 CALORIES

LUNCH:

- 1 Roasted Red Pepper Sandwich (p. 160)
  404 CALORIES
- 1/2 cup sliced fresh strawberries
  27 CALORIES
- 1 glass ice water
  FREE FOOD

LUNCH TOTAL: 431 CALORIES

DINNER & DESSERT:

- 1 serving Tilapia & Lemon Sauce (p. 205)
  334 CALORIES
- 3/4 cup Savory Brussels Sprouts (p. 243)
  76 CALORIES
- 1 big green salad (see Free Food Chart on p. 43) with 1 tablespoon reduced-fat salad dressing
  FREE FOOD
- 1 can diet soft drink
  FREE FOOD
- 1 cup Strawberry Banana Delight (p. 269)
  78 CALORIES
- 1 cup coffee (with sugar substitute and 1 tablespoon liquid nondairy creamer, if desired)
  FREE FOOD

DINNER TOTAL: 488 CALORIES

SNACKS:

- 2 Jalapenos with Olive-Cream Filling (p. 71)
  58 CALORIES
- 1/2 small pear, sliced with 1 tablespoon caramel ice cream topping
  92 CALORIES

WEEK 5, DAY 3, TOTAL: 1,401 CALORIES

> Taking time for breakfast has lots of benefits. You get energy, raise your metabolism and are less likely to overeat later. If preparing breakfast is too difficult on busy weekday mornings, a little planning can do wonders. Smoothies can be made a day early and many breakfast bakes can be prepared the night before.

day 4

BREAKFAST:

- 2 Nutmeg Waffles (p. 94)
  196 CALORIES
- 1 large scrambled egg
  101 CALORIES
- 1 small orange
  45 CALORIES
- 1 cup coffee (with sugar substitute and 1 tablespoon liquid nondairy creamer, if desired)
  FREE FOOD

BREAKFAST TOTAL: 342 CALORIES

LUNCH:

- 1 California Chicken Wrap (p. 142)
  300 CALORIES
- 1/2 cup sliced strawberries with 2 tablespoons reduced-fat frozen whipped topping
  47 CALORIES
- 1/2 cup fat-free vanilla frozen yogurt
  95 CALORIES
- 1 glass club soda
  FREE FOOD

LUNCH TOTAL: 442 CALORIES

DINNER & DESSERT:

- 1 cup Skillet Tacos (p. 205)
  267 CALORIES
- 3/4 cup Corn and Broccoli in Cheese Sauce (p. 255)
  148 CALORIES
- 1 cup brewed ice tea (with sugar substitute if desired)
  FREE FOOD
- 1 serving Lemon Pudding Cup (p. 276)
  84 CALORIES
- 1 cup hot tea (with sugar substitute if desired)
  FREE FOOD

DINNER TOTAL: 499 CALORIES

SNACKS:

- 1 piece Chunky Fruit and Nut Fudge (p. 270)
  92 CALORIES
- 2 pineapple rings
  41 CALORIES

WEEK 5, DAY 4, TOTAL: 1,416 CALORIES

day 5

BREAKFAST:

- 1/2 cup Raisin Oatmeal Mix (p. 94)
  186 CALORIES
- 1 slice whole wheat bread, toasted
  69 CALORIES
- spread with 1 teaspoon reduced-fat margarine
  FREE FOOD
- 1/2 small banana with 2 teaspoons reduced-fat creamy peanut butter
  99 CALORIES
- 1 glass ice water
  FREE FOOD

BREAKFAST TOTAL: 354 CALORIES

LUNCH:

- 1 Slow-Cooked Pork Taco (p. 149)
  301 CALORIES
- 1/2 cup cooked long-grain white rice
  103 CALORIES
- 1 cup cubed watermelon
  40 CALORIES
- Steamed fresh or frozen green beans topped with 1 teaspoon reduced-fat margarine spread
  FREE FOOD
- 1 bottle flavored water
  FREE FOOD

LUNCH TOTAL: 444 CALORIES

DINNER & DESSERT:

- 1 serving Chipotle-Rubbed Beef Tenderloin (p. 166)
  195 CALORIES
- 3/4 cup Corn 'N' Red Pepper Medley (p. 252)
  130 CALORIES
- 1 whole wheat dinner roll
  76 CALORIES
- 1 glass ice water
  FREE FOOD
- 1 piece Chunky Fruit and Nut Fudge (p. 270)
  92 CALORIES
- 1 cup hot tea (with sugar substitute if desired)
  FREE FOOD

DINNER TOTAL: 493 CALORIES

SNACKS:

- 3 Caprese Tomato Bites (p. 69)
  63 CALORIES
- 2 chocolate kisses
  49 CALORIES

WEEK 5, DAY 5, TOTAL: 1,403 CALORIES

day 6

BREAKFAST:

- 1 piece Harvest Vegetable Tart (p. 109)
  256 CALORIES
- 1/2 cup strawberry-flavored 1% milk
  75 CALORIES
- 1 glass ice water
  FREE FOOD

BREAKFAST TOTAL: 331 CALORIES

LUNCH:

- 1 serving Honey-Dijon Chicken Salad (p. 145)
  301 CALORIES
- 2/3 cups Spiced Glazed Carrots (p. 244)
  83 CALORIES
- 1/2 cup fat-free milk
  43 CALORIES

LUNCH TOTAL: 427 CALORIES

DINNER & DESSERT:

- 1 serving Pot Roast with Vegetables (p. 235)
  417 CALORIES
- 1 glass ice water
  FREE FOOD
- 1 Trail Mix Cluster (p. 270)
  79 CALORIES
- 1 cup hot tea (with sugar substitute if desired)
  FREE FOOD

DINNER TOTAL: 496 CALORIES

SNACKS:

- 1 Icy Fruit Pop (p. 76)
  66 CALORIES
- 1 clementine
  35 CALORIES
- 2 tablespoons tuna with 3 wheat crackers
  50 CALORIES

WEEK 5, DAY 6, TOTAL: 1,405 CALORIES

Drinking water has lots of benefits for your body and can keep you from feeling hungry between meals. Here are a few suggestions to help you get into the habit of drinking plenty of it:

- Keep a pitcher of water in your refrigerator so it's handy, well-chilled and inviting.
- Keep a big mug or bottle of water with you at work. You'll find yourself reaching for it automatically.
- Perk up plain water with a squeeze of lemon.

meal plan | THE COMFORT FOOD DIET

day 7

BREAKFAST:

- 1 Mini Ham 'N' Cheese Frittata (p. 88)
  106 CALORIES
- 1 cup Sunrise Slushy (p. 81)
  73 CALORIES
- 1 slice cinnamon-raisin toast with 1 teaspoon honey
  91 CALORIES
- 1 cup cubed fresh pineapple
  74 CALORIES
- 1 cup coffee (with sugar substitute and 1 tablespoon liquid nondairy creamer, if desired)
  FREE FOOD

BREAKFAST TOTAL: 344 CALORIES

LUNCH:

- 2 Open-Faced Veggie Sandwiches (p. 127)
  249 CALORIES
- 10 baked potato chips
  100 CALORIES
- 1 medium banana
  100 CALORIES
- 1 dill pickle spear
  FREE FOOD
- 1 glass ice water
  FREE FOOD

LUNCH TOTAL: 449 CALORIES

DINNER & DESSERT:

- 1 serving Tender Chicken Nuggets (p. 181)
  194 CALORIES
- 3/4 cup Broccoli with Lemon Sauce (p. 244)
  76 CALORIES
- 1 big green salad (see the Free Food Chart on p. 43) with 1 tablespoon reduced-fat salad dressing
  FREE FOOD
- 1 cup brewed ice tea (with sugar substitute if desired)
  FREE FOOD
- 1 piece Hot Berries 'N' Brownie Ice Cream Cake (p. 288)
  233 CALORIES
- 1 cup coffee (with sugar substitute and 1 tablespoon liquid nondairy creamer, if desired)
  FREE FOOD

DINNER TOTAL: 503 CALORIES

SNACKS:

- 1 ounce deli turkey breast with 3 slices snack rye bread
  84 CALORIES
- 1 cup cubed watermelon
  40 CALORIES

WEEK 5, DAY 7, TOTAL: 1,420 CALORIES

day 1

BREAKFAST:

- 1 Yummy Raisin Bite (p. 87)
  82 CALORIES
- 1 cup Orange Soy Milk Frappes (p. 82)
  70 CALORIES
- 1 large scrambled egg
  101 CALORIES
- 1 slice whole wheat bread, toasted
  69 CALORIES
- spread with 1 tablespoon no-sugar-added jam
  FREE FOOD
- 1 glass ice water
  FREE FOOD

BREAKFAST TOTAL: 322 CALORIES

LUNCH:

- 1 Mango Shrimp Pita (p. 133)
  230 CALORIES
- 1 piece string cheese
  80 CALORIES
- 1 medium pear
  96 CALORIES
- 1 can diet sodal
  FREE FOOD

LUNCH TOTAL: 406 CALORIES

DINNER & DESSERT:

- 1 serving Chipotle-Rubbed Beef Tenderloin (p. 166)
  195 CALORIES
- 2/3 cup Onion Au Gratin (p. 254)
  179 CALORIES
- Steamed broccoli topped with 1 teaspoon reduced-fat margarine spread
  FREE FOOD
- 1 glass ice water
  FREE FOOD
- 1 slice Pumpkin Chiffon Dessert (p. 282)
  125 CALORIES
- 1 cup hot tea (with sugar substitute if desired)
  FREE FOOD

DINNER TOTAL: 499 CALORIES

SNACKS:

- 3 Caprese Tomato Bites
  63 CALORIES
- 1/2 ounce Swiss cheese and 2 butter-flavored crackers
  87 CALORIES
- 2 pineapple rings
  41 CALORIES

WEEK 6, DAY 1, TOTAL: 1,418 CALORIES

day 2

BREAKFAST:

- 1 piece Asparagus Frittata (p.96)
  146 CALORIES

- 1 slice whole wheat bread, toasted
  69 CALORIES

- spread with 1 teaspoon reduced-fat margarine
  FREE FOOD

- 1 medium banana
  100 CALORIES

- 3/4 cup tomato juice
  31 CALORIES

BREAKFAST TOTAL: **346 CALORIES**

LUNCH:

- 1 Barbecue Beef Sandwich (p. 141)
  348 CALORIES

- 10 baked potato chips
  100 CALORIES

- 1 dill pickle spear
  FREE FOOD

- 1 cup brewed ice tea (with sugar substitute if desired)
  FREE FOOD

LUNCH TOTAL: **448 CALORIES**

DINNER & DESSERT:

- 1 serving Tilapia & Lemon Sauce (p. 205)
  334 CALORIES

- 3/4 cup Zippy Green Beans (p. 242)
  98 CALORIES

- 1 glass ice water
  FREE FOOD

- 1 Cocoa Mint Truffle (p. 269)
  58 CALORIES

- 1 cup coffee (with sugar substitute and 1 tablespoon liquid nondairy creamer, if desired)
  FREE FOOD

DINNER TOTAL: **490 CALORIES**

SNACKS:

- 1/2 cup Special Summer Berry Medley (p. 71)
  85 CALORIES

- 2 tablespoons tuna with 3 wheat crackers
  50 CALORIES

WEEK 6, DAY 2, TOTAL: **1,419 CALORIES**

When buying fruit juice, remember that words such as "punch," "cocktail," "beverage" or "drink" on the label mean you're likely not getting 100% juice.

day 3

BREAKFAST:

- 1/2 Open-Faced Omelet (p. 113)
  202 CALORIES

- 1 mini bagel (2-1/2 inch diameter)
  72 CALORIES

- spread with 1 tablespoon whipped cream cheese
  35 CALORIES

- 1/2 cup fat-free milk
  43 CALORIES

BREAKFAST TOTAL: **352 CALORIES**

LUNCH:

- 1 serving Warm Fajita Salad (p. 142)
  280 CALORIES

- 1 whole wheat dinner roll
  76 CALORIES

- spread with 1 teaspoon reduced-fat margarine
  FREE FOOD

- 1/3 cup 1% cottage cheese with ¼ cup unsweetened pineapple tidbits
  81 CALORIES

- 1 glass ice water
  FREE FOOD

LUNCH TOTAL: **437 CALORIES**

DINNER & DESSERT:

- 1 serving Chicken with Rosemary-Onion Sauce (p. 164)
  247 CALORIES

- 2/3 cup Roasted Potatoes with Thyme and Gorgonzola (p. 252)
  150 CALORIES

- 1 can diet soft drink
  FREE FOOD

- 1 Mini Apple Strudel (p. 272)
  100 CALORIES

- 1 cup hot tea (with sugar substitute if desired)
  FREE FOOD

DINNER TOTAL: **497 CALORIES**

SNACKS:

- 1/2 cup Zucchini with 2 tablespoons salsa
  19 CALORIES

- 1/2 cup canned sliced peaches in juice
  53 CALORIES

- 1/2 frozen waffle with 1 tablespoon sugar-free syrup
  58 CALORIES

WEEK 6, DAY 3, TOTAL: **1,416 CALORIES**

day 4

BREAKFAST:

- 2 Yogurt Pancakes (p. 118)
  242 CALORIES

- 1 sliced medium banana
  100 CALORIES

- 1 cup coffee (with sugar substitute and 1 tablespoon liquid nondairy creamer, if desired)
  FREE FOOD

BREAKFAST TOTAL: 343 CALORIES

LUNCH:

- 1 serving Seasoned Chicken Strips (p. 123)
  188 CALORIES

- 2/3 cup Creamed Kohlrabi (p. 254)
  125 CALORIES

- 1/3 cup canned baked beans
  89 CALORIES

- 1/2 cup baby carrots
  25 CALORIES

- 1 bottle flavored water
  FREE FOOD

LUNCH TOTAL: 427 CALORIES

DINNER & DESSERT:

- 2 Sesame Beef 'N' Veggie Kabobs (p. 179)
  216 CALORIES

- 1 serving Seasoned Baked Potatoes (p. 258)
  167 CALORIES

- 1 cup brewed ice tea (with sugar substitute if desired)
  FREE FOOD

- 1 serving Broiled Pineapple Dessert (p. 274)
  98 CALORIES

- 1 cup coffee (with sugar substitute and 1 tablespoon liquid nondairy creamer, if desired)
  FREE FOOD

DINNER TOTAL: 481 CALORIES

SNACKS:

- 1 Shrimp Canape (p. 70)
  43 CALORIES

- 1 cup Strawberry Mango Smoothie (p. 74)
  100 CALORIES

WEEK 6, DAY 4, TOTAL: 1,394 CALORIES

When shopping for fresh uncooked shrimp, choose those that have a firm texture with a mild aroma.

day 5

BREAKFAST:

- 1 Scrambled Egg Wrap (p. 107)
  258 CALORIES

- 1/3 cup red grapes
  43 CALORIES

- 2 pineapple rings
  41 CALORIES

- 1 bottle flavored water
  FREE FOOD

BREAKFAST TOTAL: 342 CALORIES

LUNCH:

- 1 cup Cashew Chicken (p. 139)
  301 CALORIES

- 1/2 cup cooked long-grain white rice
  103 CALORIES

- 1 clementine
  35 CALORIES

- 1 can diet soda
  FREE FOOD

LUNCH TOTAL: 439 CALORIES

DINNER & DESSERT:

- 1 cup Tortellini with Salmon-Ricotta Sauce (p. 238)
  373 CALORIES

- 1 big green salad (see Free Foods Chart on p. 43) with 1 tablespoon reduced-fat salad dressing
  FREE FOOD

- 1 glass ice water
  FREE FOOD

- 1 Heavenly Surprise Mini Cupcake (p. 280)
  130 CALORIES

- 1 cup hot tea (with sugar substitute if desired)
  FREE FOOD

DINNER TOTAL: 503 CALORIES

SNACKS:

- 1/3 cup Zucchini Fritters (p. 73)
  67 CALORIES

- 1 Cheese Straw (p. 72)
  19 CALORIES

- 1/2 cup cheese popcorn
  40 CALORIES

WEEK 6, DAY 5, TOTAL: 1,410 CALORIES

day 6

BREAKFAST:

- 1 Pepper Cheese Omelet (p. 88)
  156 CALORIES

- 1 slice whole wheat bread, toasted
  69 CALORIES

- spread with 1 teaspoon reduced-fat margarine
  FREE FOOD

- 1 cup orange juice
  110 CALORIES

BREAKFAST TOTAL: **335 CALORIES**

LUNCH:

- 1 Bistro Turkey Sandwich (p. 136)
  346 CALORIES

- 1/2 cup baby carrots
  25 CALORIES

- 2 tablespoons soy nuts
  70 CALORIES

- 1 glass ice water
  FREE FOOD

LUNCH TOTAL: **441 CALORIES**

DINNER & DESSERT:

- 1 serving Beefy Red Pepper Pasta (p. 234)
  362 CALORIES

- 1 big green salad (see Free Foods Chart on p. 43) with 1 tablespoon reduced-fat salad dressing
  FREE FOOD

- Steamed broccoli topped with 1 teaspoon reduced-fat margarine spread
  FREE FOOD

- 1 glass club soda
  FREE FOOD

- 1 Heavenly Surprise Mini Cupcake (p. 280)
  130 CALORIES

- 1 cup coffee (with sugar substitute and 1 tablespoon liquid nondairy creamer, if desired)
  FREE FOOD

DINNER TOTAL: **492 CALORIES**

SNACKS:

- 2 Artichoke Rye Toasts (p. 75)
  78 CALORIES

- 1 clementine
  35 CALORIES

- 1 whole cinnamon graham cracker
  35 CALORIES

WEEK 6, DAY 6, TOTAL: **1,418 CALORIES**

day 7

BREAKFAST:

- 1 serving Breakfast Sundaes (p. 119)
  266 CALORIES

- 1 medium apple
  72 CALORIES

- 1 glass ice water
  FREE FOOD

BREAKFAST TOTAL: **338 CALORIES**

LUNCH:

- 1 cup Creamy Pepperoni Ziti (p. 141)
  340 CALORIES

- 1 whole wheat dinner roll
  76 CALORIES
  spread with 1 teaspoon reduced-fat margarine
  FREE FOOD

- 1/2 cup sliced fresh strawberries
  27 CALORIES

- 1 glass club soda
  FREE FOOD

LUNCH TOTAL: **443 CALORIES**

DINNER & DESSERT:

- 1 Crab-Stuffed Chicken Breasts (p. 169)
  225 CALORIES

- 3/4 cup Colorful Veggie Saute (p. 245)
  51 CALORIES

- 1 big green salad (see Free Foods Chart on p. 43) with 1 tablespoon reduced-fat salad dressing
  FREE FOOD

- I cup brewed ice tea (with sugar substitute if desired)
  FREE FOOD

- 1 serving Meringue with Fresh Berries (p. 290)
  222 CALORIES

- 1 cup coffee (with sugar substitute and 1 tablespoon liquid nondairy creamer, if desired)
  FREE FOOD

DINNER TOTAL: **498 CALORIES**

SNACKS:

- 1 cup Hot Buttered Coffee (p. 77)
  67 CALORIES

- 7 miniature caramel-flavored rice cakes
  60 CALORIES

WEEK 6, DAY 7, TOTAL: **1,406 CALORIES**

When making a salad, skip the croutons and bacon bits. Try to use romaine lettuce or spinach instead of iceberg.

snacks

It's a snap to curb cravings when you indulge in a snack between meals. Best of all, a bite now and then can help keep your metabolism going. If you're a woman, enjoy two snacks per day, totaling 100 calories. Men should eat two snacks totaling no more than 200 calories.

75

72

79

See the list at right for 45 effortless ideas that are low-calorie yet deliciously satisfying. You'll also find after-school snacks and easy appetizers that come in at 100-calorie or less on pages 68 through 79. And for no-fuss munching when time is tight, see the list of light bites on page 73.

When hunger comes calling, TREAT YOURSELF to a simple bite that's FAST AND EASY but won't pack on the pounds. Each item is an ideal way to satisfy a serious SNACK ATTACK!

50 CALORIES OR LESS

- 1/2 cup sliced zucchini with 2 tablespoons salsa, 19 calories
- 1/2 cup sliced fresh strawberries, 27 calories
- 3/4 cup tomato juice, 31 calories
- 1 cup air-popped popcorn sprinkled with Italian seasoning, 31 calories
- 1 clementine, 35 calories
- 1 whole cinnamon graham cracker, 35 calories
- 1/3 cup unsweetened applesauce sprinkled with cinnamon, 35 calories
- 1/2 cup grape tomatoes with 2 tablespoons fat-free Italian salad dressing, 36 calories
- 1 cup cubed watermelon, 40 calories
- 1/2 cup cheese popcorn, 40 calories
- 2 pineapple rings, 41 calories
- 1/2 miniature bagel with 2 teaspoons fat-free cream cheese, 42 calories
- 1/3 cup grapes with 1 tablespoon fat-free whipped topping, 45 calories
- 1 medium kiwifruit, 46 calories
- 1/2 cup baby carrots with 1 tablespoon hummus, 48 calories
- 1 cup salad greens with 1 tablespoon crumbled feta cheese and 1 tablespoon fat-free creamy Caesar salad dressing, 49 calories

- 1 small cucumber, sliced, with 2 tablespoons reduced-fat French onion dip, 49 calories
- 2 chocolate kisses, 49 calories
- 2 tablespoons tuna with 3 wheat crackers, 50 calories
- 1 cup reduced-sodium V8 juice, 50 calories

51-100 CALORIES

- 1/2 cup canned sliced peaches in juice, 53 calories
- 1/2 cup broccoli florets with 2 tablespoons fat-free ranch salad dressing, 58 calories
- 1/2 frozen waffle with 1 tablespoon sugar-free syrup, 58 calories
- 2 crisp lady finger cookies, 60 calories
- 7 miniature caramel-flavored rice cakes, 60 calories
- 1/2 cup strawberry-flavored 1% milk, 75 calories
- 5 medium cooked shrimp with 2 tablespoons cocktail sauce, 77 calories
- 1/4 cup pretzel sticks with 1 tablespoon honey-mustard, 77 calories
- 1/2 cup raspberries with 1 tablespoon chocolate syrup, 80 calories
- 1 ice cream cake cone filled with 1/3 cup fat-free strawberry yogurt and 1/4 cup blueberries, 81 calories

- 1 ounce deli turkey breast with 3 slices snack rye bread, 84 calories
- 1/2 cup 1% chocolate milk, 85 calories
- 1/2 ounce Swiss cheese and 2 butter-flavored crackers, 87 calories
- 3 pieces snack rye bread topped with 1 tablespoon reduced-fat garden vegetable cream cheese and 6 cucumber slices, 89 calories
- 1/3 cup baked beans, 89 calories
- 1/4 cup miniature marshmallows with 1 tablespoon semisweet chocolate chips, 90 calories
- 1/2 small pear, sliced, with 1 tablespoon caramel ice cream topping, 92 calories
- 3/4 cup sugar-free hot cocoa prepared with fat-free milk, 92 calories
- 2 tablespoons chocolate-covered raisins, 93 calories
- 1/2 medium apple with 1/2 ounce sharp cheddar cheese, 93 calories
- 4 dates, 94 calories
- 13 almonds, 95 calories
- 1/2 cup fat-free vanilla frozen yogurt, 95 calories
- 1/2 small banana with 2 teaspoons reduced-fat creamy peanut butter, 99 calories
- 1/2 cup sugar-free chocolate pudding (prepared with fat-free milk) topped with a crushed chocolate wafer, 99 calories

24 CALORIES

MANDARIN SALSA

mandarin salsa

Yvonne Opp | GREENVILLE, PENNSYLVANIA

Sweet mandarin oranges temper the boldness of cilantro, jalapeno and onion, creating an impressive and colorful combination.

- 5 plum tomatoes, chopped
- 1 large sweet onion, chopped
- 2 jalapeno peppers, seeded and chopped
- 2 tablespoons sugar
- 2 tablespoons minced fresh cilantro
- 2 tablespoons lime juice
- 1 teaspoon salt
- 1 teaspoon minced garlic
- 1 can (15 ounces) mandarin oranges, drained

Tortilla chips

- In a small bowl, combine the first eight ingredients. Stir in mandarin oranges. Chill until serving. Drain before serving if necessary. Serve with tortilla chips.

YIELD: 4 cups.

EDITOR'S NOTE: When cutting hot peppers, disposable gloves are recommended. Avoid touching your face.

NUTRITION FACTS: 1/4 cup (calculated without chips) equals 24 calories, trace fat (trace saturated fat), 0 cholesterol, 150 mg sodium, 6 g carbohydrate, 1 g fiber, trace protein. **DIABETIC EXCHANGE:** 1/2 starch.

cranberry popcorn deluxe

Carolyn Sykora | BLOOMER, WISCONSIN

I created this recipe when I needed a festive treat for the holidays. Everyone finds the combination of popcorn, fruit and nuts irresistible!

- 8 cups air-popped popcorn
- 3/4 cup dried cranberries
- 1/4 cup slivered almonds
- 1/4 cup pecan halves
- 1/4 cup honey
- 3 tablespoons butter
- 2 tablespoons maple syrup
- 1/4 teaspoon almond extract

- In a shallow roasting pan, combine the popcorn, cranberries, almonds and pecans.

- In a small saucepan, combine the honey, butter and syrup. Cook and stir over medium heat until butter is melted. Remove from the heat; stir in extract. Drizzle over popcorn mixture and toss to coat.

- Bake at 325° for 15 minutes, stirring every 5 minutes. Cool on a wire rack, stirring occasionally. Store in an airtight container.

YIELD: 8 cups.

NUTRITION FACTS: 1/2 cup equals 96 calories, 4 g fat (2 g saturated fat), 6 mg cholesterol, 16 mg sodium, 14 g carbohydrate, 1 g fiber, 1 g protein. **DIABETIC EXCHANGES:** 1 starch, 1 fat.

CRANBERRY POPCORN DELUXE

96 CALORIES

63 CALORIES

CAPRESE TOMATO BITES

caprese tomato bites

Crystal Williams | BROOKLYN, NEW YORK
I love the classic combination of tomatoes, mozzarella and basil in these bite-size appetizers. The juicy explosion you get when you pop one into your mouth is the genuine taste of springtime.

- 1 pint cherry tomatoes, halved
- 3 tablespoons heavy whipping cream
- 1/2 pound fresh mozzarella cheese, sliced
- 6 fresh basil leaves
- 1 garlic clove, minced
- 1 tablespoon balsamic vinegar

- Scoop out and discard pulp of cherry tomatoes. Invert tomatoes onto paper towels to drain.

- In a food processor, combine the whipping cream, mozzarella cheese, basil and garlic; cover and process until blended.

- Cut a small hole in the corner of a pastry or heavy-duty resealable plastic bag. Fill with cheese mixture.

- Turn tomato halves over; drizzle with vinegar. Pipe cheese mixture into tomatoes. Refrigerate until serving.

YIELD: about 3-1/2 dozen.

NUTRITION FACTS: 3 appetizers equals 63 calories, 5 g fat (3 g saturated fat), 17 mg cholesterol, 27 mg sodium, 2 g carbohydrate, trace fiber, 3 g protein.

watermelon cooler

Cool down on a sweltering day with this special blend from our home economists. It features summer's favorite fruit.

- 1 cup ginger ale, chilled
- 2 fresh mint leaves
- 2 cups cubed seedless watermelon, frozen

- In a blender, cover and process ginger ale and mint for 15 seconds or until finely chopped. Add watermelon; cover and process until slushy. Pour into chilled glasses; serve immediately.

YIELD: 2 servings.

NUTRITION FACTS: 1 cup equals 82 calories, 0 fat (0 saturated fat), 0 cholesterol, 14 mg sodium, 24 g carbohydrate, 1 g fiber, 1 g protein. **DIABETIC EXCHANGES:** 1 fruit, 1/2 starch.

WATERMELON COOLER

82 CALORIES

38 CALORIES

CRISPY BAKED WONTONS

crispy baked wontons

Brianna Shade I BEAVERTON, OREGON

These quick, versatile wontons are great for a crunchy afternoon snack or paired with a bowl of soothing soup on a cold day. I usually make a large batch, freeze half on a floured cookie sheet, then store them in an air-tight container for a fast bite.

- 1/2 **pound ground pork**
- 1/2 **pound extra-lean ground turkey**
- 1 **small onion, chopped**
- 1 **can (8 ounces) sliced water chestnuts, drained and chopped**
- 1/3 **cup reduced-sodium soy sauce**
- 1/4 **cup egg substitute**
- 1-1/2 **teaspoons ground ginger**
- 1 **package (12 ounces) wonton wrappers**

Cooking spray

Sweet-and-sour sauce, optional

classic

- In a large skillet, cook the pork, turkey and onion over medium heat until meat is no longer pink; drain. Transfer to a large bowl. Stir in the water chestnuts, soy sauce, egg substitute and ginger.

- Position a wonton wrapper with one point toward you. (Keep remaining wrappers covered with a damp paper towel until ready to use.) Place 2 heaping teaspoons of filling in the center of wrapper. Fold bottom corner over filling; fold sides toward center over filling. Roll toward the remaining point. Moisten top corner with water; press to seal. Repeat with remaining wrappers and filling.

- Place on baking sheets coated with cooking spray; lightly coat wontons with additional cooking spray.

- Bake at 400° for 10-12 minutes or until golden brown, turning once. Serve warm with sweet-and-sour sauce if desired.

YIELD: about 4 dozen.

NUTRITION FACTS: 1 wonton (calculated without sweet-and-sour sauce) equals 38 calories, 1 g fat (trace saturated fat), 5 mg cholesterol, 103 mg sodium, 5 g carbohydrate, trace fiber, 3 g protein.

shrimp canapes

Sarah Vasques I MILFORD, NEW HAMPSHIRE

Could there be a breezier way to start a party or celebration? This light but oh-so special appetizer will disappear before your eyes!

- 2/3 **cup spreadable chive and onion cream cheese**
- 8 **slices pumpernickel bread, crusts removed**
- 32 **cooked large shrimp, peeled and deveined**
- 1/2 **cup seafood cocktail sauce**
- 1 **medium lemon, cut into wedges and halved**

- Spread cream cheese on one side of each slice of bread. Cut each slice into four triangles. Top with shrimp and seafood sauce. Garnish with lemon.

YIELD: 32 servings.

NUTRITION FACTS: 1 canape equals 43 calories, 2 g fat (1 g saturated fat), 16 mg cholesterol, 104 mg sodium, 4 g carbohydrate, 1 g fiber, 2 g protein.

SHRIMP CANAPES

43 CALORIES

SPECIAL SUMMER BERRY MEDLEY

special summer berry medley

Nancy Whitford I EDWARDS, NEW YORK

No matter how big the meal, folks always find room for this delightfully special dessert. With its hint of citrus and mint, this medley also makes a pretty side dish at casual cookouts or potlucks. Best of all, it's as fast and easy to make as it is to clean up!

   1 **cup sparkling wine *or* white grape juice**

1/2 **cup sugar**

   1 **tablespoon lemon juice**

1-1/2 **teaspoons grated lemon peel**

1/2 **teaspoon vanilla extract**

1/8 **teaspoon salt**

   3 **cups sliced fresh strawberries**

   2 **cups fresh blueberries**

   1 **cup fresh raspberries**

   1 **cup fresh blackberries**

   1 **tablespoon minced fresh mint**

- In a small heavy saucepan, bring wine and sugar to a boil. Cook, uncovered, for about 15 minutes or until reduced to 1/2 cup, stirring occasionally. Cool slightly. Stir in the lemon juice and peel, vanilla and salt.

- In a large bowl, combine berries and mint. Add syrup and toss gently to coat. Cover and refrigerate until serving.

YIELD: 12 servings.

NUTRITION FACTS: 1/2 cup equals 85 calories, trace fat (trace saturated fat), 0 cholesterol, 26 mg sodium, 18 g carbohydrate, 3 g fiber, 1 g protein. **DIABETIC EXCHANGES:** 1 fruit, 1/2 starch.

jalapenos with olive-cream filling

Kristal & Sean Peterson I WALKER, LOUISIANA

These jalapenos are great! I take them to all get-togethers and potlucks, and the people at my husband's work are always requesting them.

   1 **package (8 ounces) cream cheese, softened**

1/4 **cup chopped pimiento-stuffed olives**

   2 **tablespoons olive juice**

 16 **large jalapeno peppers, halved lengthwise and seeded**

- In a small bowl, combine the cream cheese, olives and olive juice. Spoon about 2 teaspoons into each jalapeno half. Serve immediately or refrigerate.

YIELD: 32 appetizers.

EDITOR'S NOTE: When cutting hot peppers, disposable gloves are recommended. Avoid touching your face.

NUTRITION FACTS: 2 appetizers equals 58 calories, 5 g fat (3 g saturated fat), 16 mg cholesterol, 103 mg sodium, 1 g carbohydrate, trace fiber, 1 g protein.

JALAPENOS WITH OLIVE-CREAM FILLING

cheese straws

Ann Nace | PERKASIE, PENNSYLVANIA

You'll have a hard time eating just one of these cheesy, buttery treats. Try twisting the sticks for an extra-fancy look.

        1   cup all-purpose flour
    1-1/2   teaspoons baking powder
      1/2   teaspoon salt
      1/2   cup shredded reduced-fat cheddar cheese
        2   tablespoons plus 1-1/2 teaspoons cold butter
      1/3   cup fat-free milk
        2   teaspoons paprika

- In a small bowl, combine the flour, baking powder and salt; stir in cheese. Cut in butter until mixture resembles coarse crumbs. Gradually add milk, tossing with a fork until dough forms a ball.

- On a lightly floured surface, roll the dough into a 12-in. square. Cut in half lengthwise; cut each half widthwise into 1/2-in. strips. Sprinkle with paprika.

- Place 1 in. apart on baking sheets coated with cooking spray. Bake at 425° for 6-8 minutes or until golden brown. Serve warm.

YIELD: 4 dozen.

NUTRITION FACTS: 1 cheese straw equals 19 calories, 1 g fat (1 g saturated fat), 2 mg cholesterol, 52 mg sodium, 2 g carbohydrate, trace fiber, 1 g protein.

CHEESE STRAWS

19 CALORIES

66 CALORIES

CHILI CON QUESO DIP

chili con queso dip

Sarah Mohrman | FORT WAYNE, INDIANA

This cheesy dip never lets on that it has only 2 g of fat per serving. Chilies and garlic kick up the flavor, making it a real crowd pleaser.

    1   can (14-1/2 ounces) no-salt-added diced tomatoes
    1   can (10 ounces) diced tomatoes and green chilies
    1   small onion, chopped
    2   garlic cloves, minced
    1   teaspoon olive oil
    1   package (8 ounces) fat-free cream cheese, cubed
    6   ounces reduced-fat process cheese (Velveeta), cubed
    1   teaspoon chili powder
    2   tablespoons minced fresh cilantro
        Baked tortilla chip scoops

classic

- Pour both cans of tomatoes into a colander over a small bowl; drain, reserving 1/3 cup liquid. Discard remaining liquid or save for another use.

- In a large skillet, saute onion and garlic in oil until tender. Stir in the cream cheese until melted. Add the tomatoes, process cheese, chili powder and reserved liquid. Cook and stir over low heat until cheese is melted. Stir in the cilantro.

- Transfer to a 1-1/2-qt. slow cooker or chafing dish; keep warm. Serve with tortilla chips.

YIELD: 3 cups.

NUTRITION FACTS: 1/4 cup (calculated without chips) equals 66 calories, 2 g fat (1 g saturated fat), 7 mg cholesterol, 411 mg sodium, 6 g carbohydrate, 1 g fiber, 6 g protein. **DIABETIC EXCHANGES:** 1/2 starch, 1/2 fat.

zucchini fritters

Trisha Kruse | EAGLE, IDAHO

You will not believe how fast these snacks disappear. Even confirmed veggie-haters devour these tasty fritters as fast as I can make them!

- 1/4 cup buttermilk
- 1/4 cup egg substitute
- 1/2 cup panko (Japanese) bread crumbs
- 1/2 cup seasoned bread crumbs
- 1/4 cup grated Parmesan cheese
- 1-1/2 teaspoons taco seasoning
- 1/4 teaspoon garlic salt
- 3 medium zucchini, cut into 1/4-inch slices
- 1/4 cup fat-free sour cream
- 1/4 cup fat-free ranch salad dressing
- 1/4 cup salsa

- In a shallow bowl, combine buttermilk and egg substitute. In another shallow bowl, combine the bread crumbs, cheese, taco seasoning and garlic salt. Dip zucchini in buttermilk mixture, then bread crumb mixture.

- Place zucchini slices on baking sheets coated with cooking spray. Bake at 400° for 20-25 minutes or until golden brown, turning once.

- In a small bowl, combine the sour cream, ranch dressing and salsa. Serve with zucchini.

YIELD: 10 servings (3/4 cup sauce).

NUTRITION FACTS: 1/3 cup zucchini with about 1 tablespoon sauce equals 67 calories, 1 g fat (trace saturated fat), 3 mg cholesterol, 296 mg sodium, 11 g carbohydrate, 1 g fiber, 3 g protein. **DIABETIC EXCHANGE:** 1 starch.

EFFORTLESS EDIBLES

Keep these no-fuss bites in mind when hunger comes calling.

- **1/2 cup baby carrots,** 25 calories
- **Medium peach,** 40 calories
- **Medium plum,** 40 calories
- **1 cup whole strawberries,** 45 calories
- **3/4 cup skinny latte (with fat-free milk),** 60 calories
- **Raspberries (1 cup),** 60 calories
- **Fun-Size Snickers candy bar,** 71 calories
- **2 California roll slices,** 75 calories
- **1 serving Lay's Light Original Potato Chips,** 75 calories
- **Piece of string cheese,** 80 calories
- **Hunt's Fat-Free Snack Pack Tapioca Pudding,** 80 calories
- **Crisp rice cereal bar (22 g package),** 90 calories
- **3 cups air-popped popcorn,** 94 calories
- **Weight Watchers Berries 'n Cream Yogurt,** 100 calories
- **Skinny Cow Chocolate Peanut Butter Ice Cream Sandwich,** 150 calories

ZUCCHINI FRITTERS

67 CALORIES

68 CALORIES

CHEESE PUFFS

cheese puffs

Jamie Wetter | BOSCOBEL, WISCONSIN

I found this recipe in one of my mother's old cookbooks and updated the flavor by adding cayenne and mustard. Tasty and quick for the busy holiday season, these tender, golden puffs go together in minutes and simply disappear at parties!

classic

> 1 cup water
> 2 tablespoons butter
> 1/2 teaspoon salt
> 1/8 teaspoon cayenne pepper
> 1 cup all-purpose flour
> 4 eggs
> 1-1/4 cups shredded Gruyère *or* Swiss cheese
> ·1 tablespoon Dijon mustard
> 1/4 cup grated Parmesan cheese

- In a large saucepan, bring the water, butter, salt and cayenne to a boil. Add flour all at once and stir until a smooth ball forms. Remove from the heat; let stand for 5 minutes. Add eggs, one at a time, beating well after each addition. Continue beating until mixture is smooth and shiny. Stir in Gruyère and mustard.

- Drop by rounded teaspoonfuls 2 in. apart onto greased baking sheets. Sprinkle with Parmesan cheese. Bake at 425° for 15-20 minutes or until golden brown. Serve warm or cold.

YIELD: 4 dozen.

NUTRITION FACTS: 2 appetizers equals 68 calories, 4 g fat (2 g saturated fat), 45 mg cholesterol, 120 mg sodium, 4 g carbohydrate, trace fiber, 4 g protein.

strawberry mango smoothies

Sometimes artificial sweeteners make food taste exactly that, artificial. Not so with these smoothies, they're delicious and creamy with lots of strawberry and mango flavor. Our home economists find them just perfect for breakfast or dessert as well as an afternoon snack.

> 1 cup fat-free milk
> 1/2 cup vanilla yogurt
> 1-1/2 cups halved fresh strawberries
> 1 medium mango, peeled and chopped
> 4 to 6 ice cubes

Sugar substitute equivalent to 1 tablespoon sugar

- In a blender, combine all ingredients; cover and process for 30-45 seconds or until smooth. Stir if necessary. Pour into chilled glasses; serve immediately.

YIELD: 4 servings.

EDITOR'S NOTE: This recipe was tested with Splenda no-calorie sweetener.

NUTRITION FACTS: 1 cup equals 100 calories, 1 g fat (trace saturated fat), 3 mg cholesterol, 47 mg sodium, 21 g carbohydrate, 2 g fiber, 4 g protein. **DIABETIC EXCHANGES:** 1 fruit, 1/2 fat-free milk.

STRAWBERRY MANGO SMOOTHIES

100 CALORIES

ARTICHOKE RYE TOASTS

78 CALORIES

artichoke rye toasts

Jo Ann Guzolik | WEST LEECHBURG, PENNSYLVANIA
Quick, light and cheesy, my mouthwatering artichoke bites make irresistible finger food for guests of all ages.

  24 slices snack rye bread
Refrigerated butter-flavored spray
  1 can (14 ounces) water-packed artichoke hearts, rinsed, drained and chopped
  1/2 cup grated Parmesan cheese
  1/4 cup shredded cheddar cheese
  1/8 teaspoon cayenne pepper
  4 egg whites
  1/4 teaspoon paprika

- Place the bread on ungreased baking sheets; spritz with butter-flavored spray. In a small bowl, combine the artichokes, cheeses and cayenne. In a small bowl, beat egg whites until stiff; fold into artichoke mixture.

- Spread over bread; sprinkle with paprika. Bake at 400° for 10-12 minutes or until golden brown. Serve warm. Refrigerate leftovers.

YIELD: 2 dozen.

NUTRITION FACTS: 2 slices equals 78 calories, 2 g fat (1 g saturated fat), 5 mg cholesterol, 270 mg sodium, 9 g carbohydrate, 1 g fiber, 5 g protein.

vegetable spiral sticks

Teri Albrecht | MT. AIRY, MARYLAND
I love to serve these savory wrapped vegetable sticks for parties or special occasions. They're a simple but impressive appetizer.

  3 medium carrots
  12 fresh asparagus spears, trimmed
  1 tube (11 ounces) refrigerated breadsticks
  1 egg white, lightly beaten
  1/4 cup grated Parmesan cheese
  1/2 teaspoon dried oregano

- Cut carrots lengthwise into quarters. In a large skillet, bring 2 in. of water to a boil. Add carrots; cook for 3 minutes. Add asparagus; cook 2-3 minutes longer. Drain and rinse with cold water; pat dry.

- Cut each piece of breadstick dough in half. Roll each piece into a 7-in. rope. Wrap one rope in a spiral around each vegetable. Place on a baking sheet coated with cooking spray; tuck ends of dough under vegetables to secure.

- Brush with the egg white. Combine cheese and oregano; sprinkle over sticks. Bake at 375° for 12-14 minutes or until golden brown. Serve warm.

YIELD: 2 dozen.

NUTRITION FACTS: 2 sticks equals 97 calories, 2 g fat (trace saturated fat), 2 mg cholesterol, 247 mg sodium, 15 g carbohydrate, 1 g fiber, 4 g protein. **DIABETIC EXCHANGES:** 1 starch, 1 vegetable.

VEGETABLE SPIRAL STICKS

97 CALORIES

78 CALORIES

CANNELLINI BEAN HUMMUS

cannellini bean hummus

Marina Castle | NORTH HOLLYWOOD, CALIFORNIA

My version of hummus features a delightful nuttiness from tahini, a peanut butter-like paste made from ground sesame seeds.

- 2 garlic cloves, peeled
- 1 can (15 ounces) white kidney *or* cannellini beans, rinsed and drained
- 1/4 cup tahini
- 3 tablespoons lemon juice
- 1-1/2 teaspoons ground cumin
- 1/4 teaspoon salt
- 1/4 teaspoon crushed red pepper flakes
- 2 tablespoons minced fresh parsley

Pita breads, cut into wedges

- Place garlic in a food processor; cover and process until minced. Add the beans, tahini, lemon juice, cumin, salt and pepper flakes; cover and process until smooth.

- Transfer to a small bowl; stir in parsley. Refrigerate until serving. Serve with pita wedges.

YIELD: 1-1/4 cups.

NUTRITION FACTS: 2 tablespoons (calculated without pita bread) equals 78 calories, 4 g fat (1 g saturated fat), 0 cholesterol, 114 mg sodium, 8 g carbohydrate, 2 g fiber, 3 g protein. **DIABETIC EXCHANGES:** 1 fat, 1/2 starch.

icy fruit pops

Leann Kane | FORSYTH, ILLINOIS

My grandmother made these pineapple treats for my brother and I when we were little. Today, the pops remain a cool and simple snack that delights the whole family.

- 1 can (20 ounces) crushed pineapple, undrained
- 1 cup water
- 3/4 cup thawed orange juice concentrate
- 3/4 cup thawed lemonade concentrate

Sugar substitute equivalent to 1/2 cup sugar

- 5 medium firm bananas, cut into 1/4-inch slices and quartered
- 1 can (12 ounces) diet ginger ale
- 24 maraschino cherries *or* fresh strawberries

- In a large bowl, combine the pineapple, water, orange juice concentrate, lemonade concentrate and the sugar substitute. Stir in the bananas and ginger ale.

- Place a cherry in each of twenty-four 3-oz. paper cups; fill with pineapple mixture. Insert wooden sticks. Cover and freeze until firm.

YIELD: 2 dozen.

EDITOR'S NOTE: This recipe was tested with Splenda no-calorie sweetener.

NUTRITION FACTS: 1 fruit pop equals 66 calories, trace fat (trace saturated fat), 0 cholesterol, 5 mg sodium, 17 g carbohydrate, 1 g fiber, 1 g protein. **DIABETIC EXCHANGE:** 1 fruit.

ICY FRUIT POPS

66 CALORIES

67 CALORIES

HOT BUTTERED COFFEE

hot buttered coffee

Rich and rewarding, this coffee coupling is sure to warm your spirits. To save time when entertaining, our staff suggests dishing up the butter mixture with a small scoop and letting guests mix their own drinks.

- 1/4 cup butter, softened
- 1 cup packed brown sugar
- 1 teaspoon vanilla extract
- 1/2 teaspoon ground cinnamon
- 1/4 teaspoon ground nutmeg
- 1/4 teaspoon ground allspice
- 1/8 teaspoon ground cloves

classic

EACH SERVING:

- 1 cup hot brewed coffee (French *or* other dark roast)

Cinnamon sticks and whipped cream, optional

- In a small bowl, beat butter and brown sugar until crumbly, about 2 minutes. Beat in vanilla and spices.

- For each serving, stir 1 tablespoon butter mixture into 1 cup coffee. Garnish with cinnamon stick and whipped cream if desired.

- Cover and refrigerate leftover butter mixture for up to 2 weeks.

YIELD: 20 servings (1-1/4 cups mix).

NUTRITION FACTS: 1 cup (calculated without whipped cream) equals 67 calories, 2 g fat (1 g saturated fat), 6 mg cholesterol, 32 mg sodium, 12 g carbohydrate, trace fiber, trace protein. **DIABETIC EXCHANGE:** 1 starch.

mexican salsa pizza

Carla McMahon | HERMISTON, OREGON

This recipe gets rave reviews. It's great as is, but you can kick up the heat with spicy salsa and pepper jack cheese.

- 1 prebaked 12-inch pizza crust
- 1 cup (4 ounces) shredded Monterey Jack cheese, *divided*
- 3/4 cup salsa
- 2 tablespoons minced fresh cilantro

- Place crust on an ungreased baking sheet or pizza pan. In a small bowl, combine 1/2 cup cheese, salsa and cilantro. Spread over crust to within 1/2 in. of edges. Sprinkle with remaining cheese.

- Bake at 350° for 20-25 minutes or until the cheese is melted. Cut into wedges.

YIELD: 2 dozen.

NUTRITION FACTS: 1 slice equals 64 calories, 2 g fat (1 g saturated fat), 4 mg cholesterol, 143 mg sodium, 8 g carbohydrate, trace fiber, 3 g protein. **DIABETIC EXCHANGES:** 1/2 starch, 1/2 fat.

MEXICAN SALSA PIZZA

64 CALORIES

88 CALORIES

CHOCOLATE FRUIT DIP

chocolate fruit dip

Abigail Sims | TERRELL, TEXAS

My grandma helped me experiment with chocolate sauce and yogurt combinations to create this fruit dip for a tea party we had. Our guests said it was a sweet way to start the meal.

1-1/2 cups plain yogurt
   2 tablespoons fat-free milk
 10 miniature marshmallows
   2 tablespoons semisweet chocolate chips
Assorted fresh fruit

- Line a strainer with four layers of cheesecloth or one coffee filter and place over a bowl. Place the yogurt in prepared strainer; cover yogurt with edges of cheesecloth. Refrigerate for 8 hours or overnight.

- In a small heavy saucepan, combine the milk, marshmallows and chocolate chips. Cook and stir until chips are melted and mixture is smooth. Transfer to a small bowl; cool to room temperature.

- Remove yogurt from cheesecloth and discard liquid from bowl. Gradually stir yogurt into milk mixture. Refrigerate until serving. Serve with fruit.

YIELD: 1 cup.

NUTRITION FACTS: 1/4 cup (calculated without fruit) equals 88 calories, 5 g fat (3 g saturated fat), 12 mg cholesterol, 47 mg sodium, 9 g carbohydrate, trace fiber, 4 g protein. **DIABETIC EXCHANGES:** 1 fat, 1/2 starch.

mango salsa

Kristine Sims | ST. JOSEPH, MICHIGAN

Here's a quick and easy way to put a tantalizing twist on salsa. Tangy fruit, savory onion and peppy hot sauce work in perfect harmony to create a fun appetizer that's good for you, too!

1/2 cup finely chopped tart apple
1/2 cup finely chopped peeled mango
1/2 cup canned crushed pineapple
  2 green onions, thinly sliced
  2 tablespoons minced fresh cilantro
  3 to 5 drops hot pepper sauce, optional
Tortilla chips

- In a small bowl, combine the apple, mango, pineapple, onions, cilantro and pepper sauce if desired. Chill until serving. Serve with tortilla chips.

YIELD: 1-1/2 cups.

NUTRITION FACTS: 1/2 cup (calculated without chips) equals 62 calories, trace fat (trace saturated fat), 0 cholesterol, 3 mg sodium, 16 g carbohydrate, 2 g fiber, 1 g protein. **DIABETIC EXCHANGES:** 1/2 starch, 1/2 fruit.

MANGO SALSA

62 CALORIES

87 CALORIES

GARLIC PUMPKIN SEEDS

garlic pumpkin seeds

Iola Egle | BELLA VISTA, ARKANSAS

What to do with all those pumpkin seeds after Halloween? This yummy, microwave-easy recipe will have your gang eating them up by crunchy handfuls! Save a few for yourself before they're gone.

- 1 tablespoon canola oil
- 1/2 teaspoon celery salt
- 1/2 teaspoon garlic powder
- 1/2 teaspoon seasoned salt
- 2 cups fresh pumpkin seeds

classic

- In a small bowl, combine the oil, celery salt, garlic powder and seasoned salt. Add pumpkin seeds; toss to coat. Spread a quarter of the seeds in a single layer on a microwave-safe plate. Microwave, uncovered, on high for 1 minute; stir.

- Microwave 2-3 minutes longer or until seeds are crunchy and lightly browned, stirring after each minute. Repeat with remaining pumpkin seeds. Serve warm, or cool, before storing in an airtight container.

YIELD: 2 cups.

EDITOR'S NOTE: This recipe was tested in a 1,100-watt microwave.

NUTRITION FACTS: 1/4 cup equals 87 calories, 5 g fat (1 g saturated fat), 0 cholesterol, 191 mg sodium, 9 g carbohydrate, 1 g fiber, 3 g protein. **DIABETIC EXCHANGES:** 1 fat, 1/2 starch.

cordon bleu appetizers

Susan Mello | JACKSON HEIGHTS, NEW YORK

Looking for a cheesy snack with mass appeal? Adults and kids alike love these satisfying appetizers!

- 4 ounces cream cheese, softened
- 1 teaspoon Dijon mustard
- 1 cup (4 ounces) shredded Swiss cheese
- 3/4 cup diced fully cooked ham
- 1/2 cup minced chives, *divided*
- 18 slices French bread (1/2 inch thick)

- In a small bowl, beat the cream cheese and mustard until smooth. Stir in the Swiss cheese, ham and 1/4 cup chives. Spread 1 tablespoon mixture over each bread slice; place on an ungreased baking sheet.

- Bake at 350° for 12-15 minutes or until lightly browned. Sprinkle with remaining chives.

YIELD: 1-1/2 dozen.

NUTRITION FACTS: 1 appetizer equals 86 calories, 5 g fat (3 g saturated fat), 16 mg cholesterol, 185 mg sodium, 7 g carbohydrate, trace fiber, 4 g protein. **DIABETIC EXCHANGES:** 1 fat, 1/2 starch.

CORDON BLEU APPETIZERS

86 CALORIES

breakfasts

There's no doubt about it! Breakfast is clearly the most important meal. It sets the tone for the rest of a calorie-smart day. Try to consume roughly 350 calories per day during your morning meal, and you'll find you have fewer cravings to battle.

107

82

88

The first section in this chapter has lower-calorie breakfast items. Enjoy them on their own or pair them with something a bit more substantial. The other two sections are higher-calorie recipes that will surely fill you up as you start your day.

100 calories or less

spiced bacon twists

Glenda Evans Wittner I JOPLIN, MISSOURI

A sweet and savory rub makes these tasty twists of bacon deliciously different and definitely worth the extra step to prepare.

- 1/4 cup packed brown sugar
- 1-1/2 teaspoons ground mustard
- 1/8 teaspoon ground cinnamon
- 1/8 teaspoon ground nutmeg
- Dash cayenne pepper
- 10 center-cut bacon strips

- Combine the first five ingredients; rub over bacon on both sides. Twist bacon; place on a rack in a 15-in. x 10-in. x 1-in. baking pan.

- Bake at 350° for 25-30 minutes or until firm; bake longer if desired.

YIELD: 5 servings.

NUTRITION FACTS: 2 bacon twists equals 75 calories, 4 g fat (1 g saturated fat), 15 mg cholesterol, 212 mg sodium, 6 g carbohydrate, trace fiber, 5 g protein. **DIABETIC EXCHANGES:** 1 high-fat meat, 1/2 starch.

SPICED BACON TWISTS

75 CALORIES

SUNRISE SLUSHIES

73 CALORIES

sunrise slushies

Linda Evancoe-Coble I LEOLA, PENNSYLVANIA

My daughters are perpetual dieters, so I worry about their nutrition. I came up with this yummy breakfast beverage, and they love it.

- 2 cups orange juice
- 1 cup reduced-calorie reduced-sugar cranberry juice
- 1 medium tart apple, coarsely chopped
- 1/2 cup cubed peeled mango
- 2 kiwifruit, peeled, sliced and quartered
- 2 cups halved fresh strawberries
- 8 to 10 ice cubes

- In a blender, place half of each ingredient; cover and process until smooth. Pour into glasses. Repeat with the remaining ingredients.

YIELD: 8 servings.

NUTRITION FACTS: 1 serving (1 cup) equals 73 calories, trace fat (trace saturated fat), 0 cholesterol, 2 mg sodium, 18 g carbohydrate, 2 g fiber, 1 g protein. **DIABETIC EXCHANGE:** 1 fruit.

86 CALORIES

TURKEY BREAKFAST SAUSAGE PATTIES

turkey breakfast sausage patties

Marla Swoffer | NOVATO, CALIFORNIA

After a lot of experimenting, I finally discovered the next-best-thing to pork sausage. These are especially good crumbled in a breakfast burrito with scrambled eggs, cheese and a little taco sauce.

1	pound lean ground turkey
1	teaspoon rubbed sage
1/2	teaspoon salt
1/2	teaspoon fennel seed
1/2	teaspoon dried thyme
1/8	teaspoon garlic powder
1/8	teaspoon pepper

Dash *each* white pepper, cayenne pepper, ground allspice, ground cloves and ground nutmeg

- In a large bowl, combine all ingredients. Shape into eight 2-1/2-in. patties. Cover and refrigerate for at least 1 hour.

- In a large skillet coated with cooking spray, cook patties over medium heat for 4-6 minutes on each side or until no longer pink.

YIELD: 8 servings.

NUTRITION FACTS: 1 patty equals 86 calories, 5 g fat (1 g saturated fat), 45 mg cholesterol, 201 mg sodium, trace carbohydrate, trace fiber, 10 g protein. **DIABETIC EXCHANGE:** 1 lean meat.

orange soy milk frappes

Light, frothy and filled with natural goodness, this creamy-topped orange smoothie from our food editors uses just a few ingredients, but makes a wholesome morning eye-opener.

1/2	cup vanilla soy milk
1/2	cup orange juice
5	ice cubes
2	teaspoons sugar
1/4	teaspoon vanilla extract

Dash salt

- In a blender, combine all ingredients; cover and process for 30-45 seconds or until smooth. Pour into chilled glasses; serve immediately.

YIELD: 2 servings.

NUTRITION FACTS: 1 cup equals 70 calories, 1 g fat (0 saturated fat), 0 cholesterol, 98 mg sodium, 13 g carbohydrate, 0 fiber, 2 g protein. **DIABETIC EXCHANGES:** 1/2 starch, 1/2 fruit.

ORANGE SOY MILK FRAPPES

70 CALORIES

berry & yogurt phyllo nests

This elegant dessert adds a special touch to any meal. Our team suggests adding a bit of variety by using your favorite combination of flavored yogurt and fresh fruit.

> 6 sheets phyllo dough (14 inches x 9 inches)
>
> Butter-flavored cooking spray
>
> 2-1/2 teaspoons sugar, *divided*
>
> 1/3 cup vanilla yogurt
>
> 1 teaspoon grated orange peel
>
> 1 teaspoon orange juice
>
> 1/2 cup halved fresh strawberries
>
> 1/2 cup fresh raspberries
>
> 1/2 cup fresh blueberries
>
> Fresh mint leaves, optional

- Place one sheet of phyllo dough on a work surface; spritz with butter-flavored spray. Top with another sheet of phyllo; spritz with spray. Cut into six squares. (Keep remaining phyllo covered with plastic wrap to avoid drying out.) Repeat with remaining phyllo.

- Stack three squares of layered phyllo in each of six muffin cups coated with cooking spray, rotating squares so corners do not overlap. Sprinkle 1/4 teaspoon sugar into each cup. Spritz with cooking spray. Bake at 375° for 6-8 minutes or until golden brown. Cool cups on a wire rack.

- Meanwhile, in a small bowl, whisk the yogurt, orange peel and juice, and remaining sugar. Spoon yogurt mixture into cups; top with berries. Garnish with mint if desired.

YIELD: 6 servings.

NUTRITION FACTS: 1 serving equals 72 calories, 1 g fat (trace saturated fat), 1 mg cholesterol, 54 mg sodium, 14 g carbohydrate, 2 g fiber, 2 g protein. **DIABETIC EXCHANGE:** 1 starch.

BERRY & YOGURT PHYLLO NESTS

72 CALORIES

Here are some typical breakfast foods and the number of calories they contain. Use this list as a reference when combining morning mainstays to keep within your goal of a 350-calorie breakfast.

- **1/2 cup fat-free vanilla yogurt topped with 2 tablespoons Wheaties,** 86 calories

- **1 scrambled egg with 1 slice reduced-calorie toast,** 95 calories

- **1 plain mini bagel (2-1/2" diameter),** 72 calories

- **1 hard cooked egg,** 78 calories

- **1 frozen waffle (1 square),** 98 calories

- **1 pancake (6" diameter prepared from dry, complete pancake mix),** 149 calories

- **1 large scrambled egg,** 101 calories

- **1 cup Cheerios,** 111 calories

- **1 cup Wheaties,** 107 calories

- **1 cup fat-free milk,** 86 calories

- **1/3 cup frosted bite-size Shredded Wheat with 1/3 cup fat-free milk,** 89 calories

- **1/2 small grapefruit with 1 teaspoon sugar,** 48 calories

For additional calorie calculations, check the Nutrition Facts labels on food packages.

fruit cup with citrus sauce

Edna Lee | GREELEY, COLORADO

This medley of fresh fruit is so elegant that I serve it in my prettiest crystal bowls. With its dressed-up flavor, it's perfect for a special event.

- 3/4 cup orange juice
- 1/4 cup white wine *or* white grape juice
- 2 tablespoons lemon juice
- 1 tablespoon sugar
- 1-1/2 cups fresh *or* frozen cantaloupe balls
- 1 cup halved green grapes
- 1 cup halved fresh strawberries

Fresh mint, optional

- In a small bowl, combine the orange juice, wine or grape juice, lemon juice and sugar; mix well. In a large bowl, combine the fruit; add juice mixture and toss to coat.

- Cover and refrigerate for 2-3 hours, stirring occasionally. Garnish with mint if desired.

YIELD: 6 servings.

NUTRITION FACTS: 3/4 cup equals 63 calories, trace fat (trace saturated fat), 0 cholesterol, 5 mg sodium, 14 g carbohydrate, 1 g fiber, 1 g protein. **DIABETIC EXCHANGE:** 1 fruit.

FRUIT CUP WITH CITRUS SAUCE

63 CALORIES

85 CALORIES warm grapefruit with ginger-sugar

Stephanie Levy | LANSING, NEW YORK

I greet my guests sweetly with this broiled grapefruit.

- 1 large grapefruit
- 2 teaspoons sugar
- 2 to 3 teaspoons chopped crystallized ginger

- Cut grapefruit in half horizontally. With a sharp knife, cut around the membrane in the center of each half and discard. Cut around each section to loosen the fruit. Place on a baking sheet.

- In a small bowl, combine sugar and ginger; sprinkle over top. Broil 4 in. from the heat for 4 minutes or until grapefruit is warmed and sugar is melted.

YIELD: 2 servings.

NUTRITION FACTS: 1/2 grapefruit equals 85 calories, trace fat (trace saturated fat), 0 cholesterol, 3 mg sodium, 22 g carbohydrate, 2 g fiber, 1 g protein. **DIABETIC EXCHANGES:** 1 fruit, 1/2 starch.

100 CALORIES homemade egg substitute

This egg substitute from our Test Kitchen can be used to replace whole eggs in many recipes with good results, especially in omelets and quiches.

- 2 large egg whites, lightly beaten
- 1 tablespoon nonfat dry milk powder
- 1 teaspoon canola oil
- 4 drops yellow food coloring, optional

- In a small bowl, whisk the egg whites, milk powder and oil until well blended. Add food coloring if desired.

YIELD: 1/4 cup egg substitute equivalent to 1 large egg, 1 serving.

EDITOR'S NOTE: The cholesterol in 1 large whole fresh egg is 213 mg.

NUTRITION FACTS: 1/4 cup equals 100 calories, 5 g fat (0.55 g saturated fat), 1 mg cholesterol, 150 mg sodium, 5 g carbohydrate, 0 fiber, 10 g protein. **DIABETIC EXCHANGES:** 1 lean meat, 1 fat.

fruit smoothies

Bryce Sickich | NEW PORT RICHEY, FLORIDA

This fresh, fruity smoothie is perfect for mornings when you're in a rush. The mix of flavors will start any day out right.

- 3/4 cup fat-free milk
- 1/2 cup orange juice
- 1/2 cup unsweetened applesauce
- 1 small ripe banana, halved
- 1/2 cup frozen unsweetened raspberries
- 7 to 10 ice cubes

- In a blender, combine all of the ingredients; cover and process until smooth. Pour the mixture into chilled glasses; serve immediately.

YIELD: 3 servings.

NUTRITION FACTS: 1 cup equals 97 calories, trace fat (trace saturated fat), 1 mg cholesterol, 33 mg sodium, 22 g carbohydrate, 2 g fiber, 3 g protein. **DIABETIC EXCHANGE:** 1-1/2 fruit.

FRUIT SMOOTHIES

97 CALORIES

91 CALORIES

APPLESAUCE OATMEAL PANCAKES

applesauce oatmeal pancakes

Martha Cage | WHEELING, WEST VIRGINIA

This recipe makes light, fluffy pancakes that will have the entire family asking for seconds. They're wonderful for those on restricted diets. Try them topped with homemade sugarless applesauce.

- 1 cup quick-cooking oats
- 1/4 cup whole wheat flour
- 1/4 cup all-purpose flour
- 1 tablespoon baking powder
- 1 cup fat-free milk
- 2 tablespoon sugarless applesauce *(recipe also found in Recipe Finder)*
- 4 egg whites

- In a bowl, combine the oats, flours and baking powder. In another bowl, combine milk, applesauce and egg whites; add to dry ingredients and mix well.

- Pour batter by 1/4 cupfuls onto a heated griddle coated with cooking spray. Cook until bubbles appear on the top; turn and cook until lightly browned.

YIELD: 5 servings (2 pancakes each).

NUTRITION FACTS: 2 pancakes equals 91 calories, 323 mg sodium, 1 mg cholesterol, 15 g carbohydrate, 5 g protein, trace fat. **DIABETIC EXCHANGES:** 1 starch.

90 CALORIES

VEGETABLE SCRAMBLED EGGS

vegetable scrambled eggs

Marilyn Ipson | ROGERS, ARKANSAS

These scrambled eggs are packed with a variety of veggies, giving you an instant healthy start to your day!

- 1 cup egg substitute
- 1/2 cup chopped green pepper
- 1/4 cup sliced green onions
- 1/4 cup fat-free milk
- 1/4 teaspoon salt
- 1/8 teaspoon pepper
- 1 small tomato, chopped and seeded

- In a small bowl, combine the egg substitute, green pepper, onions, milk, salt and pepper. Pour into a nonstick skillet coated with cooking spray. Cook and stir over medium heat until eggs are nearly set. Add the tomato; cook and stir until completely set.

YIELD: 2 servings.

NUTRITION FACTS: 1 serving equals 90 calories, trace fat (trace saturated fat), 1 mg cholesterol, 563 mg sodium, 8 g carbohydrate, 2 g fiber, 14 g protein. **DIABETIC EXCHANGES:** 2 lean meat, 1 vegetable.

cinnamon-honey grapefruit

Carson Sadler | SOURIS, MANITOBA

Although grapefruit is naturally delicious, it gains even more great flavor with this recipe. I often like to prepare this as a light breakfast, but it also makes an appealing addition to your morning meal.

- 1 medium grapefruit
- 2 teaspoons honey

Dash ground cinnamon

- Cut each grapefruit in half. With a sharp knife, carefully cut around each section to loosen fruit. Place cut side up in a baking pan.

- Drizzle each half with 1 teaspoon honey; sprinkle with cinnamon. Broil 4 in. from heat for 2-3 minutes or until bubbly. Serve warm.

YIELD: 2 servings.

NUTRITION FACTS: 1/2 grapefruit equals 63 calories, trace fat (trace saturated fat), 0 cholesterol, trace sodium, 16 g carbohydrate, 1 g fiber, 1 g protein. **DIABETIC EXCHANGES:** 1/2 starch, 1/2 fruit.

CINNAMON-HONEY GRAPEFRUIT

63 CALORIES

YUMMY RAISIN BITES

yummy raisin bites

Hannah Barringer | LOUDON, TENNESSEE

These scone-like snacks are good right out of the oven, but they're great at room temperature, too, when you're on the way to work or school.

- 2 cups all-purpose flour
- 3 teaspoons baking powder
- 1/2 teaspoon salt
- 1/2 teaspoon ground cinnamon
- 1/4 teaspoon ground nutmeg
- 1 cup fat-free milk
- 1/4 cup canola oil
- 1/4 cup honey
- 1/2 cup raisins

- In a large bowl, combine the flour, baking powder, salt, cinnamon and nutmeg.

- In a small bowl, combine the milk, oil and honey; add to the dry ingredients and stir just until moistened. Stir in raisins.

- Drop by tablespoonfuls onto baking sheets coated with cooking spray. Bake at 425° for 8-10 minutes or until lightly browned. Remove to wire racks.

YIELD: 2 dozen.

NUTRITION FACTS: 1 piece equals 82 calories, 2 g fat (trace saturated fat), trace cholesterol, 104 mg sodium, 14 g carbohydrate, trace fiber, 2 g protein. **DIABETIC EXCHANGES:** 1 starch, 1/2 fat.

rainbow fruit bowl

Dorothy Pritchett | WILLS POINT, TEXAS

I've discovered that mint gives melon a delicious zip. Mixed with fruit juices and served over melon, it's a pleasant blend that's both sweet and refreshing.

- 2 cups watermelon balls
- 2 cups honeydew balls
- 2 cups cantaloupe balls
- 1/2 cup orange juice
- 1/4 cup lime juice
- 2 tablespoons sugar
- 1 tablespoon snipped fresh mint
- 1 tablespoon grated orange peel
- 1 cup lemon-lime soda

- Combine the melon balls in a glass bowl. In a small bowl, whisk together juices, sugar, mint and orange peel; pour over melon and toss gently.

- Cover and refrigerate for 2 hours. Just before serving, add soda and toss gently.

YIELD: 8 servings.

NUTRITION FACTS: 3/4 cup equals 77 calories, trace fat (trace saturated fat), 0 cholesterol, 13 mg sodium, 19 g carbohydrate, 1 g fiber, 1 g protein. **DIABETIC EXCHANGES:** 1 fruit, 1/2 starch.

RAINBOW FRUIT BOWL

101-200 calories

mini ham 'n' cheese frittatas

Susan Watt | BASKING RIDGE, NEW JERSEY

I found this recipe a few years ago and tried to make it with a few changes. I'm diabetic, and this fits into my low-carb and low-fat diet. Every time I serve a brunch, the frittatas are the first thing to disappear, and nobody knows they are low fat!

- 1/4 pound cubed fully cooked ham
- 1 cup (4 ounces) shredded fat-free cheddar cheese
- 6 eggs
- 4 egg whites
- 3 tablespoons minced chives
- 2 tablespoons fat-free milk
- 1/4 teaspoon salt
- 1/4 teaspoon pepper

MINI HAM 'N' CHEESE FRITTATAS

106 CALORIES

- Divide ham evenly among eight muffin cups coated with cooking spray; top with cheese. In a large bowl, beat eggs and whites. Beat in the chives, milk, salt and pepper. Pour over cheese, filling each muffin cup three-fourths full.

- Bake at 375° for 22-25 minutes or until a knife inserted near the center comes out clean. Carefully run a knife around edges to loosen; remove from pan. Serve warm.

YIELD: 8 frittatas.

NUTRITION FACTS: 1 frittata equals 106 calories, 4 g fat (1 g saturated fat), 167 mg cholesterol, 428 mg sodium, 2 g carbohydrate, trace fiber, 14 g protein. **DIABETIC EXCHANGE:** 2 medium-fat meat.

156 CALORIES pepper cheese omelet

Susan Rekerdres | DALLAS, TEXAS

Packed with red peppers, onion, paprika and cheese, this savory omelet is simply scrumptious.

- 2 eggs
- 4 egg whites
- 2 teaspoons fat-free milk
- 1 teaspoon paprika
- 1/4 teaspoon salt
- 1/4 teaspoon pepper
- 2 tablespoons finely chopped onion
- 2 tablespoons finely chopped sweet red pepper
- 1/4 cup shredded part-skim mozzarella cheese

classic

- In a small bowl, beat the eggs, egg whites, milk, paprika, salt and pepper. Coat an 8-in. nonstick skillet with cooking spray and place over medium heat. Add half of the egg mixture. As eggs set, lift edges, letting uncooked portion flow underneath.

- When eggs are set, sprinkle half of the onion, red pepper and cheese over one side; fold omelet over filling. Cover and let stand for 1 minute or until cheese is melted. Repeat with remaining ingredients.

YIELD: 2 servings.

NUTRITION FACTS: 1 omelet equals 156 calories, 7 g fat (3 g saturated fat), 221 mg cholesterol, 537 mg sodium, 4 g carbohydrate, 1 g fiber, 17 g protein. **DIABETIC EXCHANGE:** 3 lean meat.

110 CALORIES

WAKE-UP WONTON CUPS

wake-up wonton cups

Gina Berry | CHANHASSEN, MINNESOTA

Dainty, delectable and delightfully different, these yummy breakfast bites add a fun touch to a healthy morning meal. Pepper sauce lends just a bit of heat and can be adjusted to your liking.

10	wonton wrappers

Cooking spray

4	eggs
1/2	teaspoon garlic powder
1/4	teaspoon salt
1	medium tomato, seeded and chopped
10	drops hot pepper sauce

- Press wonton wrappers into miniature muffin cups coated with cooking spray. Spritz wrappers with cooking spray. Bake at 350° for 10-12 minutes or until lightly browned.

- Meanwhile, in a small bowl, whisk the eggs, garlic powder and salt. Heat a small nonstick skillet coated with cooking spray until hot. Add egg mixture; cook and stir over medium heat until eggs are completely set.

- Spoon eggs into cups. Top each with chopped tomato and a drop of pepper sauce.

YIELD: 10 wonton cups.

NUTRITION FACTS: 2 wonton cups equals 110 calories, 4 g fat (1 g saturated fat), 171 mg cholesterol, 269 mg sodium, 11 g carbohydrate, 1 g fiber, 7 g protein. DIABETIC EXCHANGES: 1 starch, 1 medium-fat meat.

apple yogurt parfaits

Rebekah Radewahn | WAUWATOSA, WISCONSIN

Get the morning started right with this super-simple four-ingredient parfait. Try chunky or flavored applesauce for easy variations.

1	cup sweetened applesauce

Dash ground nutmeg

1/2	cup granola with raisins
1-1/3	cups vanilla yogurt

- In a small bowl, combine applesauce and nutmeg. Spoon 1 tablespoon granola into each of four parfait glasses. Layer each with 1/3 cup yogurt and 1/4 cup applesauce; sprinkle with remaining granola. Serve immediately.

YIELD: 4 servings.

NUTRITION FACTS: 1 parfait equals 170 calories, 4 g fat (2 g saturated fat), 8 mg cholesterol, 69 mg sodium, 30 g carbohydrate, 1 g fiber, 5 g protein. DIABETIC EXCHANGES: 1 starch, 1/2 milk.

APPLE YOGURT PARFAITS

170 CALORIES

138 CALORIES

ANYTIME FRITTATA

anytime frittata

Lynne Van Wagenen | SALT LAKE CITY, UTAH

We enjoy frittatas often at our house. They're a great way to use up leftover vegetables, cheese and lean meat. Enjoy this hearty recipe with fruit and biscuits for a light dinner.

1-1/4 cups egg substitute
   2 eggs
 1/2 teaspoon dried oregano
 1/8 teaspoon pepper
   1 small onion, chopped
   1 garlic clove, minced
   1 teaspoon butter
   3 plum tomatoes, chopped
 1/2 cup crumbled feta cheese
   2 tablespoons capers, drained

- In a small bowl, whisk the egg substitute, eggs, oregano and pepper; set aside. In a 10-in. oven-proof skillet, saute onion and garlic in butter for 2 minutes. Stir in tomatoes; heat through.

- Pour the reserved egg mixture into skillet. Reduce heat; cover and cook for 4-6 minutes or until nearly set.

- Sprinkle with cheese and capers. Broil 3-4 in. from the heat for 2-3 minutes or until eggs are completely set. Let stand for 5 minutes. Cut into wedges.

YIELD: 4 servings.

NUTRITION FACTS: 1 wedge equals 138 calories, 6 g fat (3 g saturated fat), 116 mg cholesterol, 465 mg sodium, 6 g carbohydrate, 2 g fiber, 14 g protein. **DIABETIC EXCHANGES:** 2 lean meat, 1 vegetable, 1/2 fat.

banana blueberry pancakes

Kelly Reinicke | WISCONSIN RAPIDS, WISCONSIN

This recipe is a favorite in our home. My kids don't even realize how healthy it is!

   1 cup whole wheat flour
 1/2 cup all-purpose flour
   2 tablespoons sugar
   2 teaspoons baking powder
 1/2 teaspoon salt
   1 egg, lightly beaten
1-1/4 cups fat-free milk
   3 medium ripe bananas, mashed
   1 teaspoon vanilla extract
1-1/2 cups fresh *or* frozen blueberries
Maple syrup, optional

- In a large bowl, combine the flours, sugar, baking powder and salt. Combine the egg, milk, bananas and vanilla; stir into dry ingredients just until moistened.

- Pour batter by 1/4 cupfuls onto a hot griddle coated with cooking spray; sprinkle with blueberries. Turn when bubbles form on top; cook until second side is golden brown. Serve with syrup if desired.

YIELD: 14 pancakes.

EDITOR'S NOTE: If using frozen blueberries, do not thaw.

NUTRITION FACTS: 2 pancakes (calculated without syrup) equals 195 calories, 2 g fat (trace saturated fat), 31 mg cholesterol, 317 mg sodium, 41 g carbohydrate, 4 g fiber, 6 g protein. **DIABETIC EXCHANGES:** 1-1/2 starch, 1 fruit.

BANANA BLUEBERRY PANCAKES

195 CALORIES

187 CALORIES

MAKEOVER MULTIGRAIN WAFFLES

makeover multigrain waffles

Betty Blair | **BARTLETT, TENNESSEE**

These delicious multigrain waffles are crispy, airy, and lower in fat, calories and cholesterol than my original recipe...but just as tasty!

- 1 cup all-purpose flour
- 1 cup whole wheat flour
- 1 cup cornmeal
- 1 tablespoon sugar
- 1 tablespoon baking powder
- 3/4 teaspoon baking soda
- 1/2 teaspoon salt
- 3 eggs
- 4 egg whites
- 3 cups buttermilk
- 1/2 cup unsweetened applesauce
- 3 tablespoons canola oil
- 2 tablespoons butter, melted

Butter and maple syrup, optional

- In a large bowl, combine the first seven ingredients. In another bowl, whisk the eggs, egg whites, buttermilk, applesauce, oil and butter; whisk into dry ingredients just until blended.

- Bake in a preheated waffle iron according to manufacturer's directions until golden brown. Serve with butter and syrup if desired.

YIELD: 28 waffles.

NUTRITION FACTS: 2 waffles (calculated without butter and syrup) equals 187 calories, 7 g fat (2 g saturated fat), 52 mg cholesterol, 336 mg sodium, 25 g carbohydrate, 2 g fiber, 7 g protein. **DIABETIC EXCHANGES:** 1-1/2 starch, 1 fat.

cherry yogurt

Serve wholesome granola over this thick, rich yogurt for a quick breakfast. Or layer it in a parfait glass with granola and fruit for something special. It will keep in the refrigerator for the entire week. Our home economists suggest looking for 100% cherry juice at the store, since the cocktail blends have added sugar.

- 4 cups (32 ounces) reduced-fat plain yogurt
- 1 cup frozen pitted dark sweet cherries, thawed and quartered
- 1/2 cup cherry juice blend
- 3 tablespoons confectioners' sugar
- 1-1/2 teaspoons vanilla extract

- Line a strainer with four layers of the cheesecloth or one coffee filter and place over a bowl. Place the yogurt in prepared strainer; cover the yogurt with the edges of cheesecloth. Refrigerate for 8 hours or overnight.

- Remove yogurt from cheesecloth and discard liquid from bowl. Place yogurt in a small bowl; stir in the remaining ingredients. Cover and refrigerate until serving.

YIELD: 3 cups.

NUTRITION FACTS: 1/2 cup equals 147 calories, 3 g fat (2 g saturated fat), 10 mg cholesterol, 115 mg sodium, 22 g carbohydrate, 1 g fiber, 9 g protein. **DIABETIC EXCHANGES:** 1 reduced-fat milk, 1/2 fruit.

CHERRY YOGURT

147 CALORIES

too-yummy-to-share scramble

Vickey Abate | GREEN ISLAND, NEW YORK
Pamper yourself one sunny morning with this scrumptious, single-serving egg dish because you're worth it! I've gotten many compliments on this recipe; basil gives it fresh flavor.

- 1/4 cup chopped sweet onion
- 1/4 cup chopped tomato
- 1/8 teaspoon dried basil

Dash salt and pepper

- 1 egg
- 1 tablespoon water
- 2 tablespoons shredded reduced-fat cheddar cheese

- In a small nonstick skillet coated with cooking spray, cook and stir the onion over medium heat until tender. Add the tomato, basil, salt and pepper; cook 1 minute longer.

- In a small bowl, whisk egg and water. Add egg mixture to the pan; cook and stir until egg is completely set. Remove from the heat. Sprinkle with cheese; cover and let stand until cheese is melted.

YIELD: 1 serving.

NUTRITION FACTS: 1 serving equals 136 calories, 8 g fat (4 g saturated fat), 222 mg cholesterol, 310 mg sodium, 7 g carbohydrate, 1 g fiber, 11 g protein.

TOO-YUMMY-TO-SHARE SCRAMBLE

BREAKFAST CREPES WITH BERRIES

breakfast crepes with berries

Jennifer Weisbrodt | OCONOMOWOC, WISCONSIN
After a long day of blackberry picking, I whipped up a sauce to dress up some crepes I had on hand. This speedy dish really hit the spot and tied everything together beautifully! The crepes make an elegant addition to any brunch, and the sauce is delectable over warm waffles.

- 1-1/2 cups fresh raspberries
- 1-1/2 cups fresh blackberries
- 1 cup (8 ounces) sour cream
- 1/2 cup confectioners' sugar
- 1 carton (6 ounces) orange creme yogurt
- 1 tablespoon lime juice
- 1-1/2 teaspoons grated lime peel
- 1/2 teaspoon vanilla extract
- 1/8 teaspoon salt
- 8 prepared crepes (9 inches)

- In a large bowl, combine the raspberries and blackberries; set aside. In a small bowl, combine the sour cream and confectioners' sugar until smooth. Stir in the yogurt, lime juice, lime peel, vanilla and salt.

- Spread 2 tablespoons sour cream mixture over each crepe; top with about 1/3 cup berries. Roll up; drizzle with remaining sour cream mixture. Serve immediately.

YIELD: 8 servings.

NUTRITION FACTS: 1 crepe equals 182 calories, 7 g fat (4 g saturated fat), 27 mg cholesterol, 144 mg sodium, 27 g carbohydrate, 3 g fiber, 3 g protein. **DIABETIC EXCHANGES:** 1-1/2 starch, 1-1/2 fat.

broccoli cheddar brunch bake

Carla Weeks | INDEPENDENCE, IOWA

This slimmed-down version of a favorite brunch dish is hearty, wholesome and boasts all the gourmet flavor of the original recipe!

- 6 tablespoons reduced-fat butter, cubed
- 8 cups chopped fresh broccoli
- 1 cup finely chopped onion
- 6 eggs, beaten
- 1-1/2 cups egg substitute
- 1-1/2 cups (6 ounces) shredded sharp cheddar cheese, *divided*
- 1 cup fat-free milk
- 1 cup half-and-half cream
- 1 teaspoon salt
- 1 teaspoon pepper

- In a Dutch oven, melt butter. Add broccoli and onion; saute until crisp-tender. In a large bowl, combine the eggs, egg substitute, 1 cup cheese, milk, cream, salt and pepper. Stir in broccoli mixture. Pour into a 3-qt. baking dish coated with cooking spray.

BROCCOLI CHEDDAR BRUNCH BAKE

- Bake, uncovered, at 350° for 40-45 minutes or until a knife inserted near the center comes out clean. Sprinkle with remaining cheese. Let stand for 10 minutes before serving.

YIELD: 12 servings.

EDITOR'S NOTE: This recipe was tested with Land O'Lakes light stick butter.

NUTRITION FACTS: 1 piece equals 178 calories, 12 g fat (7 g saturated fat), 139 mg cholesterol, 459 mg sodium, 7 g carbohydrate, 2 g fiber, 12 g protein.

raspberry pancakes

Karen Edland | MCHENRY, NORTH DAKOTA

Sometimes we have these pancakes for dinner because they are so rich. They are the best on a cool summer night!

- 2/3 cup all-purpose flour
- 1 tablespoon sugar
- 1 teaspoon baking powder
- 3/4 teaspoon baking soda
- 1/3 cup plain yogurt
- 1 large egg, beaten lightly
- 1 tablespoon butter, melted and cooled
- 1/2 cup whole milk
- 1 cup fresh raspberries

Raspberry jam

Confectioners' sugar

- Whisk together flour, sugar, baking powder and soda. (Add a pinch of salt if desired.) Set aside.

- In large bowl, whisk together yogurt, egg, butter and milk. Add to flour mixture; stir just until combined. Fold in raspberries.

- Heat a griddle over moderately high heat; brush with additional melted butter. Drop scant 1/4 cupfuls of batter onto griddle; cook for 1 minute or until bubbles form on top. Turn and cook 1 minute more. Serve with raspberry jam and sugar.

YIELD: 4 servings.

NUTRITION FACTS: 2 pancakes (calculated without jam and confectioners' sugar) equals 178 calories, 6 g fat (3 g saturated fat), 68 mg cholesterol, 405 mg sodium, 25 g carbohydrate, 3 g fiber, 6 g protein. **DIABETIC EXCHANGES:** 1-1/2 starch, 1 fat.

186 CALORIES

RAISIN OATMEAL MIX

raisin oatmeal mix

Robert Caummisar | GRAYSON, KENTUCKY

We like the sweet cinnamon flavor of this instant oatmeal. The mix makes it convenient to zap a bowl in the microwave for a speedy breakfast. If you like milk with your oatmeal, pour a little on top before serving.

    6 cups quick-cooking oats
  1/2 cup raisins
  1/2 cup chopped dried apples *or* dried banana
       chips
  1/4 cup sugar
  1/4 cup packed brown sugar
    3 teaspoons ground cinnamon
    1 teaspoon salt

ADDITIONAL INGREDIENT FOR OATMEAL:

  3/4 cup water

- In a large bowl, combine the first seven ingredients. Divide into two batches; store in airtight containers in a cool dry place for up to 1 month. **YIELD:** 7 cups of mix (two batches oatmeal mix—each batch makes 7 servings).

- **TO PREPARE OATMEAL:** In a deep microwave-safe bowl, combine 1/2 cup of the oatmeal mix and 3/4 cup water. Microwave, uncovered, on high for 45 seconds; stir. Cook 20-50 seconds longer or until bubbly. Let stand for 1-2 minutes.

YIELD: 1 serving.

EDITOR'S NOTE: This recipe was tested in a 1,100-watt microwave.

NUTRITION FACTS: 1/2 cup equals 186 calories, 2 g fat (trace saturated fat), 0 cholesterol, 175 mg sodium, 36 g carbohydrate, 4 g fiber, 6 g protein. **DIABETIC EXCHANGE:** 2-1/2 starch.

nutmeg waffles

James Christensen | ST. ANTHONY, IDAHO

Bake an extra batch of these tender, golden waffles on the weekend. Eat a couple, then freeze the others in packages of two to pop in the toaster and reheat on hurried mornings. Nutmeg adds to their warm, feel-good flavor!

  1-1/4 cups all-purpose flour
      1 teaspoon baking powder
      1 teaspoon ground cinnamon
    1/2 teaspoon salt
    1/2 teaspoon ground nutmeg
    1/4 teaspoon baking soda
      1 egg, lightly beaten
      1 cup fat-free milk
      1 teaspoon canola oil
      1 teaspoon vanilla extract

Butter and maple syrup, optional

- In a small bowl, combine the flour, baking powder, cinnamon, salt, nutmeg and baking soda. In another bowl, combine the egg, milk, oil and vanilla; stir into dry ingredients until smooth.

- Bake waffles in a preheated waffle iron according to the manufacturer's directions until golden brown. Serve with butter and syrup if desired.

YIELD: 8 waffles.

NUTRITION FACTS: 2 waffles (calculated without butter and syrup) equals 196 calories, 3 g fat (1 g saturated fat), 54 mg cholesterol, 518 mg sodium, 34 g carbohydrate, 1 g fiber, 8 g protein. **DIABETIC EXCHANGES:** 2 starch, 1/2 fat.

NUTMEG WAFFLES

196 CALORIES

197 CALORIES

CRUSTLESS SPINACH QUICHE

crustless spinach quiche

Vicki Schrupp | ST. CLOUD, MINNESOTA

My daughter is a vegetarian, so I eliminated the ham called for in my original recipe. Wedges of this healthy quiche make a fast and flavorful brunch, lunch or supper.

- 3 ounces reduced-fat cream cheese, softened
- 1 cup fat-free milk
- 1 cup egg substitute
- 1/4 teaspoon pepper
- 3 cups (12 ounces) shredded reduced-fat cheddar cheese
- 3 cups frozen chopped spinach, thawed and squeezed dry
- 1 cup frozen chopped broccoli, thawed and well drained
- 1 small onion, finely chopped
- 5 fresh mushrooms, sliced

- In a small bowl, beat cream cheese. Add the milk, egg substitute and pepper; beat until smooth. Stir in the remaining ingredients.

- Transfer to a 10-in. quiche pan coated with cooking spray. Bake at 350° for 45-50 minutes or until a knife inserted near the center comes out clean.

YIELD: 8 servings.

NUTRITION FACTS: 1 piece equals 197 calories, 12 g fat (8 g saturated fat), 38 mg cholesterol, 439 mg sodium, 8 g carbohydrate, 3 g fiber, 18 g protein. **DIABETIC EXCHANGES:** 2 medium-fat meat, 1 vegetable.

ham potato puffs

Brad Eichelberger | YORK, PENNSYLVANIA

This is a different way to use up leftover mashed potatoes. It was an instant hit with our teenagers. Serve with steamed green beans, cauliflower or broccoli.

- 1 tube (12 ounces) refrigerated buttermilk biscuits
- 1 cup cubed fully cooked ham
- 1 cup leftover mashed potatoes
- 1 cup (4 ounces) shredded cheddar cheese, *divided*
- 1/2 teaspoon dried parsley flakes
- 1/4 teaspoon garlic powder

- Press each biscuit onto the bottom and up the sides of a greased muffin cup. In a large bowl, combine the ham, potatoes, 1/2 cup cheese, parsley and garlic powder.

- Spoon 1/4 cup into each prepared cup. Sprinkle with remaining cheese. Bake at 350° for 20-25 minutes or until lightly browned. Serve warm. Refrigerate leftovers.

YIELD: 10 puffs.

NUTRITION FACTS: 1 potato puff equals 165 calories, 5 g fat (3 g saturated fat), 20 mg cholesterol, 592 mg sodium, 21 g carbohydrate, trace fiber, 8 g protein. **DIABETIC EXCHANGES:** 1-1/2 starch, 1 fat.

HAM POTATO PUFFS

165 CALORIES

asparagus frittata

James Bates | HERMISTON, OREGON

You would never guess that egg substitute takes the place of eggs in this fun variation on a traditional frittata. Chock-full of fresh asparagus, this dish is perfect for a light springtime lunch or brunch.

- 1 cup water
- 2/3 pound fresh asparagus, trimmed and cut into 1-inch pieces
- 1 medium onion, chopped
- 2 teaspoons olive oil
- 2 tablespoons minced fresh parsley
- 1-1/2 cups egg substitute
- 5 tablespoons shredded Parmesan cheese, *divided*
- 1/4 teaspoon salt
- 1/8 teaspoon pepper
- 1/4 cup shredded reduced-fat cheddar cheese

- In a small saucepan, bring water to a boil. Add asparagus; cover and boil for 3 minutes. Drain and immediately place asparagus in ice water; drain and pat dry. In a 10-in. ovenproof skillet, saute onion in oil until tender. Add parsley and asparagus; toss to coat.

- In a small bowl, combine the egg substitute, 3 tablespoons Parmesan cheese, salt and pepper. Pour over the asparagus mixture; cover and cook over medium heat for 8-10 minutes or until eggs are nearly set. Sprinkle with remaining Parmesan.

ASPARAGUS FRITTATA

146 CALORIES

- Place uncovered skillet in the broiler, 6 in. from the heat, for 2 minutes or until eggs are set. Sprinkle with cheddar cheese. Cut into quarters. Serve immediately.

YIELD: 4 servings.

NUTRITION FACTS: 1 piece equals 146 calories, 5 g fat (2 g saturated fat), 8 mg cholesterol, 533 mg sodium, 9 g carbohydrate, 2 g fiber, 16 g protein. **DIABETIC EXCHANGES:** 2 lean meat, 1 vegetable.

scrumptious scramble

156 CALORIES

Lynn Winkler | CHATSWORTH, GEORGIA

By substituting 4 egg whites for the 4 whole eggs in this recipe you save 25 calories, 3 g of fat and a whopping 141 mg cholesterol per serving! And since the eggs are seasoned with veggies and dill, you don't miss the flavor at all.

- 1/2 cup finely chopped red onion
- 1 teaspoon olive oil
- 1 medium tomato, seeded and finely chopped
- 4 eggs
- 4 egg whites
- 2 tablespoons water
- 1-1/2 teaspoons snipped fresh dill *or* 1/2 teaspoon dill weed
- 1/4 teaspoon salt
- 1/8 teaspoon pepper

- In a large nonstick skillet coated with cooking spray, saute onion in oil for 2 minutes. Add tomato; saute 1-2 minutes longer or until vegetables are tender. Transfer to a small bowl; set aside.

- Whisk the remaining ingredients. Coat the same skillet with additional cooking spray; add egg mixture. Cook and stir over medium heat until eggs are nearly set.

- Add reserved onion mixture; cook and stir until heated through and eggs are completely set.

YIELD: 3 servings.

NUTRITION FACTS: 3/4 cup equals 156 calories, 8 g fat (2 g saturated fat), 283 mg cholesterol, 359 mg sodium, 6 g carbohydrate, 1 g fiber, 14 g protein.

baked blueberry pancake

Norna Detig | LINDENWOOD, ILLINOIS

For a quick breakfast, I make this huge pancake while I fix supper the night before, then I cut it into squares. The next morning, I top them with butter and syrup before placing them in the microwave. This method takes most of the fuss out of making breakfast.

    2 cups pancake mix
1-1/2 cups fat-free milk
    1 egg
    1 tablespoon canola oil
    1 teaspoon ground cinnamon
    1 cup fresh *or* frozen blueberries
Butter and maple syrup

- In a large bowl, combine the pancake mix, milk, egg, oil and cinnamon just until blended (batter will be lumpy). Fold in blueberries.

- Spread into a greased 15-in. x 10-in. x 1-in. baking pan. Bake at 400° for 10-12 minutes or until golden brown. Serve with butter and syrup.

YIELD: 6 servings.

EDITOR'S NOTE: If using frozen blueberries, use without thawing to avoid discoloring the batter.

NUTRITION FACTS: 1 serving (calculated without butter and syrup) equals 200 calories, 4 g fat (1 g saturated fat), 36 mg cholesterol, 527 mg sodium, 34 g carbohydrate, 3 g fiber, 7 g protein. **DIABETIC EXCHANGES:** 2 starch, 1 fat.

BAKED BLUEBERRY PANCAKE

CRUNCHY APPLE SALAD

crunchy apple salad

Kathy Armstrong | POST FALLS, IDAHO

This fruit salad pairs crunchy toppings with smooth vanilla yogurt, creating a combination you'll love!

    6 tablespoons vanilla yogurt
    6 tablespoons reduced-fat whipped topping
  1/4 teaspoon plus 1/8 teaspoon ground cinnamon, *divided*
    2 medium red apples, chopped
    1 large Granny Smith apple, chopped
  1/4 cup dried cranberries
    2 tablespoons chopped walnuts

- In a large bowl, combine the yogurt, whipped topping and 1/4 teaspoon cinnamon. Add apples and cranberries; toss to coat. Refrigerate until serving. Sprinkle with walnuts and remaining cinnamon before serving.

YIELD: 5 servings.

NUTRITION FACTS: 3/4 cup equals 116 calories, 3 g fat (1 g saturated fat), 1 mg cholesterol, 13 mg sodium, 23 g carbohydrate, 3 g fiber, 2 g protein. **DIABETIC EXCHANGES:** 1 fruit, 1/2 starch, 1/2 fat.

198 CALORIES

MUSTARD HAM STRATA

mustard ham strata

Dolores Zornow | POYNETTE, WISCONSIN

I had this at a bed-and-breakfast years ago. They were kind enough to give me the recipe, and I've made it many times since.

12	slices day-old bread, crusts removed and cubed
1-1/2	cups cubed fully cooked ham
1	cup chopped green pepper
3/4	cup shredded cheddar cheese
3/4	cup shredded Monterey Jack cheese
1/3	cup chopped onion
7	eggs
3	cups whole milk
3	teaspoons ground mustard
1	teaspoon salt

- In a greased 13-in. x 9-in. baking dish, layer the bread cubes, ham, green pepper, cheeses and onion. In a large bowl, combine the eggs, milk, mustard and salt. Pour over top. Cover and refrigerate overnight.

- Remove from the refrigerator 30 minutes before baking. Bake, uncovered, at 325° for 45-50 minutes or until a knife inserted near the center comes out clean. Let stand for 5 minutes before cutting.

YIELD: 12 servings.

NUTRITION FACTS: 1 piece equals 198 calories, 11 g fat (5 g saturated fat), 153 mg cholesterol, 648 mg sodium, 11 g carbohydrate, 1 g fiber, 13 g protein.

cinnamon fruit biscuits

Ione Burham | WASHINGTON, IOWA

Because these sweet treats are so easy, I'm almost embarrassed when people ask me for the recipe. They're a snap to make with refrigerated buttermilk biscuits, sugar, cinnamon and your favorite fruit preserves.

1/2	cup sugar
1/2	teaspoon ground cinnamon
1	tube (12 ounces) refrigerated buttermilk biscuits, separated into 10 biscuits
1/4	cup butter, melted
10	teaspoons strawberry preserves

- In a small bowl, combine sugar and cinnamon. Dip top and sides of biscuits in butter, then in cinnamon-sugar.

- Place on ungreased baking sheets. With the end of a wooden spoon handle, make a deep indentation in the center of each biscuit; fill with 1 teaspoon preserves.

- Bake at 375° for 15-18 minutes or until golden brown. Cool for 15 minutes before serving (preserves will be hot).

YIELD: 10 servings.

NUTRITION FACTS: 1 biscuit equals 178 calories, 5 g fat (3 g saturated fat), 12 mg cholesterol, 323 mg sodium, 31 g carbohydrate, trace fiber, 3 g protein. **DIABETIC EXCHANGES:** 2 starch, 1 fat.

CINNAMON FRUIT BISCUITS

178 CALORIES

EGG BLOSSOMS

egg blossoms

Barbara Nowakowski

NORTH TONAWANDA, NEW YORK

These cute phyllo dough shells are filled with a savory combination of eye-opening flavors!

  4 sheets phyllo dough (14 inches x 9 inches)
  2 tablespoons butter, melted
  4 teaspoons grated Parmesan cheese
  4 eggs
  4 teaspoons finely chopped green onion
  1/4 teaspoon salt
  1/8 teaspoon pepper

SALSA:

  1 can (14-1/2 ounces) diced tomatoes, undrained
  1 small onion, chopped
  1-1/2 teaspoons sugar
  1-1/2 teaspoons white wine vinegar
  1 garlic clove, minced
  1/2 teaspoon salt
  1/4 teaspoon dried oregano

- Place one sheet of phyllo dough on a work surface; brush with butter. Top with another sheet of phyllo; brush with butter. Cut into six 4-1/2-in. squares. (Keep remaining phyllo dough covered with plastic wrap to avoid drying out.) Repeat with remaining phyllo and butter.

- Stack three squares of layered phyllo in each of four greased muffin cups, rotating squares so corners do not overlap. Sprinkle 1 teaspoon of cheese into each cup. Top with one egg. Sprinkle with green onion, salt and pepper. Place on a baking sheet. Bake at 350° for 25-30 minutes or until eggs are completely set and pastry is golden brown.

- Meanwhile, in a saucepan, combine the salsa ingredients. Bring to a boil over medium heat. Reduce heat; simmer, uncovered, for 10 minutes or until onion is tender. Serve with egg cups.

YIELD: 4 servings.

NUTRITION FACTS: 1 serving (1 each) equals 198 calories, 11 g fat (5 g saturated fat), 229 mg cholesterol, 771 mg sodium, 16 g carbohydrate, 2 g fiber, 9 g protein.

spinach feta frittata

Laura Fall-Sutton | Buhl, Idaho

When I want something special, I rely on this low-calorie favorite. It's hearty with potatoes, spinach and feta cheese, and the basil and garlic lend a delightful flavor everyone is sure to adore.

  6 egg whites
  3 eggs
  2 tablespoons water
  1/2 teaspoon coarsely ground pepper
  1/4 teaspoon salt
  1/2 cup chopped onion
  1/2 teaspoon minced garlic
  2 tablespoons olive oil
  2 medium red potatoes, cut into 1/4-inch cubes
  1 package (10 ounces) frozen chopped spinach, thawed and squeezed dry
  3/4 cup crumbled feta cheese
  2 tablespoons minced fresh basil

- In a bowl, whisk the egg whites, eggs, water, pepper and salt; set aside. In a 10-in. ovenproof skillet, saute onion and garlic in oil for 2 minutes. Add potatoes; cook and stir until almost tender, about 10 minutes. Reduce heat; sprinkle with spinach, feta cheese and basil.

- Top with egg mixture. Cover and cook for 4-6 minutes or until nearly set. Uncover; broil 3-4 in. from the heat for 2-3 minutes or until eggs are completely set. Let stand for 5 minutes. Cut into wedges.

YIELD: 6 servings.

NUTRITION FACTS: 1 slice equals 178 calories, 9 g fat (3 g saturated fat), 114 mg cholesterol, 358 mg sodium, 12 g carbohydrate, 3 g fiber, 12 g protein. **DIABETIC EXCHANGES:** 2 vegetable, 1-1/2 fat, 1 lean meat.

crepes with berries

Leica Merriam | **PROVIDENCE, UTAH**

The freshness of sweet berries paired with apricot preserves makes these crepes a perfect breakfast treat.

- 2 tablespoons sugar
- 4 cups blueberries, blackberries *and/or* raspberries
- 1 cup fat-free milk
- 1 egg
- 3 egg whites
- 1/2 teaspoon almond extract
- 1/2 teaspoon vanilla extract
- 2/3 cup all-purpose flour
- 1/4 cup cornmeal
- 16 teaspoons reduced-sugar apricot preserves
- 1 cup (8 ounces) vanilla yogurt

• Sprinkle sugar over berries; gently toss to mix. Cover and refrigerate. In a blender, combine the milk, egg, egg whites and extracts; cover and process until blended. Add the flour and cornmeal; cover and process until blended. Cover and refrigerate for 1 hour.

CREPES WITH BERRIES

• Coat a 7-in. skillet with cooking spray. Heat skillet over medium heat. Pour about 2 tablespoons batter into the center of skillet. Lift and tilt pan to evenly coat bottom. Cook until top appears dry; turn and cook 15-20 seconds longer. Remove to a plate; keep warm. Repeat with remaining batter, coating with additional cooking spray as needed.

• Spread each crepe with 1 teaspoon apricot preserves. Fold each crepe into quarters; place two crepes on an individual plate. Top with 2 tablespoons yogurt and 1/2 cup berry mixture. Serve immediately.

YIELD: 8 servings.

NUTRITION FACTS: 2 crepes equals 178 calories, 1 g fat (1 g saturated fat), 29 mg cholesterol, 64 mg sodium, 35 g carbohydrate, 2 g fiber, 7 g protein. **DIABETIC EXCHANGES:** 1-1/2 starch, 1 fruit.

whole wheat pancakes

157 CALORIES

Line Walter | **WAYNE, PENNSYLVANIA**

These light and fluffy pancakes allow you to enjoy your favorite Saturday morning treat, while still maintaining a healthy diet. Whole wheat flour and toasted wheat germ make them hearty and delicious.

- 2 cups whole wheat flour
- 1/2 cup toasted wheat germ
- 1 teaspoon baking soda
- 1/2 teaspoon salt
- 2 eggs
- 3 cups buttermilk
- 1 tablespoon canola oil

classic

• In a large bowl, combine the flour, wheat germ, baking soda and salt. In another bowl, whisk the eggs, buttermilk and oil. Stir into dry ingredients just until blended.

• Pour batter by 1/4 cupfuls onto a hot griddle coated with cooking spray; turn when bubbles form on top of pancakes. Cook until second side is golden brown.

YIELD: 20 pancakes.

NUTRITION FACTS: 2 pancakes equals 157 calories, 4 g fat (1 g saturated fat), 45 mg cholesterol, 335 mg sodium, 24 g carbohydrate, 4 g fiber, 9 g protein. **DIABETIC EXCHANGES:** 1-1/2 starch, 1 fat.

cappuccino smoothies

Michelle Cluney | LAKE MARY, FLORIDA

Topped with miniature marshmallows, this icy cappuccino beverage is a twist on traditional fruit smoothies. My mom and I created it when trying to fix an easy, healthy snack.

> 1 cup (8 ounces) cappuccino *or* coffee yogurt
> 1/3 cup whole milk
> 3 tablespoons confectioners' sugar, optional
> 1 tablespoon chocolate syrup
> 1-1/2 cups ice cubes
> 1/2 cup miniature marshmallows, *divided*

- In a blender, combine the yogurt, milk, sugar if desired and chocolate syrup. Add ice cubes and 1/4 cup marshmallows; cover and process until blended. Pour into chilled glasses; top with the remaining marshmallows. Serve immediately.

YIELD: 3 servings.

NUTRITION FACTS: 1 cup equals 166 calories, 3 g fat (2 g saturated fat), 11 mg cholesterol, 69 mg sodium, 30 g carbohydrate, trace fiber, 5 g protein.

CAPPUCCINO SMOOTHIES

VEGETABLE FRITTATA

vegetable frittata

Pauline Howard | LAGO VISTA, TEXAS

This breakfast dish is perfect if you want to incorporate fresh veggies into your morning meal.

> 1 cup egg substitute
> 1 cup sliced fresh mushrooms
> 1/2 cup chopped fresh broccoli
> 1/4 cup shredded reduced-fat cheddar cheese
> 2 tablespoons finely chopped onion
> 2 tablespoons finely chopped green pepper
> 2 tablespoons grated Parmesan cheese
> 1/8 teaspoon salt

Dash pepper

- In a large bowl, combine all of the ingredients. Pour into a shallow 2-cup baking dish coated with cooking spray.

- Bake, uncovered, at 350° for 20-25 minutes or until a knife inserted near the center comes out clean. Serve immediately.

YIELD: 2 servings.

NUTRITION FACTS: 1/2 frittata equals 141 calories, 5 g fat (3 g saturated fat), 14 mg cholesterol, 571 mg sodium, 6 g carbohydrate, 1 g fiber, 19 g protein. **DIABETIC EXCHANGE:** 3 lean meat.

197 CALORIES

VERY VEGGIE OMELET

very veggie omelet

Jan Houberg | REDDICK, ILLINOIS

I enjoy serving this fluffy omelet to my husband, who always appreciates a new twist on breakfast. It's chock-full of garden goodness.

 classic

1	small onion, chopped
1/4	cup chopped green pepper
1	tablespoon butter
1	small zucchini, chopped
3/4	cup chopped tomato
1/4	teaspoon dried oregano
1/8	teaspoon pepper
4	egg whites
1/4	cup water
1/4	teaspoon cream of tartar
1/4	teaspoon salt
1/4	cup egg substitute
1/2	cup shredded reduced-fat cheddar cheese, *divided*

- In a large nonstick skillet, saute onion and green pepper in butter until tender. Add the zucchini, tomato, oregano and pepper. Cook and stir for 5-8 minutes or until vegetables are tender and liquid is nearly evaporated. Set aside and keep warm.

- In a bowl, beat egg whites, water, cream of tartar and salt until stiff peaks form. Place egg substitute in another bowl; fold in egg white mixture. Pour into a 10-in. ovenproof skillet coated with cooking spray. Cook over medium heat for 5 minutes or until bottom is lightly browned.

- Bake at 350° for 9-10 minutes or until a knife inserted near the center comes out clean. Spoon vegetable mixture over one side; sprinkle with half of the cheese. To fold, score middle of omelet with a sharp knife; fold omelet over filling. Transfer to a warm platter. Sprinkle with remaining cheese. Cut in half to serve.

YIELD: 2 servings.

NUTRITION FACTS: 1 omelet half equals 197 calories, 9 g fat (5 g saturated fat), 21 mg cholesterol, 639 mg sodium, 10 g carbohydrate, 2 g fiber, 19 g protein. **DIABETIC EXCHANGES:** 3 lean meat, 2 vegetable, 1-1/2 fat.

fruit crepes

Jean Murtagh | SOLON, OHIO

These delicious crepes can be served for breakfast or as a yummy treat. The combination of flavors makes them one-of-a-kind.

classic

2	egg whites
2/3	cup fat-free milk
2	teaspoons canola oil
1/2	cup all-purpose flour
1/4	teaspoon salt
1/4	cup reduced-sugar orange marmalade
1	cup unsweetened raspberries, blackberries *or* blueberries

FRUIT CREPES

173 CALORIES

Sugar substitute equivalent to 8 teaspoons sugar

1/2 cup fat-free sour cream

1/8 teaspoon ground cinnamon

- In a large bowl, combine the egg whites, milk and oil. Combine flour and salt; add to milk mixture and mix well. Cover and refrigerate for 1 hour.

- In a large saucepan, heat marmalade until melted; remove from the heat. Fold in berries and sugar substitute; set aside. In a small bowl, combine sour cream and cinnamon; set aside.

- Heat an 8-in. nonstick skillet coated with cooking spray; add 2 tablespoons batter. Lift and tilt pan to evenly coat bottom. Cook until top appears dry and bottom is light brown. Remove to a wire rack. Repeat with remaining batter.

- Spread each crepe with 1 tablespoon sour cream mixture; roll up and place in an ungreased 11-in. x 7-in. baking dish. Spoon fruit mixture over top. Bake, uncovered, at 375° for 15 minutes.

YIELD: 4 servings.

NUTRITION FACTS: 2 crepes equals 173 calories, 3 g fat (0 saturated fat), 1 mg cholesterol, 231 mg sodium, 32 g carbohydrate, 2 g fiber, 7 g protein. DIABETIC EXCHANGES: 2 starch, 1/2 fat.

makeover sunday brunch casserole

Alice Hofmann | SUSSEX, WISCONSIN

The Taste of Home test kitchen dramatically improved the nutritional value of my recipe for this hearty brunch casserole. It's wonderful because they kept its core flavors and ingredients intact.

6 bacon strips

1 small onion, chopped

1 small green pepper, chopped

1 teaspoon canola oil

2 cartons (8 ounces *each*) egg substitute

4 eggs

1 cup fat-free milk

4 cups frozen shredded hash brown potatoes, thawed

1 cup (4 ounces) shredded reduced-fat cheddar cheese

3/4 teaspoon salt

1/2 teaspoon pepper

1/4 teaspoon dill weed

- In a large skillet, cook bacon over medium heat until crisp. Remove to paper towels; drain. Crumble bacon and set aside. In the same skillet, saute onion and green pepper in oil until tender; remove with a slotted spoon.

- In a large bowl, whisk the egg substitute, eggs and milk. Stir in the hash browns, cheese, salt, pepper, dill, onion mixture and reserved bacon.

- Transfer to a 13-in. x 9-in. dish coated with cooking spray. Bake, uncovered, at 350° for 30-35 minutes or until a knife inserted near the center comes out clean.

YIELD: 8 servings.

NUTRITION FACTS: 1 piece equals 181 calories, 8 g fat (3 g saturated fat), 122 mg cholesterol, 591 mg sodium, 11 g carbohydrate, 1 g fiber, 16 g protein. DIABETIC EXCHANGES: 2 lean meat, 1 starch.

MAKEOVER SUNDAY BRUNCH CASSEROLE

181 CALORIES

turkey sausage patties

Janice Wuertzer | DUBUQUE, IOWA

Eat smart, starting with this homemade turkey sausage. If you like garlic, try substituting it for the sage.

- 1 small onion, finely chopped
- 1/4 cup dry bread crumbs
- 1 teaspoon rubbed sage
- 1/2 teaspoon salt
- 1/2 teaspoon paprika
- 1/4 teaspoon pepper
- 1 pound lean ground turkey
- 2 teaspoons canola oil

- In a large bowl, combine the onion, bread crumbs, sage, salt, paprika and pepper. Crumble turkey over mixture and mix well. Shape into six patties. Cover and refrigerate for 2 hours.

- In a large nonstick skillet over medium heat, cook patties in oil for 7 minutes on each side or until meat is no longer pink.

YIELD: 6 patties.

NUTRITION FACTS: 1 patty equals 150 calories, 8 g fat (2 g saturated fat), 60 mg cholesterol, 307 mg sodium, 4 g carbohydrate, trace fiber, 14 g protein. **DIABETIC EXCHANGES:** 2 lean meat, 1/2 fat.

TURKEY SAUSAGE PATTIES

orange whole wheat pancakes

150 CALORIES

Earl Brunner | LAS VEGAS, NEVADA

Friends and family will flip over these light whole wheat pancakes with a sunny twist of citrus that I adapted from a traditional pancake recipe. Feel free to mix raisins or dried cranberries into the batter.

- 3 egg whites
- 1 cup orange juice
- 1/3 cup unsweetened applesauce
- 1/4 teaspoon orange extract
- 1-1/4 cups whole wheat flour
- 2 tablespoons sugar
- 2 teaspoons baking powder
- 1/2 teaspoon salt
- 1/2 cup orange marmalade

- In a blender, combine the first four ingredients. Cover and process until smooth. In a large bowl, combine the flour, sugar, baking powder and salt; make a well. Add orange juice mixture; stir just until moistened.

- Pour batter by 2 tablespoonfuls onto a hot griddle coated with cooking spray. Turn when bubbles form on top of pancake; cook until second side is golden brown. Serve with marmalade.

YIELD: 16 pancakes.

NUTRITION FACTS: 2 pancakes with 1 tablespoon marmalade equals 150 calories, trace fat (trace saturated fat), 0 cholesterol, 238 mg sodium, 35 g carbohydrate, 3 g fiber, 4 g protein. **DIABETIC EXCHANGE:** 2 starch.

baked southern grits

158 CALORIES

Karen Mau | JACKSBORO, TENNESSEE

I turn a southern favorite into a tasty low-fat dish with this recipe. Jalapeno peppers add a welcome kick while reduced-fat cheese creates a rich texture.

- 4 cups water
- 1 cup quick-cooking grits

4 egg whites

2 eggs

1-1/2 cups (6 ounces) shredded reduced-fat cheddar cheese

1/2 cup fat-free milk

1 to 2 jalapeno peppers, seeded and chopped

1/2 teaspoon garlic salt

1/4 teaspoon white pepper

4 green onions, chopped, *divided*

- In a large saucepan, bring water to a boil. Add grits; cook and stir over medium heat for 5 minutes or until thickened. Remove from the heat.

- In a small bowl, whisk egg whites and eggs. Stir a small amount of hot grits into eggs; return all to the pan, stirring constantly. Stir in the cheese, milk, jalapenos, garlic salt, pepper and half of the onions.

- Transfer to a 2-qt. baking dish coated with cooking spray. Bake, uncovered, at 350° for 30-35 minutes or until golden brown. Sprinkle with remaining onions.

YIELD: 8 servings.

EDITOR'S NOTE: When cutting hot peppers, disposable gloves are recommended. Avoid touching your face.

NUTRITION FACTS: 3/4 cup equals 158 calories, 6 g fat (3 g saturated fat), 68 mg cholesterol, 300 mg sodium, 17 g carbohydrate, 1 g fiber, 11 g protein. **DIABETIC EXCHANGES:** 1 starch, 1 lean meat, 1/2 fat.

frittata florentine

Jenny Flake | NEWPORT BEACH, CALIFORNIA
This recipe has huge flavor and is good for you! Thanks to the eggs, cheese and spinach, you get a dose of phosphorus and calcium, too, which contribute to healthier bones.

6 egg whites

3 eggs

1/2 teaspoon dried oregano

1/4 teaspoon garlic powder

1/4 teaspoon salt

1/4 teaspoon pepper

1 small onion, finely chopped

176 CALORIES

FRITTATA FLORENTINE

1/4 cup finely chopped sweet red pepper

2 turkey bacon strips, chopped

1 tablespoon olive oil

1 cup fresh baby spinach

3 tablespoons thinly sliced fresh basil leaves

1/2 cup shredded part-skim mozzarella cheese

- In a small bowl, whisk the first six ingredients; set aside. In an 8-in. ovenproof skillet, saute onion, red pepper and bacon in oil until tender. Reduce heat; top with spinach.

- Pour reserved egg mixture over spinach. As eggs set, push cooked edges toward the center, letting uncooked portion flow underneath until eggs are nearly set. Sprinkle with basil and cheese.

- Broil 3-4 in. from the heat for 2-3 minutes or until eggs are completely set. Let stand for 5 minutes. Cut frittata into four wedges.

YIELD: 4 servings.

NUTRITION FACTS: 1 wedge equals 176 calories, 11 g fat (4 g saturated fat), 174 mg cholesterol, 451 mg sodium, 4 g carbohydrate, 1 g fiber, 15 g protein.

201-300 calories

hash brown breakfast casserole

Cindy Schneider | SARASOTA, FLORIDA

This savory, scrumptious recipe uses egg substitute for lower fat and cholesterol. Serve with fresh fruit for a morning meal that will keep you and your family satisfied until lunch!

    4   cups frozen shredded hash brown potatoes, thawed
1-1/2   cups egg substitute
    1   cup finely chopped cooked chicken breast
  1/2   teaspoon garlic powder
  1/2   teaspoon pepper
  3/4   cup shredded reduced-fat cheddar cheese

- In a large bowl, combine the hash browns, egg substitute, chicken, garlic powder and pepper. Transfer to an 8-in. square baking dish coated with cooking spray; sprinkle with cheese.

- Bake, uncovered, at 350° for 40-45 minutes or until set.

YIELD: 4 servings.

NUTRITION FACTS: 1 piece equals 220 calories, 6 g fat (3 g saturated fat), 42 mg cholesterol, 355 mg sodium, 16 g carbohydrate, 1 g fiber, 26 g protein. **DIABETIC EXCHANGES:** 3 very lean meat, 1 starch.

HASH BROWN BREAKFAST CASSEROLE

220 CALORIES

HONEY WHEAT PANCAKES

253 CALORIES

honey wheat pancakes

Martina Bias | BELLEVILLE, ILLINOIS

Even my kids love these wholesome pancakes! These thick and tender flapjacks have a delightful hint of honey and cinnamon you'll love.

1-1/2   cups reduced-fat biscuit/baking mix
  1/2   cup whole wheat flour
  1/4   cup wheat germ
    1   teaspoon baking powder
    1   teaspoon ground cinnamon
    2   eggs, lightly beaten
1-1/2   cups buttermilk
    1   medium ripe banana, mashed
    2   tablespoons honey
Assorted fresh fruit *and/or* maple syrup, optional

- In a small bowl, combine the first five ingredients. Combine the eggs, buttermilk, banana and honey; add to dry ingredients just until moistened.

- Pour batter by 1/4 cupfuls onto a hot griddle coated with cooking spray; turn when bubbles form on top. Cook until the second side is golden brown. Serve with fruit and/or syrup if desired.

YIELD: 12 pancakes.

NUTRITION FACTS: 2 pancakes (calculated without optional toppings) equals 253 calories, 5 g fat (1 g saturated fat), 73 mg cholesterol, 502 mg sodium, 44 g carbohydrate, 3 g fiber, 9 g protein. **DIABETIC EXCHANGES:** 3 starch, 1/2 fat.

black forest crepes

Mary Relyea I CANASTOTA, NEW YORK

Cherries and chocolate just naturally taste great together, but the combination is even better when enhanced by tender crepes and a creamy filling.

1 package (8 ounces) reduced-fat cream cheese, softened

1/2 cup reduced-fat sour cream

1/2 teaspoon vanilla extract

2/3 cup confectioners' sugar

8 prepared crepes (9 inches)

1 can (20 ounces) reduced-sugar cherry pie filling, warmed

1/4 cup chocolate syrup

- In a small bowl, beat the cream cheese, sour cream and vanilla until smooth. Gradually beat in confectioners' sugar. Spread about 3 tablespoons over each crepe to within 1/2 in. of edges and roll up.

- Arrange in an ungreased 13-in. x 9-in. baking dish. Bake, uncovered, at 350° for 5-7 minutes or until warm. To serve, top each crepe with 1/4 cup pie filling and drizzle with 1-1/2 teaspoons chocolate syrup.

YIELD: 8 servings.

NUTRITION FACTS: 1 filled crepe equals 256 calories, 9 g fat (6 g saturated fat), 31 mg cholesterol, 222 mg sodium, 39 g carbohydrate, 1 g fiber, 6 g protein. **DIABETIC EXCHANGES:** 2-1/2 starch, 1-1/2 fat.

BLACK FOREST CREPES

256 CALORIES

258 CALORIES

SCRAMBLED EGG WRAPS

scrambled egg wraps

Jane Shapton I IRVINE, CALIFORNIA

This tasty morning meal will fill your family up with protein and veggies. Try using flavored wraps to jazz things up a bit.

1 medium sweet red pepper, chopped

1 medium green pepper, chopped

2 teaspoons canola oil

classic

5 plum tomatoes, seeded and chopped

6 eggs

1/2 cup soy milk

1/4 teaspoon salt

6 flour tortillas (8 inches), warmed

- In a large nonstick skillet, saute the peppers in oil until tender. Add tomatoes; saute 1-2 minutes longer.

- Meanwhile, in a large bowl, whisk the eggs, soy milk and salt. Reduce heat to medium; add egg mixture to skillet. Cook and stir until eggs are completely set. Spoon 2/3 cup mixture down the center of each tortilla; roll up.

YIELD: 6 servings.

NUTRITION FACTS: 1 wrap equals 258 calories, 10 g fat (2 g saturated fat), 212 mg cholesterol, 427 mg sodium, 30 g carbohydrate, 1 g fiber, 12 g protein. **DIABETIC EXCHANGES:** 1-1/2 starch, 1 lean meat, 1 vegetable, 1 fat.

224 CALORIES

SPRING BRUNCH BAKE

spring brunch bake

Nancy Zimmerman | CAPE MAY COURT HOUSE, NEW JERSEY

This is a delicious way to use up leftover ham and fresh asparagus! Fluffy and moist, this dish will be a welcomed sight at any meal.

- 8 cups cubed French bread
- 2 cups cut fresh asparagus (1-inch pieces)
- 1 cup cubed fully cooked lean ham
- 3/4 cup shredded part-skim mozzarella cheese
- 6 egg whites
- 3 eggs
- 1-1/2 cups fat-free milk
- 2 tablespoons lemon juice
- 1/4 teaspoon garlic powder

- In a large bowl, combine the bread, asparagus, ham and cheese. Whisk the egg whites, eggs, milk, lemon juice and garlic powder; pour over bread mixture and stir until blended. Transfer to a 13-in. x 9-in. baking dish coated with cooking spray.

- Cover and bake at 350° for 25 minutes. Uncover and bake 8-10 minutes longer or until a knife inserted near the center comes out clean. Let stand for 10 minutes before serving.

YIELD: 6 servings.

NUTRITION FACTS: 1 piece equals 224 calories, 6 g fat (3 g saturated fat), 124 mg cholesterol, 640 mg sodium, 20 g carbohydrate, 2 g fiber, 21 g protein.

blueberry oat pancakes

Candy Summerhill | ALEXANDER, ARKANSAS

I grind my own oats in this recipe, which boosts the health value. But oats aren't the only power food in these fluffy pancakes: You get plenty of bursting-with-flavor blueberries in every bite, too!

- 3/4 cup quick-cooking oats, *divided*
- 3 tablespoons orange juice
- 1 egg, lightly beaten
- 2/3 cup fat-free evaporated milk
- 1/4 cup reduced-fat sour cream
- 2 tablespoons unsweetened applesauce
- 1/2 teaspoon vanilla extract
- 1/2 cup whole wheat flour
- 1/4 cup all-purpose flour
- 3 tablespoons brown sugar
- 1 teaspoon baking powder
- 1/2 teaspoon ground cinnamon
- 1/4 teaspoon salt
- 1/4 teaspoon baking soda
- 1 cup fresh *or* frozen unsweetened blueberries

- In a small bowl, combine 1/4 cup oats and orange juice; let stand for 5 minutes. Stir in the egg, milk, sour cream, applesauce and vanilla; set aside.

BLUEBERRY OAT PANCAKES

221 CALORIES

- Place remaining oats in a small food processor; cover and process until ground. Transfer to a large bowl; add the flours, brown sugar, baking powder, cinnamon, salt and baking soda. Stir in the wet ingredients just until mixture is moistened.

- Pour batter by 1/4 cupfuls onto a hot griddle coated with cooking spray; sprinkle with blueberries. Turn when bubbles form on top; cook until second side is golden brown.

YIELD: 10 pancakes.

NUTRITION FACTS: 2 pancakes equals 221 calories, 3 g fat (1 g saturated fat), 48 mg cholesterol, 327 mg sodium, 41 g carbohydrate, 4 g fiber, 9 g protein. **DIABETIC EXCHANGES:** 2 starch, 1/2 fruit, 1/2 fat.

256 CALORIES

HARVEST VEGETABLE TART

harvest vegetable tart

Ruth Lee | TROY, ONTARIO

When guests lay eyes on this gorgeous lightened-up veggie tart, everyone approves. I've been serving this for 30 years, and its robust taste and aroma always get a warm reception.

- 1/2 cup all-purpose flour
- 1/4 cup whole wheat flour
- 1/4 cup cornmeal
- 2 tablespoons grated Parmesan cheese
- 1/2 teaspoon salt
- 1/8 teaspoon cayenne pepper
- 1/4 cup cold butter, cubed
- 3 to 4 tablespoons cold water

FILLING:
- 1/2 cup thinly sliced green onions
- 2 garlic cloves, minced
- 1 tablespoon olive oil
- 5 slices peeled eggplant (3-1/2 inches x 1/4 inch)
- 2 tablespoons grated Parmesan cheese, *divided*
- 1 small tomato, cut into 1/4-inch slices
- 3 green pepper rings
- 3 sweet red pepper rings
- 1/2 cup frozen corn
- 2 eggs, lightly beaten
- 2/3 cup fat-free evaporated milk
- 3/4 teaspoon salt
- 1/4 teaspoon pepper

- In a bowl, combine the first six ingredients. Cut in butter until crumbly. Gradually add water, tossing with a fork until dough forms a ball. Cover and refrigerate for at least 30 minutes.

- Roll out pastry to fit a 9-in. tart pan with removable bottom. Transfer pastry to pan; trim even with edge of pan. Line unpricked pastry shell with a double thickness of heavy-duty foil. Bake at 450° for 8 minutes. Remove foil; bake 5 minutes longer.

- In a large nonstick skillet coated with cooking spray, cook onions and garlic in oil for 2 minutes. Add eggplant; cook for 4-5 minutes or until softened. Cool for 5 minutes. Spoon into crust. Sprinkle with 1 tablespoon Parmesan cheese. Top with tomato slices and pepper rings. Sprinkle with corn.

- In a small bowl, whisk the eggs, milk, salt and pepper; pour over vegetables. Sprinkle with remaining Parmesan cheese. Bake at 350° for 30-35 minutes or until a knife inserted near the center comes out clean.

YIELD: 6 servings.

NUTRITION FACTS: 1 piece equals 256 calories, 13 g fat (6 g saturated fat), 95 mg cholesterol, 691 mg sodium, 27 g carbohydrate, 3 g fiber, 9 g protein. **DIABETIC EXCHANGES:** 2 fat, 1-1/2 starch, 1 vegetable.

brunch enchiladas

Gail Sykora | **MENOMONEE FALLS, WISCONSIN**
Here's a fun change-of-pace way to start the day!

2 cups cubed fully cooked ham

1/2 cup chopped green onions

10 fat-free flour tortillas (8 inches)

2 cups (8 ounces) shredded reduced-fat cheddar cheese

1 tablespoon all-purpose flour

2 cups fat-free milk

1-1/2 cups egg substitute

- Combine ham and onions; place 1/3 cup down the center of each tortilla. Top with 2 tablespoons cheese. Roll up and place in a greased 13-in. x 9-in. baking dish.

- In another large bowl, combine the flour, milk and egg substitute until smooth. Pour over tortillas. Cover and refrigerate for 8 hours or overnight.

- Remove from the refrigerator 30 minutes before baking. Cover and bake at 350° for 25 minutes. Uncover; bake for 10 minutes. Sprinkle with remaining cheese; bake 3 minutes longer or until the cheese is melted. Let stand for 10 minutes before serving.

YIELD: 10 enchiladas.

NUTRITION FACTS: 1 enchilada equals 258 calories, 7 g fat (4 g saturated fat), 32 mg cholesterol, 838 mg sodium, 29 g carbohydrate, 1 g fiber, 19 g protein.

BRUNCH ENCHILADAS

258 CALORIES

203 CALORIES

FRUITED DUTCH BABY

fruited dutch baby

Shirley Robertson | **VERSAILLES, MISSOURI**
This traditional oven-baked pancake is a sensational way to showcase fruit and is ideal for a holiday breakfast or brunch. If you prefer, sprinkle it with powdered sugar, or serve it with canned pie filling or other fruit.

1 tablespoon butter

3/4 cup all-purpose flour

1 tablespoon sugar

1/4 teaspoon salt

3 eggs, lightly beaten

3/4 cup 2% milk

1-1/2 cups sliced fresh strawberries

2 medium firm bananas, sliced

Whipped cream, optional

1/4 cup flaked coconut, toasted

classic

- Place butter in a 9-in. pie plate. Place in a 400° oven for 5 minutes or until melted. Meanwhile, in a large bowl, combine the flour, sugar and salt. Stir in eggs and milk until smooth. Pour into prepared pie plate. Bake for 15-20 minutes or until golden brown.

- In a large bowl, combine strawberries and bananas. Using a slotted spoon, place fruit in center of pancake. Top with whipped cream if desired. Sprinkle with coconut. Serve immediately.

YIELD: 6 servings.

NUTRITION FACTS: 1 piece (calculated without whipped cream) equals 203 calories, 7 g fat (4 g saturated fat), 114 mg cholesterol, 170 mg sodium, 30 g carbohydrate, 2 g fiber, 7 g protein. **DIABETIC EXCHANGES:** 1-1/2 starch, 1 fat, 1/2 fruit.

multigrain pancakes

Ann Harris | **LANCASTER, CALIFORNIA**

My husband and I love foods prepared with whole grains. However, our children prefer white bread. So I created this recipe to appeal to their love of pancakes while giving them a taste of whole grain goodness.

- 1/2 cup all-purpose flour
- 1/4 cup whole wheat flour
- 1/4 cup cornmeal
-   2 tablespoons sugar
- 1/2 teaspoon baking soda
- 1/2 teaspoon salt
-   1 egg
-   1 cup buttermilk
-   2 tablespoons butter, melted

Maple syrup

- In a large bowl, combine the first six ingredients. In a small bowl, whisk the egg, buttermilk and butter. Stir into dry ingredients just until moistened.

- Pour batter by 1/4 cupfuls onto a greased hot griddle; turn when bubbles form on top. Cook until the second side is golden brown. Serve with syrup.

YIELD: 8 pancakes.

NUTRITION FACTS: 2 pancakes (calculated without syrup) equals 231 calories, 8 g fat (4 g saturated fat), 70 mg cholesterol, 575 mg sodium, 33 g carbohydrate, 2 g fiber, 7 g protein. **DIABETIC EXCHANGES:** 2 starch, 1-1/2 fat.

MULTIGRAIN PANCAKES

START-RIGHT STRATA

start-right strata

Cecile Brown | **CHILLICOTHE, TEXAS**

I substituted reduced-fat ingredients and reworked this recipe to fit my diet...and my tastes! Served with melon or grapes on the side, it's ideal for overnight guests.

-   4 slices white bread, torn into pieces
-   4 breakfast turkey sausage links, casings removed, crumbled
- 1/3 cup chopped onion
-   1 cup fat-free milk
- 3/4 cup egg substitute
- 1/2 cup reduced-fat sour cream
- 1/4 cup shredded reduced-fat cheddar cheese
- 1/4 cup salsa

- Place bread in an 8-in. square baking dish coated with cooking spray; set aside.

- In a small nonstick skillet, cook the sausage and onion over medium heat until meat is no longer pink; drain. Spoon over bread. In a small bowl, combine the milk, egg substitute and sour cream. Stir in cheese. Pour over the meat mixture. Cover and refrigerate overnight.

- Remove from the refrigerator 30 minutes before baking. Bake, uncovered, at 325° for 35-40 minutes or until a knife inserted near the center comes out clean. Let stand for 10 minutes before cutting. Serve with salsa.

YIELD: 4 servings.

NUTRITION FACTS: 1 piece with 1 tablespoon salsa equals 247 calories, 10 g fat (4 g saturated fat), 39 mg cholesterol, 580 mg sodium, 21 g carbohydrate, 1 g fiber, 17 g protein. **DIABETIC EXCHANGES:** 2 lean meat, 1-1/2 starch, 1 fat.

203 CALORIES

CHOCOLATE CREPES WITH RASPBERRY SAUCE

chocolate crepes with raspberry sauce

Rebecca Baird | SALT LAKE CITY, UTAH

Everyone at the table will feel special eating this scrumptious treat. Seemingly rich and decadent, these crepes have just 2 grams of fat per serving!

  1 cup fat-free milk
1/2 cup fat-free evaporated milk
  2 egg whites
  1 egg
  1 cup all-purpose flour
1/4 cup plus 1/3 cup sugar, *divided*
1/4 cup baking cocoa
1/2 teaspoon salt
4-1/2 teaspoons cornstarch
  1 cup water
4-1/2 cups fresh *or* frozen raspberries, thawed, *divided*

Reduced-fat whipped cream in a can

  1 teaspoon confectioners' sugar

- In a small bowl, combine the milk, evaporated milk, egg whites and egg. Combine the flour, 1/4 cup sugar, cocoa and salt; add to milk mixture and mix well. Cover and refrigerate for 1 hour.

- In a small saucepan, combine cornstarch and remaining sugar; set aside. Place water and 3-1/2 cups raspberries in a blender; cover and process for 2-3 minutes or until pureed.

- Strain puree into cornstarch mixture and discard seeds. Bring to a boil; cook and stir for 2 minutes or until thickened. Transfer to a bowl; refrigerate until chilled.

- Coat an 8-in. nonstick skillet with cooking spray; heat over medium heat. Stir crepe batter; pour a scant 3 tablespoons into center of skillet. Lift and tilt pan to coat bottom evenly. Cook until top appears dry; turn and cook 15-20 seconds longer. Remove to a wire rack.

- Repeat with remaining batter, coating skillet with cooking spray as needed. When cool, stack crepes with waxed paper or paper towels in between.

- To serve, spoon a scant 3 tablespoons sauce over each crepe; roll up. Top each with 1 tablespoon whipped cream. Garnish with remaining raspberries and sprinkle with confectioners' sugar.

YIELD: 8 servings.

NUTRITION FACTS: 2 filled crepes equals 203 calories, 2 g fat (1 g saturated fat), 30 mg cholesterol, 202 mg sodium, 42 g carbohydrate, 6 g fiber, 7 g protein.

285 CALORIES # veggie breakfast pizza

Bev Lehrman | GIJOCA, BRAZIL

I love Mexican food so I combined several recipes to come up with this one. I often serve it for breakfast on Saturdays, when we can enjoy more time around the table. Our kids look forward to getting up just for this!

classic

1-1/4 teaspoons active dry yeast
 3/4 cup warm water (110° to 115°)
  1 tablespoon sugar
  1 tablespoon olive oil
  1 teaspoon salt
2-1/4 cups all-purpose flour
TOPPINGS:
  1 cup salsa
  2 medium tomatoes, seeded and chopped
  1 large onion, chopped
  1 small green pepper, chopped
  1 tablespoon olive oil

6 eggs, beaten
1/2 teaspoon seasoned salt
1/4 teaspoon salt
1/4 teaspoon garlic pepper blend
1 cup (4 ounces) shredded part-skim mozzarella cheese

- In a large bowl, dissolve yeast in warm water. Add the sugar, oil, salt and 1-1/4 cups flour. Beat until smooth. Stir in enough remaining flour to form a soft dough (dough will be sticky). Turn onto a lightly floured surface, knead until smooth and elastic, about 6-8 minutes.

- Place in a bowl coated with cooking spray, turning once to coat the top. Cover and let rise in a warm place for 30 minutes.

- Punch dough down; roll into a 13-in. circle. Transfer to a 12-in. pizza pan coated with cooking spray. Build up edges slightly. Prick dough thoroughly with a fork. Bake at 425° for 8-10 minutes or until golden brown.

- Meanwhile, drain salsa, discarding the liquid. In a large skillet over medium heat, cook and stir the tomatoes, onion and green pepper in oil until crisp-tender. Combine eggs and seasonings; add to the pan. Cook and stir until eggs are set.

- Spoon salsa and egg mixture over crust; sprinkle with cheese. Bake for 3-5 minutes or until cheese is melted.

YIELD: 8 slices.

NUTRITION FACTS: 1 slice equals 285 calories, 10 g fat (3 g saturated fat), 168 mg cholesterol, 731 mg sodium, 34 g carbohydrate, 2 g fiber, 13 g protein. **DIABETIC EXCHANGES:** 2 starch, 1 lean meat, 1 vegetable, 1 fat.

open-faced omelet

Pamela Shank | PARKERSBURG, WEST VIRGINIA

This is a recipe I used to make with bacon, ham and regular cheese. It's easy to substitute the high fat for low fat or fat free ingredients. Plus it is a very pretty dish when served because of all the colors!

2 small red potatoes, diced
1/4 cup sliced fresh mushrooms
1 tablespoon chopped green pepper

1 tablespoon chopped sweet red pepper
1 green onion, chopped
1 tablespoon olive oil
2/3 cup egg substitute
1/4 cup shredded reduced-fat cheddar cheese, *divided*
2 tablespoons fat-free sour cream
1/4 cup chopped tomatoes

- Place potatoes in a small saucepan and cover with water. Bring to a boil. Reduce heat; cover and cook for 5-7 minutes or until tender. Drain.

- In a small skillet, saute the mushrooms, peppers, onion and potatoes in oil until tender. Coat a nonstick skillet with cooking spray and place over medium heat. Add egg substitute. As eggs set, push cooked edges toward the center, letting uncooked portion flow underneath. When the eggs are set, spoon vegetable mixture over eggs; sprinkle with 2 tablespoons cheese.

- Transfer to a serving plate. Top with sour cream, tomatoes and remaining cheese.

YIELD: 2 servings.

NUTRITION FACTS: 1/2 omelet equals 202 calories, 10 g fat (3 g saturated fat), 13 mg cholesterol, 276 mg sodium, 15 g carbohydrate, 2 g fiber, 14 g protein. **DIABETIC EXCHANGES:** 2 lean meat, 1 starch, 1 fat.

OPEN-FACED OMELET

202 CALORIES

prosciutto egg panini

Erin Renouf Mylroie | SANTA CLARA, UTAH

With mustard, maple syrup and prosciutto, this is a yummy twist on the usual bacon-and-egg sandwich. Your family will agree that this is one breakfast worth waking up for!

- 3 eggs
- 2 egg whites
- 6 tablespoons milk
- 1 green onion, thinly sliced
- 1 tablespoon Dijon mustard
- 1 tablespoon maple syrup
- 8 slices sourdough bread
- 8 thin slices prosciutto *or* deli ham
- 1/2 cup shredded sharp cheddar cheese
- 8 teaspoons butter

- In a small bowl, whisk the eggs, egg whites, milk and onion. Coat a large skillet with cooking spray and place over medium heat. Add egg mixture; cook and stir over medium heat until completely set.

- Combine mustard and syrup; spread over four bread slices. Layer with scrambled eggs, prosciutto and cheese; top with remaining bread. Butter outsides of sandwiches.

- Cook on a panini maker or indoor grill for 3-4 minutes or until bread is browned and cheese is melted. Cut each panini in half to serve.

YIELD: 8 servings.

NUTRITION FACTS: 1/2 panini equals 228 calories, 10 g fat (5 g saturated fat), 111 mg cholesterol, 640 mg sodium, 21 g carbohydrate, 1 g fiber, 13 g protein. **DIABETIC EXCHANGES:** 1-1/2 starch, 1-1/2 fat, 1 lean meat.

260 CALORIES

ENERGIZING GRANOLA

PROSCIUTTO EGG PANINI

228 CALORIES

energizing granola

Nina Wiseman | BATAVIA, OHIO

This tasty breakfast or snack combo packs a healthy punch of vitamin E, and flaxseed offers omega-3 fatty acids. It's perfect for the whole gang.

- 2-1/2 cups old-fashioned oats
- 3/4 cup chopped walnuts
- 1/2 cup unsalted sunflower kernels
- 1/3 cup packed brown sugar
- 1/4 cup flaked coconut
- 1/4 cup toasted wheat germ
- 2 tablespoons sesame seeds
- 2 tablespoons ground flaxseed
- 1/3 cup water
- 2 tablespoons honey

2 tablespoons molasses

1 tablespoon canola oil

3/4 teaspoon vanilla extract

1/2 teaspoon salt

1/2 teaspoon ground cinnamon

1/3 cup dried cranberries

1/3 cup golden raisins

1/4 cup dried banana chips

- In a large bowl, combine the first eight ingredients. In a small saucepan, combine the water, honey, molasses and oil. Heat for 3-4 minutes over medium until heated through. Remove from the heat; stir in the vanilla, salt and cinnamon. Pour over the oat mixture; stir to coat.

- Transfer to a 15-in. x 10-in. x 1-in. baking pan coated with cooking spray. Bake at 350° for 25-30 minutes or until lightly browned, stirring every 10 minutes. Cool completely on a wire rack. Stir in dried fruits. Store in an airtight container.

YIELD: 6 cups.

NUTRITION FACTS: 1/2 cup equals 260 calories, 12 g fat (2 g saturated fat), 0 cholesterol, 110 mg sodium, 35 g carbohydrate, 4 g fiber, 7 g protein. **DIABETIC EXCHANGES:** 2-1/2 starch, 1-1/2 fat.

carrot cake doughnuts

Tamera Danforth | THE DALLES, OREGON

For an easy doughnut recipe that everyone will love, I make these treats. I adore carrot cake so I wanted to carry the flavor over to the doughnuts. My experiments worked and these are my family's favorite.

2 tablespoons butter, softened

1 cup sugar

2 eggs

1 teaspoon grated orange peel

3-1/2 cups all-purpose flour

4 teaspoons baking powder

1-1/2 teaspoons ground cinnamon

1 teaspoon baking soda

3/4 teaspoon *each* salt, ground nutmeg and cloves

244 CALORIES

CARROT CAKE DOUGHNUTS

1/3 cup milk

1 cup shredded carrot

Oil for deep-fat frying

GLAZE:

1 cup confectioners' sugar

2 tablespoons orange juice

1 tablespoon finely shredded carrot

1/2 teaspoon vanilla extract

1/4 cup finely chopped walnuts

- In a large bowl, cream butter and sugar. Add eggs, one at a time, beating well after each addition. Stir in the orange peel.

- Combine the flour, baking powder, cinnamon, baking soda, salt, nutmeg and cloves; add to creamed mixture alternately with milk. Fold in carrot.

- Turn the dough onto a lightly floured surface; roll out to 1/2-in. thickness. Cut dough with a floured 2-1/2-in. doughnut cutter.

- In an electric skillet or deep-fat fryer, heat oil to 375°. Fry doughnuts, a few at a time, for 1-1/2 to 2 minutes on each side or until golden brown. Drain on paper towels.

- For glaze, combine the confectioners' sugar, orange juice, carrot and vanilla; drizzle over cooled doughnuts. Sprinkle with walnuts.

YIELD: 1-1/2 dozen.

NUTRITION FACTS: 1 doughnut equals 244 calories, 9 g fat (2 g saturated fat), 27 mg cholesterol, 281 mg sodium, 38 g carbohydrate, 1 g fiber, 4 g protein.

- As the eggs set, lift edges, letting uncooked portion flow underneath. Cook until eggs are completely set, about 8-10 minutes. Cut into wedges.

YIELD: 4 servings.

EDITOR'S NOTE: When cutting hot peppers, disposable gloves are recommended. Avoid touching your face.

NUTRITION FACTS: 1 wedge equals 201 calories, 10 g fat (3 g saturated fat), 268 mg cholesterol, 559 mg sodium, 10 g carbohydrate, 2 g fiber, 17 g protein. **DIABETIC EXCHANGES:** 2 lean meat, 2 vegetable, 1 fat.

201 CALORIES

CALICO PEPPER FRITTATA

calico pepper frittata

Loretta Kelcinski | KUNKLETOWN, PENNSYLVANIA

My garden-fresh frittata has all-day appeal. I serve it for breakfast, brunch, lunch and even dinner. It's made in a skillet, so there's no need to heat up the oven.

- 1 medium green pepper, chopped
- 1 medium sweet red pepper, chopped
- 1 jalapeno pepper, seeded and chopped
- 1 medium onion, chopped
- 1 garlic clove, minced
- 1 tablespoon olive oil
- 5 eggs
- 1-1/4 cups egg substitute
- 1 tablespoon grated Romano cheese
- 1/2 teaspoon salt
- 1/8 teaspoon pepper

- In a large nonstick skillet, saute peppers, onion and garlic in oil until crisp-tender. In a large bowl, whisk eggs and egg substitute. Pour into the skillet. Sprinkle with cheese, salt and pepper.

good-for-you morning muffins

The Taste of Home economists cut the fat from these carrot-flavored muffins, and also made them more nutritious, too. With the help of flaxseed, applesauce and whole wheat flour, the tasty result has nearly 50% less fat, 82 fewer calories and twice the amount of fiber than the original recipe.

- 1 cup all-purpose flour
- 1 cup whole wheat flour
- 3/4 cup ground flaxseed
- 3/4 cup sugar

GOOD-FOR-YOU MORNING MUFFINS

203 CALORIES

2-3/4 teaspoons baking powder

2 teaspoons ground cinnamon

3/4 teaspoon salt

1/4 teaspoon baking soda

4 egg whites

1 egg

1/2 cup unsweetened applesauce

1/3 cup orange juice

1/4 cup canola oil

2 teaspoons vanilla extract

2 cups grated carrots

1/2 cup chopped pecans

1/2 cup flaked coconut

1/2 cup raisins

1 medium tart apple, peeled and shredded

- In a large bowl, combine the first eight ingredients. In another bowl, beat the egg whites, egg, applesauce, orange juice, oil and vanilla. Stir into dry ingredients just until moistened. Fold in the carrots, pecans, coconut, raisins and apple.

- Coat muffin cups with cooking spray or use foil liners; fill three-fourths full. Bake at 350° for 15-18 minutes or until a toothpick comes out clean. Cool for 5 minutes before removing from pans to wire racks.

YIELD: 1-1/2 dozen.

NUTRITION FACTS: 1 muffin equals 203 calories, 9 g fat (2 g saturated fat), 12 mg cholesterol, 207 mg sodium, 29 g carbohydrate, 4 g fiber, 5 g protein. DIABETIC EXCHANGES: 2 starch, 2 fat.

peach-stuffed french toast

Julie Robinson | LITTLE CHUTE, WISCONSIN

With its make-ahead convenience and scrumptious flavor, this recipe is ideal for special brunches and busy hostesses with a hungry crowd to feed!

1 loaf (1 pound) French bread, cut into 20 slices

1 can (15 ounces) sliced peaches in extra-light syrup, drained and chopped

1/4 cup chopped pecans

267 CALORIES

PEACH-STUFFED FRENCH TOAST

4 eggs

4 egg whites

1-1/2 cups fat-free milk

3 tablespoons sugar

1-1/4 teaspoons ground cinnamon, *divided*

1 teaspoon vanilla extract

1/4 cup all-purpose flour

2 tablespoons brown sugar

2 tablespoons cold butter

Reduced-calorie pancake syrup, optional

- Arrange half of the bread in a 13-in. x 9-in. baking dish coated with cooking spray. Top with peaches, pecans and remaining bread.

- In a small bowl, whisk the eggs, egg whites, milk, sugar, 1 teaspoon cinnamon and vanilla; pour over bread. Cover and refrigerate for 8 hours or overnight.

- Remove from the refrigerator 30 minutes before baking. Bake, uncovered, at 400° for 20 minutes.

- In a small bowl, combine the flour, brown sugar and remaining cinnamon; cut in butter until crumbly. Sprinkle over French toast. Bake 5-10 minutes longer or until a knife inserted near the center comes out clean. Serve with syrup if desired.

YIELD: 10 servings.

NUTRITION FACTS: 1 serving (1 piece) equals 267 calories, 8 g fat (3 g saturated fat), 92 mg cholesterol, 368 mg sodium, 39 g carbohydrate, 2 g fiber, 10 g protein. DIABETIC EXCHANGES: 2-1/2 starch, 1-1/2 fat.

yogurt pancakes

Cheryll Baber | HOMEDALE, IDAHO

Get your day off to a great start with these delicious yogurt pancakes. Simply whip up a quick batch on the weekend.

- 2 cups all-purpose flour
- 2 tablespoons sugar
- 2 teaspoons baking powder
- 1 teaspoon baking soda
- 2 eggs
- 2 cups (16 ounces) plain yogurt
- 1/4 cup water

Semisweet chocolate chips, dried cranberries, sliced ripe bananas and coarsely chopped pecans, optional

- In a small bowl, combine the flour, sugar, baking powder and baking soda. In another bowl, whisk the eggs, yogurt and water. Stir into dry ingredients just until moistened.

- Pour batter by 1/4 cupfuls onto a hot griddle coated with cooking spray. Sprinkle with chocolate chips or cranberries if desired. Turn when bubbles form on top; cook until the second side is golden brown. Serve with bananas or pecans, if desired.

- To freeze, arrange cooled pancakes in a single layer on sheet pans. Freeze overnight or until frozen. Transfer to a resealable plastic freezer bag. May be frozen for up to 2 months.

YOGURT PANCAKES

242 CALORIES

- **TO USE FROZEN PANCAKES:** Place pancake on a microwave-safe plate; microwave on high for 40-50 seconds or until heated through.

YIELD: 12 pancakes.

NUTRITION FACTS: 2 pancakes (calculated without optional ingredients) equals 242 calories, 5 g fat (2 g saturated fat), 81 mg cholesterol, 403 mg sodium, 40 g carbohydrate, 1 g fiber, 9 g protein. **DIABETIC EXCHANGE:** 3 starch.

206 CALORIES

GOOD-MORNING GRANOLA

good-morning granola

Mary Bilyeu | ANN ARBOR, MICHIGAN

This is ridiculously easy to make and has lots of healthy ingredients. It's a great way to start your day and keep you going. With pretty packaging, it makes a nice gift or bake sale item.

- 4 cups old-fashioned oats
- 1/2 cup toasted wheat germ
- 1/2 cup sliced almonds
- 2 teaspoons ground cinnamon
- 1/8 teaspoon salt
- 1/2 cup orange juice
- 1/2 cup honey
- 2 teaspoons canola oil
- 1 teaspoon vanilla extract
- 1 cup dried cherries
- 1 cup dried cranberries

Reduced-fat plain yogurt, optional

- In a large bowl, combine the first five ingredients; set aside. In a small saucepan, combine the orange juice, honey and oil. Bring to a boil, stirring constantly. Remove from the heat; stir in vanilla. Pour over oat mixture and mix well.

- Transfer to a 15-in. x 10-in. x 1-in. baking pan coated with cooking spray. Bake at 350° for 20-25 minutes or until golden brown, stirring every 10 minutes. Cool completely on a wire rack.

- Stir in dried fruits. Store in an airtight container. Serve with yogurt if desired.

YIELD: 7-1/2 cups.

NUTRITION FACTS: 1/2 cup (calculated without yogurt) equals 206 calories, 4 g fat (trace saturated fat), 0 cholesterol, 21 mg sodium, 40 g carbohydrate, 4 g fiber, 5 g protein.

breakfast sundaes

266 CALORIES

Linda Franceschi | ELDRED, NEW YORK

Kids of all ages will love the layers of creamy yogurt, crunchy granola, banana slices and mandarin oranges in this dish. It sweetens the morning meal but also serves as a healthy dessert or after-school snack. Spooned into clear parfait glasses, this yummy treat makes a pretty presentation.

- 2 cups (16 ounces) fat-free raspberry yogurt *or* flavored yogurt of your choice
- 1 cup reduced-fat granola cereal
- 2 medium firm bananas, sliced
- 1 can (15 ounces) mandarin oranges, drained

- In four parfait glasses or bowls, layer 2 tablespoons each of yogurt, granola, bananas and oranges. Repeat layers. Serve immediately.

YIELD: 4 servings.

NUTRITION FACTS: 1 serving equals 266 calories, 2 g fat (trace saturated fat), 3 mg cholesterol, 130 mg sodium, 57 g carbohydrate, 6 g fiber, 9 g protein.

sausage-potato bake

Ruth Rigoni | HURLEY, WISCONSIN

I not only make this dish for breakfast, but sometimes for a main meal. You can substitute finely diced lean ham or crumbled turkey bacon for the sausage for a change of pace.

- 1/2 pound bulk pork sausage
- 3 large potatoes, peeled and thinly sliced
- 1/2 teaspoon salt
- 1/4 teaspoon pepper
- 1 jar (2 ounces) diced pimientos, drained
- 3 eggs
- 1 cup 2% milk
- 2 tablespoons minced chives
- 3/4 teaspoon dried thyme *or* oregano

Additional minced chives, optional

- In a large skillet, cook sausage over medium heat until no longer pink; drain.

- Arrange half of the potatoes in a greased 8-in. square baking dish; sprinkle with salt, pepper and half of the sausage. Top with remaining potatoes and sausage; sprinkle with pimientos. In a small bowl, whisk the eggs, milk, chives and thyme; pour over the top.

- Cover and bake at 375° for 45-50 minutes or until a knife inserted near the center comes out clean. Uncover; bake 10 minutes longer or until lightly browned. Let stand for 10 minutes before cutting. Sprinkle with additional chives if desired.

YIELD: 6 servings.

NUTRITION FACTS: 1 serving equals 202 calories, 11 g fat (4 g saturated fat), 124 mg cholesterol, 407 mg sodium, 18 g carbohydrate, 1 g fiber, 9 g protein.

SAUSAGE-POTATO BAKE

202 CALORIES

273 CALORIES

FLAXSEED OATMEAL PANCAKES

flaxseed oatmeal pancakes

Sharon Hansen | PONTIAC, ILLINOIS

I came up with this healthy and tasty recipe because my husband loves pancakes. They have a great texture and cinnamon taste.

- 1/3 cup whole wheat flour
- 3 tablespoons quick-cooking oats
- 1 tablespoon flaxseed
- 1/2 teaspoon baking powder
- 1/4 teaspoon ground cinnamon
- 1/8 teaspoon baking soda

Dash salt

- 1 egg, *separated*
- 1/2 cup buttermilk
- 1 tablespoon brown sugar
- 1 tablespoon canola oil
- 1/2 teaspoon vanilla extract

- In a large bowl, combine the first seven ingredients. In a small bowl, whisk the egg yolk, buttermilk, brown sugar, oil and vanilla; carefully stir into the dry ingredients just until moistened.

- In a small bowl, beat egg white on medium speed until stiff peaks form. Fold into batter.

- Pour batter by 1/4 cupfuls onto a hot griddle coated with cooking spray; turn when bubbles form on top. Cook until the second side is golden brown.

YIELD: 4 pancakes.

NUTRITION FACTS: 2 pancakes equals 273 calories, 13 g fat (2 g saturated fat), 108 mg cholesterol, 357 mg sodium, 31 g carbohydrate, 5 g fiber, 10 g protein.

228 CALORIES

dried fruit muesli

Your day will start just right when you prepare this comforting chilled cereal created by our Test Kitchen staff. Filled with wholesome ingredients, it sits in the fridge overnight for the perfect pick-me-up when the alarm clock rings.

- 1 cup quick-cooking oats
- 1 cup fat-free milk
- 1/4 cup orange juice
- 1/4 cup chopped dried apricots
- 1/4 cup dried cranberries
- 1/4 cup chopped dried apples
- 2 tablespoons chopped almonds
- 2 tablespoons honey
- 1/8 teaspoon salt
- 1/8 teaspoon ground cinnamon

- In a large bowl, combine all of the ingredients. Cover and refrigerate for at least 8 hours or overnight.

YIELD: 4 servings.

NUTRITION FACTS: 1/2 cup equals 228 calories, 4 g fat (trace saturated fat), 1 mg cholesterol, 112 mg sodium, 43 g carbohydrate, 4 g fiber, 7 g protein. **DIABETIC EXCHANGES:** 1-1/2 starch, 1 fruit, 1/2 fat-free milk, 1/2 fat.

meatless sausage egg bake

This eye-opener from our Test Kitchen is sure to please every palate at your breakfast table. Crumbled vegetarian patties make the potato casserole a hearty option that doesn't pack on the pounds.

1 small onion, chopped

1 small green pepper, chopped

1 small sweet red pepper, chopped

2 teaspoons canola oil

12 egg whites

6 eggs

1 cup fat-free milk

1 package (16 ounces) frozen shredded hash brown potatoes, thawed

1 package (8 ounces) frozen vegetarian breakfast sausage patties, thawed and crumbled

1 cup (4 ounces) shredded reduced-fat cheddar cheese

1 teaspoon salt

1/2 teaspoon pepper

- In a small nonstick skillet, saute onion and peppers in oil until tender. In a large bowl, beat the egg whites, eggs and milk. Stir in hash browns, crumbled sausage, cheese, salt, pepper and onion mixture.

- Transfer to a 13-in. x 9-in. baking dish coated with cooking spray. Bake, uncovered, at 350° for 35-45 minutes or until a knife inserted near the center comes out clean. Let stand for 10 minutes before cutting.

YIELD: 8 servings.

NUTRITION FACTS: 1 piece equals 256 calories, 11 g fat (3 g saturated fat), 170 mg cholesterol, 733 mg sodium, 19 g carbohydrate, 4 g fiber, 22 g protein. **DIABETIC EXCHANGES:** 3 lean meat, 1 starch, 1/2 fat.

MEATLESS SAUSAGE EGG BAKE

256 CALORIES

FRUITY DESSERT TACOS

227 CALORIES

fruity dessert tacos

Diane Halferty I CORPUS CHRISTI, TEXAS

Here's a dessert you can feel good about eating! Fresh fruit and zippy jalapenos make a tasty filling for sweetened tortillas. Fruit-flavored yogurt or honey can be drizzled over the tortillas if desired.

1/2 cup cubed fresh pineapple

1/2 cup sliced peeled kiwifruit

1/2 cup sliced fresh strawberries

3 teaspoons sugar, *divided*

1 teaspoon chopped seeded jalapeno pepper, optional

1/2 teaspoon ground cinnamon

2 whole wheat tortillas (8 inches)

Butter-flavored cooking spray

- In a small bowl, combine the pineapple, kiwifruit, strawberries, 1 teaspoon sugar and jalapeno if desired. Combine cinnamon and remaining sugar; set aside.

- Spray both sides of each tortilla with cooking spray. In a nonstick skillet, heat tortillas for 45-60 seconds on each side or until golden brown. Sprinkle both sides with cinnamon-sugar mixture.

- Place half of fruit mixture on each tortilla; fold in half.

YIELD: 2 servings.

EDITOR'S NOTE: When cutting hot peppers, disposable gloves are recommended. Avoid touching your face.

NUTRITION FACTS: 1 taco equals 227 calories, 4 g fat (trace saturated fat), 0 cholesterol, 172 mg sodium, 43 g carbohydrate, 5 g fiber, 5 g protein.

lunches

Enjoying a meal in the middle of the day is a great way to keep your metabolism up and keep hunger at bay. Try to stick to 450 calories when planning your lunches. Round out your meal with a low-calorie snack or even a Free Food, and don't forget to drink plenty of water.

127

139

136

The first section in this chapter has lower-calorie items you might pair with a piece of fruit or a salad. The other sections offer foods that are slightly higher in calories. These satisfying dishes just need a beverage. See the chart on page 139 for the calorie counts of typical lunch foods.

seasoned chicken strips

Becky Oliver | FAIRPLAY, COLORADO

These strips are designed for kids, but tasty enough for company. The tender bites are moist and juicy and would also be great on a salad.

- 1/3 cup egg substitute
- 1 tablespoon prepared mustard
- 1 garlic clove, minced
- 3/4 cup dry bread crumbs
- 2 teaspoons dried basil
- 1 teaspoon paprika
- 1/2 teaspoon salt
- 1/4 teaspoon pepper
- 1 pound chicken tenderloins

classic

- In a shallow bowl, combine the egg substitute, mustard and garlic. In another shallow bowl, combine the bread crumbs, basil, paprika, salt and pepper. Dip chicken in egg mixture, then roll in crumbs.

- Place on a baking sheet coated with cooking spray. Bake at 400° for 10-15 minutes or until golden brown and juices run clear.

YIELD: 4 servings.

NUTRITION FACTS: 3 ounces cooked chicken equals 188 calories, 2 g fat (trace saturated fat), 67 mg cholesterol, 525 mg sodium, 14 g carbohydrate, 1 g fiber, 30 g protein. **DIABETIC EXCHANGES:** 3 lean meat, 1 starch.

SEASONED CHICKEN STRIPS

188 CALORIES

206 CALORIES

MAKEOVER HASH BROWN SOUP

makeover hash brown soup

Judith Webb | BLUE SPRINGS, MISSOURI

This rich and creamy soup has all the goodness you'd expect, but is surprisingly good for you. If you ask me, it's the perfect recipe to chase away chills on a cool autumn day.

- 2 green onions, chopped
- 2 teaspoons canola oil
- 1 package (28 ounces) frozen O'Brien potatoes, thawed
- 2 cups 2% milk
- 1 can (10-3/4 ounces) reduced-fat reduced-sodium condensed cream of chicken soup, undiluted
- 6 turkey bacon strips, diced and cooked
- 1/2 cup shredded cheddar cheese

- In a small skillet, saute onions in oil until tender. In a 5-qt. slow cooker, combine the potatoes, milk, soup and onion mixture. Cover and cook on low for 6-7 hours or until heated through. Top each serving with 2 tablespoons bacon and 1 tablespoon cheese.

YIELD: 8 servings.

NUTRITION FACTS: 3/4 cup equals 206 calories, 9 g fat (4 g saturated fat), 26 mg cholesterol, 520 mg sodium, 24 g carbohydrate, 2 g fiber, 8 g protein.

236 CALORIES

OPEN-FACED PORTOBELLO SANDWICHES

open-faced portobello sandwiches

Rosemarie Smith | BOUNTIFUL, UTAH

This is a great meatless lunch that doesn't leave you feeling deprived. People are always surprised at how hearty the mushrooms are. The warm, chewy sandwich boasts an earthy flavor and still manages to keep calories at bay!

- 4 teaspoons prepared pesto
- 2 slices Italian bread (3/4-inch thick), toasted
- 3 oil-packed sun-dried tomatoes, cut into strips
- 2 slices part-skim mozzarella cheese (3/4 ounce each)
- 2 large portobello mushrooms, stems removed

- Spread 2 teaspoons pesto sauce on each slice of toast; top with tomatoes and cheese. Place mushrooms on a microwave-safe plate; cover with a microwave-safe paper towel. Microwave on high for 1 minute or until tender.

- Cut mushrooms into 1/2-in. slices; place on cheese. Cook on high 15-20 seconds longer or until the cheese is melted.

YIELD: 2 servings.

EDITOR'S NOTE: This recipe was tested in a 1,100-watt microwave.

NUTRITION FACTS: 1 sandwich equals 236 calories, 11 g fat (4 g saturated fat), 15 mg cholesterol, 382 mg sodium, 22 g carbohydrate, 3 g fiber, 12 g protein. **DIABETIC EXCHANGES:** 1 starch, 1 medium-fat meat, 1 vegetable, 1 fat.

taco chicken wraps

Melissa Green | LOUISVILLE, KENTUCKY

The flavorful filling in these wraps has a definite kick, but you can adjust the chilies and peppers to suit your family's taste. I serve them alongside Spanish rice.

- 1 can (10 ounces) diced tomatoes and green chilies, drained
- 1 can (9-3/4 ounces) chunk white chicken, drained
- 1 cup (4 ounces) shredded cheddar-Monterey Jack cheese
- 2 tablespoons diced jalapeno pepper
- 2 teaspoons taco seasoning
- 6 flour tortillas (6 inches), warmed

Taco sauce and sour cream, optional

- In a small bowl, combine the tomatoes, chicken, cheese, jalapeno and taco seasoning. Place about 1/3 cupful down the center of each tortilla. Roll up and place seam side down in a greased 11-in. x 7-in. baking dish.

- Bake, uncovered, at 350° for 10-15 minutes or until heated through. Serve with taco sauce and sour cream if desired.

YIELD: 6 servings.

EDITOR'S NOTE: When cutting hot peppers, disposable gloves are recommended. Avoid touching your face.

NUTRITION FACTS: 1 wrap equals 211 calories, 9 g fat (4 g saturated fat), 38 mg cholesterol, 818 mg sodium, 17 g carbohydrate, 1 g fiber, 16 g protein.

TACO CHICKEN WRAPS

211 CALORIES

222 CALORIES

ZESTY HAMBURGER SOUP

zesty hamburger soup

Kelly Milan | LAKE JACKSON, TEXAS

This is a soup even the kids will love! The flavors blend together wonderfully, making it perfect for the entire family.

1	pound lean ground beef (90% lean)
2	cups sliced celery
1	cup chopped onion
2	teaspoons minced garlic
4	cups hot water
2	medium red potatoes, peeled and cubed
2	cups frozen corn
1-1/2	cups uncooked small shell pasta
4	pickled jalapeno slices
4	cups V8 juice
2	cans (10 ounces *each*) diced tomatoes with green chilies
1	to 2 tablespoons sugar

- In a Dutch oven, cook the beef, celery and onion over medium heat until meat is no longer pink. Add garlic, cook 1 minute longer. Drain. Stir in the water, potatoes, corn, pasta and jalapeno.

- Bring to a boil. Reduce heat; cover and simmer for 10-15 minutes or until pasta is tender. Stir in the remaining ingredients. Cook and stir until heated through.

YIELD: 10 servings (3-3/4 quarts).

NUTRITION FACTS: 1-1/2 cups equals 222 calories, 5 g fat (2 g saturated fat), 28 mg cholesterol, 542 mg sodium, 33 g carbohydrate, 4 g fiber, 14 g protein. **DIABETIC EXCHANGES:** 2 vegetable, 1-1/2 starch, 1 lean meat.

potato-bar chili

Alcy Thorne | LOS MOLINOIS, CALIFORNIA

This is a creative twist on traditional chili. The potatoes make it a delicious, and filling, main dish.

1-1/2	pounds lean ground beef (90% lean)
2	medium onions, chopped
1	medium green pepper, chopped
1	can (28 ounces) diced tomatoes, undrained
1	can (16 ounces) chili beans, undrained
2	tablespoons sugar
2	teaspoons chili powder
1/4	teaspoon salt
1/4	teaspoon pepper

Baked potatoes

- In a Dutch oven, cook the beef, onions and green pepper over medium heat until meat is no longer pink; drain. Add the tomatoes, beans, sugar and seasonings.

- Bring to a boil. Reduce heat; simmer, uncovered, for 20 minutes. Serve with potatoes.

YIELD: 7 cups.

NUTRITION FACTS: 1/2 cup equals 134 calories, 4 g fat (2 g saturated fat), 30 mg cholesterol, 237 mg sodium, 13 g carbohydrate, 3 g fiber, 12 g protein. **DIABETIC EXCHANGES:** 1 starch, 1 lean meat.

POTATO-BAR CHILI

134 CALORIES

189 CALORIES

POTATO CORN CHOWDER

potato corn chowder

No one would guess that this hearty, chunky soup from our Test Kitchen is made with tofu and soy milk. Double the recipe for family meals.

2/3	cup fresh *or* frozen corn, thawed
1/3	cup chopped onion
1/4	cup chopped sweet red pepper
1/4	cup chopped green pepper
1	teaspoon canola oil
1	medium red potato, diced
2/3	cup reduced-sodium chicken broth
1/2	cup silken firm tofu
1/2	cup soy milk
1/4	teaspoon salt
1/8	teaspoon pepper

- In a small saucepan, saute the corn, onion and peppers in oil until onion is tender. Add potato and broth. Bring to a boil. Reduce heat; cover and simmer for 8-10 minutes or until potato is tender.

- Process tofu in a blender until smooth. Gradually stir tofu and soy milk into soup. Bring to a boil. Reduce heat; simmer, uncovered, for 10-15 minutes or until thickened, stirring occasionally. Season with salt and pepper.

YIELD: 2 servings.

NUTRITION FACTS: 1 cup equals 189 calories, 5 g fat (trace saturated fat), 0 cholesterol, 544 mg sodium, 29 g carbohydrate, 4 g fiber, 9 g protein. **DIABETIC EXCHANGES:** 1 starch, 1 reduced-fat milk.

california pizzas

Sheila Martin | LA QUINTA, CALIFORNIA

This is a delicious lunch or light dinner for two. Tortillas make the convenient crust for these crispy personal pizzas topped with fresh vegetables and cheese.

1/2	cup chopped onion
1/2	cup chopped green pepper
2	teaspoons canola oil
2	flour tortillas (6 inches)
1/4	teaspoon dried oregano
1/8	teaspoon garlic powder
1	medium tomato, sliced
1/2	cup shredded part-skim mozzarella cheese

- In a small skillet, saute onion and green pepper in oil until tender. Place the tortillas on an ungreased baking sheet. Top with onion mixture, oregano, garlic powder, tomato and cheese.

- Bake at 400° for 8-10 minutes or until cheese is melted. Cut each pizza into four wedges.

YIELD: 2 servings.

NUTRITION FACTS: 1 pizza equals 245 calories, 13 g fat (3 g saturated fat), 16 mg cholesterol, 364 mg sodium, 23 g carbohydrate, 2 g fiber, 11 g protein. **DIABETIC EXCHANGES:** 1 starch, 1 medium-fat meat, 1 vegetable.

CALIFORNIA PIZZAS

245 CALORIES

SPICY SAUSAGE AND PENNE

spicy sausage and penne

Brian Albright | SEWARD, NEBRASKA

I got the inspiration for this recipe from a dish at a local restaurant. It's a quick meal-in-one that I fix often. You can also substitute whatever pasta or veggies you have on hand for this versatile skillet supper.

- 1 cup uncooked penne pasta
- 1 cup frozen mixed vegetables
- 1/2 pound smoked turkey sausage, cut into 1/4-inch slices
- 2 tablespoons all-purpose flour
- 1/4 teaspoon garlic powder
- 1/4 teaspoon ground mustard
- 1/4 teaspoon crushed red pepper flakes
- 1-1/4 cups fat-free milk
- 1/3 cup shredded part-skim mozzarella cheese

- In a large saucepan, cook pasta according to package directions, adding the vegetables during the last 6 minutes of cooking.

- Meanwhile, in a large nonstick skillet coated with cooking spray, brown sausage; remove from skillet and keep warm.

- In a small bowl, combine the flour, garlic powder, mustard and pepper flakes; gradually whisk in milk until smooth. Add milk mixture to the skillet; stirring to loosen browned bits from pan. Bring to a boil; cook and stir for 1-2 minutes or until thickened.

- Drain pasta and vegetables; stir into the pan. Add cheese and reserved sausage; cook and stir until cheese is melted.

YIELD: 4 servings.

NUTRITION FACTS: 1 cup equals 228 calories, 5 g fat (2 g saturated fat), 42 mg cholesterol, 650 mg sodium, 27 g carbohydrate, 3 g fiber, 18 g protein. **DIABETIC EXCHANGES:** 2 lean meat, 1-1/2 starch.

open-faced veggie sandwiches

Karen Mello | FAIRHAVEN, MASSACHUSETTS

Since I'm a vegetarian, I love these broiled sandwiches. Even non-vegetarians like their fresh taste. The veggie-topped muffin halves make a quick lunch or a great snack and are very affordable!

- 4 teaspoons spicy brown *or* horseradish mustard
- 4 English muffins, split
- 1/2 cup *each* chopped fresh broccoli, cauliflower and sweet red pepper
- 1 cup (4 ounces) shredded cheddar cheese

- Spread mustard on cut sides of muffins. Top each with vegetables and cheese. Broil 4-6 in. from the heat for 3 minutes or until the cheese is melted.

YIELD: 4 servings.

NUTRITION FACTS: 2 English muffin halves equals 249 calories, 9 g fat (6 g saturated fat), 30 mg cholesterol, 506 mg sodium, 30 g carbohydrate, 2 g fiber, 11 g protein. **DIABETIC EXCHANGES:** 2 starch, 1 lean meat.

OPEN-FACED VEGGIE SANDWICHES

195 CALORIES

TURKEY LUNCHEON SALAD

turkey luncheon salad

Joan Cannon | NOBLESVILLE, INDIANA

I received this recipe as a newlywed and made it healthier by using brown rice as well as fat-free mayo and sour cream. Think ladies' luncheon—with a light, refreshing Asian twist!

- 2 cups cubed cooked turkey breast
- 2 cups cooked brown rice
- 1 can (14 ounces) bean sprouts, drained
- 1 can (8 ounces) sliced water chestnuts, drained
- 1 celery rib, chopped
- 1 small carrot, shredded
- 1/4 cup finely chopped onion
- 1/2 cup fat-free mayonnaise
- 1/2 cup fat-free sour cream
- 1 tablespoon reduced-sodium soy sauce
- 3/4 teaspoon salt
- 7 lettuce leaves
- 1/4 cup dried cranberries

- In a large bowl, combine the first seven ingredients. In a small bowl, combine the mayonnaise, sour cream, soy sauce and salt; pour over salad and gently stir to coat. Serve over lettuce leaves. Sprinkle with cranberries.

YIELD: 7 servings.

NUTRITION FACTS: 1 cup equals 195 calories, 2 g fat (trace saturated fat), 39 mg cholesterol, 545 mg sodium, 29 g carbohydrate, 4 g fiber, 16 g protein. **DIABETIC EXCHANGES:** 1-1/2 starch, 1 lean meat, 1 vegetable.

southwestern chicken soup

Harold Tartar | WEST PALM BEACH, FLORIDA

This is the perfect recipe to make when you're short on time because the slow cooker does most of the work for you!

- 1-1/4 pounds boneless skinless chicken breasts, cut into thin strips
- 1 tablespoon canola oil
- 2 cans (14-1/2 ounces *each*) reduced-sodium chicken broth
- 1 package (16 ounces) frozen corn, thawed
- 1 can (14-1/2 ounces) diced tomatoes, undrained
- 1 medium onion, chopped
- 1 medium green pepper, chopped
- 1 medium sweet red pepper, chopped
- 1 can (4 ounces) chopped green chilies
- 1-1/2 teaspoons seasoned salt, optional
- 1 teaspoon ground cumin
- 1/2 teaspoon garlic powder

- In a large skillet, saute the chicken in oil until lightly browned. Transfer to a 5-qt. slow cooker with a slotted spoon. Stir in the remaining ingredients. Cover and cook on low for 7-8 hours or until chicken and vegetables are tender. Stir before serving.

YIELD: 10 servings.

NUTRITION FACTS: 1 cup equals 143 calories, 3 g fat (1 g saturated fat), 31 mg cholesterol, 364 mg sodium, 15 g carbohydrate, 3 g fiber, 15 g protein. **DIABETIC EXCHANGES:** 2 lean meat, 1 starch.

SOUTHWESTERN CHICKEN SOUP

143 CALORIES

184 CALORIES

GREEN TEA TERIYAKI CHICKEN

green tea teriyaki chicken

Tender chicken is treated to a delightful sauce with green tea for a low-fat entree that really stands out. Serve it with fragrant rice, like jasmine, for a restaurant-quality meal. Thanks goes to our Test Kitchen for this sensational dish!

3-1/2 teaspoons green tea leaves, *divided*
   1 cup boiling water
   4 green onions, chopped, *divided*
   3 tablespoons honey
   2 tablespoons cider vinegar
   2 tablespoons reduced-sodium soy sauce
   4 garlic cloves, minced
 1/2 teaspoon minced fresh gingerroot
 1/8 teaspoon sesame oil
   4 boneless skinless chicken breast halves (4 ounces *each*)

• Place 2-1/2 teaspoons tea leaves in a small bowl; add boiling water. Cover and steep for 5-6 minutes.

• Strain and discard leaves; pour tea into a large skillet. Add half of the onions. Stir in the honey, vinegar, soy sauce, garlic, ginger and sesame oil. Bring to a boil. Reduce heat; simmer, uncovered, until the sauce is reduced to roughly 3/4 cup.

• Add chicken and remaining tea leaves; cover and cook over medium heat for 4-5 minutes on each side or until a meat thermometer reads 170°. Cut chicken into thin slices; serve with sauce. Garnish with remaining onions.

YIELD: 4 servings.

NUTRITION FACTS: 1 chicken breast half with 3 tablespoons sauce equals 184 calories, 3 g fat (1 g saturated fat), 63 mg cholesterol, 359 mg sodium, 16 g carbohydrate, trace fiber, 24 g protein. **DIABETIC EXCHANGES:** 3 lean meat, 1 starch.

salmon chowder

Cindy St. Martin | PORTLAND, OREGON
The salmon in this recipe is a change from traditional chowder, but it sure is delicious!

   2 pounds red potatoes, peeled and cubed
   1 large onion, chopped
   6 cups reduced-sodium chicken broth
   1 pound salmon fillets, cut into 1-inch pieces
 1/2 pound sliced bacon, cooked and crumbled
   2 cups whole milk
   1 cup half-and-half cream
   1 tablespoon butter
 1/2 teaspoon salt
Pepper to taste

• In a Dutch oven, combine the potatoes, onion and broth. Bring to a boil. Reduce heat; cover and cook for 10-15 minutes or until potatoes are tender. Add salmon and bacon; cook over medium heat until fish flakes easily with a fork.

• Reduce heat; stir in the milk, cream, butter, salt and pepper; heat through (do not boil). Thicken if desired.

YIELD: 14 servings.

NUTRITION FACTS: 1 cup equals 198 calories, 10 g fat (4 g saturated fat), 38 mg cholesterol, 466 mg sodium, 14 g carbohydrate, 1 g fiber, 12 g protein. **DIABETIC EXCHANGES:** 1 starch, 1 lean meat, 1 fat.

SALMON CHOWDER

198 CALORIES

spiced butternut squash soup

Julie Hession | LAS VEGAS, NEVADA

I like making this recipe year round, but it's best in the fall and winter months when butternut squash is in season. I love it because it's hearty and filling, but very healthy as well as easy to make. Serve it with some good crusty bread for a complete meal!

- 2 medium butternut squash (about 3 pounds *each*)
- 2 large onions, sliced
- 1 tablespoon olive oil
- 1 tablespoon butter
- 2 cinnamon sticks (3 inches)
- 2 tablespoons brown sugar
- 1 tablespoon minced fresh gingerroot
- 2 garlic cloves, minced
- 3 cans (14-1/2 ounces *each*) reduced-sodium chicken broth
- 2-1/4 cups water
- 1-1/4 teaspoons salt
- 1 tablespoon minced fresh parsley

- Cut squash in half; discard seeds. Place squash cut side down in a 15-in. x 10-in. x 1-in. baking pan coated with cooking spray. Bake at 400° for 40-50 minutes or until tender. Cool slightly; scoop out pulp and set aside.

- In a Dutch oven over medium heat, cook and stir onions in oil and butter for 2 minutes. Add the cinnamon, brown sugar, ginger and garlic; cook 2 minutes longer or until onions are tender. Stir in the broth, water, salt and reserved squash. Bring to a boil. Reduce heat; cover and simmer for 10 minutes.

- Cool the soup slightly. Discard cinnamon. In a blender, process soup in batches until smooth. Carefully, return all to the pan and heat through. Sprinkle each serving with parsley.

YIELD: 12 servings (3 quarts).

NUTRITION FACTS: 1 cup equals 133 calories, 2 g fat (1 g saturated fat), 3 mg cholesterol, 596 mg sodium, 28 g carbohydrate, 7 g fiber, 4 g protein. **DIABETIC EXCHANGES:** 2 starch, 1/2 fat.

SPICED BUTTERNUT SQUASH SOUP

133 CALORIES

165 CALORIES open-face tuna melts

Marilyn Smelser | ALBANY, OREGON

I created this recipe when I got married 20 years ago and have served it countless times since then. Sometimes I add a little chili powder, heap the tuna mixture over tortilla chips and microwave for a light take on nachos.

- 2 cans (6 ounces *each*) light water-packed tuna, drained and flaked
- 3/4 cup chopped sweet red pepper
- 1/2 cup chopped fresh mushrooms
- 1/2 cup shredded reduced-fat cheddar cheese
- 1/4 cup sliced pimiento-stuffed olives
- 4-1/2 teaspoons reduced-fat mayonnaise
- 4 English muffins, split and toasted
- 8 thin slices tomato

- In a large bowl, combine tuna, red pepper, mushrooms, cheese and olives. Fold in the mayonnaise. Spread over English muffin halves. Top each with a tomato slice.

- Broil 6 in. from the heat for 7-9 minutes or until lightly browned. Serve immediately.

YIELD: 8 servings.

NUTRITION FACTS: 1 serving equals 165 calories, 5 g fat (2 g saturated fat), 24 mg cholesterol, 413 mg sodium, 16 g carbohydrate, 2 g fiber, 14 g protein. **DIABETIC EXCHANGES:** 2 lean meat, 1 starch.

MEDITERRANEAN SALAD SANDWICHES

mediterranean salad sandwiches

Candice Garcia | WINTER HAVEN, FLORIDA

These hearty, fresh-flavored sandwiches taste like a summer salad on a bun. Add iced tea, some carrot sticks and call it an easy lunch!

  2 tablespoons olive oil, *divided*
  1 garlic clove, minced
1/4 teaspoon salt
  4 large portobello mushrooms, stems removed
  2 cups spring mix salad greens
  1 medium tomato, chopped
1/2 cup chopped roasted sweet red peppers
1/4 cup crumbled reduced-fat feta cheese
  2 tablespoons chopped pitted Greek olives
  1 tablespoon red wine vinegar
1/2 teaspoon dried oregano
  4 slices sourdough bread, toasted and halved

- In a small bowl, combine 1 tablespoon oil, garlic and salt; brush over mushrooms.

- Using long-handled tongs, dip a paper towel in cooking oil and lightly coat the grill rack. Grill mushrooms, covered, over medium heat for 12-16 minutes, turning frequently or until tender.

- In a large bowl, combine the salad greens, tomato, peppers, cheese and olives. In a small bowl, whisk the vinegar, oregano and remaining oil. Pour over salad mixture; toss to coat. Layer each of four half slices of toast with a mushroom and 3/4 cup salad mixture; top with remaining toast.

YIELD: 4 servings.

NUTRITION FACTS: 1 serving equals 225 calories, 9 g fat (2 g saturated fat), 3 mg cholesterol, 495 mg sodium, 26 g carbohydrate, 3 g fiber, 8 g protein. DIABETIC EXCHANGES: 2 vegetable, 2 fat, 1 starch.

veggie cheese soup

Jean Hall | RAPID CITY, SOUTH DAKOTA

My niece makes this in a slow cooker by putting in all the ingredients but the cheese. When the veggies are tender, she adds the cubed cheese.

     1 medium onion, chopped
     1 celery rib, chopped
     2 small red potatoes, cut into 1/2-inch cubes
2-3/4 cups water
     2 teaspoons reduced-sodium chicken bouillon granules
     1 tablespoon cornstarch
   1/4 cup cold water
     1 can (10-3/4 ounces) reduced-fat reduced-sodium condensed cream of chicken soup, undiluted
     3 cups frozen California-blend vegetables, thawed
   1/2 cup chopped fully cooked lean ham
     8 ounces reduced-fat process cheese (Velveeta), cubed

- In a large nonstick saucepan coated with a cooking spray, cook onion and celery over medium heat until onion is tender. Stir in the potatoes, water and bouillon. Bring to a boil. Reduce heat; cover and simmer for 10 minutes.

- Combine cornstarch and cold water until smooth; gradually stir into soup. Return to a boil; cook and stir for 1-2 minutes or until slightly thickened. Stir in condensed soup until blended.

- Reduce heat; add vegetables and ham. Cook and stir until vegetables are tender. Stir in cheese until melted.

YIELD: 9 servings.

NUTRITION FACTS: 3/4 cup equals 115 calories, 4 g fat (2 g saturated fat), 15 mg cholesterol, 682 mg sodium, 13 g carbohydrate, 1 g fiber, 8 g protein.

236 CALORIES

CHICKEN CAESAR SALAD

chicken caesar salad

Kay Andersen | BEAR, DELAWARE

This main-dish salad may sound fancy, but in reality it couldn't be easier to make.

- 2 boneless skinless chicken breast halves (1/2 pound)
- 2 teaspoons olive oil
- 1/4 teaspoon garlic salt
- 1/4 teaspoon pepper
- 1/4 teaspoon paprika
- 1/8 teaspoon dried basil
- 1/8 teaspoon dried oregano
- 4 cups torn romaine
- 1 small tomato, thinly sliced
- 1/4 cup fat-free creamy Caesar salad dressing

Caesar salad croutons, optional

- Brush chicken with oil. Combine the garlic salt, pepper, paprika, basil and oregano; sprinkle over chicken. Grill, uncovered, over medium heat for 12-15 minutes or until juices run clear, turning several times.

- Arrange romaine and tomato on plates. Cut chicken into strips; place over salads. Drizzle with dressing. Sprinkle with croutons if desired.

YIELD: 2 servings.

NUTRITION FACTS: 1 serving equals 236 calories, 8 g fat (1 g saturated fat), 63 mg cholesterol, 653 mg sodium, 17 g carbohydrate, 4 g fiber, 26 g protein. **DIABETIC EXCHANGES:** 3 lean meat, 2 vegetable, 1 starch, 1 fat.

sausage lentil soup

Suzanne Dabkowski | BLYTHEWOOD, SOUTH CAROLINA

I found this good-for-you recipe in a men's magazine and lightened it up. It comes together without much effort. Best of all, it's loaded with fiber and vitamins, and it makes good use of low-fat ingredients.

- 1 medium onion, chopped
- 1 celery rib, chopped
- 1/4 pound reduced-fat smoked sausage, halved and thinly sliced
- 1 medium carrot, halved and thinly sliced
- 2 garlic cloves, minced
- 2 cans (14-1/2 ounces *each*) reduced-sodium chicken broth
- 1/3 cup water
- 1 cup dried lentils, rinsed
- 1/2 teaspoon dried oregano
- 1/4 teaspoon ground cumin
- 1/4 teaspoon pepper
- 1 can (14-1/2 ounces) stewed tomatoes, cut up
- 1 tablespoon Worcestershire sauce
- 1 cup chopped fresh spinach

- In a large saucepan coated with cooking spray, cook and stir onion and celery over medium-high heat for 2 minutes. Add the sausage, carrot and garlic; cook 2-3 minutes longer or until onion is tender.

SAUSAGE LENTIL SOUP

180 CALORIES

- Stir in the broth, water, lentils, oregano, cumin and pepper. Bring to a boil. Reduce heat; cover and simmer for 25-30 minutes or until lentils and vegetables are tender.

- Stir in the tomatoes, Worcestershire sauce and spinach; cook until heated through and spinach is wilted.

YIELD: 6 servings.

NUTRITION FACTS: 1 cup equals 180 calories, 1 g fat (trace saturated fat), 7 mg cholesterol, 639 mg sodium, 31 g carbohydrate, 12 g fiber, 14 g protein. **DIABETIC EXCHANGES:** 2 lean meat, 1 starch, 1 vegetable.

MANGO SHRIMP PITAS

mango shrimp pitas

Beverly O'Ferrall | LINKWOOD, MARYLAND

Mango, ginger and curry combine with a splash of lime juice to coat this juicy, grilled shrimp. Stuffed in pitas, the shrimp combo makes for a fabulous lunch!

1/2	cup mango chutney
3	tablespoons lime juice
1	teaspoon grated fresh gingerroot
1/2	teaspoon curry powder
1	pound uncooked large shrimp, peeled and deveined
2	pita breads (6 inches), halved
8	Bibb *or* Boston lettuce leaves
1	large tomato, thinly sliced

- In a small bowl, combine the chutney, lime juice, ginger and curry. Pour 1/2 cup marinade into a large resealable plastic bag; add the shrimp. Seal bag and turn to coat; refrigerate for at least 15 minutes. Cover and refrigerate remaining marinade.

- Drain and discard marinade. Thread shrimp onto four metal or soaked wooden skewers. Using long-handled tongs, dip a paper towel in cooking oil and lightly coat the grill rack. Grill shrimp, covered, over medium heat or broil 4 in. from the heat for 6-8 minutes or until shrimp turn pink, turning frequently.

- Fill pita halves with lettuce, tomato and shrimp; spoon reserved chutney mixture over filling.

YIELD: 4 servings.

NUTRITION FACTS: 1 filled pita half equals 230 calories, 2 g fat (trace saturated fat), 138 mg cholesterol, 410 mg sodium, 29 g carbohydrate, 1 g fiber, 22 g protein. **DIABETIC EXCHANGES:** 3 lean meat, 2 starch.

201 CALORIES

chicken chili

Lisa Goodman | BLOOMINGTON, MINNESOTA

Loaded with hearty beans and chicken, this zippy chili really warms up my entire family on chilly winter days. Leftovers taste even better the next day!

4-1/2	cups reduced-sodium chicken broth
2	cans (15 ounces *each*) black beans, rinsed and drained
1/2	cup *each* chopped green, yellow and sweet red pepper
1/4	cup chopped onion
1	tablespoon chili powder
1-1/2	teaspoons paprika
1	to 1-1/2 teaspoons pepper
1	to 1-1/2 teaspoons crushed red pepper flakes
1	to 1-1/2 teaspoons ground cumin
1/2	teaspoon salt-free seasoning blend

Dash cayenne pepper

2	cups cubed cooked chicken breast

- In a 3-qt. saucepan, bring broth to a boil. Reduce heat; add the beans, peppers, onion and seasonings. Cover and simmer 15 minutes. Add chicken; simmer for 30 minutes.

YIELD: 7 servings.

NUTRITION FACTS: 1 cup equals 201 calories, 3 g fat (0 saturated fat), 36 mg cholesterol, 474 mg sodium, 20 g carbohydrate, 7 g fiber, 21 g protein. **DIABETIC EXCHANGES:** 2 lean meat, 1 starch, 1/2 vegetable.

mom's classic clam chowder

Christine Schenher | SAN CLEMENTE, CALIFORNIA

When my family lived in Michigan, this was truly a comforting soup when blustery winds blew into town. The steaming bowls warmed up icy toes just right!

- 3/4 cup *each* chopped onion, celery and carrots
- 1/2 cup chopped green pepper
- 1/4 cup butter, cubed
- 1 carton (32 ounces) reduced-sodium chicken broth
- 1 bottle (8 ounces) clam juice
- 2 teaspoons reduced-sodium chicken bouillon granules
- 1 bay leaf
- 1/2 teaspoon dried parsley flakes
- 1/2 teaspoon salt
- 1/4 teaspoon curry powder
- 1/4 teaspoon pepper
- 1 medium potato, peeled and cubed
- 2/3 cup all-purpose flour
- 2 cups 2% milk, *divided*

classic

MOM'S CLASSIC CLAM CHOWDER

155 CALORIES

227 CALORIES

MEDITERRANEAN CHICKEN SANDWICHES

- 4 cans (6-1/2 ounces *each*) minced clams, undrained
- 1 cup half-and-half cream

- In a Dutch oven over medium heat, cook the onion, celery, carrots and green pepper in butter until tender. Stir in the broth, clam juice, bouillon and seasonings. Add potato. Bring to a boil. Reduce heat; simmer, uncovered, for 15-20 minutes or until potato is tender.

- In a small bowl, combine flour and 1 cup milk until smooth. Gradually stir into soup. Bring to a boil; cook and stir for 1-2 minutes or until thickened.

- Stir in the clams, cream and the remaining milk; heat through (do not boil). Discard bay leaf before serving.

YIELD: 12 servings (3 quarts).

NUTRITION FACTS: 1 cup equals 155 calories, 7 g fat (4 g saturated fat), 34 mg cholesterol, 726 mg sodium, 15 g carbohydrate, 1 g fiber, 8 g protein. **DIABETIC EXCHANGES:** 1 starch, 1 lean meat, 1 fat.

mediterranean chicken sandwiches

Marcia Fuller | SHERIDAN, MONTANA

I copied this delightful recipe when I was in Italy visiting my Aunt Elsa. The refreshing sandwich filling is nicely flavored with oregano and mint. I like it tucked into chewy pita bread. However, you can save a few calories by eating the chicken mixture as is and leaving out the pita bread altogether.

1-1/4 pounds boneless skinless chicken breasts, cut into 1-inch strips

2 medium tomatoes, seeded and chopped

1/2 cup sliced quartered seeded cucumber

1/2 cup sliced sweet onion

2 tablespoons cider vinegar

1 tablespoon olive oil

1 tablespoon minced fresh oregano *or* 1 teaspoon dried oregano

1 to 2 teaspoons minced fresh mint *or* 1/2 teaspoon dried mint

1/4 teaspoon salt

6 whole wheat pita pocket halves, warmed

6 lettuce leaves

- In a large nonstick skillet coated with cooking spray, cook chicken for 5 minutes or until no longer pink. Remove from the skillet; cool slightly.

- In a large bowl, combine the chicken, tomatoes, cucumber and onion. In a small bowl, whisk the vinegar, oil, oregano, mint and salt. Pour over chicken mixture; toss gently.

- Cover and refrigerate for at least 1 hour. Line pita halves with lettuce; fill with chicken mixture, using a slotted spoon.

YIELD: 6 servings.

NUTRITION FACTS: 1 filled pita half equals 227 calories, 4 g fat (1 g saturated fat), 55 mg cholesterol, 335 mg sodium, 22 g carbohydrate, 3 g fiber, 26 g protein. **DIABETIC EXCHANGES:** 3 lean meat, 1 starch, 1 vegetable.

spicy three-bean chili

Melissa Mendez | GILBERT, MINNESOTA

Even my meat-loving family devours this hearty meatless chili. It's fast, simple to make and freezes so well. You can even serve it with chips as a warm salsa at casual get-togethers.

1 medium green pepper, chopped

1 medium sweet yellow pepper, chopped

1 jalapeno pepper, seeded and chopped

1 medium onion, chopped

1 tablespoon olive oil

3 garlic cloves, minced

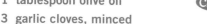

SPICY THREE-BEAN CHILI

2 cans (14-1/2 ounces *each*) diced tomatoes with mild green chilies, undrained

1 can (10 ounces) diced tomatoes with green chilies, undrained

1 can (16 ounces) kidney beans, rinsed and drained

1 can (15 ounces) black beans, rinsed and drained

1 cup vegetable broth

1 teaspoon chili powder

3/4 teaspoon ground cumin

1/2 teaspoon cayenne pepper

1 can (16 ounces) spicy fat-free refried beans

1/3 cup shredded reduced-fat cheddar cheese

1/3 cup thinly sliced green onions

- In a Dutch oven coated with cooking spray, saute the peppers and onion in oil until tender. Add garlic; cook 1 minute longer. Stir in the tomatoes, kidney beans, black beans, broth, chili powder, cumin and cayenne. Bring to a boil. Reduce heat; simmer, uncovered for 10 minutes.

- Stir in refried beans; simmer 10 minutes longer. Garnish each serving with 2 teaspoons each of cheese and sliced green onions.

YIELD: 8 servings (2-1/2 quarts).

EDITOR'S NOTE: When cutting hot peppers, disposable gloves are recommended. Avoid touching your face.

NUTRITION FACTS: 1-1/4 cups equals 201 calories, 3 g fat (1 g saturated fat), 3 mg cholesterol, 803 mg sodium, 34 g carbohydrate, 8 g fiber, 10 g protein. **DIABETIC EXCHANGES:** 2 starch, 1 lean meat, 1 vegetable.

251-350 calories

garden vegetable wraps

Barbara Blake | WEST BRATTLEBORO, VERMONT

My husband and I love these light and tasty wraps. I found the recipe years ago, and it was an instant hit.

- 1/2 cup reduced-fat garlic-herb cheese spread
- 4 flour tortillas (10 inches)
- 1-1/4 cups chopped seeded tomatoes
- 1-1/4 cups julienned fresh spinach
- 3/4 cup chopped sweet red pepper
- 2 bacon strips, cooked and crumbled
- 1/4 teaspoon coarsely ground pepper

- Spread 2 tablespoons cheese spread over each tortilla. Sprinkle with tomatoes, spinach, red pepper, bacon and pepper. Roll up tightly.

YIELD: 4 servings.

NUTRITION FACTS: 1 wrap equals 314 calories, 10 g fat (5 g saturated fat), 21 mg cholesterol, 614 mg sodium, 37 g carbohydrate, 8 g fiber, 12 g protein. **DIABETIC EXCHANGES:** 2-1/2 starch, 2 fat, 1 vegetable.

GARDEN VEGETABLE WRAPS

314 CALORIES

346 CALORIES

BISTRO TURKEY SANDWICHES

bistro turkey sandwiches

Veronica Callaghan | GLASTONBURY, CONNECTICUT

Sweet and savory flavors combine in this sandwich. You can substitute the apples with pears for a tasty change.

- 1 small red onion, thinly sliced
- 4 teaspoons brown sugar, *divided*
- 1 tablespoon olive oil
- 1/4 teaspoon salt
- 1/8 teaspoon cayenne pepper
- 1/4 cup Dijon mustard
- 1 tablespoon apple cider *or* unsweetened apple juice
- 6 wheat sandwich buns, split
- 6 Bibb *or* Boston lettuce leaves
- 1 medium pear, peeled and thinly sliced
- 1 pound cooked turkey breast, thinly sliced
- 1/4 cup loosely packed basil leaves
- 6 tablespoons crumbled Gorgonzola cheese

- In a small skillet over medium heat, cook onion and 1 teaspoon brown sugar in oil for 8-10 minutes or until golden brown, stirring frequently. Stir in salt and cayenne.

- Combine the mustard, apple cider and remaining brown sugar; spread over bun bottoms. Layer with lettuce, pear, turkey, basil and cheese. Top with caramelized onion. Replace tops.

YIELD: 6 servings.

NUTRITION FACTS: 1 sandwich equals 346 calories, 8 g fat (3 g saturated fat), 71 mg cholesterol, 708 mg sodium, 35 g carbohydrate, 4 g fiber, 31 g protein. **DIABETIC EXCHANGES:** 3 lean meat, 2 starch, 1/2 fat.

asian chicken with pasta

Rebecca Sams | OAK HARBOR, OHIO

Mild flavors make this a dish even picky eaters will like. The coleslaw mix brings a pleasing crunch to the veggie-filled recipe.

- 1/2 **pound uncooked angel hair pasta**
- 1 **pound chicken tenderloins, cut into 1-inch cubes**
- 1/3 **cup prepared balsamic vinaigrette**
- 1/3 **cup prepared Italian salad dressing**
- 1 **package (12 ounces) broccoli coleslaw mix**
- 1/2 **pound sliced fresh mushrooms**
- 3/4 **cup julienned sweet red pepper**
- 1/2 **cup sliced onion**
- 1/2 **teaspoon garlic powder**
- 1/2 **teaspoon ground ginger**
- 1/4 **teaspoon salt**
- 1/8 **teaspoon pepper**

- Cook pasta according to package directions. Meanwhile, in a large skillet, saute chicken in vinaigrette and salad dressing until no longer pink. Remove and keep warm.

- In the same skillet, saute the coleslaw mix, mushrooms, red pepper and onion until tender. Add the seasonings. Stir in the chicken; heat through. Drain pasta. Add to chicken mixture; toss to coat.

YIELD: 6 servings.

NUTRITION FACTS: 1-1/2 cups equals 320 calories, 8 g fat (1 g saturated fat), 44 mg cholesterol, 474 mg sodium, 38 g carbohydrate, 4 g fiber, 25 g protein. **DIABETIC EXCHANGES:** 3 lean meat, 2 starch, 1 vegetable, 1 fat.

ASIAN CHICKEN WITH PASTA

320 CALORIES

317 CALORIES

EASY BEEF BARLEY SOUP

easy beef barley soup

Carole Lanthier | COURTICE, ONTARIO

This soup is really simple and takes very little time to put together. You can serve it for a comforting lunch or for supper with homemade bread, which I do on occasion.

- 1/2 **pound lean ground beef (90% lean)**
- 2 **large fresh mushrooms, sliced**
- 1 **celery rib, chopped**
- 1 **small onion, chopped**
- 2 **teaspoons all-purpose flour**
- 3 **cans (14-1/2 ounces *each*) reduced-sodium beef broth**
- 2 **medium carrots, sliced**
- 1 **large potato, peeled and cubed**
- 1/2 **teaspoon pepper**
- 1/8 **teaspoon salt**
- 1/3 **cup medium pearl barley**
- 1 **can (5 ounces) evaporated milk**
- 2 **tablespoons tomato paste**

- In a Dutch oven over medium heat, cook and stir the beef, mushrooms, celery and onion until meat is no longer pink; drain. Stir in flour until blended; gradually add broth. Stir in the carrots, potato, pepper and salt. Bring to a boil. Stir in barley.

- Reduce heat; cover and simmer for 45-50 minutes or until barley is tender. Whisk in milk and tomato paste; heat through.

YIELD: 4 servings.

NUTRITION FACTS: 1-3/4 cups equals 317 calories, 7 g fat (3 g saturated fat), 45 mg cholesterol, 753 mg sodium, 42 g carbohydrate, 6 g fiber, 21 g protein. **DIABETIC EXCHANGES:** 2-1/2 starch, 2 lean meat, 1 vegetable.

ASIAN TURKEY LETTUCE WRAPS

275 CALORIES

asian turkey lettuce wraps

Susan Riley | ALLEN, TEXAS

A bag of frozen chopped vegetables make these wraps a snap. Add some Asian chile sauce if you want to spice it up a bit.

1-1/4 **pounds extra-lean ground turkey**

1 **package (16 ounces) frozen stir-fry vegetable blend, thawed**

1/3 **cup reduced-sodium teriyaki sauce**

1/4 **cup hoisin sauce**

3 **tablespoons reduced-fat creamy peanut butter**

2 **tablespoons minced fresh gingerroot**

1 **tablespoon rice vinegar**

1 **tablespoon sesame oil**

3 **garlic cloves, minced**

4 **green onions, chopped**

10 **Boston lettuce leaves**

Additional hoisin sauce, optional

- In a large nonstick skillet coated with cooking spray, cook and stir turkey over medium-high heat until no longer pink.

- Coarsely chop mixed vegetables; add to the pan. Stir in the teriyaki sauce, hoisin sauce, peanut butter, ginger, vinegar and oil. Cook and stir over medium-high heat for 5 minutes. Add garlic; cook 1 minute longer.

- Remove from the heat; stir in onions. Place a scant 1/2 cup turkey mixture on each lettuce leaf; fold lettuce over filling. Serve with additional hoisin sauce if desired.

YIELD: 5 servings.

NUTRITION FACTS: 2 wraps (calculated without additional hoisin sauce) equals 275 calories, 8 g fat (1 g saturated fat), 45 mg cholesterol, 686 mg sodium, 19 g carbohydrate, 4 g fiber, 34 g protein. **DIABETIC EXCHANGES:** 3 lean meat, 1 starch, 1 vegetable, 1 fat.

pumpkin sloppy joes

Donna Musser | PEARL CITY, ILLINOIS

Here's a wonderful harvest version of an old standby.

1/2 **pound lean ground beef (90% lean)**

3 **tablespoons finely chopped onion**

1/4 **cup ketchup**

2 **tablespoons tomato juice**

1/4 **teaspoon chili powder**

Dash ground cloves and nutmeg

Dash pepper

2/3 **cup canned pumpkin**

2 **hamburger buns, split**

- In a large skillet, cook beef and onion over medium heat until meat is no longer pink; drain.

- Add the ketchup, tomato juice, chili powder, cloves, nutmeg and pepper. Bring to a boil. Stir in pumpkin. Reduce heat; cover and simmer for 15-20 minutes or until heated through. Serve on buns.

YIELD: 2 servings.

NUTRITION FACTS: 1 sandwich equals 350 calories, 11 g fat (4 g saturated fat), 56 mg cholesterol, 730 mg sodium, 36 g carbohydrate, 3 g fiber, 27 g protein. **DIABETIC EXCHANGES:** 3 lean meat, 2-1/2 starch.

PUMPKIN SLOPPY JOES

350 CALORIES

301 CALORIES

CASHEW CHICKEN

cashew chicken

Linda Avila | TOONE, TENNESSEE

Whenever my friends and I get together for a potluck, they always ask me to bring this dish. The recipe came from my brother; it has a distinct Asian flavor from all of the spices.

- 3 tablespoons reduced-sodium soy sauce, *divided*
- 1 tablespoon sherry *or* reduced-sodium chicken broth
- 3/4 teaspoon sesame oil, *divided*
- 1 pound boneless skinless chicken breasts, cut into 1-inch pieces
- 1 tablespoon cornstarch
- 1/3 cup reduced-sodium chicken broth
- 1 tablespoon sugar
- 1 tablespoon rice vinegar
- 1 tablespoon hoisin sauce
- 1/2 teaspoon minced fresh gingerroot
- 1/4 teaspoon salt
- 2 teaspoons canola oil, *divided*
- 1-1/2 cups fresh snow peas
- 2 medium carrots, julienned
- 1 can (8 ounces) sliced water chestnuts, drained
- 1/4 cup unsalted cashews, toasted

Hot cooked rice, optional

- In a large resealable plastic bag, combine 2 tablespoons soy sauce, sherry or broth and 1/2 teaspoon sesame oil; add the chicken. Seal bag and turn to coat. Refrigerate for 30 minutes.

- In a small bowl, combine cornstarch and broth until smooth. Stir in the sugar, vinegar, hoisin sauce, ginger, salt, and remaining soy sauce and sesame oil; set aside.

- Drain chicken and discard marinade. In a large nonstick wok or skillet, stir-fry chicken in 1 teaspoon oil until no longer pink. Remove and keep warm.

- In the same pan, stir-fry peas and carrots in remaining oil until crisp-tender. Add water chestnuts.

- Return chicken to the pan. Stir sauce mixture and stir into chicken mixture. Bring to a boil; cook and stir for 1 minute or until thickened. Sprinkle with cashews. Serve with rice if desired.

YIELD: 4 servings.

NUTRITION FACTS: 1 cup (calculated without cooked rice) equals 301 calories, 10 g fat (2 g saturated fat), 63 mg cholesterol, 590 mg sodium, 25 g carbohydrate, 4 g fiber, 28 g protein.

Below are a few items you might rely on when preparing a basic lunch. When packing a lunch or adding something to your afternoon menu, use this list to make sure you stick to your goal of 450 calories.

- **1 slice whole wheat bread,** 69 calories
- **1 slice reduced-calorie wheat bread,** 48 calories
- **1 large pita (6-1/2" diameter),** 165 calories
- **1 flour tortilla (approximately 6" diameter),** 150 calories
- **1 whole wheat dinner roll,** 76 calories
- **1 hamburger bun,** 79 calories
- **1 hard roll,** 83 calories
- **1 slice American cheese (1 ounce),** 93 calories
- **1 slice Swiss cheese (1 ounce),** 106 calories
- **1 slice cheddar cheese (1 ounce),** 113 calories

For the calorie counts of other typical lunch side dishes, see the Smart Snacks list on page 67. You might also check the Free Foods Chart on page 45.

For calorie calculations of other foods, see the Nutrition Facts labels on food packages.

grilled pepper jack chicken sandwiches

Linda Foreman | LOCUST GROVE, OKLAHOMA

This is a great meal for summer days. Basic, yet packed with flavor, this sandwich gets a kick from zesty cheese and savory bacon.

> 2 boneless skinless chicken breast halves (4 ounces *each*)
>
> 1 teaspoon poultry seasoning
>
> 2 center-cut bacon strips, cooked and halved
>
> 2 slices (1/2 ounce *each*) pepper Jack cheese
>
> 2 hamburger buns, split
>
> 2 lettuce leaves
>
> 1 slice onion, separated into rings
>
> 2 slices tomato

Dill pickle slices, optional

- Sprinkle chicken with poultry seasoning. Using long-handled tongs, dip a paper towel in cooking oil and lightly coat the grill rack. Grill chicken, covered, over medium heat or broil 4 in. from the heat for 4-7 minutes on each side or until a meat thermometer reads 170°. Top with bacon and cheese; cover and grill 1-2 minutes longer or until cheese is melted.

- Serve on buns with lettuce, onion, tomato and pickles if desired.

YIELD: 2 servings.

GRILLED PEPPER JACK CHICKEN SANDWICHES

335 CALORIES

NUTRITION FACTS: 1 sandwich (calculated without pickles) equals 335 calories, 11 g fat (4 g saturated fat), 85 mg cholesterol, 456 mg sodium, 25 g carbohydrate, 2 g fiber, 33 g protein. **DIABETIC EXCHANGES:** 4 lean meat, 1-1/2 starch.

289 CALORIES

SIMON'S FAMOUS TUNA SALAD

simon's famous tuna salad

Simon Seitz | HIGHLAND, NEW YORK

This nicely seasoned tuna salad makes for a simple and satisfying lunch. Crunchy carrots give it a unique and tasty twist you'll love.

> 3 cans (6 ounces *each*) light water-packed tuna, drained and flaked
>
> 3/4 cup fat-free mayonnaise
>
> 1/4 cup chopped celery
>
> 1/4 cup chopped carrot
>
> 1/2 teaspoon onion powder
>
> 1/2 teaspoon garlic powder
>
> 1/4 teaspoon dill weed
>
> 10 slices whole wheat bread, toasted
>
> 5 lettuce leaves

- In a large bowl, combine the first seven ingredients. For each sandwich, layer a slice of toast with a lettuce leaf and 1/2 cup tuna salad. Top with a second slice of toast.

YIELD: 5 servings.

NUTRITION FACTS: 1 sandwich equals 289 calories, 4 g fat (1 g saturated fat), 34 mg cholesterol, 907 mg sodium, 29 g carbohydrate, 5 g fiber, 34 g protein.

creamy pepperoni ziti

Charlane Gathy | LEXINGTON, KENTUCKY

You can easily feed a crowd with this no-fuss casserole that's ready in about 40 minutes. Its comforting sauce will become a fast favorite at your next potluck or weeknight dinner.

- 1 package (16 ounces) ziti *or* small tube pasta
- 1 can (10-3/4 ounces) condensed cream of mushroom soup, undiluted
- 3/4 cup shredded part-skim mozzarella cheese
- 3/4 cup chopped pepperoni
- 1/2 cup *each* chopped onion, mushrooms, green pepper and tomato
- 1/2 cup half-and-half cream
- 1/4 cup chicken broth
- 1/4 teaspoon salt
- 1/4 teaspoon garlic powder
- 1/4 teaspoon pepper
- 1/2 cup grated Parmesan cheese

- Cook pasta according to package directions; drain. In a large bowl, combine the pasta, soup, mozzarella cheese, pepperoni, onion, mushrooms, green pepper, tomato, cream, broth and seasonings.

- Transfer to a greased 13-in. x 9-in. baking dish. Sprinkle with Parmesan cheese. Cover and bake at 350° for 20 minutes. Uncover; bake 5-10 minutes longer or until bubbly.

YIELD: 9 servings.

NUTRITION FACTS: 1 cup equals 340 calories, 12 g fat (6 g saturated fat), 27 mg cholesterol, 696 mg sodium, 43 g carbohydrate, 2 g fiber, 15 g protein. **DIABETIC EXCHANGES:** 3 starch, 1 high-fat meat, 1/2 fat.

CREAMY PEPPERONI ZITI

BARBECUE BEEF SANDWICHES

barbecue beef sandwiches

Sharon Zagar | GARDNER, ILLINOIS

A quick, tangy sauce gives these family-pleasing sandwiches lots of zip. I've had this recipe for years and have given it out many, many times.

- 1-1/2 pounds lean ground beef (90% lean)
- 2 celery ribs, sliced
- 1 large onion, chopped
- 1 can (8 ounces) tomato sauce
- 1/4 cup ketchup
- 2 tablespoons brown sugar
- 2 tablespoons barbecue sauce
- 1 tablespoon prepared mustard
- 1 tablespoon Worcestershire sauce
- 6 hamburger buns, split

- In a large nonstick skillet, cook the beef, celery and onion over medium heat until meat is no longer pink; drain.

- Stir in the tomato sauce, ketchup, brown sugar, barbecue sauce, mustard and Worcestershire sauce. Bring to a boil. Reduce heat; simmer, uncovered, for 10-15 minutes to allow flavors to blend. Spoon 3/4 cup onto each bun.

YIELD: 6 servings.

NUTRITION FACTS: 1 sandwich equals 348 calories, 11 g fat (4 g saturated fat), 56 mg cholesterol, 719 mg sodium, 35 g carbohydrate, 2 g fiber, 27 g protein. **DIABETIC EXCHANGES:** 3 lean meat, 2 starch.

warm fajita salad

Bobbie Jo Yokley | FRANKLIN, KENTUCKY

When I didn't have tortillas in the house to wrap up the pork in this recipe, I made it into a healthy salad instead. It was delicious!

- 1 cup lime juice
- 1/4 cup reduced-sodium chicken broth
- 1/4 cup reduced-sodium soy sauce
- 2 garlic cloves, minced
- 1 tablespoon canola oil
- 1 teaspoon sugar
- 1 teaspoon Liquid Smoke, optional
- 3/4 teaspoon ground cumin
- 1/2 teaspoon dried oregano
- 1/4 teaspoon ground ginger
- 1/4 teaspoon hot pepper sauce
- 1 pound boneless pork loin, trimmed and cut into thin strips
- 1 large onion, sliced
- 1 medium green pepper, cut into strips
- 1 medium sweet yellow pepper, cut into strips
- 1 tablespoon lemon juice
- 6 cups torn romaine
- 12 cherry tomatoes, quartered

- In a large resealable plastic bag, combine the lime juice, broth, soy sauce, garlic, oil, sugar and seasonings. Set aside 2 tablespoons; cover and refrigerate. Add pork to

WARM FAJITA SALAD

280 CALORIES

300 CALORIES

CALIFORNIA CHICKEN WRAPS

remaining marinade; toss to coat. Cover and refrigerate for 30 minutes to 3 hours, turning occasionally.

- Drain pork, discarding marinade. Heat reserved marinade in a large skillet over medium-high heat. Add the pork, onion and peppers; stir-fry for 3-4 minutes or until pork is no longer pink. Drizzle with lemon juice. Remove from the heat.

- Arrange lettuce on four individual plates; top with meat mixture and tomatoes.

YIELD: 4 servings.

NUTRITION FACTS: 1 cup equals 280 calories, 11 g fat (3 g saturated fat), 67 mg cholesterol, 707 mg sodium, 21 g carbohydrate, 4 g fiber, 27 g protein. **DIABETIC EXCHANGES:** 3 lean meat, 2 vegetable, 1 fat, 1/2 starch.

california chicken wraps

Donna Munch | EL PASO, TEXAS

The combination of hummus and feta give these wraps unbeatable flavor. Hummus is a fantastic alternative to mayonnaise; try it on your favorite sandwich today!

- 1/3 cup prepared hummus
- 4 whole wheat tortillas (8 inches)
- 2 cups cubed cooked chicken breast
- 1/4 cup chopped roasted sweet red peppers
- 1/4 cup crumbled feta cheese
- 1/4 cup thinly sliced fresh basil leaves

- Spread hummus on tortillas; top with chicken, peppers, cheese and basil. Roll up.

YIELD: 4 servings.

NUTRITION FACTS: 1 wrap equals 300 calories, 8 g fat (2 g saturated fat), 58 mg cholesterol, 408 mg sodium, 26 g carbohydrate, 3 g fiber, 27 g protein. **DIABETIC EXCHANGES:** 3 lean meat, 2 starch.

toasted sandwich with a twist

Lisa Davey | COLUMBUS, OHIO

This ham and turkey sandwich gets a unique spin with raisin bread. Yes, it's different, but oh-so delicious.

  1 slice deli ham (3/4 ounce)
  2 slices deli turkey (1/2 ounce *each*)
1-1/2 teaspoons reduced-fat butter
  2 slices raisin bread
  1 slice Swiss cheese (3/4 ounce)

- In a small nonstick skillet coated with cooking spray, brown the ham and turkey. Meanwhile, spread butter over one side of each slice of bread. Remove ham and turkey from skillet.

- On unbuttered side of one slice of bread, layer cheese, ham and turkey; top with remaining bread, buttered side up. In the skillet, toast sandwich for 1-2 minutes on each side or until bread is lightly browned.

YIELD: 1 serving.

NUTRITION FACTS: 1 sandwich equals 299 calories, 11 g fat (6 g saturated fat), 50 mg cholesterol, 678 mg sodium, 31 g carbohydrate, 4 g fiber, 21 g protein. **DIABETIC EXCHANGES:** 2 starch, 2 lean meat, 1/2 fat.

TOASTED SANDWICH WITH A TWIST

299 CALORIES

304 CALORIES

TURKEY SLOPPY JOES

turkey sloppy joes

Lisa Ann Panzino-DiNunzio | VINELAND, NEW JERSEY

Letting all the flavors combine in the slow cooker is the key to these mildly sweet sloppy joes. This recipe is sure to be a keeper, and since it calls for turkey, you can feel good about serving it to your whole family.

  2 pounds lean ground turkey
  1 medium onion, finely chopped
  1 small green pepper, chopped
  2 cans (8 ounces *each*) no-salt-added tomato sauce
  1 cup water
  2 envelopes sloppy joe mix
  1 tablespoon brown sugar
 10 hamburger buns, split

- In a large nonstick skillet coated with cooking spray, cook the turkey, onion and pepper over medium heat until meat is no longer pink; drain. Transfer to a 3-qt. slow cooker.

- Stir in the tomato sauce, water, sloppy joe mix and brown sugar. Cover and cook on low for 4-5 hours or until flavors are blended. Spoon 1/2 cup onto each bun.

YIELD: 10 servings.

NUTRITION FACTS: 1 sandwich equals 304 calories, 9 g fat (3 g saturated fat), 72 mg cholesterol, 870 mg sodium, 33 g carbohydrate, 2 g fiber, 20 g protein.

OPEN-FACED MEATBALL SANDWICHES

277 CALORIES

open-faced meatball sandwiches

Karen Barthel | NORTH CANTON, OHIO

My husband and I love classic meatball subs, but I wanted to create a version that's fast to fix after a long day. This recipe comes together in a snap, and the meatballs are freezer-friendly as well.

- 1/4 cup egg substitute
- 1/2 cup soft bread crumbs
- 1/4 cup finely chopped onion
- 2 garlic cloves, minced
- 1/2 teaspoon onion powder
- 1/2 teaspoon dried oregano
- 1/2 teaspoon dried basil
- 1/4 teaspoon pepper

Dash salt

- 1-1/4 pounds lean ground beef (90% lean)
- 2 cups garden-style pasta sauce
- 4 hoagie buns, split
- 2 tablespoons shredded part-skim mozzarella cheese

Shredded Parmesan cheese, optional

- In a large bowl, combine the first nine ingredients. Crumble beef over mixture and mix well. Shape into 40 meatballs. In a large skillet coated with cooking spray, brown meatballs in batches; drain.

- Place meatballs in a large saucepan. Add pasta sauce; bring to a boil. Reduce heat; cover and simmer for 10-15 minutes or until meat is no longer pink. Spoon meatballs and sauce onto bun halves; sprinkle with mozzarella and Parmesan cheese if desired.

YIELD: 8 servings.

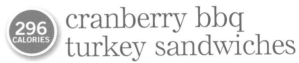

NUTRITION FACTS: 1 sandwich (calculated without Parmesan cheese) equals 277 calories, 10 g fat (4 g saturated fat), 47 mg cholesterol, 506 mg sodium, 28 g carbohydrate, 3 g fiber, 20 g protein.

296 CALORIES

cranberry bbq turkey sandwiches

Susan Matthews | ROCKFORD, ILLINOIS

This slightly sweet sandwich is a great way to use up leftover turkey. Keep the meat warm in a slow cooker at your next potluck, and you're sure to impress friends and family.

- 1 can (14 ounces) jellied cranberry sauce
- 1 cup reduced-sodium beef broth
- 1/4 cup sugar
- 1/4 cup ketchup
- 2 tablespoons cider vinegar
- 1 tablespoon Worcestershire sauce
- 1 teaspoon yellow mustard
- 1/4 teaspoon garlic powder
- 1/8 teaspoon seasoned salt
- 1/8 teaspoon paprika
- 6 cups shredded cooked turkey breast
- 12 sandwich buns, split

- In a large saucepan, combine the first 10 ingredients. Bring to a boil. Reduce heat; simmer, uncovered, for 20 minutes or until sauce is thickened.

- Stir in turkey; simmer 4-5 minutes longer or until heated through. Spoon 1/2 cup onto each bun.

YIELD: 12 servings.

NUTRITION FACTS: 1 sandwich equals 296 calories, 3 g fat (1 g saturated fat), 61 mg cholesterol, 388 mg sodium, 41 g carbohydrate, 1 g fiber, 25 g protein. **DIABETIC EXCHANGES:** 3 lean meat, 2-1/2 starch.

honey-dijon chicken salad

Janelle Hensley | HARRISONBURG, VIRGINIA

This delightful main-dish salad has an easy sauce/ dressing that lends a sweet-tangy flavor to the mix. You can add or substitute vegetables to suit your taste.

- 1/2 pound chicken tenderloins, cut into 1-1/2-inch pieces
- 2 tablespoons honey, *divided*
- 2 tablespoons Dijon mustard, *divided*
- 3 cups torn leaf lettuce
- 2 hard-cooked eggs, chopped
- 2 tablespoons *each* chopped green, sweet orange and yellow pepper
- 1 tablespoon chopped onion
- 2 teaspoons sesame seeds

- Place chicken in a 1-1/2-qt. baking dish coated with cooking spray. Combine 1 tablespoon each of honey and mustard; pour over chicken. Cover and bake at 350° for 20-25 minutes or until meat is no longer pink.

- In a large bowl, combine the lettuce, eggs, peppers, onion and sesame seeds; divide between two plates. Top with chicken. Combine remaining honey and mustard; drizzle over chicken.

YIELD: 2 servings.

NUTRITION FACTS: 1 serving equals 301 calories, 9 g fat (2 g saturated fat), 279 mg cholesterol, 498 mg sodium, 25 g carbohydrate, 2 g fiber, 35 g protein. **DIABETIC EXCHANGES:** 4 lean meat, 2 vegetable, 1 starch.

HONEY-DIJON CHICKEN SALAD

301 CALORIES

255 CALORIES

GREEK SALAD PITAS

greek salad pitas

Alexis Worchesky-Lasek | WEST FRIENDSHIP, MARYLAND

Veggie lovers, here's a full-flavored recipe just for you! This hearty, meatless pita is stuffed with plenty of chopped vegetables and savory Greek accents.

- 2/3 cup chopped seeded cucumber
- 2/3 cup chopped sweet red pepper
- 2/3 cup chopped tomato
- 2/3 cup chopped zucchini
- 1/4 cup crumbled feta cheese
- 2 tablespoons chopped ripe olives
- 2 teaspoons red wine vinegar
- 2 teaspoons lemon juice
- 3/4 teaspoon dried oregano
- 1/8 teaspoon salt
- 1/8 teaspoon pepper
- 4 lettuce leaves
- 2 pita breads (6 inches), halved

- In a small bowl, combine cucumber, red pepper, tomato, zucchini, feta cheese and olives. In another bowl, whisk the vinegar, lemon juice, oregano, salt and pepper. Pour over vegetables and toss to coat. Spoon into lettuce-lined pita halves.

YIELD: 2 servings.

NUTRITION FACTS: 2 filled pita halves equals 255 calories, 4 g fat (2 g saturated fat), 8 mg cholesterol, 688 mg sodium, 45 g carbohydrate, 5 g fiber, 10 g protein. **DIABETIC EXCHANGES:** 2 starch, 2 vegetable, 1/2 fat.

barbecued turkey sandwiches

Barbara Smith | COLUMBUS, OHIO

These moist shredded turkey sandwiches are a welcome break from beef barbecue or sloppy joes. The turkey cooks in a tangy sauce made with ketchup, vinegar, Worcestershire sauce and mustard.

- 1/4 cup chopped onion
- 1 tablespoon butter
- 3 cups shredded cooked turkey
- 1/2 cup water
- 1/2 cup ketchup
- 1/4 cup red wine vinegar
- 1 tablespoon sugar
- 2 teaspoons Worcestershire sauce
- 1 teaspoon prepared mustard
- 1 teaspoon paprika
- 6 kaiser rolls, split

- In a large nonstick skillet, saute onion in butter until tender. Add the turkey, water, ketchup, vinegar, sugar, Worcestershire sauce, mustard and paprika. Bring to a boil. Reduce heat; simmer, uncovered, for 15 minutes or until sauce is thickened. Serve on rolls.

YIELD: 6 servings.

NUTRITION FACTS: 1 sandwich equals 340 calories, 8 g fat (3 g saturated fat), 56 mg cholesterol, 637 mg sodium, 39 g carbohydrate, 2 g fiber, 27 g protein. **DIABETIC EXCHANGES:** 3 lean meat, 2-1/2 starch, 1/2 fat.

BARBECUED TURKEY SANDWICHES

340 CALORIES

ITALIAN BLTS

272 CALORIES

italian blts

Joyce Moul | YORK HAVEN, PENNSYLVANIA

The brilliant method of toasting BLTs in a coating of crispy bread crumbs takes these calorie-smart sandwiches from satisfying to spectacular.

- 2 turkey bacon strips, diced
- 4 slices Italian bread (1/2-inch thick)
- 2 slices reduced-fat provolone cheese
- 2 lettuce leaves
- 1 small tomato, sliced   *classic*
- 4 teaspoons fat-free Italian salad dressing
- 1/3 cup panko (Japanese) bread crumbs

Butter-flavored cooking spray

- 1/2 teaspoon olive oil

- In a small skillet, cook the bacon over medium heat until crisp. Layer two bread slices with cheese, bacon, lettuce and tomato; top with remaining bread.

- Brush outsides of sandwiches with salad dressing. Place bread crumbs in a shallow bowl. Coat sandwiches with bread crumbs; spray with butter-flavored cooking spray.

- In a large skillet over medium heat, toast sandwiches in oil for 2-3 minutes on each side or until the bread is lightly browned.

YIELD: 2 servings.

NUTRITION FACTS: 1 sandwich equals 272 calories, 11 g fat (4 g saturated fat), 25 mg cholesterol, 761 mg sodium, 30 g carbohydrate, 2 g fiber, 13 g protein. **DIABETIC EXCHANGES:** 2 starch, 2 lean meat.

jamaican-style beef stew

James Hayes | RIDGECREST, CALIFORNIA

This delicious stew makes a hearty lunch with a lighter touch. The leaner cut of meat, herbs, seasonings and fresh vegetables make it so flavorful, you'll want another bowl for dinner!

- 1 tablespoon canola oil
- 1 tablespoon sugar
- 1-1/2 pounds beef top sirloin steak, cut into 3/4-inch cubes
- 5 plum tomatoes, finely chopped
- 3 large carrots, cut into 1/2-inch slices
- 3 celery ribs, cut into 1/2-inch slices
- 4 green onions, chopped
- 3/4 cup reduced-sodium beef broth
- 1/4 cup barbecue sauce
- 1/4 cup reduced-sodium soy sauce
- 2 tablespoons steak sauce
- 1 tablespoon garlic powder
- 1 teaspoon dried thyme
- 1/4 teaspoon ground allspice
- 1/4 teaspoon pepper
- 1/8 teaspoon hot pepper sauce
- 1 tablespoon cornstarch
- 2 tablespoons cold water

Hot cooked rice *or* mashed potatoes, optional

JAMAICAN-STYLE BEEF STEW

- In a Dutch oven, heat oil over medium-high hea[t]; [add] sugar; cook and stir for 1 minute or until lightly bro[wned]. Add beef and brown on all sides.

- Stir in the vegetables, broth, barbecue sauce, soy sauce, steak sauce and seasonings. Bring to a boil. Reduce heat; cover and simmer for 1 to 1-1/4 hours or until meat and vegetables are tender.

- Combine cornstarch and water until smooth; stir into stew. Bring to a boil; cook and stir for 2 minutes or until thickened. Serve with rice or potatoes if desired.

YIELD: 5 servings.

NUTRITION FACTS: 1 cup (calculated without rice or potatoes) equals 285 calories, 9 g fat (2 g saturated fat), 56 mg cholesterol, 892 mg sodium, 18 g carbohydrate, 3 g fiber, 32 g protein.

grecian gold medal wraps

Margee Berry | TROUT LAKE, WASHINGTON

For a healthy dish, I created these wraps with fat-free yogurt and whole wheat tortillas.

- 1/2 cup canned white kidney *or* cannellini beans, rinsed and drained
- 1/3 cup crumbled feta cheese
- 1/3 cup fat-free plain yogurt
- 1/4 cup chopped red onion
- 2 teaspoons lemon juice
- 2 small tomatoes, chopped
- 4 whole wheat tortillas (8 inches), room temperature
- 1 package (6 ounces) ready-to-use grilled chicken breast strips
- 2/3 cup torn romaine
- 2 tablespoons chopped pitted Greek olives

- In a small bowl, mash beans with a fork. Stir in the feta cheese, yogurt, onion and lemon juice. Fold in tomatoes. Spread 1/4 cup onto each tortilla. Top with chicken, romaine and olives; roll up.

YIELD: 4 servings.

NUTRITION FACTS: 1 wrap equals 279 calories, 7 g fat (2 g saturated fat), 33 mg cholesterol, 774 mg sodium, 33 g carbohydrate, 5 g fiber, 18 g protein. **DIABETIC EXCHANGES:** 2 starch, 2 lean meat, 1 fat.

270 CALORIES

OPEN-FACED SALMON SANDWICHES

open-faced salmon sandwiches

Katnee Cabeceiras | SO. PRAIRIE, WASHINGTON

I keep several cans of salmon in my pantry at all times so I never have to worry about drop-in guests. This recipe is so tasty and quick...and it doubles easily for company.

- 1 egg, lightly beaten
- 1 small onion, finely chopped
- 1 small green pepper, finely chopped
- 1/3 cup soft bread crumbs
- 1 tablespoon lemon juice
- 1 teaspoon reduced-sodium teriyaki sauce
- 1/4 teaspoon dried parsley flakes
- 1/4 teaspoon dried basil
- 1/4 teaspoon pepper
- 1 can (14-3/4 ounces) salmon, drained, bones and skin removed
- 2 English muffins, split and toasted

Lettuce leaves and tomato slices, optional

- In a small bowl, combine the first nine ingredients. Add salmon and mix well. Shape into four patties.

- In a large nonstick skillet coated with cooking spray, cook patties over medium heat for 4-5 minutes on each side or until lightly browned. Serve on English muffin halves with lettuce and tomato if desired.

YIELD: 4 servings.

NUTRITION FACTS: 1 sandwich equals 270 calories, 10 g fat (2 g saturated fat), 99 mg cholesterol, 757 mg sodium, 19 g carbohydrate, 2 g fiber, 26 g protein. **DIABETIC EXCHANGES:** 3 lean meat, 1 starch.

turkey a la king

Pat Lemke | BRANDON, WISCONSIN

I like to make this dish with leftover turkey. It's a nice change from casseroles and so simple. Serve it over rice, noodles, biscuits or toast.

- 1-3/4 cups sliced fresh mushrooms
- 1 celery rib, chopped
- 1/4 cup chopped onion
- 1/4 cup chopped green pepper
- 2 tablespoons butter
- 1/4 cup all-purpose flour
- 1 cup reduced-sodium chicken broth
- 1 cup fat-free milk
- 2 cups cubed cooked turkey breast
- 1 cup frozen peas
- 1/2 teaspoon salt
- 2 cups hot cooked rice

- In a large nonstick skillet, saute the mushrooms, celery, onion and pepper in butter until tender.

- Combine flour and broth until smooth; stir into vegetable mixture. Stir in milk. Bring to a boil. Cook and stir for 2 minutes or until thickened. Add the turkey, peas and salt; heat through. Serve with rice.

YIELD: 4 servings.

NUTRITION FACTS: 1-1/4 cups turkey mixture with 1/2 cup rice equals 350 calories, 7 g fat (4 g saturated fat), 76 mg cholesterol, 594 mg sodium, 40 g carbohydrate, 3 g fiber, 30 g protein. **DIABETIC EXCHANGES:** 3 lean meat, 2 starch, 1-1/2 fat, 1 vegetable.

TURKEY A LA KING

350 CALORIES

301 CALORIES

SLOW-COOKED PORK TACOS

slow-cooked pork tacos

Kathleen Wolf | NAPERVILLE, ILLINOIS

Often I'll substitute Bibb lettuce leaves for the tortillas to make crunchy lettuce wraps, and I find that any extras are perfect for burritos.

- 1 boneless pork sirloin roast (2 pounds), cut into 1-inch pieces
- 1-1/2 cups salsa verde
- 1 medium sweet red pepper, chopped
- 1 medium onion, chopped
- 1/4 cup chopped dried apricots
- 2 tablespoons lime juice
- 2 garlic cloves, minced
- 1 teaspoon ground cumin
- 1/2 teaspoon salt
- 1/4 teaspoon white pepper

Dash hot pepper sauce

- 10 flour tortillas (8 inches), warmed

Reduced-fat sour cream, thinly sliced green onions, cubed avocado, shredded reduced-fat cheddar cheese and chopped tomato, optional

- In a 3-qt. slow cooker, combine the first 11 ingredients. Cover and cook on high for 4-5 hours or until meat is very tender.

- Shred pork with two forks. Place about 1/2 cup pork mixture down the center of each tortilla. Serve with toppings if desired.

YIELD: 10 tacos.

NUTRITION FACTS: 1 taco (calculated without optional toppings) equals 301 calories, 8 g fat (2 g saturated fat), 54 mg cholesterol, 616 mg sodium, 32 g carbohydrate, 1 g fiber, 24 g protein. DIABETIC EXCHANGES: 3 lean meat, 2 starch.

pastrami deli wraps

Nila Grahl | GURNEE, ILLINOIS

I sometimes add horseradish when I make this wonderful wrap for my husband.

- 1/4 cup reduced-fat spreadable cream cheese
- 1/4 cup coarsely chopped roasted sweet red pepper
- 4 spinach tortillas (8 inches)
- 4 lettuce leaves
- 4 slices deli pastrami
- 4 slices reduced-fat provolone cheese
- 1/4 cup thinly sliced red onion
- 1 small sweet red pepper, julienned
- 1/2 cup chopped cucumber

- Place cream cheese and roasted pepper in a small food processor. Cover and process until blended. Spread over tortillas. Layer with remaining ingredients; roll up. Secure with toothpicks.

YIELD: 4 servings.

NUTRITION FACTS: 1 wrap equals 271 calories, 10 g fat (4 g saturated fat), 29 mg cholesterol, 697 mg sodium, 29 g carbohydrate, 1 g fiber, 15 g protein. DIABETIC EXCHANGES: 2 medium-fat meat, 1-1/2 starch, 1 vegetable, 1 fat.

PASTRAMI DELI WRAPS

271 CALORIES

trimmed-down cream of tomato soup

Linda Parkhurst | BROOKLYN, MICHIGAN

A surefire chill chaser, this delightful soup has all of the creamy goodness of a full-fat version I used to enjoy. The seasoned crackers are a great touch.

- 1 can (14-1/2 ounces) stewed tomatoes
- 4 ounces reduced-fat cream cheese, cubed
- 1 medium onion, chopped
- 2 tablespoons butter
- 2 garlic cloves, minced
- 3 cans (10-3/4 ounces *each*) reduced-sodium condensed tomato soup, undiluted
- 4 cans (5-1/2 ounces *each*) reduced-sodium V8 juice
- 3 tablespoons tomato paste
- 1 cup fat-free half-and-half
- 1/2 teaspoon dried basil

SEASONED OYSTER CRACKERS:

- 3 cups oyster crackers
- 2 tablespoons canola oil
- 1 tablespoon ranch salad dressing mix
- 1/2 teaspoon garlic powder
- 1/2 teaspoon dill weed
- 9 tablespoons shredded part-skim mozzarella cheese

TRIMMED-DOWN CREAM OF TOMATO SOUP

303 CALORIES

- In a food processor, combine stewed tomatoes and cream cheese; cover and process until smooth. Set aside.

- In a large saucepan, saute onion in butter until crisp-tender; Add garlic; cook 1 minute longer. Whisk in tomato soup, V8 and tomato paste until blended. Gradually stir in cream cheese mixture, half-and-half and basil. Cook and stir until heated through (do not boil).

- In a large bowl, combine the oyster crackers, oil, dressing mix, garlic powder and dill; toss to coat. Ladle soup into bowls; sprinkle with crackers and cheese.

YIELD: 9 servings (3 cups crackers).

NUTRITION FACTS: 1 cup soup with 1/3 cup oyster crackers equals 303 calories, 12 g fat (5 g saturated fat), 20 mg cholesterol, 893 mg sodium, 39 g carbohydrate, 3 g fiber, 8 g protein. **DIABETIC EXCHANGES:** 2-1/2 starch, 2 fat.

fruited turkey wraps

332 CALORIES

Lisa Renshaw | KANSAS CITY, MISSOURI

This colorful wrap tastes great and is so good for you. It's packed with lean protein, fruit and veggies and wrapped in whole-grain goodness!

- 1/2 cup fat-free mayonnaise
- 1 tablespoon orange juice
- 1 teaspoon grated orange peel
- 3/4 teaspoon curry powder
- 4 whole wheat tortillas (8 inches), room temperature
- 2 cups finely shredded Chinese *or* napa cabbage
- 1/2 cup thinly sliced red onion
- 1 can (11 ounces) mandarin oranges, drained
- 2/3 cup dried cranberries
- 1/2 pound thinly sliced deli smoked turkey

- Combine the mayonnaise, orange juice, peel and curry; spread over tortillas. Top with the cabbage, onion, oranges, cranberries and turkey. Roll up.

YIELD: 4 servings.

NUTRITION FACTS: 1 wrap equals 332 calories, 5 g fat (trace saturated fat), 23 mg cholesterol, 845 mg sodium, 54 g carbohydrate, 5 g fiber, 17 g protein.

312 CALORIES

BUFFALO TURKEY BURGERS

buffalo turkey burgers

Mary Pax-Shipley | BEND, OREGON

There's nothing bland about these juicy turkey burgers! Celery and blue cheese salad dressing help tame the hot sauce. For an even skinnier version, skip the bun and add sliced onion and chopped tomato.

  2 tablespoons Louisiana-style hot sauce, *divided*
  2 teaspoons ground cumin
  2 teaspoons chili powder
  2 garlic cloves, minced
1/2 teaspoon salt
1/8 teaspoon pepper
  1 pound lean ground turkey
  4 whole wheat hamburger buns, split
  1 cup shredded lettuce
  2 celery ribs, chopped
  2 tablespoons fat-free blue cheese salad dressing

- In a large bowl, combine 1 tablespoon hot sauce, cumin, chili powder, garlic, salt and pepper. Crumble turkey over mixture and mix well. Shape into four patties.

- In a large nonstick skillet coated with cooking spray, cook patties over medium heat for 4-5 minutes on each side or until a meat thermometer reads 165° and juices run clear.

- Serve on buns with lettuce, celery, blue cheese dressing and remaining hot sauce.

YIELD: 4 servings.

NUTRITION FACTS: 1 burger equals 312 calories, 12 g fat (3 g saturated fat), 90 mg cholesterol, 734 mg sodium, 28 g carbohydrate, 5 g fiber, 24 g protein. **DIABETIC EXCHANGES:** 3 lean meat, 2 starch, 1/2 fat.

hearty bean burritos

This super-easy entree bursts with flavor, thanks to tasty spices, tomatoes and a cream-cheese filling. Our kitchen staff recommend them for lunch or dinner.

1/2 cup instant brown rice
  1 small green pepper, chopped
  2 teaspoons canola oil
  1 can (15 ounces) pinto beans, rinsed and drained
  1 cup no-salt-added diced tomatoes
  4 ounces fat-free cream cheese, cubed
1/2 teaspoon chili powder
1/4 teaspoon ground cumin
1/8 teaspoon ground coriander
1/8 teaspoon dried oregano
  6 whole wheat tortillas (8 inches), warmed
3/4 cup shredded reduced-fat cheddar cheese

- Cook rice according to package directions. Meanwhile, in a large nonstick skillet, saute pepper in oil until tender. In a large bowl, coarsely mash beans. Add the beans, tomatoes, cream cheese and seasonings to the skillet. Cook and stir until heated through; stir in rice.

- Spoon scant 1/2 cup filling off center on each tortilla. Sprinkle with 2 tablespoons cheese. Fold sides and ends over filling and roll up. Serve immediately.

YIELD: 6 servings.

NUTRITION FACTS: 1 burrito equals 314 calories, 8 g fat (2 g saturated fat), 12 mg cholesterol, 479 mg sodium, 43 g carbohydrate, 6 g fiber, 15 g protein. **DIABETIC EXCHANGES:** 3 starch, 1 lean meat, 1 fat.

HEARTY BEAN BURRITOS

314 CALORIES

351-450 calories

chicken fried rice

David Tiren | CATONSVILLE, MARYLAND
I use leftover chicken and rice to make this classic Chinese recipe that is enhanced with soy sauce and green onions.

- 1/4 cup chopped fresh mushrooms
- 1 tablespoon canola oil
- 1-1/2 cups cold cooked long grain rice
- 3/4 cup cubed cooked chicken
- 2 tablespoons reduced-sodium soy sauce
- 1 egg, lightly beaten
- 1 green onion, sliced

- In a large skillet or wok, stir-fry mushrooms in oil until tender. Stir in the rice, chicken and soy sauce. Cook over low heat for 8-10 minutes, stirring occasionally.

- Add egg and onion; cook and stir for 1-2 minutes or until egg is set.

YIELD: 2 servings.

NUTRITION FACTS: 1 cup equals 368 calories, 14 g fat (2 g saturated fat), 153 mg cholesterol, 684 mg sodium, 36 g carbohydrate, 1 g fiber, 23 g protein.

CHICKEN FRIED RICE

368 CALORIES

358 CALORIES

CHICKEN CAESAR DELUXE PIZZA

chicken caesar deluxe pizza

Erin Hamann | REESEVILLE, WISCONSIN
Here is my favorite pizza recipe. The tomatoes really add color, and it's definitely worth the time it takes to put together!

- 1 pound boneless skinless chicken breasts, cubed
- 1 teaspoon dried rosemary, crushed
- 1 tablespoon olive oil
- 1-3/4 cups all-purpose flour
- 1 cup whole wheat flour
- 4 teaspoons sugar
- 1 package (1/4 ounce) quick-rise yeast
- 3/4 teaspoon salt
- 1 teaspoon dried basil
- 1-1/4 cups warm water (120° to 130°)
- 3/4 cup reduced-fat Caesar vinaigrette
- 2 cups fresh baby spinach
- 1 small green pepper, chopped
- 1/2 cup chopped fresh mushrooms
- 1/3 cup finely chopped onion
- 1-3/4 cups shredded part-skim mozzarella cheese
- 4 plum tomatoes, chopped

- In a large skillet over medium heat, cook chicken and rosemary in oil until chicken is no longer pink; set aside.

- In a large bowl, combine 1-1/4 cups all-purpose flour, whole wheat flour, sugar, yeast, salt and basil. Add water; beat just until moistened. Stir in enough remaining all-purpose flour to form a soft dough (dough will be sticky). Turn onto a lightly floured surface; knead until smooth and elastic, about 5 minutes. Cover and rest for 10 minutes.

- Press dough onto the bottom and up the sides of a 15-in. x 10-in. x 1-in. baking pan coated with cooking spray. Bake at 400° for 7-9 minutes or until lightly browned.

- Spread vinaigrette over crust. Layer with spinach, green pepper, mushrooms, onion and chicken. Sprinkle with cheese and tomatoes. Bake for 20-25 minutes or until crust is golden brown and cheese is melted.

YIELD: 8 pieces.

NUTRITION FACTS: 1 piece equals 358 calories, 11 g fat (4 g saturated fat), 47 mg cholesterol, 794 mg sodium, 39 g carbohydrate, 4 g fiber, 24 g protein. **DIABETIC EXCHANGES:** 3 lean meat, 2-1/2 starch, 1 fat.

fully loaded chili

Cynthia Baca | CRANBERRY TOWNSHIP, PENNSYLVANIA

With lean ground beef, four types of beans and lots of seasonings and toppings, this chili is truly "fully loaded." But those aren't the only heavyweights in here; every serving provides a hefty 26 g protein and 11 g fiber.

- 1 **pound lean ground beef (90% lean)**
- 1 **medium onion, chopped**
- 1 **medium green pepper, chopped**
- 1-3/4 **cups water**
- 2 **cans (8 ounces _each_) tomato sauce**
- 1 **can (16 ounces) kidney beans, rinsed and drained**
- 1 **can (15-1/2 ounces) great northern beans, rinsed and drained**
- 1 **can (15 ounces) garbanzo beans _or_ chickpeas, rinsed and drained**
- 1 **can (15 ounces) black beans, rinsed and drained**

- 1 **tablespoon baking cocoa**
- 2 **teaspoons Louisiana-style hot sauce**
- 1/2 **teaspoon pepper**
- 1/2 **teaspoon chili powder**
- 1/4 **teaspoon garlic powder**
- 1/8 **teaspoon cayenne pepper**

GARNISHES:
- 1/2 **cup reduced-fat sour cream**
- 1/2 **cup crushed baked tortilla chip scoops**
- 1/2 **cup shredded reduced-fat cheddar cheese**

- In a Dutch oven over medium heat, cook the beef, onion and pepper until meat is no longer pink; drain.

- Stir in the water, tomato sauce, beans, cocoa, hot sauce and seasonings. Bring to a boil. Reduce heat; cover and simmer for 30 minutes.

- Garnish each serving with 1 tablespoon each of sour cream, crushed chips and cheese.

YIELD: 8 servings (2 quarts).

NUTRITION FACTS: 1 cup equals 351 calories, 9 g fat (4 g saturated fat), 38 mg cholesterol, 762 mg sodium, 42 g carbohydrate, 11 g fiber, 26 g protein.

FULLY LOADED CHILI

351 CALORIES

fruited turkey salad pitas

Donna Noel | GRAY, MAINE

Leftover turkey gets dressed up with this tasty idea that feeds a crowd. Apples, pecans and celery give this delightful turkey salad a nice crunch.

- 1/2 cup reduced-fat plain yogurt
- 1/2 cup reduced-fat mayonnaise
- 2 tablespoons lemon juice
- 1/2 teaspoon pepper
- 4 cups cubed cooked turkey breast
- 2 celery ribs, thinly sliced
- 1 medium apple, peeled and chopped
- 1/2 cup finely chopped fresh spinach
- 1/3 cup dried cranberries
- 1/3 cup chopped pecans
- 8 pita breads (6 inches), halved
- 16 romaine leaves
- 8 slices red onion, separated into rings

- In a small bowl, combine the yogurt, mayonnaise, lemon juice and pepper. In a large bowl, combine the turkey, celery, apple, spinach, cranberries and pecans. Add yogurt mixture and stir to coat. Cover and refrigerate until chilled.

- Line pita halves with lettuce and onion; fill each with 1/2 cup turkey mixture.

YIELD: 8 servings.

NUTRITION FACTS: 2 filled pita halves equals 393 calories, 11 g fat (2 g saturated fat), 66 mg cholesterol, 501 mg sodium, 45 g carbohydrate, 3 g fiber, 29 g protein. **DIABETIC EXCHANGES:** 3 starch, 3 lean meat, 1 fat.

FRUITED TURKEY SALAD PITAS

393 CALORIES

371 CALORIES

BLACK BEAN CORN CHOWDER

black bean corn chowder

Shelly Platten | AMHERST, WISCONSIN

This thick Southwestern-style chowder is seasoned with salsa, lime juice and cumin. I first made this for a special lunch with my daughter. We like it with baked tortilla chips.

- 1/2 cup half-and-half cream
- 1 can (15 ounces) black beans, rinsed and drained, *divided*
- 1/2 cup chopped onion
- 1 teaspoon olive oil
- 2 garlic cloves, minced
- 1/2 cup salsa
- 1/3 cup fresh *or* frozen corn
- 1 tablespoon lime juice
- 3/4 teaspoon ground cumin
- 1/2 medium ripe avocado, peeled and chopped

Sour cream and shredded cheddar cheese, optional

- In a blender, combine cream and 3/4 cup black beans; cover and process until smooth. Set aside.

- In a small saucepan, saute onion in oil until tender. Add garlic; cook 1 minute longer. Stir in the salsa, corn, lime juice, cumin and remaining beans.

- Reduce heat; stir in cream mixture. Cook, uncovered, for 2-3 minutes or until heated through. Stir in avocado. Serve with sour cream and cheese if desired.

YIELD: 2 servings.

NUTRITION FACTS: 1 cup (prepared with fat-free half-and-half; calculated without sour cream and cheese) equals 371 calories, 10 g fat (1 g saturated fat), 0 cholesterol, 741 mg sodium, 52 g carbohydrate, 12 g fiber, 15 g protein.

makeover
gourmet enchiladas

Beth Dauenhauer | PUEBLO, COLORADO

The Taste of Home kitchen pros created a healthier version of my dish by tweaking the original. With this better-for-you recipe, now we can enjoy great enchilada flavor more often!

- 1 pound lean ground beef (90% lean)
- 1 pound extra-lean ground turkey

MAKEOVER GOURMET ENCHILADAS

358 CALORIES

- 1 large onion, chopped
- 1-1/2 cups (12 ounces) 2% cottage cheese
- 1-1/2 cups (12 ounces) reduced-fat sour cream
- 2 cans (4 ounces *each*) chopped green chilies
- 1/2 teaspoon ground cumin
- 1/2 teaspoon ground coriander

SAUCE:
- 1 medium onion, chopped
- 2 cans (8 ounces *each*) tomato sauce
- 1 cup salsa
- 1 tablespoon chili powder
- 1 teaspoon dried oregano
- 1/2 teaspoon garlic powder
- 1/2 teaspoon dried thyme
- 12 whole wheat tortilla (8 inches), warmed
- 3/4 cup shredded cheddar cheese, *divided*

- In a large skillet, cook the beef, turkey and onion over medium heat until meat is no longer pink; drain. Stir in the cottage cheese, sour cream, chilies, cumin and coriander; set aside.

- For sauce, in a large nonstick skillet coated with cooking spray, saute onion until tender. Stir in the tomato sauce, salsa, chili powder, oregano, garlic powder and thyme. Bring to a boil. Reduce heat; simmer, uncovered, for 15-20 minutes or until slightly thickened.

- Place a heaping 1/2 cup meat mixture down the center of each tortilla. Roll up and place seam side down in two 13-in. x 9-in. baking dishes coated with cooking spray. Pour sauce over top.

- Cover and freeze one dish for up to 3 months. Bake the remaining dish, uncovered, at 350° for 30-35 minutes or until heated through. Sprinkle with 6 tablespoons cheese; bake 5 minutes longer or until cheese is melted.

- **TO USE FROZEN ENCHILADAS:** Thaw in refrigerator overnight. Remove from the refrigerator 30 minutes before baking. Cover and bake as directed.

YIELD: 2 dishes (6 servings each).

NUTRITION FACTS: 1 enchilada equals 358 calories, 12 g fat (5 g saturated fat), 55 mg cholesterol, 715 mg sodium, 33 g carbohydrate, 3 g fiber, 28 g protein. **DIABETIC EXCHANGES:** 3 lean meat, 2 starch, 1 vegetable, 1 fat.

417 CALORIES

PULLED PORK SUBS

pulled pork subs

Denise Davis I PORTER, MAINE

Honey and ground ginger are the flavor boosters behind my slow-cooked sandwiches. A bottle of barbecue sauce ties it all together in a pinch.

- 1 small onion, finely chopped
- 1 boneless pork shoulder butt roast (2-1/2 pounds)
- 1 bottle (18 ounces) barbecue sauce
- 1/2 cup water
- 1/4 cup honey
- 6 garlic cloves, minced
- 1 teaspoon seasoned salt
- 1 teaspoon ground ginger
- 8 submarine buns, split

- Place onion and roast in a 5-qt. slow cooker. In a small bowl, combine the barbecue sauce, water, honey, garlic, seasoned salt and ginger; pour over meat. Cover and cook on high for 5-6 hours or until meat is tender.

- Remove meat; cool slightly. Shred meat with two forks and return to the slow cooker; heat through. Serve on buns. Cut sandwiches in half.

YIELD: 16 servings.

NUTRITION FACTS: 1/2 sub sandwich equals 417 calories, 13 g fat (4 g saturated fat), 81 mg cholesterol, 867 mg sodium, 44 g carbohydrate, 2 g fiber, 29 g protein.

grilled chicken salad

Mary Campe I LAKEWOOD, COLORADO

Perfect for two, this pretty entree salad features strips of hearty grilled chicken. Tomatoes, dried cranberries, olives and walnuts add wonderful flavor to each forkful.

- 2 boneless skinless chicken breast halves (6 ounces *each*)
- 3 cups torn mixed salad greens
- 1 small tomato, chopped
- 1/4 cup dried cranberries
- 1/4 cup shredded reduced-fat cheddar cheese
- 1/4 cup sliced ripe olives
- 2 green onions, chopped
- 2 tablespoons chopped walnuts
- 1/4 cup fat-free Italian salad dressing

- Using long-handled tongs, dip a paper towel in cooking oil and lightly coat the grill rack. Grill chicken, covered, over medium heat or broil 4 in. from the heat for 8-10 minutes on each side or until a meat thermometer reads 170° and chicken juices run clear.

- Divide salad greens between two serving plates; top with tomato, cranberries, cheese, olives, onions and walnuts. Slice the chicken; arrange the chicken over salads. Serve with Italian dressing.

YIELD: 2 servings.

NUTRITION FACTS: 1 serving equals 383 calories, 14 g fat (4 g saturated fat), 105 mg cholesterol, 776 mg sodium, 24 g carbohydrate, 5 g fiber, 42 g protein. **DIABETIC EXCHANGES:** 5 lean meat, 1-1/2 starch, 1 vegetable, 1 fat.

GRILLED CHICKEN SALAD

383 CALORIES

BAKED POTATO PIZZA

- Arrange potato slices in a single layer over dough; sprinkle with salt and pepper. Top with cheeses. Bake at 400° for 22-28 minutes or until crust is golden and cheese is melted.

- Sprinkle with bacon, onions and chives. Serve with sour cream if desired.

YIELD: 12 pieces.

EDITOR'S NOTE: This recipe was tested with Land O'Lakes light stick butter.

NUTRITION FACTS: 2 pieces (calculated without sour cream) equals 359 calories, 11 g fat (5 g saturated fat), 36 mg cholesterol, 799 mg sodium, 48 g carbohydrate, 1 g fiber, 14 g protein.

baked potato pizza

Charlotte Gehle | BROWNSTOWN, MICHIGAN

I wanted to recreate a light version of a restaurant pizza my friends and I used to get all the time in college. Here's what I came up with!

- 3 medium potatoes, peeled and cut into 1/8-inch slices
- 1 loaf (1 pound) frozen pizza dough, thawed
- 3 tablespoons reduced-fat butter
- 4 garlic cloves, minced
- 1/4 teaspoon salt
- 1/4 teaspoon pepper
- 1 cup (4 ounces) shredded part-skim mozzarella cheese
- 1/4 cup shredded Parmigiano-Reggiano cheese
- 6 turkey bacon strips, cooked and crumbled
- 2 green onions, chopped
- 2 tablespoons minced chives

Reduced-fat sour cream, optional

- Place potatoes in a small saucepan and cover with water. Bring to a boil. Reduce heat; cover and simmer for 15 minutes or until tender. Drain and pat dry.

- Unroll dough onto a 14-in. pizza pan coated with cooking spray; flatten dough and build up edges slightly. In a microwave-safe bowl, melt the butter with garlic; brush over the dough.

turkey avocado sandwiches

Dave Bremson | PLANTATION, FLORIDA

I like to jazz up a plain turkey sandwich with vegetables and fresh cilantro from my garden. I combine zesty taco sauce with fat-free cream cheese for a low-calorie spread. A little hot pepper sauce quickly kicks the heat up a notch.

- 3 ounces fat-free cream cheese
- 2 teaspoons taco sauce
- 4 drops hot pepper sauce
- 4 slices whole wheat bread
- 4 ounces sliced cooked turkey
- 1/2 medium ripe avocado, peeled and sliced
- 1 medium ripe tomato, sliced
- 2 to 4 tablespoons minced fresh cilantro
- 2 lettuce leaves

- In a large bowl, beat cream cheese until smooth; beat in taco sauce and pepper sauce. Spread on each slice of bread.

- Layer the turkey, avocado and tomato on two slices of bread; sprinkle with cilantro. Top with lettuce and remaining bread.

YIELD: 2 servings.

NUTRITION FACTS: 1 sandwich equals 399 calories, 11 g fat (2 g saturated fat), 52 mg cholesterol, 617 mg sodium, 40 g carbohydrate, 7 g fiber, 33 g protein. **DIABETIC EXCHANGES:** 3 lean meat, 2 starch, 1 vegetable, 1 fat.

fettuccine with mushrooms and tomatoes

Phyllis Schmalz | KANSAS CITY, KANSAS

Not only is this comforting dish fast, but it's elegant enough to serve guests.

- 1 package (12 ounces) fettuccine
- 1 pound fresh mushrooms, halved
- 1 large onion, chopped
- 1 large green pepper, chopped
- 1 teaspoon olive oil
- 4 garlic cloves, minced
- 3 tablespoons all-purpose flour
- 3 cups 1% milk
- 1 teaspoon salt
- 1/4 teaspoon pepper
- 1/2 cup sun-dried tomatoes (not packed in oil), thinly sliced
- 1 cup (4 ounces) shredded reduced-fat Swiss cheese
- 1/4 cup grated Parmesan cheese

- Cook the fettuccine according to package directions. In a large nonstick skillet, saute the mushrooms, onion and green pepper in oil for 4-6 minutes or until vegetables are tender. Add garlic; cook 1 minute longer.

FETTUCCINE WITH MUSHROOMS AND TOMATOES

- In a small bowl, combine the flour, milk, salt and pepper until smooth; gradually stir into mushroom mixture. Add tomatoes. Bring to a boil; cook and stir for 2 minutes or until thickened. Stir in cheeses. Drain fettuccine; toss with the sauce.

YIELD: 6 servings.

NUTRITION FACTS: 1-1/3 cups equals 387 calories, 8 g fat (4 g saturated fat), 17 mg cholesterol, 662 mg sodium, 60 g carbohydrate, 5 g fiber, 23 g protein.

veggie chicken pitas

Bill Parkis | WILMINGTON, NORTH CAROLINA

These delicious pita pockets make for great on-the-go lunches...just be sure to bring a napkin!

- 1 medium red onion, sliced
- 1 cup julienned carrots
- 1 cup chopped fresh broccoli
- 1 cup fresh snow peas
- 2 tablespoons olive oil
- 1/2 teaspoon minced garlic
- 1 cup cubed cooked chicken
- 1 jar (7 ounces) roasted sweet red peppers, drained and chopped
- 1/4 cup white wine *or* chicken broth
- 1/2 teaspoon dried oregano
- 1/2 teaspoon cayenne pepper
- 5 pita breads (6 inches), halved
- 1/3 cup shredded part-skim mozzarella cheese
- 1/3 cup shredded cheddar cheese

- In a large skillet, saute the onion, carrots, broccoli and peas in oil for 4-5 minutes or until tender. Add garlic; cook 1 minute longer.

- Stir in the chicken, red peppers, wine, oregano and cayenne. Bring to a boil. Reduce heat; simmer, uncovered, for 5-6 minutes or until heated through. Spoon mixture into pita breads; sprinkle with cheeses.

YIELD: 5 servings.

NUTRITION FACTS: 2 stuffed pita halves equals 373 calories, 12 g fat (4 g saturated fat), 37 mg cholesterol, 595 mg sodium, 43 g carbohydrate, 4 g fiber, 19 g protein. **DIABETIC EXCHANGES:** 2 starch, 2 lean meat, 2 vegetable, 1 fat.

slow-cooked pork barbecue

Connie Johnson | SPRINGFIELD, MISSOURI

I need only six ingredients to fix these sweet and tender pork sandwiches. I think they're perfect just the way they are, but feel free to adjust the sauce ingredients to suit your family's tastes.

- 1 boneless pork loin roast (3 to 4 pounds)
- 1-1/2 teaspoons seasoned salt
- 1 teaspoon garlic powder
- 1 cup barbecue sauce
- 1 cup cola
- 10 sandwich buns, split

- Cut roast in half; place in a 5-qt. slow cooker. Sprinkle with seasoned salt and garlic powder. Cover and cook on low for 4 hours or until meat is tender.

- Remove meat; skim fat from cooking juices. Shred meat with a fork and return to the slow cooker. Combine barbecue sauce and cola; pour over meat. Cover and cook on high for 1-2 hours or until sauce is thickened. Serve on rolls.

YIELD: 10 servings.

NUTRITION FACTS: 1 sandwich equals 410 calories, 11 g fat (3 g saturated fat), 68 mg cholesterol, 886 mg sodium, 41 g carbohydrate, 1 g fiber, 35 g protein.

SLOW-COOKED PORK BARBECUE

FIESTA RANCH BURGERS

fiesta ranch burgers

Carol Brewer | FAIRBORN, OHIO

Depending on how spicy you like your burgers, add more or less chipotle pepper, which also gives a nice smoky flavor.

- 2 egg whites, lightly beaten
- 1/2 cup canned diced tomatoes, drained
- 1/2 cup canned black beans, rinsed and drained
- 1 small onion, chopped
- 1 tablespoon lime juice
- 1 to 2 tablespoons chopped chipotle peppers in adobo sauce
- 1 garlic clove, minced
- 1/4 teaspoon salt
- 1-1/4 pounds lean ground turkey
- 1/3 cup fat-free ranch salad dressing
- 1 tablespoon minced fresh cilantro
- 5 lettuce leaves
- 5 hamburger buns, split

- In a large bowl, combine the first eight ingredients. Crumble turkey over mixture and mix well. Shape into five burgers.

- Broil 4 in. from the heat for 7-9 minutes on each side or until a meat thermometer reads 165° and juices run clear. In a small bowl, combine the salad dressing and cilantro. Serve burgers with dressing on lettuce-lined buns.

YIELD: 5 servings.

NUTRITION FACTS: 1 burger equals 357 calories, 12 g fat (3 g saturated fat), 90 mg cholesterol, 745 mg sodium, 34 g carbohydrate, 3 g fiber, 27 g protein. **DIABETIC EXCHANGES:** 3 lean meat, 2 starch.

404 CALORIES

ROASTED PEPPER CHICKEN SANDWICHES

roasted pepper chicken sandwiches

Laura Merkle | DOVER, DELAWARE

This is a wonderful, flavorful sandwich perfect for a special lunch, when hosting a weekend luncheon or if you need a casual dinner. It always gets rave reviews.

- 1 tablespoon lemon juice
- 1 tablespoon Dijon mustard
- 2 teaspoons olive oil
- 1 garlic clove, minced
- 1/4 teaspoon dried thyme
- 1/4 teaspoon dried marjoram
- 4 boneless skinless chicken breast halves (4 ounces *each*)

PEPPER MIXTURE:

- 1 large onion, thinly sliced
- 1 teaspoon sugar
- 3/4 teaspoon fennel seed, crushed
- 1/4 teaspoon crushed red pepper flakes
- 1/8 teaspoon salt
- 1/8 teaspoon pepper
- 4 garlic cloves, minced
- 1 jar (7 ounces) roasted sweet red peppers, drained and sliced
- 1 tablespoon red wine vinegar

SANDWICHES:

- 1 loaf (8 ounces) focaccia bread
- 4 teaspoons fat-free mayonnaise
- 4 slices reduced-fat Swiss cheese

- In a large resealable plastic bag, combine the first six ingredients; add chicken. Seal bag and turn to coat; refrigerate for 1 hour.

- In a large nonstick skillet coated with cooking spray, cook and stir the onion, sugar and seasonings over medium heat until tender. Add garlic; cook for 1 minute. Stir in roasted peppers and vinegar; cook 2 minutes longer. Remove from the heat; keep warm.

- Coat grill rack with cooking spray before starting the grill. Drain chicken if necessary, discarding any excess marinade. Grill chicken, covered, over medium heat for 4-7 minutes on each side or until a meat thermometer reads 170°. Cut into 1/2-in. strips.

- Cut focaccia bread in half lengthwise; spread mayonnaise over cut side of bread bottom. Layer with cheese, chicken strips and pepper mixture. Replace bread top; lightly press down. Grill, covered, for 2-3 minutes or until cheese is melted. Cut into four sandwiches.

YIELD: 4 servings.

NUTRITION FACTS: 1 sandwich equals 404 calories, 11 g fat (3 g saturated fat), 73 mg cholesterol, 795 mg sodium, 41 g carbohydrate, 2 g fiber, 35 g protein. **DIABETIC EXCHANGES:** 4 lean meat, 2 starch, 1 vegetable.

summer veggie subs

Jennie Todd | LANCASTER, PENNSYLVANIA

Every Sunday night during the summer, a local park near our home holds free outdoor concerts. We've been going for years. These subs are perfect for picnics, so I've taken them to the park several times.

- 4 medium sweet red peppers
- 1/2 cup fat-free mayonnaise
- 2 tablespoons minced fresh basil
- 1 tablespoon minced fresh parsley
- 1 tablespoon minced fresh tarragon
- 2 loaves French bread (1 pound *each*), halved lengthwise

classic

2 cups fresh baby spinach

2 cups thinly sliced cucumbers

2 cups alfalfa sprouts

4 medium tomatoes, sliced

2 medium ripe avocados, peeled and sliced

3/4 pound thinly sliced deli turkey

6 slices reduced-fat Swiss cheese, halved

- Broil peppers 4 in. from the heat until skins blister, about 5 minutes. With tongs, rotate peppers a quarter turn. Broil and rotate until all sides are blistered and blackened. Immediately place peppers in a large bowl; cover and let stand for 15-20 minutes.

- Peel off and discard charred skin. Remove stems and seeds. Julienne peppers.

- Combine the mayonnaise, basil, parsley and tarragon; spread over bread bottoms. Top with spinach, cucumbers, sprouts, roasted peppers, tomatoes, avocados, turkey and cheese. Replace tops. Cut each loaf into six slices.

YIELD: 12 servings.

NUTRITION FACTS: 1 slice equals 357 calories, 9 g fat (2 g saturated fat), 19 mg cholesterol, 894 mg sodium, 53 g carbohydrate, 6 g fiber, 20 g protein.

SUMMER VEGGIE SUBS

357 CALORIES

399 CALORIES

grilled italian meatball burgers

Priscilla Gilbert | INDIAN HARBOUR BEACH, FLORIDA

I just love these burgers! They're a big hit with children and adults alike. I serve them with sliced green peppers, tomato and onion on the side as well as a jar of crushed red peppers, but kids seem to enjoy them best "as is."

1 egg, lightly beaten

1/3 cup seasoned bread crumbs

3 garlic cloves, minced

1 teaspoon dried oregano

1 teaspoon dried basil

1/4 teaspoon salt

1/4 teaspoon dried thyme

1-1/2 pounds lean ground beef (90% lean)

1/2 pound Italian turkey sausage links, casings removed

3/4 cup shredded part-skim mozzarella cheese

8 kaiser rolls, split

1 cup roasted garlic Parmesan spaghetti sauce, warmed

- In a large bowl, combine the first seven ingredients. Crumble beef and sausage over mixture and mix well. Shape into eight burgers.

- Using long-handled tongs, dip a paper towel in cooking oil and lightly coat the grill rack. Grill burgers, covered, over medium heat or broil 4 in. from the heat for 5-7 minutes on each side or until a meat thermometer reads 165° and juices run clear.

- Sprinkle burgers with cheese; cover, grill or broil 2-3 minutes longer or until cheese is melted. Remove and keep warm.

- Grill or broil rolls, uncovered, for 1-2 minutes or until toasted. Serve burgers on rolls with spaghetti sauce.

YIELD: 8 servings.

NUTRITION FACTS: 1 burger equals 399 calories, 14 g fat (5 g saturated fat), 102 mg cholesterol, 743 mg sodium, 35 g carbohydrate, 2 g fiber, 30 g protein.

dinners

Only the Taste of Home Comfort Food Diet lets you savor classic fare such as cheesy pizzas, bubbling casseroles and juicy pork chops...and still lose weight! Aim for about 500 calories for an entire supper, so when planning your menu, be sure to save a few calories for a side dish and dessert.

183

179

195

The first section in this chapter has lower-calorie entrees you might pair with side dishes, a green salad, bread, desserts, etc. The two remaining entree areas are largely higher-calorie one-dish meals that simply need a beverage for a complete supper.

savory onion chicken

Julia Anderson I RINGGOLD, GEORGIA

Dinner doesn't get any easier than this tasty chicken entree. Buy chicken that's already cut up to save even more time on busy weeknights.

- 1/4 cup all-purpose flour, *divided*
- 1 broiler/fryer chicken (3 to 4 pounds), skin removed and cut up
- 2 tablespoons olive oil
- 1 envelope onion soup mix
- 1 bottle (12 ounces) beer *or* nonalcoholic beer

- Place 2 tablespoons flour in a large resealable plastic bag. Add chicken, a few pieces at a time, and shake to coat. In a large skillet, brown chicken in oil on all sides. Remove and keep warm.

- Add soup mix and remaining flour, stirring to loosen browned bits from pan. Gradually whisk in beer. Bring to a boil; cook and stir for 2 minutes or until thickened. Return chicken to the pan. Bring to a boil. Reduce heat; cover and simmer for 12-15 minutes or until chicken juices run clear.

YIELD: 6 servings.

NUTRITION FACTS: 1 serving equals 231 calories, 11 g fat (2 g saturated fat), 73 mg cholesterol, 469 mg sodium, 7 g carbohydrate, trace fiber, 25 g protein. **DIABETIC EXCHANGES:** 3 lean meat, 1 fat, 1/2 starch.

SAVORY ONION CHICKEN

231 CALORIES

227 CALORIES

SIZZLING BEEF KABOBS

sizzling beef kabobs

Kathy Spang I MANHEIM, PENNSYLVANIA

A mild soy sauce marinade lends an appealing flavor to these tender beef and veggie kabobs. With colorful chunks of yellow squash and sweet red and green peppers, they're perfect for parties!

- 1/3 cup canola oil
- 1/4 cup soy sauce
- 2 tablespoons red wine vinegar classic
- 2 teaspoons garlic powder
- 2 pounds beef top sirloin steak, cut into 1-inch pieces
- 2 medium yellow summer squash, cut into 1/2-inch slices
- 1 large onion, cut into 1-inch chunks
- 1 large green pepper, cut into 1-inch pieces
- 1 large sweet red pepper, cut into 1-inch pieces

- In a large resealable plastic bag, combine the oil, soy sauce, vinegar and garlic powder; add beef. Seal bag and turn to coat; refrigerate for at least 1 hour.

- Drain and discard marinade. On eight metal or soaked wooden skewers, alternately thread beef and vegetables. Grill, covered, over medium-hot heat or broil 4-6 in. from the heat for 8-10 minutes or until meat reaches desired doneness, turning occasionally.

YIELD: 8 servings.

NUTRITION FACTS: 1 kabob equals 227 calories, 12 g fat (3 g saturated fat), 63 mg cholesterol, 326 mg sodium, 6 g carbohydrate, 2 g fiber, 23 g protein. **DIABETIC EXCHANGES:** 3 lean meat, 1 vegetable, 1 fat.

honey-glazed ham

Jacquie Stolz | LITTLE SIOUX, IOWA

Here's an easy solution for feeding a large group. The simple ham is perfect for family dinners when time in the kitchen is as valuable as space in the oven.

1 boneless fully cooked ham (4 pounds)

1-1/2 cups ginger ale

1/4 cup honey

1/2 teaspoon ground mustard *classic*

1/2 teaspoon ground cloves

1/4 teaspoon ground cinnamon

Sour cream, optional

- Cut ham in half; place in a 5-qt. slow cooker. Pour ginger ale over ham. Cover and cook on low for 4-5 hours or until heated through.

- Combine the honey, mustard, cloves and cinnamon; stir until smooth. Spread over ham; cook 30 minutes longer. Garnish with sour cream if desired.

YIELD: 14 servings.

NUTRITION FACTS: 4 ounces ham equals 166 calories, 5 g fat (2 g saturated fat), 66 mg cholesterol, 1,347 mg sodium, 8 g carbohydrate, trace fiber, 24 g protein.

HONEY-GLAZED HAM

166 CALORIES

247 CALORIES

CHICKEN WITH ROSEMARY-ONION SAUCE

chicken with rosemary-onion sauce

Donna Roberts | MANHATTAN, KANSAS

This is a great dish to serve guests because it tastes like you cooked forever. There is nothing more aromatic or flavorful than chicken with rosemary.

4 boneless skinless chicken breast halves (6 ounces *each*)

1/2 teaspoon salt

1/4 teaspoon pepper

3 teaspoons butter, *divided*

1 medium onion, chopped

1 garlic clove, minced

4 teaspoons all-purpose flour

1/2 cup reduced-sodium chicken broth

1/2 cup fat-free milk

1 teaspoon dried rosemary, crushed

- Sprinkle chicken with salt and pepper. In a large nonstick skillet, brown chicken in 1 teaspoon butter. Transfer to an 11-in. x 7-in. baking dish coated with cooking spray.

- In the same skillet, saute onion and garlic in remaining butter until tender. Stir in flour until blended. Gradually stir in broth and milk. Add rosemary. Bring to a boil; cook and stir for 2 minutes or until thickened.

- Pour sauce over chicken. Cover and bake at 350° for 20-25 minutes or until chicken juices run clear.

YIELD: 4 servings.

NUTRITION FACTS: 1 chicken breast half with 1/4 cup sauce equals 247 calories, 7 g fat (3 g saturated fat), 102 mg cholesterol, 501 mg sodium, 8 g carbohydrate, 1 g fiber, 37 g protein. **DIABETIC EXCHANGES:** 5 lean meat, 1/2 starch, 1/2 fat.

crumb-topped haddock

Debbie Solt | LEWISTOWN, PENNSYLVANIA

With only five ingredients, this creamy dinner with a crispy topping is a breeze to make.

- 2 pounds haddock *or* cod fillets
- 1 can (10-3/4 ounces) condensed cream of shrimp soup, undiluted
- 1 teaspoon grated onion
- 1 teaspoon Worcestershire sauce
- 1 cup crushed butter-flavored crackers (about 25 crackers)

- Arrange the fillets in a greased 13-in. x 9-in. baking dish. Combine the soup, onion and Worcestershire sauce; pour over fish.

- Bake, uncovered, at 375° for 20 minutes. Sprinkle with cracker crumbs. Bake 15 minutes longer or until fish flakes easily with a fork.

YIELD: 6 servings.

NUTRITION FACTS: 1 serving equals 248 calories, 7 g fat (2 g saturated fat), 94 mg cholesterol, 631 mg sodium, 14 g carbohydrate, trace fiber, 31 g protein. **DIABETIC EXCHANGES:** 4 lean meat, 1 starch, 1 fat.

CRUMB-TOPPED HADDOCK

248 CALORIES

196 CALORIES

MARINATED FLANK STEAK

marinated flank steak

Lisa Ruehlow | BLAINE, MINNESOTA

A handful of kitchen staples come together quickly in this flavorful marinade that will really perk up easy-to-cook flank steak. Try placing the strips on a salad with your favorite dressing.

classic

- 3 tablespoons canola oil
- 2 tablespoons lemon juice
- 2 tablespoons Worcestershire sauce
- 1 tablespoon dried minced garlic
- 1 tablespoon Greek seasoning
- 1 tablespoon brown sugar
- 1 teaspoon onion powder
- 1 beef flank steak (1-1/2 pounds)

- In a large resealable plastic bag, combine the first seven ingredients; add the steak. Seal bag and turn to coat; refrigerate for 6 hours or overnight.

- Drain and discard marinade. Using long-handled tongs, dip a paper towel in cooking oil and lightly coat the grill rack. Grill steak, covered, over medium heat or broil 4 in. from heat for 9-11 minutes on each side or until steak reaches desired doneness (for medium-rare, a meat thermometer should read 145°; medium, 160°; well-done, 170°).

- To serve, thinly slice across the grain.

YIELD: 6 servings.

NUTRITION FACTS: 3 ounces cooked beef equals 196 calories, 11 g fat (4 g saturated fat), 54 mg cholesterol, 269 mg sodium, 2 g carbohydrate, trace fiber, 22 g protein. **DIABETIC EXCHANGES:** 3 lean meat, 1 fat.

224 CALORIES

SOUTHWESTERN GOULASH

...otle-rubbed ...f tenderloin

Go ahead, rub it in! Our home economists found that coating traditional tenderloin with lively, peppery flavors gives it a south-of-the-border twist. Your gang is bound to be impressed.

- 1 beef tenderloin roast (2 pounds)
- 2 teaspoons canola oil
- 3 teaspoons coarsely ground pepper
- 3 garlic cloves, minced
- 2-1/2 teaspoons brown sugar
- 1 teaspoon salt
- 1 teaspoon ground coriander
- 1/2 teaspoon ground chipotle pepper
- 1/4 teaspoon cayenne pepper

- Brush beef with oil. Combine the remaining ingredients; rub over meat. Cover and refrigerate for 2 hours.

- Place beef on a rack coated with cooking spray in a shallow roasting pan. Bake, uncovered, at 400° for 45-55 minutes or until meat reaches desired doneness (for medium-rare, a meat thermometer should read 145°; medium, 160°; well-done, 170°). Let stand for 10 minutes before slicing.

YIELD: 8 servings.

NUTRITION FACTS: 3 ounces cooked beef equals 195 calories, 9 g fat (3 g saturated fat), 71 mg cholesterol, 351 mg sodium, 2 g carbohydrate, trace fiber, 24 g protein. **DIABETIC EXCHANGE:** 3 lean meat.

CHIPOTLE-RUBBED BEEF TENDERLOIN

195 CALORIES

southwestern goulash

Vikki Rebholz | WEST CHESTER, OHIO
I had some extra cilantro in the fridge and didn't want to throw it away. Instead, I came up with this delightful and filling family recipe. Everyone just loved it!

- 1 cup uncooked elbow macaroni
- 1 pound lean ground beef (90% lean)
- 1 medium onion, chopped
- 1 can (28 ounces) diced tomatoes, undrained
- 2/3 cup frozen corn
- 1 can (8 ounces) tomato sauce
- 1 can (4 ounces) chopped green chilies
- 1/2 teaspoon ground cumin
- 1/2 teaspoon pepper
- 1/4 teaspoon salt
- 1/4 cup minced fresh cilantro

- Cook macaroni according to the package directions. Meanwhile, in a Dutch oven over medium heat, cook beef and onion until meat is no longer pink; drain. Stir in the tomatoes, corn, tomato sauce, chilies, cumin, pepper and salt. Bring to a boil. Reduce heat; simmer, uncovered, for 3-4 minutes or until heated through.

- Drain macaroni; add to meat mixture. Stir in cilantro and heat through.

YIELD: 6 servings.

NUTRITION FACTS: 1-1/3 cups equals 224 calories, 6 g fat (2 g saturated fat), 37 mg cholesterol, 567 mg sodium, 24 g carbohydrate, 4 g fiber, 19 g protein. **DIABETIC EXCHANGES:** 2 lean meat, 2 vegetable, 1 starch.

grilled pork chops with cilantro salsa

Lisa Ruehlow | BLAINE, MINNESOTA

These quick and easy chops make a very colorful statement when they hit the table. Your family will rave!

1-1/2	cups cubed cantaloupe
1	cup chopped tomatoes
1/2	cup chopped green pepper
2	tablespoons limeade concentrate
2	tablespoons chopped green onion
2	tablespoons minced fresh cilantro
1/4	teaspoon salt
6	bone-in pork loin chops (7 ounces *each* and 1/2 inch thick)

Pepper to taste

- In a large bowl combine the cantaloupe, tomatoes, green pepper, limeade, onion, cilantro and salt. Cover and refrigerate until serving.

- Season pork with pepper. Using long-handled tongs, dip a paper towel in cooking oil and lightly coat the grill rack. Grill, covered, over medium heat or broil 4 in. from the heat for 6-7 minutes on each side or until a meat thermometer reads 160°. Serve with salsa.

YIELD: 6 servings.

NUTRITION FACTS: 1 pork chop with 1/3 cup salsa equals 240 calories, 9 g fat (3 g saturated fat), 86 mg cholesterol, 168 mg sodium, 9 g carbohydrate, 1 g fiber, 31 g protein. **DIABETIC EXCHANGES:** 4 lean meat, 1/2 starch.

GRILLED PORK CHOPS WITH CILANTRO SALSA

240 CALORIES

214 CALORIES

PECAN-CRUSTED CHICKEN

pecan-crusted chicken

Molly Lloyd | BOURNEVILLE, OHIO

These moist, tender chicken breasts have a crunchy coating of pecans and sesame seeds. They're perfect with a side of green beans.

1/4	cup milk
1/2	cup all-purpose flour
1/2	cup finely chopped pecans
2	tablespoons sesame seeds
1-1/2	teaspoons paprika
1-1/2	teaspoons pepper
1	teaspoon salt
8	boneless skinless chicken breast halves (4 ounces *each*), partially flattened
2	tablespoons canola oil

- Place milk in a shallow bowl. In another shallow bowl, combine the flour, pecans, sesame seeds, paprika, pepper and salt. Dip chicken in milk, then coat in flour mixture.

- In a large nonstick skillet, brown chicken in oil on both sides. Transfer to a 15-in. x 10-in. x 1-in. baking pan coated with cooking spray. Bake, uncovered, at 350° for 15-20 minutes or until no longer pink.

YIELD: 8 servings.

NUTRITION FACTS: 1 chicken breast half equals 214 calories, 10 g fat (2 g saturated fat), 63 mg cholesterol, 252 mg sodium, 5 g carbohydrate, 1 g fiber, 24 g protein. **DIABETIC EXCHANGES:** 3 lean meat, 1-1/2 fat.

216 CALORIES

SPINACH-TOMATO PHYLLO BAKE

spinach-tomato phyllo bake

Shirley Kacmarik | GLASGOW, SCOTLAND

This flaky phyllo bake has an excellent mix of flavors. The low-fat main dish features tomatoes, feta and spinach with a pleasant amount of dill and nutmeg for a special meal.

    4 eggs, lightly beaten
    2 packages (10 ounces *each*) frozen chopped spinach, thawed and squeezed dry
    1 cup (4 ounces) crumbled feta cheese
1/2 cup 1% cottage cheese
    3 green onions, sliced
    1 teaspoon dill weed
1/2 teaspoon salt
1/4 teaspoon pepper
1/4 teaspoon ground nutmeg
  10 sheets phyllo dough (14 inches x 9 inches)
Butter-flavored cooking spray
    3 large tomatoes, sliced

- In a large bowl, combine the first nine ingredients; set aside.
- Spritz one sheet of phyllo dough with butter-flavored cooking spray. Place in an 8-in. square baking dish coated with cooking spray, allowing one end of dough to hang over edge of dish. Repeat with four more phyllo sheets, staggering the overhanging phyllo around edges of dish. (Keep remaining phyllo covered with plastic wrap and a damp towel to prevent it from drying out.)

- Spoon a third of the spinach mixture into crust. Layer with half of the tomatoes, another third of the spinach mixture, remaining tomatoes and remaining spinach mixture. Spritz and layer remaining phyllo dough as before.

- Gently fold ends of dough over filling and toward center of baking dish; spritz with butter-flavored spray. Cover edges with foil. Bake at 350° for 55-60 minutes or until a meat thermometer reads 160°. Let stand for 15 minutes before cutting.

YIELD: 6 servings.

NUTRITION FACTS: 1 piece equals 216 calories, 9 g fat (3 g saturated fat), 153 mg cholesterol, 652 mg sodium, 21 g carbohydrate, 5 g fiber, 15 g protein. **DIABETIC EXCHANGES:** 2 medium-fat meat, 2 vegetable, 1 starch.

italian cabbage casserole

Debra Sanders | BREVARD, NORTH CAROLINA

If your gang likes stuffed cabbage, they'll love this filling, beefy recipe. You'll find that it has all the flavor, but with a lot less work than stuffed cabbage!

    1 medium head cabbage, coarsely shredded
    1 pound lean ground beef (90% lean)
    1 large green pepper, chopped
    1 medium onion, chopped
    1 can (14-1/2 ounces) diced tomatoes, undrained

ITALIAN CABBAGE CASSEROLE

223 CALORIES

1 can (8 ounces) tomato sauce

3 tablespoons tomato paste

1-1/2 teaspoons dried oregano

1/2 teaspoon garlic powder

1/2 teaspoon pepper

1/8 teaspoon salt

1/2 cup shredded part-skim mozzarella cheese

- Place cabbage in a steamer basket; place in a large saucepan over 1 in. of water. Bring to a boil; cover and steam for 6-8 minutes or until tender. Drain and set aside.

- In a large nonstick skillet over medium heat, cook and stir the beef, green pepper and onion until meat is no longer pink; drain. Stir in the tomatoes, tomato sauce, tomato paste and seasonings. Bring to a boil. Reduce heat; simmer, uncovered, for 10 minutes.

- Place half of the cabbage in an 11-in. x 7-in. baking dish coated with cooking spray; top with half of beef mixture. Repeat layers (dish will be full). Sprinkle with cheese. Bake, uncovered, at 350° for 15-20 minutes or until heated through.

YIELD: 6 servings.

NUTRITION FACTS: 1-1/3 cups equals 223 calories, 7 g fat (3 g saturated fat), 42 mg cholesterol, 438 mg sodium, 20 g carbohydrate, 7 g fiber, 21 g protein. **DIABETIC EXCHANGES:** 2 lean meat, 1 starch, 1 vegetable.

crab-stuffed chicken breasts

Mary Plummer | DE SOTO, KANSAS

This is an elegant light chicken dish filled with crabmeat and crunchy water chestnuts.

6 boneless skinless chicken breast halves (5 ounces *each*)

1/2 teaspoon salt

1/4 teaspoon pepper

1/2 cup canned crabmeat, drained, flaked and cartilage removed

1/4 cup sliced water chestnuts, drained and chopped

2 tablespoons dry bread crumbs

225 CALORIES

CRAB-STUFFED CHICKEN BREASTS

2 tablespoons reduced-fat mayonnaise

1 tablespoon minced fresh parsley

1 teaspoon Dijon mustard

6 teaspoons marinade for chicken, *divided*

2 green onions, thinly sliced, *divided*

3 slices reduced-fat Swiss cheese, *divided*

- Flatten chicken to 1/4-in. thickness; sprinkle with salt and pepper. In a small bowl, combine the crab, water chestnuts, bread crumbs, mayonnaise, parsley, mustard, 2 teaspoons marinade for chicken and half of the onions.

- Chop one cheese slice; stir into crab mixture. Spread over chicken; roll up and secure with toothpicks.

- In a large nonstick skillet coated with cooking spray, brown chicken on all sides. Place seam side down in a shallow 3-qt. baking dish coated with cooking spray. Brush with remaining marinade for chicken.

- Bake, uncovered, at 350° for 25 minutes. Cut each remaining cheese slice into six strips; place two cheese strips over each chicken breast. Bake 5-10 minutes longer or until a meat thermometer reads 170°. Discard toothpicks. Sprinkle remaining onions over chicken.

YIELD: 6 servings.

EDITOR'S NOTE: This recipe was tested with Lea & Perrins Marinade for Chicken.

NUTRITION FACTS: 1 stuffed chicken breast half equals 225 calories, 7 g fat (2 g saturated fat), 95 mg cholesterol, 469 mg sodium, 5 g carbohydrate, trace fiber, 35 g protein. **DIABETIC EXCHANGES:** 5 lean meat.

roast dinner

udley | BEMIDJI, MINNESOTA

Since this healthy dish is slow cooked, you can use less-expensive roasts and have the same mouthwatering results you would get with more costly cuts. Change up the veggies for variety, nutrition and taste!

- 1 pound red potatoes (about 4 medium), cubed
- 1/4 pound small fresh mushrooms
- 1-1/2 cups fresh baby carrots
- 1 medium green pepper, chopped
- 1 medium parsnip, chopped
- 1 small red onion, chopped
- 1 beef rump roast *or* bottom round roast (3 pounds)
- 1 can (14-1/2 ounces) beef broth
- 3/4 teaspoon salt
- 3/4 teaspoon dried oregano
- 1/4 teaspoon pepper
- 3 tablespoons cornstarch
- 1/4 cup cold water

classic

- Place vegetables in a 5-qt. slow cooker. Cut roast in half; place in slow cooker. Combine the broth, salt, oregano and pepper; pour over meat.Cover and cook on low for 8 hours or until meat is tender.

- Remove meat and vegetables to a serving platter; keep warm. Skim fat from cooking juices; transfer to a small saucepan. Bring liquid to a boil.

BEEF ROAST DINNER

245 CALORIES

- Combine cornstarch and water until smooth. Gradually stir into the pan. Bring to a boil; cook and stir for 2 minutes or until thickened. Serve with meat and vegetables.

YIELD: 10 servings.

NUTRITION FACTS: 4 ounces cooked beef with 2/3 cup vegetables and 1/4 cup gravy equals 245 calories, 7 g fat (2 g saturated fat), 82 mg cholesterol, 427 mg sodium, 16 g carbohydrate, 2 g fiber, 29 g protein. **DIABETIC EXCHANGES:** 4 lean meat, 1 starch.

220 CALORIES

ZIPPY SPAGHETTI SAUCE

zippy spaghetti sauce

Elaine Priest | DOVER, PENNSYLVANIA

This spaghetti sauce is perfect for putting together a flavorful supper. Serve it with any kind of pasta for a fabulous dinner option.

- 2 pounds lean ground beef (90% lean)
- 1 cup chopped onion
- 1/2 cup chopped green pepper
- 2 cans (15 ounces *each*) tomato sauce
- 1 can (28 ounces) diced tomatoes, undrained
- 1 can (12 ounces) tomato paste
- 1/2 pound sliced fresh mushrooms
- 1 cup grated Parmesan cheese
- 1/2 to 3/4 cup dry red wine *or* beef broth
- 1/2 cup sliced pimiento-stuffed olives
- 1/4 cup dried parsley flakes
- 1 to 2 tablespoons dried oregano
- 2 teaspoons Italian seasoning
- 2 teaspoons minced garlic

classic

1/2 teaspoon salt

1 teaspoon pepper

Hot cooked spaghetti

- In a large skillet, cook the beef, onion and green pepper over medium heat until meat is no longer pink; drain. Transfer to a 5-qt. slow cooker.

- Stir in the tomato sauce, tomatoes, tomato paste, mushrooms, Parmesan cheese, wine or broth, olives, parsley, oregano, Italian seasoning, garlic, salt and pepper.

- Cover and cook on low for 6-8 hours. Serve with spaghetti.

YIELD: about 3 quarts.

NUTRITION FACTS: 1 cup equals 220 calories, 9 g fat (3 g saturated fat), 49 mg cholesterol, 729 mg sodium, 15 g carbohydrate, 3 g fiber, 20 g protein. **DIABETIC EXCHANGES:** 2 lean meat, 1 starch, 1/2 fat.

prosciutto-pepper pork chops

Donna Prisco | RANDOLPH, NEW JERSEY

This dish is quick, fast and most importantly, delicious. It's especially easy to make for two, six, eight or more.

4 boneless pork loin chops (4 ounces *each*)

1/8 teaspoon garlic powder

1/8 teaspoon pepper

2 teaspoons canola oil

4 thin slices prosciutto *or* deli ham

PROSCIUTTO-PEPPER PORK CHOPS

237 CALORIES

1/2 cup julienned roasted sweet red peppers

2 slices reduced-fat provolone cheese, cut in half

- Sprinkle pork chops with garlic powder and pepper. In a large nonstick skillet, cook chops in oil over medium heat for 4-5 minutes on each side or until a meat thermometer reads 160°.

- Top each pork chop with prosciutto, red peppers and cheese. Cover and cook for 1-2 minutes or until cheese is melted.

YIELD: 4 servings.

NUTRITION FACTS: 1 pork chop equals 237 calories, 12 g fat (4 g saturated fat), 72 mg cholesterol, 483 mg sodium, 1 g carbohydrate, trace fiber, 28 g protein. **DIABETIC EXCHANGES:** 4 lean meat, 1/2 fat.

210 CALORIES

savory baked chicken

Bonnie Baumgardner | SYLVA, NORTH CAROLINA

A crispy golden breading flavored with robust mustard and lemon envelopes this main course.

2 tablespoons spicy brown mustard

1 teaspoon lemon juice

1/8 teaspoon dried savory

1/8 teaspoon grated lemon peel

1/8 teaspoon salt

1/8 teaspoon pepper

2/3 cup crushed seasoned stuffing

2 boneless skinless chicken breast halves (4 ounces *each*)

classic

- In a shallow bowl, combine the first six ingredients. Place the stuffing in another bowl. Dip chicken in mustard mixture, then coat with stuffing.

- Place the chicken in an 11-in. x 7-in. baking dish coated with cooking spray. Spritz chicken with cooking spray. Bake, uncovered, at 350° for 15-20 minutes or until a meat thermometer reads 170°.

YIELD: 2 servings.

NUTRITION FACTS: 1 chicken breast half equals 210 calories, 3 g fat (1 g saturated fat), 63 mg cholesterol, 664 mg sodium, 15 g carbohydrate, 1 g fiber, 25 g protein. **DIABETIC EXCHANGES:** 3 lean meat, 1 starch.

FAVORITE SKILLET LASAGNA

favorite skillet lasagna

Lorie Miner I KAMAS, UTAH

You simply won't believe my stovetop supper is light!
Best of all, the meal-in-one is on the table in about 30
minutes. What could be better?

- 1/2 pound Italian turkey sausage links, casings
  removed
- 1 small onion, chopped
- 1 jar (14 ounces) spaghetti sauce
- 2 cups uncooked whole wheat egg noodles
- 1 cup water
- 1/2 cup chopped zucchini
- 1/2 cup fat-free ricotta cheese
- 2 tablespoons grated Parmesan cheese
- 1 tablespoon minced fresh parsley *or* 1 teaspoon
  dried parsley flakes
- 1/2 cup shredded part-skim mozzarella cheese

- In a large nonstick skillet, cook sausage and onion
  over medium heat until no longer pink; drain. Stir in
  the spaghetti sauce, egg noodles, water and zucchini.
  Bring to a boil. Reduce heat; cover and simmer for 8-10
  minutes or until pasta is tender, stirring occasionally.

- Combine the ricotta, Parmesan and parsley. Drop
  by tablespoonfuls over pasta mixture. Sprinkle with
  mozzarella cheese; cover and cook 3-5 minutes longer or
  until cheese is melted.

YIELD: 5 servings.

NUTRITION FACTS: 1 cup equals 250 calories, 10 g fat (3 g saturated fat), 41 mg cholesterol, 783 mg sodium, 24 g carbohydrate, 3 g fiber, 17 g protein. **DIABETIC EXCHANGES:** 2 lean meat,
1-1/2 starch, 1 fat.

bavarian pork loin

Edie DeSpain I LOGAN, UTAH

I received the recipe for this tender pork roast from an
aunt, who made it all the time. It is a delicious taste
sensation with sauerkraut, carrots, onions and apples.

- 1 boneless whole pork loin roast (3 to 4 pounds)
- 1 can (14 ounces) Bavarian sauerkraut, rinsed
  and drained
- 1-3/4 cups chopped carrots
- 1 large onion, finely chopped
- 1/2 cup unsweetened apple juice
- 2 teaspoons dried parsley flakes
- 3 large tart apples, peeled and quartered

- Cut roast in half; place in a 5-qt. slow cooker. In a small
  bowl, combine the sauerkraut, carrots, onion, apple juice
  and parsley; spoon over roast. Cover and cook on low for
  4 hours.

- Add apples to slow cooker. Cover and cook 2 to 2-1/2
  hours longer or until a meat thermometer reads 160°.

- Remove roast; let stand for 5 minutes before slicing.
  Serve with sauerkraut mixture.

YIELD: 10 servings.

NUTRITION FACTS: 4 ounces cooked pork with 1/2 cup sauerkraut
mixture equals 235 calories, 6 g fat (2 g saturated fat), 68 mg
cholesterol, 294 mg sodium, 17 g carbohydrate, 2 g fiber, 27 g
protein. **DIABETIC EXCHANGES:** 4 lean meat, 1 starch.

BAVARIAN PORK LOIN

225 CALORIES

BRISKET WITH CRANBERRY GRAVY

brisket with cranberry gravy

Noelle LaBrecque I ROUND ROCK, TEXAS

With just a few minutes of hands-on work, this tender beef brisket simmers into a delectable entree. The meat and gravy are great for sandwiches the next day.

classic

- 1 medium onion, sliced
- 1 fresh beef brisket (3 pounds), halved
- 1 can (14 ounces) jellied cranberry sauce
- 1/2 cup thawed cranberry juice concentrate
- 2 tablespoons cornstarch
- 1/4 cup water

- Place the onion in a 5-qt. slow cooker; top with brisket. Combine the cranberry sauce and cranberry juice concentrate; pour over beef.

- Cover and cook on low for 5-1/2 to 6 hours or until meat is tender.

- Remove brisket and keep warm. Strain cooking juices, discarding onion; skim fat.

- In a small saucepan, combine cornstarch and water until smooth; stir in the cooking juices. Bring to a boil over medium heat, stirring constantly. Cook and stir for 2 minutes or until thickened. Thinly slice brisket across the grain; serve with gravy.

YIELD: 12 servings.

EDITOR'S NOTE: This is a fresh beef brisket, not corned beef.

NUTRITION FACTS: 3 ounces equals 225 calories, 5 g fat (2 g saturated fat), 48 mg cholesterol, 46 mg sodium, 21 g carbohydrate, 1 g fiber, 23 g protein. **DIABETIC EXCHANGES:** 3 lean meat, 1-1/2 starch.

beef 'n' turkey meat loaf

Fern Nead I FLORENCE, KENTUCKY

Shredded potatoes bulk up this hefty meat loaf, seasoned with garlic and thyme.

- 2 egg whites
- 2/3 cup ketchup, *divided*
- 1 medium potato, peeled and finely shredded
- 1 medium green pepper, finely chopped
- 1 small onion, grated
- 3 garlic cloves, minced
- 1 teaspoon salt
- 1 teaspoon dried thyme
- 1/2 teaspoon pepper
- 3/4 pound lean ground beef (90% lean)
- 3/4 pound lean ground turkey

classic

- In a large bowl, combine egg whites and 1/3 cup ketchup. Stir in the potato, green pepper, onion, garlic, salt, thyme and pepper. Crumble beef and turkey over mixture and mix well. Shape into a 10-in. x 4-in. loaf.

- Line a 15-in. x 10-in. x 1-in. baking pan with heavy-duty foil and coat the foil with cooking spray. Place loaf in pan. Bake, uncovered, at 375° for 45 minutes; drain. Brush with remaining ketchup. Bake 5-10 minutes longer or until a meat thermometer reads 165°. Let stand for 10 minutes before slicing.

YIELD: 6 servings.

NUTRITION FACTS: 1 slice equals 240 calories, 9 g fat (3 g saturated fat), 79 mg cholesterol, 808 mg sodium, 16 g carbohydrate, 2 g fiber, 23 g protein.

BEEF 'N' TURKEY MEAT LOAF

240 CALORIES

spinach lasagna

Christine Laba | ARLINGTON, VIRGINIA

No one in your house will suspect that tofu is buried in the layers of this delicious lasagna!

classic

- 9 lasagna noodles
- 1 medium onion, chopped
- 3 garlic cloves, minced
- 1 tablespoon olive oil
- 2 cups sliced fresh mushrooms
- 1 package (14 ounces) firm tofu
- 1 carton (15 ounces) part-skim ricotta cheese
- 1/2 cup minced fresh parsley
- 1 teaspoon salt, *divided*
- 2 packages (10 ounces *each*) frozen chopped spinach, thawed and squeezed dry
- 1-3/4 cups marinara *or* meatless spaghetti sauce
- 1 cup (4 ounces) shredded part-skim mozzarella cheese
- 1/3 cup shredded Parmesan cheese

- Cook noodles according to package directions. Meanwhile, in a large nonstick skillet, saute onion and garlic in oil for 1 minute. Add mushrooms; saute until tender. Set aside.

- Drain tofu, reserving 2 tablespoons liquid. Place tofu and reserved liquid in a food processor; cover and process until blended. Add ricotta cheese; cover and process for 1-2 minutes or until smooth. Transfer to a large bowl; stir in the parsley, 1/2 teaspoon salt and mushroom mixture. Combine spinach and remaining salt; set aside.

- Drain noodles. Spread half of the marinara sauce into a 13-in. x 9-in. baking dish coated with cooking spray. Layer with three noodles, half of the tofu mixture and half of the spinach mixture. Repeat layers of noodles, tofu and spinach. Top with remaining noodles and marinara sauce. Sprinkle with cheeses.

- Bake, uncovered, at 350° for 30-35 minutes or until heated through and cheese is melted. Let stand for 10 minutes before cutting.

YIELD: 12 servings.

NUTRITION FACTS: 1 piece equals 227 calories, 8 g fat (4 g saturated fat), 18 mg cholesterol, 429 mg sodium, 25 g carbohydrate, 3 g fiber, 15 g protein. **DIABETIC EXCHANGES:** 1-1/2 starch, 1 lean meat, 1 vegetable, 1/2 fat.

SPINACH LASAGNA

227 CALORIES

---

226 CALORIES # maple-glazed chicken

Taryn Kuebelbeck | PLYMOUTH, MINNESOTA

Tender and loaded with appeal, this entree will please everyone at the table.

- 4 boneless skinless chicken breast halves (5 ounces *each*)
- 1/4 teaspoon salt
- 1/8 teaspoon pepper
- 1 tablespoon canola oil
- 1/2 teaspoon cornstarch
- 1/2 cup apple cider *or* unsweetened apple juice
- 2 tablespoons maple syrup
- 1/2 teaspoon onion powder

- Flatten chicken to 1/2-in. thickness. Sprinkle with salt and pepper. In a skillet, cook chicken in oil for 5-6 minutes on each side or until no longer pink.

- Meanwhile, in a small bowl, combine cornstarch and cider until smooth. Stir in syrup and onion powder; add to skillet. Bring to a boil; cook and stir for 2 minutes or until thickened. Add chicken and turn to coat.

YIELD: 4 servings.

NUTRITION FACTS: 1 chicken breast half with 2 tablespoons glaze equals 226 calories, 7 g fat (1 g saturated fat), 78 mg cholesterol, 220 mg sodium, 11 g carbohydrate, trace fiber, 29 g protein. **DIABETIC EXCHANGE:** 4 lean meat, 1 starch, 1/2 fat.

red pepper & parmesan tilapia

Michelle Martin | DURHAM, NORTH CAROLINA

My husband and I are always looking for light fish recipes because of the health benefits involved. This one's a hit with him, and we've tried it at dinner parties, too. It's a staple!

- 1/4 cup egg substitute
- 1/2 cup grated Parmesan cheese
- 1 teaspoon Italian seasoning
- 1/2 to 1 teaspoon crushed red pepper flakes
- 1/2 teaspoon pepper
- 4 tilapia fillets (6 ounces *each*)

- Place egg substitute in a shallow bowl. In another shallow bowl, combine the cheese, Italian seasoning, pepper flakes and pepper. Dip fillets in egg substitute, then cheese mixture.

- Place in a 15-in. x 10-in. x 1-in. baking pan coated with cooking spray. Bake at 425° for 10-15 minutes or until fish flakes easily with a fork.

YIELD: 4 servings.

NUTRITION FACTS: 1 fillet equals 179 calories, 4 g fat (2 g saturated fat), 89 mg cholesterol, 191 mg sodium, 1 g carbohydrate, trace fiber, 35 g protein. **DIABETIC EXCHANGE:** 5 lean meat.

RED PEPPER & PARMESAN TILAPIA

179 CALORIES

221 CALORIES

ASIAN CHICKEN DINNER

asian chicken dinner

Carolyn Zimmerman | FAIRBURY, ILLINOIS

This quick microwave dish for two is perfect for a busy day. Soy sauce and chicken broth bring out the flavors of the chicken and veggies.

- 1/2 pound boneless skinless chicken breasts, cut into 1/2-inch strips
- 1 small onion, thinly sliced
- 1 tablespoon canola oil
- 1 cup frozen California-blend vegetables
- 3/4 cup uncooked instant rice
- 3/4 cup reduced-sodium chicken broth
- 1 tablespoon reduced-sodium soy sauce

- In a shallow 1-qt. microwave-safe dish, combine the chicken, onion and oil. Cover and microwave on high for 2 minutes.

- Stir in the remaining ingredients. Cover and cook for 4-5 minutes or until chicken is no longer pink and rice is tender. Let stand, covered, for 5 minutes. Fluff rice with a fork.

YIELD: 2 servings.

EDITOR'S NOTE: This recipe was tested in a 1,100-watt microwave.

NUTRITION FACTS: 1-1/2 cups equals 221 calories, 10 g fat (1 g saturated fat), 63 mg cholesterol, 587 mg sodium, 6 g carbohydrate, 2 g fiber, 26 g protein. **DIABETIC EXCHANGES:** 3 lean meat, 1-1/2 fat, 1 vegetable.

228 CALORIES

JAMBALAYA

jambalaya

Sherry Huntwork | GRETNA, NEBRASKA

Sausage, chicken and shrimp keep this dish hearty and satisfying. Made easy with canned items and other kitchen staples, it's perfect for casual get-togethers.

- 1 pound smoked Polish sausage, cut into 1/2-inch slices
- 1/2 pound boneless skinless chicken breasts, cut into 1-inch cubes
- 1 can (14-1/2 ounces) beef broth
- 1 can (14-1/2 ounces) diced tomatoes, undrained
- 2 celery ribs, chopped
- 1/3 cup tomato paste
- 4 garlic cloves, minced
- 1 tablespoon dried parsley flakes
- 1-1/2 teaspoons dried basil
- 1 teaspoon cayenne pepper
- 1/2 teaspoon salt
- 1/2 teaspoon dried oregano
- 1 pound cooked medium shrimp, peeled and deveined
- 2 cups cooked rice

classic

- In a 5-qt. slow cooker, combine the first 12 ingredients. Cover and cook on low for 6-7 hours or until chicken is no longer pink.

175

- Stir in shrimp and rice. Cover and cook 15 minutes longer or until heated through.

YIELD: 12 servings.

NUTRITION FACTS: 1 cup equals 228 calories, 11 g fat (4 g saturated fat), 95 mg cholesterol, 692 mg sodium, 12 g carbohydrate, 1 g fiber, 18 g protein. **DIABETIC EXCHANGES:** 2 lean meat, 1 starch, 1 fat.

242 CALORIES

chicken in creamy gravy

Jean Little | CHARLOTTE, NORTH CAROLINA

This lighter dinner takes advantage of convenient cream of chicken and broccoli soup for the savory sauce. It comes together in a snap.

- 4 boneless skinless chicken breast halves (4 ounces *each*)
- 1 tablespoon canola oil
- 1 can (10-3/4 ounces) condensed cream of broccoli soup, undiluted
- 1/4 cup fat-free milk
- 1 tablespoon minced fresh parsley
- 2 teaspoons lemon juice
- 1/8 teaspoon pepper
- 1/8 teaspoon Worcestershire sauce
- 4 lemon slices

Hot cooked spaghetti, optional

Additional minced fresh parsley, optional

- In a nonstick skillet, cook chicken in oil until browned on both sides, about 10 minutes and a meat thermometer reads 170°; drain.

- In a bowl, combine the soup, milk, parsley, lemon juice, pepper and Worcestershire sauce. Pour over chicken. Top each chicken breast with a lemon slice. Reduce heat; cover and simmer for about 5 minutes or heated through. Serve with spaghetti if desired. Sprinkle with additional parsley if desired.

YIELD: 4 servings.

NUTRITION FACTS: 1 serving (calculated without spaghetti) equals 242 calories, 12 g fat (3 g saturated fat), 73 mg cholesterol, 643 mg sodium, 8 g carbohydrate, 1 g fiber, 26 g protein. **DIABETIC EXCHANGES:** 3 lean meat, 1 fat, 1/2 starch.

BAKED PARMESAN ROUGHY

baked parmesan roughy

Patti Bailey | CHANUTE, KANSAS

This light and crispy fish entree is a favorite with my family and friends. It's table-ready in 30 minutes but special enough to serve company.

- 3/4 cup crushed cornflakes
- 1/2 cup grated Parmesan cheese
- 1/2 teaspoon salt
-   2 eggs, lightly beaten
-   2 tablespoons 2% milk
-   2 pounds orange roughy fillets

- In a large resealable plastic bag, combine the cornflakes, cheese and salt. In a shallow bowl, combine eggs and milk. Dip fish fillets in egg mixture, then shake in cornflake mixture.

- Transfer to a greased 15-in. x 10-in. x 1-in. baking pan. Bake at 450° for 15-20 minutes or until fish flakes easily with a fork.

YIELD: 6 servings.

NUTRITION FACTS: 1 fillet equals 211 calories, 5 g fat (2 g saturated fat), 168 mg cholesterol, 513 mg sodium, 10 g carbohydrate, trace fiber, 30 g protein. **DIABETIC EXCHANGES:** 4 lean meat, 1/2 starch, 1/2 fat.

garlic chicken and gravy

Our Test Kitchen prepares this family classic in less than 30 minutes using just one skillet.

-   4 boneless skinless chicken breast halves (4 ounces *each*)
- 1/4 teaspoon salt
- 1/4 teaspoon pepper
-   5 garlic cloves, peeled and chopped
-   2 tablespoons butter
- 1/2 cup plus 2 tablespoons chicken broth, *divided*
- 1/2 cup white wine *or* additional chicken broth
- 1/2 teaspoon dried basil
- 1/4 teaspoon dried oregano
-   1 tablespoon all-purpose flour

- Sprinkle chicken with salt and pepper. In a large skillet, cook chicken and garlic in butter over medium-high heat for 5 minutes or until browned. Add 1/2 cup broth, wine or additional broth, basil and oregano. Bring to a boil. Reduce heat; cover and simmer for 7-9 minutes or until chicken is no longer pink.

- Remove chicken with a slotted spoon and keep warm. In a small bowl, combine flour and remaining broth until smooth; stir into pan juices. Bring to a boil; cook and stir for 1-2 minutes or until thickened. Serve over chicken.

YIELD: 4 servings.

NUTRITION FACTS: 1 chicken breast half with 3 tablespoons gravy equals 208 calories, 8 g fat (4 g saturated fat), 78 mg cholesterol, 407 mg sodium, 3 g carbohydrate, trace fiber, 24 g protein. **DIABETIC EXCHANGES:** 3 lean meat, 1-1/2 fat.

GARLIC CHICKEN AND GRAVY

skillet beef stroganoff

Aljene Wendling | SEATTLE, WASHINGTON
I don't recall where I got this recipe, but I've been making it for 40 years. The recipe card is covered with food stains as a result of so much use. I like the addition of using horseradish, which gives the stroganoff that extra zing.

- 5 cups sliced fresh mushrooms
- 1 large onion, sliced
- 1 tablespoon reduced-fat butter
- 1/3 to 1/2 cup hot water
- 1 tablespoon prepared horseradish
- 1/2 teaspoon salt
- 1/8 teaspoon pepper
- 1/4 cup all-purpose flour
- 1 beef flank steak (1-1/4 pounds), cut into 2-inch strips
- 1 cup (8 ounces) reduced-fat sour cream

Hot cooked noodles

- In a large skillet, saute the mushrooms and onion in butter until tender. With a slotted spoon, transfer to a large bowl; stir in the water, horseradish, salt and pepper. Set aside.

- Place flour in a large resealable plastic bag. Add beef, a few pieces at a time. Seal bag; shake to coat.

- In the same skillet, brown beef in batches. Return all of the beef to the pan; top with mushroom mixture.

SKILLET BEEF STROGANOFF

- Bring to a boil. Reduce heat; cover and simmer for 1-1/4 to 1-1/2 hours or until beef is tender, stirring once. Remove from the heat; stir in sour cream. Serve with hot cooked noodles.

YIELD: 6 servings.

EDITOR'S NOTE: This recipe was tested with Land O'Lakes light stick butter.

NUTRITION FACTS: 2/3 cup (calculated without noodles) equals 246 calories, 11 g fat (6 g saturated fat), 62 mg cholesterol, 302 mg sodium, 11 g carbohydrate, 1 g fiber, 24 g protein. **DIABETIC EXCHANGES:** 3 lean meat, 1 starch, 1 fat.

honey-grilled chicken breasts

Jennifer Petersen | MURRAY, UTAH
Orange juice and soy sauce make such a tasty combination in this recipe from my mother-in-law. And the longer this chicken marinates, the fuller the flavor!

- 1/2 cup orange juice
- 1/3 cup honey
- 1/4 cup lemon juice
- 1/4 cup reduced-sodium soy sauce
- 2 tablespoons minced fresh gingerroot
- 12 garlic cloves, minced
- 1/2 teaspoon pepper
- 1/4 teaspoon salt
- 8 boneless skinless chicken breast halves (6 ounces *each*)

- In a small bowl, combine the first eight ingredients. Pour 1/2 cup marinade into a large resealable plastic bag; add chicken. Seal bag and turn to coat; refrigerate for 8 hours or overnight. Cover and refrigerate remaining marinade.

- Drain and discard marinade. Using long-handled tongs, dip a paper towel in cooking oil and lightly coat the grill rack. Grill, covered, over medium heat or broil 4 in. from the heat for 5-7 minutes on each side or until a meat thermometer reads 170°, basting frequently with reserved marinade.

YIELD: 8 servings.

NUTRITION FACTS: 1 chicken breast half equals 221 calories, 4 g fat (1 g saturated fat), 94 mg cholesterol, 331 mg sodium, 10 g carbohydrate, trace fiber, 35 g protein. **DIABETIC EXCHANGES:** 5 lean meat, 1/2 starch.

sesame beef 'n' veggie kabobs

Frances Klingemann | OMAHA, NEBRASKA

This is a favorite with my entire family. Chalk it up to the fact that this recipe delivers great flavor, tender chunks of meat and a presentation as pretty as a picture!

- 1/2 cup reduced-sodium soy sauce
- 1/4 cup white wine *or* unsweetened apple juice
- 3 medium green peppers, cut into 1-inch pieces, *divided*
- 1 medium onion, cut into wedges
- 1 garlic clove, peeled
- 1/2 teaspoon ground ginger
- 1 tablespoon sesame seeds
- 2 pounds beef top sirloin steak, cut into 1-inch pieces
- 32 medium fresh mushrooms
- 32 cherry tomatoes
- 1 tablespoon canola oil

- In a blender, combine the soy sauce, wine, 1/2 cup green pepper, onion, garlic and ginger; cover and process until smooth. Stir in sesame seeds.

- Cover and refrigerate 1/3 cup mixture for basting. Pour remaining mixture into a large resealable plastic bag; add the beef. Seal bag and turn to coat; refrigerate overnight. Refrigerate remaining peppers.

216 CALORIES

SESAME BEEF 'N' VEGGIE KABOBS

- Drain and discard marinade. On 16 metal or soaked wooden skewers, alternately thread the beef, mushrooms, tomatoes and remaining peppers. Brush lightly with oil.

- Using long-handled tongs, dip a paper towel in cooking oil and lightly coat the grill rack. Grill, covered, over medium heat or broil 4 in. from the heat for 10-15 minutes or until beef reaches desired doneness, turning occasionally and basting with reserved marinade.

YIELD: 8 servings.

NUTRITION FACTS: 2 kabobs equals 216 calories, 7 g fat (2 g saturated fat), 46 mg cholesterol, 364 mg sodium, 10 g carbohydrate, 3 g fiber, 28 g protein. **DIABETIC EXCHANGES:** 3 lean meat, 2 vegetable.

Consider these typical dinner foods and their calorie counts to help you stay within a heart-smart 500-calorie meal.

- **1 cup cooked spaghetti,** 100 calories
- **1 ground sirloin beef patty (4 ounces), broiled,** 175 calories
- **2 roasted chicken drumsticks, skin removed,** 154 calories

- **1 prime beef tenderloin steak (4 ounces), broiled,** 200 calories
- **1 boneless pork loin chop (4 ounces), broiled,** 154 calories
- **1 salmon fillet (4 ounces), broiled,** 184 calories

- **4 ounces large shell-on shrimp, peeled, deveined and cooked,** 90 calories
- **1 boneless, skinless chicken breast half (4 ounces), broiled,** 130 calories
  Weight given is before cooking.

For additional calorie calculations, check the Nutrition Facts labels on food packages.

157 CALORIES

SWEET & SPICY CHICKEN DRUMMIES

sweet & spicy chicken drummies

Lynette Hanus I FAYETTEVILLE, GEORGIA
We were on a camping trip, and a fellow camper contributed these chicken legs for dinner. They were fabulous! I was so impressed, I asked him for the recipe.

2	cups sugar
1/4	cup paprika
2	tablespoons salt
2	teaspoons pepper
1	teaspoon garlic powder
1	teaspoon chili powder
1/2	teaspoon cayenne pepper
20	chicken drumsticks (5 ounces *each*)

- In a large resealable plastic bag, combine the sugar, paprika, salt, pepper, garlic powder, chili powder and cayenne. Add the drumsticks, a few at a time; seal and shake to coat.

- Place chicken in two greased 15-in. x 10-in. x 1-in. baking pans. Cover and refrigerate for 8 hours or overnight. (A small amount of meat juices will form in the pan.)

- Bake, uncovered, at 325° for 50-60 minutes or until chicken juices run clear and a meat thermometer reads 180°.

YIELD: 20 drumsticks.

NUTRITION FACTS: 1 drumstick equals 157 calories, 6 g fat (2 g saturated fat), 47 mg cholesterol, 398 mg sodium, 11 g carbohydrate, trace fiber, 15 g protein. **DIABETIC EXCHANGES:** 2 lean meat, 1/2 starch, 1/2 fat.

gingered pork tenderloin

Michelle Sanders I FRASER LAKE, BRITISH COLUMBIA
This pork tenderloin is absolutely delicious and great for entertaining. The quick prep is done ahead of time, and the grilling is so simple. This dish is fool-proof.

2	tablespoons reduced-sodium soy sauce
1/4	cup sherry *or* reduced-sodium chicken broth
2	tablespoons canola oil
2	tablespoons minced fresh gingerroot
2	teaspoons sugar
2	garlic cloves, minced
2	pork tenderloins (1 pound *each*)

- In a large resealable plastic bag, combine the first six ingredients; add pork. Seal bag and turn to coat; refrigerate for 8 hours or overnight.

- Drain and discard marinade. Prepare grill for indirect heat using a drip pan. Using long-handled tongs, dip a paper towel in cooking oil and lightly coat the grill rack. Place pork over drip pan and grill, covered, over indirect medium-hot heat for 25-40 minutes or until a meat thermometer reads 160°.

- Let stand for 5 minutes before slicing.

YIELD: 6 servings.

NUTRITION FACTS: 4 ounces cooked pork equals 214 calories, 8 g fat (2 g saturated fat), 84 mg cholesterol, 194 mg sodium, 2 g carbohydrate, trace fiber, 30 g protein. **DIABETIC EXCHANGES:** 4 lean meat, 1/2 fat.

GINGERED PORK TENDERLOIN

214 CALORIES

213 CALORIES

SPICY GOULASH

spicy goulash

Melissa Polk | WEST LAFAYETTE, INDIANA

Ground cumin, chili powder and a can of Mexican diced tomatoes jazz up my goulash recipe. Even the elbow macaroni is prepared in the slow cooker.

- 1 pound lean ground beef (90% lean)
- 4 cans (14-1/2 ounces *each*) Mexican diced tomatoes, undrained
- 2 cans (16 ounces *each*) kidney beans, rinsed and drained
- 2 cups water
- 1 medium onion, chopped
- 1 medium green pepper, chopped
- 1/4 cup red wine vinegar
- 2 tablespoons chili powder
- 1 tablespoon Worcestershire sauce
- 2 teaspoons beef bouillon granules
- 1 teaspoon dried basil
- 1 teaspoon dried parsley flakes
- 1 teaspoon ground cumin
- 1/4 teaspoon pepper
- 2 cups uncooked elbow macaroni

- In a large skillet, cook beef over medium heat until no longer pink; drain. Transfer to a 5-qt. slow cooker. Stir in the tomatoes, beans, water, onion, green pepper, vinegar, chili powder, Worcestershire sauce, bouillon and seasonings. Cover and cook on low for 5-6 hours or until heated through.

- Stir in macaroni; cover and cook 30 minutes longer until macaroni is tender.

YIELD: 12 servings.

NUTRITION FACTS: 1 cup equals 213 calories, 4 g fat (1 g saturated fat), 24 mg cholesterol, 585 mg sodium, 30 g carbohydrate, 6 g fiber, 15 g protein. **DIABETIC EXCHANGES:** 2 lean meat, 1-1/2 starch, 1 vegetable.

tender chicken nuggets

Lynne Hahn | WINCHESTER, CALIFORNIA

Four ingredients are all it takes to create these moist golden bites that are healthier than fast food. I serve them with ranch dressing and barbecue sauce for dipping.

- 1/2 cup seasoned bread crumbs
- 2 tablespoons grated Parmesan cheese
- 1 egg white
- 1 pound boneless skinless chicken breasts, cut into 1-inch cubes

classic

- In a large resealable plastic bag, combine bread crumbs and cheese. In a shallow bowl, beat the egg white. Dip chicken pieces in egg white, then place in bag and shake to coat.

- Place chicken in a 15-in. x 10-in. x 1-in. baking pan coated with cooking spray. Bake, uncovered, at 400° for 12-15 minutes or until no longer pink, turning once.

YIELD: 4 servings.

NUTRITION FACTS: 3 ounces cooked chicken equals 194 calories, 3 g fat (1 g saturated fat), 68 mg cholesterol, 250 mg sodium, 10 g carbohydrate, trace fiber, 30 g protein. **DIABETIC EXCHANGES:** 3 lean meat, 1/2 starch.

TENDER CHICKEN NUGGETS

194 CALORIES

210 CALORIES

PORK CHOPS WITH ONION GRAVY

pork chops with onion gravy

Amy Radyshewsky | GREAT FALLS, MONTANA

I came up with this recipe as a quick dinner for a finicky husband who's not too fond of pork chops. These are so tender and good, he always gives them a thumbs up!

4	boneless pork loin chops (1/2 inch thick and 4 ounces *each*)
1/4	teaspoon pepper
1/8	teaspoon salt
1	small onion, sliced and separated into rings
1	tablespoon canola oil
1/4	cup reduced-sodium chicken broth
1	envelope pork gravy mix
1/8	teaspoon garlic powder
3/4	cup water

• Sprinkle pork chops with pepper and salt. In a large skillet, cook chops and onion in oil over medium heat for 2-3 minutes on each side or until chops are lightly browned; drain.

• Add broth. Bring to a boil. Reduce heat; cover and simmer for 7-8 minutes on each side or until a meat thermometer reads 160°.

• In a small bowl, whisk the gravy mix, garlic powder and water. Pour over pork. Bring to a boil. Reduce heat; simmer, uncovered, for 3-4 minutes or until thickened, stirring occasionally.

YIELD: 4 servings.

NUTRITION FACTS: 1 pork chop with 3 tablespoons gravy equals 210 calories, 10 g fat (3 g saturated fat), 55 mg cholesterol, 528 mg sodium, 6 g carbohydrate, trace fiber, 22 g protein. **DIABETIC EXCHANGES:** 3 lean meat, 1/2 starch, 1/2 fat.

cornmeal oven-fried chicken

Deborah Williams | PEORIA, ARIZONA

This dish perks up the dinner table. The flavorful cornmeal/bread crumb coating is a crisp and tasty variation from the usual.

1/2	cup dry bread crumbs
1/2	cup cornmeal
1/3	cup grated Parmesan cheese
1/4	cup minced fresh parsley *or* 4 teaspoons dried parsley flakes
3/4	teaspoon garlic powder
1/2	teaspoon salt
1/2	teaspoon onion powder
1/2	teaspoon dried thyme
1/2	teaspoon pepper
1/2	cup buttermilk
1	broiler/fryer chicken (3 to 4 pounds), cut up and skin removed
1	tablespoon butter, melted

classic

CORNMEAL OVEN-FRIED CHICKEN

244 CALORIES

- In a large resealable plastic bag, combine the first nine ingredients. Place the buttermilk in a shallow bowl. Dip chicken in buttermilk, then add to bag, a few pieces at a time, and shake to coat.

- Place in a 13-in. x 9-in. baking pan coated with cooking spray. Bake at 375° for 10 minutes; drizzle with butter. Bake 30-40 minutes longer or until juices run clear.

YIELD: 6 servings.

NUTRITION FACTS: 1 serving equals 244 calories, 9 g fat (3 g saturated fat), 82 mg cholesterol, 303 mg sodium, 11 g carbohydrate, 1 g fiber, 27 g protein. **DIABETIC EXCHANGES:** 3 lean meat, 1 starch, 1/2 fat.

giant mushroom burger

224 CALORIES

Janice Delagrange | MT. AIRY, MARYLAND

I add mushrooms and onion to well-seasoned lean ground beef before forming it into one giant, family-pleasing patty. After grilling it, all I need to do is slice it up. Serve it alongside a green salad for a fast family meal.

- 1-1/2 pounds lean ground beef (90% lean)
- 1 can (4 ounces) mushroom stems and pieces, drained
- 1/4 cup egg substitute
- 1/2 cup chopped onion
- 1/4 cup ketchup
- 1 teaspoon Italian seasoning
- 1 teaspoon fennel seed, crushed
- 1/4 teaspoon pepper
- 1/4 teaspoon Worcestershire sauce

- In a large bowl, combine all ingredients. Pat into a 9-in. circle on a large sheet of waxed paper. Invert onto a greased wire grill basket; peel off waxed paper.

- Grill, covered, over medium heat for 10-13 minutes a side or until a meat thermometer reads 160° and meat juices run clear. Cut into six wedges.

YIELD: 6 servings.

NUTRITION FACTS: 1 serving equals 224 calories, 11 g fat (4 g saturated fat), 41 mg cholesterol, 305 mg sodium, 6 g carbohydrate, 1 g fiber, 25 g protein. **DIABETIC EXCHANGES:** 3 lean meat, 1 vegetable.

tomato walnut tilapia

Phyl Broich-Wessling | GARNER, IOWA

Tomato, bread crumbs and crunchy walnuts dress up tilapia fillets in this delightful recipe. I often serve it with cooked julienne carrots and green beans.

- 4 tilapia fillets (4 ounces each)
- 1/4 teaspoon salt
- 1/4 teaspoon pepper
- 1 tablespoon butter
- 1 medium tomato, thinly sliced

TOPPING:
- 1/2 cup soft bread crumbs
- 1/4 cup chopped walnuts
- 2 tablespoons lemon juice
- 1-1/2 teaspoons butter, melted

- Sprinkle fillets with salt and pepper. In a large ovenproof skillet coated with cooking spray, cook fillets in butter over medium-high heat for 2-3 minutes on each side or until lightly browned.

- Place tomato slices over fish. Combine the topping ingredients; spoon over tomato. Broil 3-4 in. from the heat for 2-3 minutes or until topping is lightly browned and fish flakes easily with a fork.

YIELD: 4 servings.

NUTRITION FACTS: 1 fillet equals 205 calories, 10 g fat (3 g saturated fat), 67 mg cholesterol, 265 mg sodium, 7 g carbohydrate, 1 g fiber, 24 g protein. **DIABETIC EXCHANGES:** 3 very lean meat, 2 fat, 1/2 starch.

TOMATO WALNUT TILAPIA

205 CALORIES

187 CALORIES

MAKEOVER LI'L CHEDDAR MEAT LOAVES

makeover li'l cheddar meat loaves

Jodie Mitchell | DENVER, PENNSYLVANIA

My husband loves my meat loaf recipe. Thanks to the Taste of Home staff, it's now lower in calories and fat, and makes a healthier dinner option than it ever made before.

- 2 egg whites, beaten
- 3/4 cup fat-free milk
- 1 cup (4 ounces) shredded reduced-fat cheddar cheese
- 3/4 cup quick-cooking oats
- 1 medium onion, chopped
- 1 medium carrot, shredded
- 1/2 teaspoon salt
- 3/4 pound lean ground beef (90% lean)
- 2/3 cup ketchup
- 2 tablespoons brown sugar
- 1-1/2 teaspoons prepared mustard

- In a large bowl, whisk egg whites and milk. Stir in the cheese, oats, onion, carrot and salt. Crumble beef over mixture and mix well.

- Shape into eight loaves; place in a 13-in. x 9-in. baking dish coated with cooking spray. In a small bowl, combine the ketchup, brown sugar and mustard; spoon over loaves.

- Bake, uncovered, at 350° for 25-30 minutes or until no pink remains and a meat thermometer reads 160°.

YIELD: 8 servings.

NUTRITION FACTS: 1 meat loaf equals 187 calories, 7 g fat (3 g saturated fat), 36 mg cholesterol, 550 mg sodium, 18 g carbohydrate, 1 g fiber, 15 g protein. **DIABETIC EXCHANGES:** 2 lean meat, 1 starch.

241 CALORIES

pork roast with gravy

classic

Jean Virzi Lowrey | DUBACH, LOUISIANA

Low in calories, this is one of my favorite entrees.

- 1 boneless pork sirloin roast (2-1/2 pounds)
- 1-1/2 teaspoons canola oil
- 3/4 cup white wine *or* chicken broth
- 2 tablespoons reduced-sodium soy sauce
- 2 tablespoons brown sugar
- 1 teaspoon minced fresh gingerroot
- 1 garlic clove, minced
- 1/2 teaspoon chicken bouillon granules
- 4-1/2 teaspoons cornstarch
- 4-1/2 teaspoons cold water

- In a Dutch oven, brown roast in oil on all sides. In a small bowl, combine the wine or broth, soy sauce, brown sugar, ginger, garlic and bouillon; pour over roast.

- Bring to a boil. Reduce heat to low; cover and cook for 45-60 minutes or until a meat thermometer reads 160°, basting occasionally with pan juices.

- Remove roast to a serving platter and keep warm. Pour drippings and loosened browned bits into a measuring cup; skim fat. Add enough water to measure 1-1/2 cups. Return to the pan.

- Combine cornstarch and water until smooth; stir into juices. Bring to a boil; cook and stir for 1-2 minutes or until thickened. Slice roast; serve with gravy.

YIELD: 8 servings.

NUTRITION FACTS: 4 ounces cooked pork with 3 tablespoons gravy equals 241 calories, 9 g fat (3 g saturated fat), 85 mg cholesterol, 262 mg sodium, 5 g carbohydrate, trace fiber, 29 g protein. **DIABETIC EXCHANGE:** 4 lean meat.

SWEET 'N' SOUR PORK CHOPS

sweet 'n' sour pork chops

Gina Young | LAMAR, COLORADO

The recipe for these moist, tender pork chops was given to me years ago by my best friend. It's become one of my family's favorites, and we enjoy it often. Hope you do, too!

6	boneless pork loin chops (4 ounces *each*)
3/4	teaspoon pepper
1/2	cup water
1/3	cup cider vinegar
1/4	cup packed brown sugar
2	tablespoons reduced-sodium soy sauce
1	tablespoon Worcestershire sauce
1	tablespoon cornstarch
2	tablespoons cold water

- Sprinkle pork chops with pepper. In a large nonstick skillet coated with cooking spray, cook pork over medium heat for 4-6 minutes on each side or until lightly browned. Remove and keep warm.

- Add the water, vinegar, brown sugar, soy sauce and Worcestershire sauce to skillet; stir to loosen browned bits. Bring to a boil. Combine cornstarch and cold water until smooth; stir into skillet. Bring to a boil; cook and stir for 2 minutes or until thickened.

- Return chops to the pan. Reduce heat; cover and simmer for 4-5 minutes or until meat is tender.

YIELD: 6 servings.

NUTRITION FACTS: 1 pork chop with 3 tablespoons sauce equals 198 calories, 6 g fat (2 g saturated fat), 55 mg cholesterol, 265 mg sodium, 12 g carbohydrate, trace fiber, 22 g protein. **DIABETIC EXCHANGES:** 3 lean meat, 1 starch.

orange-maple glazed chicken

Lillian Julow | GAINESVILLE, FLORIDA

Pick up a medium-size orange for the zest and juice in this tasty recipe that creatively combines citrus with maple syrup and balsamic vinegar.

1/3	cup orange juice
1/3	cup maple syrup
2	tablespoons balsamic vinegar
1-1/2	teaspoons Dijon mustard
1	teaspoon salt, *divided*
3/4	teaspoon pepper, *divided*
1	tablespoon minced fresh basil *or* 1 teaspoon dried basil
1/2	teaspoon grated orange peel
6	boneless skinless chicken breast halves (6 ounces *each*)

- In a small saucepan, combine the orange juice, syrup, vinegar, mustard, 1/2 teaspoon salt and 1/4 teaspoon pepper. Bring to a boil; cook until liquid is reduced to 1/2 cup, about 5 minutes. Stir in basil and orange peel. Remove from the heat; set aside.

- Sprinkle chicken with remaining salt and pepper. Grill chicken, covered, over medium heat for 5-7 minutes on each side or until a meat thermometer reads 170°, basting frequently with orange juice mixture.

YIELD: 6 servings.

NUTRITION FACTS: 1 chicken breast half equals 240 calories, 4 g fat (1 g saturated fat), 94 mg cholesterol, 508 mg sodium, 15 g carbohydrate, trace fiber, 34 g protein. **DIABETIC EXCHANGES:** 5 lean meat, 1 starch.

ORANGE-MAPLE GLAZED CHICKEN

simple salsa chicken

Jan Cooper | TROY, ALABAMA

The flavors in this dish will hide the fact that it is so easy to make. Everyone will enjoy this one!

- 2 **boneless skinless chicken breast halves (5 ounces** *each***)**
- 1/8 **teaspoon salt**
- 1/3 **cup salsa**
- 2 **tablespoons taco sauce**
- 1/3 **cup shredded reduced-fat Mexican cheese blend**

- Place chicken in a shallow 2-qt. baking dish coated with cooking spray. Sprinkle with salt. Combine salsa and taco sauce; drizzle over chicken. Sprinkle with cheese.

- Cover and bake at 350° for 25-30 minutes or until the chicken juices run clear.

YIELD: 2 servings.

NUTRITION FACTS: 1 chicken breast half equals 226 calories, 7 g fat (3 g saturated fat), 92 mg cholesterol, 601 mg sodium, 5 g carbohydrate, trace fiber, 34 g protein. **DIABETIC EXCHANGE:** 5 lean meat.

SIMPLE SALSA CHICKEN

226 CALORIES

212 CALORIES

GARLIC-GINGER TURKEY TENDERLOINS

garlic-ginger turkey tenderloins

This good-for-you Asian entree can be on your family's plates quicker than Chinese takeout...and for a lot less money! Shared by our Test Kitchen, it has a ginger-and-brown sugar soy sauce that spices things up.

- 1 **package (20 ounces) turkey breast tenderloins**
- 3 **tablespoons brown sugar,** *divided*
- 8 **teaspoons reduced-sodium soy sauce,** *divided*
- 2 **tablespoons minced fresh gingerroot**
- 6 **garlic cloves, minced**
- 1/2 **teaspoon pepper**
- 1 **tablespoon cornstarch**
- 1 **cup reduced-sodium chicken broth**

- Place turkey in a shallow 3-qt. baking dish coated with cooking spray. In a small bowl, combine 2 tablespoons brown sugar, 6 teaspoons soy sauce, ginger, garlic and pepper. Set half aside; sprinkle remaining mixture over turkey.

- Bake, uncovered, at 375° for 25-30 minutes or until a meat thermometer reads 170°. Let stand for 5 minutes before slicing.

- Meanwhile, in a small saucepan, combine the cornstarch and broth until smooth. Stir in reserved soy sauce mixture and remaining brown sugar and soy sauce. Bring to a boil; cook and stir for 2 minutes or until thickened. Serve with turkey.

YIELD: 4 servings.

NUTRITION FACTS: 4 ounces cooked turkey with 2 tablespoons sauce equals 212 calories, 2 g fat (1 g saturated fat), 69 mg cholesterol, 639 mg sodium, 14 g carbohydrate, trace fiber, 35 g protein. **DIABETIC EXCHANGES:** 4 lean meat, 1 starch.

sweet 'n' sour meat loaf

235 CALORIES

Dorothy Havner | SAN RAFAEL, CALIFORNIA
I've made this recipe many times, and everyone who tastes it raves about it. One bite of this moist meat loaf, and you will too!

- 1/4 cup tomato sauce
- 1 tablespoon brown sugar
- 1 tablespoon cider vinegar
- 1/4 teaspoon prepared mustard
- 1 tablespoon beaten egg *or* egg substitute
- 2 tablespoons finely chopped onion
- 1 tablespoon crushed butter-flavored crackers
- 1 tablespoon minced fresh parsley
- 1/4 teaspoon salt

Dash pepper

- 1/2 pound lean ground turkey

- In a small bowl, combine the tomato sauce, brown sugar, vinegar and mustard; set aside. In another bowl, combine the egg, onion, crackers, parsley, salt, pepper and 2 tablespoons reserved tomato mixture. Crumble turkey over mixture and mix well. Shape into a 4-in. x 3-in. oval.

- Place in an 8-in. square baking dish coated with cooking spray; top with remaining tomato mixture. Bake, uncovered, at 350° for 45-50 minutes or until meat is no longer pink and a meat thermometer reads 165°. Let stand for 10 minutes before slicing.

YIELD: 2 servings.

NUTRITION FACTS: 1/2 meat loaf equals 235 calories, 11 g fat (3 g saturated fat), 122 mg cholesterol, 587 mg sodium, 11 g carbohydrate, 1 g fiber, 22 g protein. **DIABETIC EXCHANGES:** 3 lean meat, 1 starch.

mahi mahi with nectarine salsa

Michelle Augustine | CINCINNATI, OHIO
A ripe nectarine inspired me to put together a fruity salsa to serve with fish fillets. I received six thumbs up from our three children for this easy, nutritious main dish.

247 CALORIES

MAHI MAHI WITH NECTARINE SALSA

- 1 medium nectarine, peeled and chopped
- 1/4 cup chopped onion
- 2 tablespoons chopped cucumber
- 1 tablespoon minced fresh cilantro
- 2 teaspoons chopped seeded jalapeno pepper
- 2 teaspoons lime juice
- 1/4 teaspoon salt
- 1/4 teaspoon pepper
- 1/4 teaspoon Louisiana-style hot sauce

FISH FILLETS:
- 2 mahi mahi fillets (6 ounces *each*)
- 1 tablespoon olive oil

Dash salt

- For the salsa, in a small bowl, combine the first nine ingredients. Cover and refrigerate until serving.

- Drizzle fillets with oil; sprinkle with salt. Using long-handled tongs, dip a paper towel in cooking oil and lightly coat the grill rack. Grill fillets, covered, over medium heat or broil 4 in. from the heat for 3-5 minutes on each side or until fish just turns opaque. Serve with salsa.

YIELD: 2 servings.

EDITOR'S NOTE: When cutting hot peppers, disposable gloves are recommended. Avoid touching your face.

NUTRITION FACTS: 1 serving equals 247 calories, 8 g fat (1 g saturated fat), 124 mg cholesterol, 520 mg sodium, 10 g carbohydrate, 2 g fiber, 33 g protein. **DIABETIC EXCHANGES:** 5 lean meat, 1-1/2 fat, 1/2 fruit.

326 CALORIES

ZESTY LIGHT TACOS

chipotle-sparked mustard salmon

Helen Conwell | FAIRHOPE, ALABAMA
This delicious salmon packs huge flavor.

- 6 salmon fillets (4 ounces *each*)
- 1/4 cup reduced-fat mayonnaise
- 1/4 cup prepared horseradish
- 1/4 cup stone-ground mustard
- 1/4 teaspoon lemon-pepper seasoning
- 1 teaspoon minced chipotle pepper in adobo sauce
- 1 teaspoon snipped fresh dill

- Place salmon in a foil-lined 15-in. x 10-in. x 1-in. baking pan. Combine the mayonnaise, horseradish, mustard, lemon-pepper and chipotle pepper; spread over fillets.

- Bake at 350° for 15-20 minutes or until fish flakes easily with a fork. Sprinkle with dill.

YIELD: 6 servings.

NUTRITION FACTS: 1 fillet equals 260 calories, 16 g fat (3 g saturated fat), 70 mg cholesterol, 407 mg sodium, 4 g carbohydrate, 1 g fiber, 23 g protein. **DIABETIC EXCHANGES:** 3 lean meat, 1-1/2 fat.

CHIPOTLE-SPARKED MUSTARD SALMON

260 CALORIES

zesty light tacos

Maureen Mack | MILWAUKEE, WISCONSIN
This colorful main dish is very high in fiber. A complete protein with black beans and brown rice, it's perfect for vegetarians. If you need to cut down on sodium, use reduced-sodium beans and tomatoes.

- 1 cup uncooked brown rice
- 1 medium red onion, halved and sliced
- 1 medium green pepper, thinly sliced
- 1 tablespoon canola oil
- 1 can (15 ounces) black beans, rinsed and drained
- 1 can (14-1/2 ounces) diced tomatoes with mild green chilies, undrained
- 1/2 cup frozen corn
- 1/2 cup taco sauce
- 1 teaspoon chili powder
- 3/4 teaspoon cayenne pepper
- 8 whole wheat tortillas (8 inches), warmed

Optional toppings: shredded lettuce, chopped tomatoes, pickled jalapeno slices, shredded reduced-fat cheddar cheese and reduced-fat sour cream

- Cook rice according to package directions. Meanwhile, in a large nonstick skillet, saute onion and pepper in oil until tender. Stir in the beans, tomatoes, corn, taco sauce, chili powder and cayenne; heat through. Stir in cooked rice.

- Spoon 3/4 cup mixture down the center of each tortilla. Add toppings if desired.

YIELD: 8 servings.

NUTRITION FACTS: 1 taco (calculated without toppings) equals 326 calories, 6 g fat (trace saturated fat), 0 cholesterol, 565 mg sodium, 57 g carbohydrate, 7 g fiber, 10 g protein.

veggie cheese ravioli

Gertrudis Miller | EVANSVILLE, INDIANA

Have the best of both worlds with this easy weeknight dish. It tastes really light and refreshing, but the cheese ravioli makes it hearty and filling.

- 1 package (9 ounces) refrigerated cheese ravioli
- 2 small zucchini, julienned
- 1 medium onion, chopped
- 1 can (14-1/2 ounces) diced tomatoes, undrained
- 2 tablespoons chopped ripe olives
- 3/4 teaspoon Italian seasoning
- 3 tablespoons shredded Parmesan cheese

- Cook ravioli according to package directions. Meanwhile, in a large nonstick skillet coated with cooking spray, cook and stir zucchini and onion until tender. Stir in the tomatoes, olives and Italian seasoning. Bring to a boil. Reduce heat; simmer, uncovered, for 5 minutes.

- Drain ravioli and add to the pan; stir gently to combine. Sprinkle with cheese.

YIELD: 3 servings.

NUTRITION FACTS: 1-1/2 cups equals 322 calories, 8 g fat (4 g saturated fat), 37 mg cholesterol, 649 mg sodium, 48 g carbohydrate, 6 g fiber, 17 g protein.

VEGGIE CHEESE RAVIOLI

GREEK PIZZAS

greek pizzas

Doris Allers | PORTAGE, MICHIGAN

Pita breads make crispy crusts for these individual pizzas. Topped with feta and ricotta cheese as well as spinach, tomatoes and basil, the fast pizzas are a hit with everyone who tries them.

- 4 pita breads (6 inches)
- 1 cup reduced-fat ricotta cheese
- 1/2 teaspoon garlic powder
- 1 package (10 ounces) frozen chopped spinach, thawed and squeezed dry
- 3 medium tomatoes, sliced
- 3/4 cup crumbled feta cheese
- 3/4 teaspoon dried basil

- Place pita breads on a baking sheet. Combine the ricotta cheese and garlic powder; spread over pitas. Top with spinach, tomatoes, feta cheese and basil.

- Bake at 400° for 12-15 minutes or until bread is lightly browned.

YIELD: 4 servings.

NUTRITION FACTS: 1 pizza equals 320 calories, 7 g fat (4 g saturated fat), 26 mg cholesterol, 642 mg sodium, 46 g carbohydrate, 6 g fiber, 17 g protein. **DIABETIC EXCHANGES:** 2 starch, 2 vegetable, 1 lean meat, 1 fat.

grilled stuffed pork tenderloin

Bobbie Carr | LAKE OSWEGO, OREGON

We serve this stuffed tenderloin with a tossed green salad and a glass of wine. It's very good and so easy to prepare using packaged stuffing mix.

       2 pork tenderloins (3/4 pound *each*)
     3/4 cup dry red wine *or* reduced-sodium beef broth
     1/3 cup packed brown sugar
     1/4 cup ketchup
       2 tablespoons reduced-sodium soy sauce
       2 garlic cloves, minced
       1 teaspoon curry powder
     1/2 teaspoon minced fresh gingerroot
     1/4 teaspoon pepper
   1-1/4 cups water
       2 tablespoons butter
       1 package (6 ounces) stuffing mix

- Cut a lengthwise slit down the center of each tenderloin to within 1/2 in. of bottom. In a large resealable plastic bag, combine the wine or broth, brown sugar, ketchup, soy sauce, garlic, curry, ginger and pepper; add pork. Seal bag and turn to coat; refrigerate for 2-3 hours.

GRILLED STUFFED PORK TENDERLOIN

296 CALORIES

- In a small saucepan, bring water and butter to a boil. Stir in stuffing mix. Remove from the heat; cover and let stand for 5 minutes. Cool.

- Drain and discard marinade. Open tenderloins so they lie flat; spread stuffing down the center of each. Close tenderloins; tie at 1-1/2-in. intervals with kitchen string.

- Using long-handled tongs, dip a paper towel in cooking oil and lightly coat the grill rack. Prepare grill for indirect heat using a drip pan. Place pork over drip pan; grill pork, covered, over indirect medium-hot heat for 25-40 minutes or until a meat thermometer reads 160°. Let stand for 5 minutes before slicing.

YIELD: 6 servings.

NUTRITION FACTS: 1 serving equals 296 calories, 9 g fat (4 g saturated fat), 73 mg cholesterol, 678 mg sodium, 24 g carbohydrate, 1 g fiber, 27 g protein. **DIABETIC EXCHANGES:** 3 lean meat, 1-1/2 starch, 1 fat.

 281 CALORIES

easy chicken strips

Crystal Sheckles-Gibson | BEESPRING, KENTUCKY

I came up with this recipe one night when I was looking for a new, fast way to serve chicken. The strips make great appetizers, especially when served with barbecue or sweet-and-sour sauce for dunking. I've been told they're restaurant-quality.

     1/4 cup all-purpose flour
     3/4 teaspoon seasoned salt   classic
   1-1/4 cups crushed cornflakes
     1/3 cup butter, melted
   1-1/2 pounds boneless skinless chicken breasts, cut into 1-inch strips

- In a shallow bowl, combine flour and seasoned salt. Place cornflakes and butter in separate shallow bowls. Coat chicken with flour mixture, then dip in butter and coat with cornflakes.

- Transfer to an ungreased baking sheet. Bake at 400° for 15-20 minutes or until chicken is no longer pink.

YIELD: 6 servings.

NUTRITION FACTS: 1 serving equals 281 calories, 12 g fat (7 g saturated fat), 87 mg cholesterol, 430 mg sodium, 18 g carbohydrate, trace fiber, 24 g protein. **DIABETIC EXCHANGES:** 3 lean meat, 2 fat, 1 starch.

crispy cod with veggies

Take the chill off brisk evenings and warm your body and soul with this light but nourishing entree from our Test Kitchen. Round out the meal with whole wheat bread.

- 2 cups broccoli coleslaw mix
- 1/2 cup chopped fresh tomato
- 4 teaspoons chopped green onion
- 2 garlic cloves, minced
- 2 cod fillets (6 ounces *each*)

Pepper to taste

- 1/4 cup crushed potato sticks
- 3 tablespoons seasoned bread crumbs
- 2 tablespoons grated Parmesan cheese
- 4 teaspoons butter, melted

- In a large bowl, combine the coleslaw mix, tomato, onion and garlic; spread into an 11-in. x 7-in. baking pan coated with cooking spray. Top with cod fillets; sprinkle with pepper.

- Combine the potato sticks, bread crumbs, cheese and butter; sprinkle over fillets. Bake, uncovered, at 450° for 25-30 minutes or until fish flakes easily with a fork.

YIELD: 2 servings.

NUTRITION FACTS: 1 fillet with 1 cup vegetables equals 316 calories, 12 g fat (6 g saturated fat), 89 mg cholesterol, 445 mg sodium, 18 g carbohydrate, 3 g fiber, 34 g protein. **DIABETIC EXCHANGES:** 5 very lean meat, 2 fat, 1 vegetable, 1/2 starch.

CRISPY COD WITH VEGGIES

316 CALORIES

347 CALORIES

BUSY MOM'S CHICKEN FAJITAS

busy mom's chicken fajitas

Sarah Newman | BROOKLYN CENTER, MINNESOTA
Staying at home with a 9-month-old makes preparing dinner a challenge, but my slow cooker provides an easy way to make a low-fat meal. The tender meat in these fajitas is a hit, and the veggies and beans offer a healthy dose of fiber!

- 1 pound boneless skinless chicken breast halves
- 1 can (16 ounces) kidney beans, rinsed and drained
- 1 can (14-1/2 ounces) diced tomatoes with mild green chilies, drained
- 1 *each* medium green, sweet red and yellow peppers, julienned
- 1 medium onion, halved and sliced
- 2 teaspoons ground cumin
- 2 teaspoons chili powder
- 1 garlic clove, minced
- 1/4 teaspoon salt
- 6 flour tortillas (8 inches), warmed

Shredded lettuce and chopped tomatoes, optional

- In a 3-qt. slow cooker, combine chicken, kidney beans, tomatoes, peppers, onion and seasonings. Cover and cook on low for 5-6 hours or until chicken is tender.

- Remove chicken; cool slightly. Shred chicken and return to the slow cooker; heat through.

- Spoon about 3/4 cup chicken mixture down the center of each tortilla. Top with lettuce and tomatoes if desired.

YIELD: 6 servings.

NUTRITION FACTS: 1 fajita (calculated without optional toppings) equals 347 calories, 5 g fat (1 g saturated fat), 42 mg cholesterol, 778 mg sodium, 49 g carbohydrate, 7 g fiber, 26 g protein.

343 CALORIES

EASY CHICKEN ALFREDO

easy chicken alfredo

TerryAnn Moore | VINELAND, NEW JERSEY

As rich as traditional Alfredo sauce, this tasty version is lower in calories and takes just minutes to prepare.

classic

- 3 ounces uncooked fettuccine
- 1/2 cup 1% cottage cheese
- 3 tablespoons evaporated milk
- 1 tablespoon butter-flavored sprinkles
- 1 garlic clove, minced
- 2 tablespoons grated Parmesan cheese
- 2 teaspoons minced fresh parsley
- 1/8 teaspoon coarsely ground pepper
- 3/4 cup cubed cooked chicken breast
- 2 tablespoons chopped sun-dried tomatoes (not packed in oil)
- 1 tablespoon sliced ripe olives

- Cook fettuccine according to the package directions. Meanwhile, in a small food processor, combine cottage cheese, evaporated milk, butter sprinkles and garlic; cover and process until smooth.

- Transfer to a microwave-safe bowl. Stir in the Parmesan cheese, parsley and pepper. Add the chicken, tomatoes and olives. Cover and microwave on high for 2-3 minutes or until heated through. Drain fettuccine; serve with chicken mixture.

YIELD: 2 servings.

EDITOR'S NOTE: This recipe was tested in a 1,100-watt microwave.

NUTRITION FACTS: 3/4 cup pasta with 2/3 cup chicken mixture equals 343 calories, 7 g fat (3 g saturated fat), 54 mg cholesterol, 770 mg sodium, 38 g carbohydrate, 2 g fiber, 32 g protein. **DIABETIC EXCHANGES:** 3 lean meat, 2-1/2 starch.

glazed beef tournedos

Janet Singleton | BELLEVUE, OHIO

I found this wonderful, quick recipe in a book years ago. It's been a favorite for special occasions ever since! I like to serve it with twice-baked potatoes and a spinach salad.

- 3 tablespoons steak sauce
- 2 tablespoons ketchup
- 2 tablespoons orange marmalade
- 1 tablespoon lemon juice
- 1 tablespoon finely chopped onion
- 1 garlic clove, minced
- 4 beef tenderloin steaks (6 ounces *each*)

- In a small bowl, combine the steak sauce, ketchup, orange marmalade, lemon juice, onion and garlic. Set aside 1/4 cup for serving.

- Using long-handled tongs, dip a paper towel in cooking oil and lightly coat the grill rack. Grill steaks, uncovered, over medium heat or broil 4 in. from the heat for 5-7 minutes on each side or until the meat reaches desired doneness (for medium-rare, a meat thermometer should read 145°; medium, 160°; well-done, 170°), basting frequently with remaining sauce.

- Just before serving, brush steaks with reserved sauce.

YIELD: 4 servings.

NUTRITION FACTS: 1 serving equals 308 calories, 12 g fat (5 g saturated fat), 106 mg cholesterol, 385 mg sodium, 12 g carbohydrate, trace fiber, 36 g protein. **DIABETIC EXCHANGES:** 5 lean meat, 1 starch.

GLAZED BEEF TOURNEDOS

308 CALORIES

dinners | 251-350 CALORIES

292 CALORIES

COUNTRY-STYLE PORK LOIN

country-style pork loin

Corina Flansberg I CARSON CITY, NEVADA
This slow cooker recipe is a perfect end to the day. Serve the homemade gravy with mashed potatoes as a comforting side and the meal is complete!

- 1 boneless whole pork loin roast (3 pounds)
- 1/2 cup all-purpose flour
- 1 teaspoon onion powder
- 1 teaspoon ground mustard
- 2 tablespoons canola oil
- 2 cups reduced-sodium chicken broth
- 1/4 cup cornstarch
- 1/4 cup cold water

Hot mashed potatoes, optional

- Cut pork roast in half. In a large resealable plastic bag, combine the flour, onion powder and mustard. Add pork, one portion at a time, and shake to coat.

- In a large skillet, brown pork in oil over medium-high heat on all sides. Transfer to a 5-qt. slow cooker. Pour broth over pork. Cover and cook on low for 5-6 hours or until tender. Remove pork and keep warm.

- For gravy, strain cooking juices and skim fat; pour 2-1/2 cups cooking juices into a large saucepan. Combine cornstarch and water until smooth; stir into juices. Bring to a boil; cook and stir for 2 minutes or until thickened. Slice pork; serve with gravy and mashed potatoes if desired.

YIELD: 8 servings.

NUTRITION FACTS: 5 ounces cooked pork with 1/4 cup gravy (calculated without potatoes) equals 292 calories, 12 g fat (3 g saturated fat), 85 mg cholesterol, 192 mg sodium, 10 g carbohydrate, trace fiber, 34 g protein. **DIABETIC EXCHANGES:** 5 lean meat, 1/2 starch, 1/2 fat.

spicy turkey quesadillas

A bit of spice livens up cranberries and turkey while fat-free cream cheese rounds out the flavors in this easy appetizer. You'll love this recipe from our Test Kitchen!

- 3 ounces fat-free cream cheese
- 1/4 cup chopped fresh *or* frozen cranberries, thawed
- 1 tablespoon chopped green chilies **classic**
- 1-1/2 teaspoons honey
- 1 teaspoon Louisiana-style hot sauce
- 4 flour tortillas (6 inches)
- 1 cup diced cooked turkey breast

- In a small bowl, beat cream cheese until smooth. Stir in the cranberries, green chilies, honey and hot sauce until blended. Spread over one side of each tortilla. Place turkey on two tortillas; top with remaining tortillas.

- Cook in a large nonstick skillet over medium heat for 2-3 minutes on each side or until lightly browned. Cut quesadillas into wedges.

YIELD: 2 servings.

NUTRITION FACTS: 1 quesadilla equals 343 calories, 7 g fat (1 g saturated fat), 64 mg cholesterol, 751 mg sodium, 35 g carbohydrate, 1 g fiber, 33 g protein. **DIABETIC EXCHANGES:** 3 lean meat, 2 starch.

SPICY TURKEY QUESADILLAS

343 CALORIES

(318 CALORIES) moist & tender turkey breast

Heidi Vawdrey | RIVERTON, UTAH

This easy dish will be very popular in your home. Your family will love the taste and you will love how quickly it comes together in the slow cooker.

- 1 bone-in turkey breast (6 to 7 pounds)
- 4 fresh rosemary sprigs
- 4 garlic cloves, peeled
- 1 tablespoon brown sugar
- 1/2 teaspoon coarsely ground pepper
- 1/4 teaspoon salt

- Place turkey breast in a 6-qt. slow cooker. Place rosemary and garlic around turkey. Combine the brown sugar, pepper and salt; sprinkle over turkey. Cover and cook on low for 4-6 hours or until turkey is tender.

YIELD: 12 servings.

NUTRITION FACTS: 7 ounces cooked turkey equals 318 calories, 12 g fat (3 g saturated fat), 122 mg cholesterol, 154 mg sodium, 2 g carbohydrate, trace fiber, 47 g protein.

stir-fried walnut chicken

Sharon Allen | ALLENTOWN, PENNSYLVANIA

I prepare this simple stir-fry often because I can't get enough of the tasty results. The meal-in-one recipe is perfect for busy weeknights.

- 1 teaspoon plus 3 tablespoons cornstarch, *divided*
- 2 teaspoons plus 3 tablespoons reduced-sodium soy sauce, *divided*
- 1 pound boneless skinless chicken breasts, cut into strips
- 1-1/2 cups reduced-sodium chicken broth
- 1-1/2 teaspoons grated fresh gingerroot
- 5 teaspoons vegetable oil, *divided*
- 1 medium onion, quartered
- 1 garlic clove, minced
- 1 medium sweet red pepper, julienned
- 1/2 cup fresh broccoli florets

(318 CALORIES)

STIR-FRIED WALNUT CHICKEN

- 1/2 cup chopped carrot
- 1 can (8 ounces) sliced water chestnuts, drained
- 3 cups cooked long grain rice
- 1/4 cup chopped walnuts, toasted

- In a small bowl, combine 1 teaspoon cornstarch and 2 teaspoons soy sauce until smooth. Place the chicken in a large resealable plastic bag; add soy sauce mixture. Seal bag and turn to coat; refrigerate for 30 minutes.

- In another bowl, combine the remaining cornstarch and soy sauce until smooth. Stir in chicken broth and ginger; set aside.

- In a large nonstick skillet or wok, stir-fry the chicken in 2 teaspoons hot oil until no longer pink; remove and keep warm. In the same pan, stir-fry onion and garlic in remaining oil until tender. Add the red pepper, broccoli, carrot and water chestnuts; cook and stir until vegetables are crisp-tender.

- Stir broth mixture and stir into vegetables. Bring to a boil; cook and stir for 1-2 minutes or until thickened. Return chicken to the pan; heat through. Serve with rice. Sprinkle with walnuts.

YIELD: 6 servings.

NUTRITION FACTS: 3/4 cup chicken mixture with 1/2 cup rice equals 318 calories, 9 g fat (1 g saturated fat), 42 mg cholesterol, 572 mg sodium, 38 g carbohydrate, 3 g fiber, 21 g protein. **DIABETIC EXCHANGES:** 2 starch, 2 lean meat, 1-1/2 fat, 1 vegetable.

stovetop beef 'n' shells

Donna Roberts | MANHATTAN, KANSAS

I fix this supper when I'm pressed for time because it's as tasty as it is fast. Team it with a tossed salad, bread and fruit for a complete meal.

- 4 ounces uncooked medium pasta shells
- 1 pound lean ground beef (90% lean)
- 1 medium onion, chopped
- 1 garlic clove, minced
- 1 can (15 ounces) crushed tomatoes
- 1 can (8 ounces) tomato sauce
- 1 teaspoon sugar
- 1/2 teaspoon salt
- 1/2 teaspoon pepper

- Cook pasta according to package directions. Meanwhile, in a large saucepan, cook beef and onion over medium heat until the meat is no longer pink. Add garlic; cook 1 minute longer. Drain.

- Stir in the tomatoes, tomato sauce, sugar, salt and pepper. Bring to a boil. Reduce heat; simmer, uncovered, for 10-15 minutes. Drain pasta; stir into beef mixture and heat through.

YIELD: 4 servings.

NUTRITION FACTS: 1-1/4 cups equals 339 calories, 9 g fat (4 g saturated fat), 56 mg cholesterol, 772 mg sodium, 36 g carbohydrate, 4 g fiber, 29 g protein. **DIABETIC EXCHANGES:** 3 lean meat, 2-1/2 starch.

STOVETOP BEEF 'N' SHELLS

339 CALORIES

252 CALORIES

SMOTHERED CHICKEN ITALIANO

smothered chicken italiano

Mary Kretschmer | MIAMI, FLORIDA

This is one of my husband's favorites and has become an "old reliable" to serve dinner guests. It's impressive and tasty but so easy to prepare.

- 1/2 teaspoon dried oregano
- 1/4 teaspoon garlic powder
- 1/4 teaspoon salt, *divided*
- 1/4 teaspoon pepper, *divided*
- 4 boneless skinless chicken breast halves (4 ounces *each*)
- 2 teaspoons canola oil
- 1 cup part-skim ricotta cheese
- 1 cup crushed tomatoes
- 4 slices part-skim mozzarella cheese

- In a small bowl, combine the oregano, garlic powder, 1/8 teaspoon salt and 1/8 teaspoon pepper; rub over chicken. In a large nonstick skillet coated with cooking spray, brown chicken in oil for 3-4 minutes on each side.

- Transfer to an 11-in. x 7-in. baking dish coated with cooking spray. Combine ricotta cheese and remaining salt and pepper; spoon over chicken. Top with tomatoes.

- Bake, uncovered, at 350° for 15 minutes. Top with the mozzarella cheese. Bake 5-10 minutes longer or until a meat thermometer reads 170°.

YIELD: 4 servings.

NUTRITION FACTS: 1 serving equals 252 calories, 11 g fat (5 g saturated fat), 85 mg cholesterol, 341 mg sodium, 6 g carbohydrate, 1 g fiber, 32 g protein. **DIABETIC EXCHANGES:** 4 lean meat, 1/2 fat.

round steak with potatoes

Taryn Kuebelbeck | PLYMOUTH, MINNESOTA

Have a delicious meat-and-potatoes dinner tonight! Baking the round steak for an extended amount of time in this recipe ensures tenderness.

- 2 pounds beef top round steak
- 1 teaspoon salt
- 1/2 teaspoon pepper
- 2 tablespoons canola oil
- 1 can (10-3/4 ounces) condensed golden mushroom soup, undiluted
- 1-1/4 cups water
- 1 cup chopped celery
- 1 cup chopped sweet red pepper
- 1/2 cup chopped onion
- 1/4 teaspoon dried thyme
- 12 small red potatoes

- Cut steak into six pieces; sprinkle with salt and pepper. In a Dutch oven, brown meat in oil on both sides. Stir in the soup, water, celery, red pepper, onion and thyme. Cover and bake at 350° for 1 hour.

- Add potatoes; cover and bake 1-1/2 hours longer or until steak and vegetables are tender.

YIELD: 6 servings.

NUTRITION FACTS: 1 serving equals 344 calories, 11 g fat (2 g saturated fat), 87 mg cholesterol, 829 mg sodium, 22 g carbohydrate, 3 g fiber, 37 g protein.

ROUND STEAK WITH POTATOES

344 CALORIES

---

269 CALORIES

BAKED CHICKEN CHIMICHANGAS

baked chicken chimichangas

Rickey Madden | CLINTON, SOUTH CAROLINA

I developed this quick and easy recipe through trial and error. I used to garnish it with sour cream, too, but eliminated it in order to lighten the recipe. My friends all love it when I cook these, and they're much healthier than fried chimichangas.

- 1-1/2 cups cubed cooked chicken breast
- 1-1/2 cups picante sauce, *divided*
- 1/2 cup shredded reduced-fat cheddar cheese
- 2/3 cup chopped green onions, *divided*
- 1 teaspoon ground cumin
- 1 teaspoon dried oregano
- 6 flour tortillas (8 inches), warmed
- 1 tablespoon butter, melted

- In a small bowl, combine the chicken, 3/4 cup picante sauce, cheese, 1/4 cup green onions, cumin and oregano. Spoon 1/2 cup mixture down the center of each tortilla. Fold sides and ends over filling and roll up. Place seam side down in a 15-in. x 10-in. x 1-in. baking pan coated with cooking spray. Brush with butter.

- Bake, uncovered, at 375° for 20-25 minutes or until heated through. Top with remaining picante sauce and onions.

YIELD: 6 servings.

NUTRITION FACTS: 1 chimichanga equals 269 calories, 8 g fat (3 g saturated fat), 39 mg cholesterol, 613 mg sodium, 31 g carbohydrate, 1 g fiber, 17 g protein. **DIABETIC EXCHANGES:** ...an meat, 1-1/2 starch, 1 vegetable, 1/2 fat.

292 CALORIES

VERMONT TURKEY LOAF

vermont turkey loaf

Kari Caven I COEUR D'ALENE, IDAHO

The maple glaze on this turkey loaf makes it deliciously different from other meat loaves. I can easily double the recipe for company or bake an extra loaf and freeze it for a hectic weeknight.

- 1/3 cup coarsely chopped onion
- 1/3 cup coarsely chopped fresh mushrooms
- 1/3 cup coarsely chopped carrot
- 1/3 cup dry bread crumbs
- 1/4 teaspoon salt
- 1/4 teaspoon pepper
- 1/2 pound lean ground turkey
- 1 tablespoon maple syrup
- 1 teaspoon Dijon mustard

- In a small skillet coated with cooking spray, saute the onion, mushrooms and carrot until tender; cool slightly.

- In a small bowl, combine the vegetables, bread crumbs, salt and pepper. Crumble turkey over mixture and mix well. Shape into a 6-in. x 3-in. loaf.

- Place in an 8-in. square baking dish coated with cooking spray. Bake, uncovered, at 375° for 15 minutes.

- In a small bowl, combine syrup and mustard; pour half over the turkey loaf. Bake 5-10 minutes longer or until a meat thermometer reads 165° and juices run clear. Serve with remaining syrup mixture.

YIELD: 2 servings.

NUTRITION FACTS: 1/2 meat loaf equals 292 calories, 11 g fat (3 g saturated fat), 90 mg cholesterol, 629 mg sodium, 25 g carbohydrate, 2 g fiber, 23 g protein. **DIABETIC EXCHANGES:** 3 lean meat, 1 starch, 1 vegetable.

homemade fish sticks

Jennifer Rowland I ELIZABETHTOWN, KENTUCKY

I'm a nutritionist and needed a healthy fish fix. Moist inside and crunchy outside, these are great with oven fries or roasted veggies and low-fat homemade tartar sauce.

- 1/2 cup all-purpose flour
- 1 egg, beaten
- 1/2 cup dry bread crumbs
- 1/2 teaspoon salt
- 1/2 teaspoon paprika
- 1/2 teaspoon lemon-pepper seasoning
- 3/4 pound cod fillets, cut into 1-inch strips

Butter-flavored cooking spray

classic

- Place flour and egg in separate shallow bowls. In another shallow bowl, combine the bread crumbs and seasonings. Dip the fish fillets in the flour, then egg, then roll in the crumb mixture.

- Place on a baking sheet coated with cooking spray. Spritz fish sticks with butter-flavored spray. Bake at 400° for 10-12 minutes or until fish flakes easily with a fork, turning once.

YIELD: 2 servings.

NUTRITION FACTS: 1 serving equals 278 calories, 4 g fat (1 g saturated fat), 129 mg cholesterol, 718 mg sodium, 25 g carbohydrate, 1 g fiber, 33 g protein. **DIABETIC EXCHANGES:** 4 lean meat, 1-1/2 starch.

HOMEMADE FISH STICKS

278 CALORIES

picante beef roast

Margaret Thiel I LEVITTOWN, PENNSYLVANIA

Before putting your roast in the slow cooker, trim the fat to avoid greasy gravy. If your roast weighs 3 or more pounds, cut it in half to ensure even cooking.

- 1 beef rump roast *or* bottom round roast (3 pounds), trimmed and halved
- 1 jar (16 ounces) picante sauce
- 1 can (15 ounces) tomato sauce
- 1 envelope taco seasoning
- 3 tablespoons cornstarch
- 1/4 cup water

- Cut roast in half; place in a 5-qt. slow cooker. In a large bowl, combine the picante sauce, tomato sauce and taco seasoning; pour over roast.

- Cover and cook on low for 8-9 hours or until the meat is tender.

- Remove meat to a serving platter; keep warm. Skim fat from cooking juices; transfer 3 cups to a small saucepan. Bring liquid to a boil.

- Combine cornstarch and water until smooth. Gradually stir into pan. Bring to a boil; cook and stir for 2 minutes or until thickened. Slice roast; serve with gravy.

YIELD: 8 servings.

NUTRITION FACTS: 5 ounces cooked beef with 1/3 cup gravy equals 267 calories, 8 g fat (3 g saturated fat), 102 mg cholesterol, 983 mg sodium, 11 g carbohydrate, trace fiber, 34 g protein.

PICANTE BEEF ROAST

267 CALORIES

340 CALORIES

MAKEOVER TATER-TOPPED CASSEROLE

makeover tater-topped casserole

Scott Woodward I ELKHORN, WISCONSIN

I love Tater Tots, and my casserole recipe is a delicious way to use them, but I wanted it to be healthier. Luckily, the Taste of Home experts slashed the fat from this favorite dish while keeping all the tots!

- 1 pound lean ground beef (90% lean)
- 1/2 pound extra-lean ground turkey
- 1 package (16 ounces) frozen mixed vegetables, thawed and drained
- 3/4 cup french-fried onions
- 1 can (10-3/4 ounces) reduced-fat reduced-sodium condensed cream of celery soup, undiluted
- 1 can (10-3/4 ounces) reduced-fat reduced-sodium condensed cream of chicken soup, undiluted
- 1/2 cup fat-free milk
- 4 cups frozen Tater Tots, thawed

classic

- In a large skillet, cook the ground beef and turkey over medium heat until no longer pink. In a 13-in. x 9-in. baking dish coated with cooking spray, layer the meat mixture, vegetables and onions.

- In a small bowl, combine soups and milk; spread over onions. Top with Tater Tots. Bake, uncovered, at 350° for 55-60 minutes or until golden brown.

YIELD: 8 servings.

NUTRITION FACTS: 1 cup equals 340 calories, 14 g fat (4 g saturated fat), 44 mg cholesterol, 657 mg sodium, 33 g carbohydrate, 4 g fiber, 22 g protein.

buffalo chicken burgers with tangy slaw

Jeanne Holt | MENDOTA HEIGHTS, MINNESOTA

With a homemade sauce and slaw, these burgers are my way of enjoying the flavors of chicken wings while avoiding some of the fat and calories.

SLAW:

- 1/4 cup thinly sliced celery
- 1/4 cup shredded apple
- 2 tablespoons fat-free blue cheese salad dressing
- 1 teaspoon finely chopped walnuts

SAUCE:

- 3 tablespoons Louisiana-style hot sauce
- 2 teaspoons ketchup
- 2 teaspoons reduced-fat butter, melted

BURGERS:

- 2 tablespoons chopped sweet red pepper
- 2 tablespoons plus 4 teaspoons thinly sliced green onions, *divided*
- 1 tablespoon unsweetened applesauce
- 1/4 teaspoon salt
- 1/4 teaspoon garlic salt
- 1/4 teaspoon pepper
- 1 pound ground chicken
- 4 lettuce leaves
- 4 hamburger buns, split

BUFFALO CHICKEN BURGERS WITH TANGY SLAW

312 CALORIES

- In a small bowl, combine the celery, apple, salad dressing and walnuts. In another small bowl, combine the hot sauce, ketchup and butter; set aside.

- In a large bowl, combine the red pepper, 2 tablespoons green onion, applesauce, salt, garlic salt and pepper. Crumble chicken over mixture and mix well. Shape into four burgers.

- Broil 6 in. from the heat for 5-7 minutes on each side or until a meat thermometer reads 165° and juices run clear, basting occasionally with reserved sauce. Serve on lettuce-lined buns; top each with 2 tablespoons slaw and sprinkle with remaining green onion.

YIELD: 4 servings.

EDITOR'S NOTE: This recipe was tested with Land O'Lakes light stick butter.

NUTRITION FACTS: 1 burger equals 312 calories, 12 g fat (4 g saturated fat), 78 mg cholesterol, 682 mg sodium, 29 g carbohydrate, 2 g fiber, 23 g protein. **DIABETIC EXCHANGES:** 3 lean meat, 2 starch.

beef macaroni skillet

291 CALORIES

Carmen Edwards | MIDLAND, TEXAS

This casserole favorite is tasty and filling. It's easy to prepare, even after a long day at work.

- 1/2 pound lean ground beef (90% lean)
- 1/3 cup chopped onion
- 1/4 cup chopped green pepper
- 1-1/2 cups spicy hot V8 juice
- 1/2 cup uncooked elbow macaroni
- 1 teaspoon Worcestershire sauce
- 1/4 teaspoon pepper

- In a large skillet, cook the beef, onion and green pepper over medium heat until meat is no longer pink; drain. Stir in the remaining ingredients. Bring to a boil. Reduce heat; cover and simmer for 18-20 minutes or until the macaroni is tender.

YIELD: 2 servings.

NUTRITION FACTS: 1-1/4 cups equals 291 calories, 9 g fat (4 g saturated fat), 56 mg cholesterol, 689 mg sodium, 25 g carbohydrate, 2 g fiber, 26 g protein. **DIABETIC EXCHANGES:** 3 lean meat, 2 vegetable, 1 starch.

MEXICALI CASSEROLE

mexicali casserole

Gertrudis Miller | EVANSVILLE, INDIANA

Kids will love this hearty yet mild-tasting Mexican-style casserole. It's also popular at potluck dinners.

- 1 **pound lean ground turkey**
- 1-1/2 **cups chopped onions**
- 1/2 **cup chopped green pepper**
- 1 **garlic clove, minced**
- 1 **teaspoon chili powder**
- 1/2 **teaspoon salt**
- 1 **can (16 ounces) kidney beans, rinsed and drained**
- 1 **can (14-1/2 ounces) diced tomatoes, undrained**
- 1 **cup water**
- 2/3 **cup uncooked long grain rice**
- 1/3 **cup sliced ripe olives**
- 1/2 **cup shredded reduced-fat cheddar cheese**

- In a large skillet coated with cooking spray, cook the turkey, onions and green pepper over medium heat until meat is no longer pink and vegetables are tender. Add garlic; cook 1 minute longer; drain. Sprinkle with chili powder and salt. Stir in the beans, tomatoes, water, rice and olives.

- Transfer to a 2-1/2-qt. baking dish coated with cooking spray. Cover and bake at 375° for 50-55 minutes or until rice is tender. Uncover; sprinkle with cheddar cheese. Bake 5 minutes longer or until cheese is melted.

YIELD: 6 servings.

NUTRITION FACTS: 1 serving equals 348 calories, 10 g fat (3 g saturated fat), 66 mg cholesterol, 508 mg sodium, 41 g carbohydrate, 9 g fiber, 24 g protein. **DIABETIC EXCHANGES:** 3 lean meat, 2 starch, 2 vegetable.

cacciatore chicken breasts

JoAnn McCauley | DUBUQUE, IOWA

This easy recipe is my version of traditional Chicken Cacciatore. The tasty sauce and chicken can be served over rice or noodles. If you want to lower the sodium, use garlic powder instead of garlic salt.

- 1/2 **medium onion, sliced and separated into rings**
- 1/2 **medium green pepper, sliced**
- 1 **tablespoon olive oil**
- 2 **boneless skinless chicken breast halves (5 ounces *each*)**
- 3/4 **cup canned stewed tomatoes**
- 2 **tablespoons white wine *or* chicken broth**
- 1/4 **teaspoon garlic salt**
- 1/4 **teaspoon dried rosemary, crushed**
- 1/8 **teaspoon pepper**

- In a large skillet, saute onion and green pepper in oil until crisp-tender. Remove and keep warm. Cook chicken over medium-high heat for 4-5 minutes on each side or until juices run clear. Remove and keep warm.

- Add tomatoes, wine or broth, garlic salt, rosemary and pepper to the skillet; cook and stir until heated through. Add onion mixture. Serve over chicken.

YIELD: 2 servings.

NUTRITION FACTS: 1 chicken breast half with 3/4 cup vegetables equals 272 calories, 10 g fat (2 g saturated fat), 78 mg cholesterol, 462 mg sodium, 12 g carbohydrate, 2 g fiber, 30 g protein. **DIABETIC EXCHANGES:** 4 lean meat, 2 vegetable, 1-1/2 fat.

CACCIATORE CHICKEN BREASTS

turkey 'n' squash lasagna

Nancy Beall | COLORADO SPRINGS, COLORADO

I came up with this lasagna recipe when spaghetti squash was on sale at the supermarket, and it was a hit with all my friends. I used ground turkey because I'm trying to cook healthier.

1 medium spaghetti squash (2 to 2-1/2 pounds)
1 pound lean ground turkey
1 large onion, chopped
1 tablespoon olive oil, *divided*
2 garlic cloves, minced
2 cans (28 ounces *each*) crushed tomatoes
1 can (6 ounces) tomato paste
1/3 cup minced fresh parsley
1 teaspoon sugar
1 teaspoon dried basil
1 teaspoon dried oregano
1/2 teaspoon salt
1/4 teaspoon pepper
1 egg, lightly beaten
1 carton (15 ounces) reduced-fat ricotta cheese
3/4 cup plus 2 tablespoons grated Parmesan cheese, *divided*
2 medium zucchini, sliced
6 lasagna noodles, cooked and drained
2 cups (8 ounces) shredded part-skim mozzarella cheese, *divided*

- With a sharp knife, pierce spaghetti squash 10 times. Place on a microwave-safe plate; microwave on high for 5-6 minutes. Turn; cook 4-5 minutes longer or until fork-tender. Cover and let stand for 15 minutes. Cut squash in half lengthwise; discard seeds. Scoop out squash, separating strands with a fork; set aside.

- In a large saucepan, cook the ground turkey and onion in 1-1/2 teaspoons oil over medium heat until meat is no longer pink. Add garlic; cook 1 minute longer. Drain. Stir in the tomatoes, tomato paste, parsley, sugar and seasonings. Bring to a boil. Reduce heat; cover and simmer for 30 minutes.

- In a small bowl, combine the egg, ricotta and 3/4 cup Parmesan until blended. In a small skillet, saute zucchini in remaining oil until crisp-tender.

- Spread 1-1/2 cups meat sauce into a 13-in. x 9-in. baking dish coated with cooking spray. Layer with three noodles and half of the zucchini, spaghetti squash and ricotta mixture. Sprinkle with 1-1/2 cups mozzarella and half of remaining sauce. Top with the remaining noodles, zucchini, spaghetti squash, ricotta mixture and sauce (dish will be full).

- Place dish on a baking sheet. Bake, uncovered, at 350° for 45-55 minutes or until edges are bubbly. Sprinkle with remaining mozzarella and Parmesan cheeses. Bake 5 minutes longer or until cheese is melted. Let stand for 10 minutes before cutting.

YIELD: 12 servings.

EDITOR'S NOTE: This recipe was tested in a 1,100-watt microwave.

NUTRITION FACTS: 1 serving equals 311 calories, 12 g fat (5 g saturated fat), 72 mg cholesterol, 548 mg sodium, 31 g carbohydrate, 5 g fiber, 22 g protein. **DIABETIC EXCHANGES:** 2 starch, 2 lean meat, 1 fat.

TURKEY 'N' SQUASH LASAGNA

311 CALORIES

eef barley stew

Lisa Kolenich | REGINA, SASKATCHEWAN

Hearty and easy to fix, this thick stew has a comforting, chili-like flavor. It's my best barley recipe. I'm sure you'll agree that it's a tasty dish.

- 1/2 pound lean ground beef (90% lean)
- 1/2 cup sliced celery
- 1/3 cup chopped onion
- 1-3/4 cups water
- 2 teaspoons reduced-sodium beef bouillon granules
- 1-1/2 teaspoons chili powder
- 1/4 teaspoon pepper
- 1/2 cup quick-cooking barley
- 1 can (14-1/2 ounces) diced tomatoes, undrained

- In a large saucepan, cook the beef, celery and onion over medium heat until meat is no longer pink and vegetables are tender; drain.

- Stir in the water, beef bouillon, chili powder and pepper. Bring to a boil. Stir in the barley. Reduce heat; cover and simmer for 10-12 minutes or until barley is tender. Stir in tomatoes; heat through.

YIELD: 4 cups.

NUTRITION FACTS: 1-1/3 cups equals 269 calories, 7 g fat (3 g saturated fat), 37 mg cholesterol, 456 mg sodium, 33 g carbohydrate, 9 g fiber, 20 g protein. **DIABETIC EXCHANGES:** 2 lean meat, 1-1/2 starch, 1 vegetable.

BEEF BARLEY STEW

269 CALORIES

342 CALORIES

CHICKEN ORZO SKILLET

chicken orzo skillet

Kathleen Farrell | ROCHESTER, NEW YORK

As a busy homemaker with a home-based business, I try to make quick dinners that are healthy for my husband and two young children. I combined two recipes to come up with this family favorite.

- 1 cup uncooked orzo pasta
- 1 pound boneless skinless chicken breasts, cubed
- 3 teaspoons olive oil, *divided*
- 3 garlic cloves, minced
- 2 cans (14-1/2 ounces *each*) stewed tomatoes, cut up
- 1 can (15 ounces) white kidney *or* cannellini beans, rinsed and drained
- 1-1/2 teaspoons Italian seasoning
- 1/2 teaspoon salt
- 1 package (16 ounces) frozen broccoli florets, thawed

- Cook orzo according to package directions. Meanwhile, in a large nonstick skillet coated with cooking spray, cook chicken in 2 teaspoons oil for 6-7 minutes or until no longer pink. Remove and keep warm.

- In the same skillet, cook garlic in remaining oil for 1 minute or until tender. Stir in the tomatoes, beans, Italian seasoning and salt. Bring to a boil. Stir in broccoli and chicken; heat through. Drain orzo; stir into chicken mixture.

YIELD: 6 servings.

NUTRITION FACTS: 1-1/2 cups equals 342 calories, 5 g fat (1 g saturated fat), 42 mg cholesterol, 589 mg sodium, 49 g carbohydrate, 7 g fiber, 25 g protein.

slow-cooked mac 'n' cheese

Shelby Molina | **WHITEWATER, WISCONSIN**

Slow-Cooked Mac 'n' Cheese: the words alone are enough to make most mouths water. This recipe is a great example of comfort food at its finest.

- 2 cups uncooked elbow macaroni
- 1 can (12 ounces) reduced-fat evaporated milk
- 1-1/2 cups fat-free milk
- 1/3 cup egg substitute
- 1 tablespoon butter, melted
- 8 ounces reduced-fat process cheese (Velveeta), cubed
- 2 cups (8 ounces) shredded sharp cheddar cheese, *divided*

- Cook macaroni according to package directions; drain and rinse in cold water. In a large bowl, combine the evaporated milk, milk, egg substitute and butter. Stir in the process cheese, 1-1/2 cups sharp cheddar cheese and macaroni.

- Transfer to a 3-qt. slow cooker coated with cooking spray. Cover and cook on low for 2-3/4 to 3 hours or until center is set, stirring once. Sprinkle with remaining sharp cheddar cheese.

YIELD: 9 servings.

NUTRITION FACTS: 3/4 cup equals 300 calories, 12 g fat (9 g saturated fat), 45 mg cholesterol, 647 mg sodium, 29 g carbohydrate, 1 g fiber, 19 g protein. **DIABETIC EXCHANGES:** 2 starch, 2 medium-fat meat.

SLOW-COOKED MAC 'N' CHEESE

ORANGE ROUGHY WITH RICE

orange roughy with rice

Orange roughy is a great fish for this mild yet tasty meal from our Test Kitchen. Flounder, sole or red snapper will also work well in this recipe.

- 1 package (5.7 ounces) instant creamy chicken-flavored rice and sauce mix
- 2 cups water
- 1 tablespoon butter, optional
- 1 cup fresh broccoli florets
- 1/4 teaspoon onion salt
- 1/4 teaspoon pepper
- 1/8 teaspoon dill weed
- 1/8 teaspoon paprika
- 4 orange roughy fillets (6 ounces *each*)
- 1 tablespoon olive oil

- In a large saucepan, combine the rice mix, water and butter if desired. Bring to a boil; stir in the broccoli. Reduce heat; cover and simmer for 7 minutes or until rice is tender.

- Meanwhile, combine the onion salt, pepper, dill and paprika; sprinkle over fillets. In a large skillet, cook fillets in oil over medium heat for 4-6 minutes on each side or until fish flakes easily with a fork.

- Remove rice from the heat; let stand for 2 minutes. Serve with fish.

YIELD: 4 servings.

NUTRITION FACTS: 1 fillet with 3/4 cup rice (calculated without butter) equals 320 calories, 8 g fat (1 g saturated fat), 34 mg cholesterol, 719 mg sodium, 31 g carbohydrate, 2 g fiber, 30 g protein. **DIABETIC EXCHANGES:** 4 lean meat, 2 starch, 1/2 fat.

302 CALORIES

TERIYAKI PORK

teriyaki pork

Molly Gee | PLAINWELL, MICHIGAN

I season pork strips and a medley of crisp-tender vegetables with a soy sauce and garlic marinade for this savory stir-fry. It's a nutritious and tasty dinner.

- 3/4 **cup reduced-sodium chicken broth,** *divided*
- 1/3 **cup reduced-sodium soy sauce**
- 2 **tablespoons red wine vinegar**
- 2 **teaspoons honey**
- 2 **teaspoons garlic powder**
- 1 **pound boneless pork loin chops, cut into thin strips**
- 1 **tablespoon canola oil**
- 2 **cups fresh broccoli florets**
- 3 **medium carrots, sliced**
- 3 **celery ribs, sliced**
- 4 **cups shredded cabbage**
- 6 **green onions, sliced**
- 1 **tablespoon cornstarch**

Hot cooked rice, optional

- In a small bowl, combine 1/4 cup broth, soy sauce, vinegar, honey and garlic powder. Pour 1/3 cup marinade into a large resealable plastic bag; add the pork. Seal bag and turn to coat; refrigerate for 1 hour. Cover and refrigerate remaining marinade.

- Drain and discard marinade. In large nonstick skillet or wok, stir-fry pork in oil for 2-3 minutes or until no longer pink. Remove and keep warm. In the same pan, stir-fry broccoli and carrots in reserved marinade for 2 minutes. Add celery; stir-fry for 2 minutes. Add cabbage and green onions; stir-fry 2-3 minutes longer or until vegetables are crisp-tender.

- Combine cornstarch and remaining broth until smooth; stir into vegetable mixture. Bring to a boil; cook and stir until thickened. Return pork to the pan; heat through. Serve with rice if desired.

YIELD: 4 servings.

NUTRITION FACTS: 1-1/2 cups stir-fry mixture (calculated without rice) equals 302 calories, 11 g fat (3 g saturated fat), 63 mg cholesterol, 802 mg sodium, 20 g carbohydrate, 5 g fiber, 30 g protein. **DIABETIC EXCHANGES:** 3 lean meat, 1 starch, 1/2 fat.

330 CALORIES

hamburger shepherd's pie

Elaine Williams | SURREY, BRITISH COLUMBIA

Transform leftovers into a light but filling one-dish meal sized for two. This is a simple and scrumptious recipe.

- 1/2 **pound lean ground beef (90% lean)**
- 2 **tablespoons chopped onion**
- 1 **cup frozen cut green beans, thawed**
- 2/3 **cup condensed tomato soup, undiluted**
- 1/4 **teaspoon Italian seasoning**
- 1/8 **teaspoon pepper**
- 1 **cup mashed potatoes (prepared with milk)**

Dash paprika

- In a small skillet, cook beef and onion over medium heat until meat is no longer pink; drain. Add the beans, soup, Italian seasoning and pepper. Transfer to a 7-in. pie plate coated with cooking spray.

- Spread the mashed potatoes over the top; sprinkle with paprika. Bake, uncovered, at 350° for 30-35 minutes or until heated through.

YIELD: 2 servings.

NUTRITION FACTS: 1/2 pie equals 330 calories, 10 g fat (4 g saturated fat), 71 mg cholesterol, 927 mg sodium, 35 g carbohydrate, 5 g fiber, 26 g protein.

267 CALORIES

SKILLET TACOS

skillet tacos

Maria Gobel I GREENFIELD, WISCONSIN

If you like Mexican food, then you'll love this fast and healthy alternative to traditional tacos. With its Southwestern flair and popular ingredients, it's a can't-miss dinner.

1/4	pound lean ground turkey
2	tablespoons chopped onion
2	tablespoons chopped green pepper
1	can (8 ounces) tomato sauce
1/2	cup uncooked elbow macaroni
1/2	cup water
1/4	cup picante sauce
2	tablespoons shredded fat-free cheddar cheese
1/4	cup crushed baked tortilla chip scoops
1/4	cup chopped avocado

Iceberg lettuce wedges and fat-free sour cream, optional

- In a large nonstick skillet coated with cooking spray, cook the turkey, onion and green pepper over medium heat until turkey is no longer pink.

- Stir in the tomato sauce, uncooked macaroni, water and picante sauce. Bring to a boil. Reduce heat; cover and simmer for 10-15 minutes or until macaroni is tender.

- Divide between two plates; top with cheese, chips and avocado. Serve with lettuce and sour cream if desired.

YIELD: 2 servings.

NUTRITION FACTS: 1 cup (calculated without optional ingredients) equals 267 calories, 9 g fat (2 g saturated fat), 46 mg cholesterol, 795 mg sodium, 30 g carbohydrate, 3 g fiber, 18 g protein. **DIABETIC EXCHANGES:** 2 lean meat, 1-1/2 starch, 1 vegetable, 1/2 fat.

tilapia & lemon sauce

Susan Taul I BIRMINGHAM, ALABAMA

Serve this dish with any tossed salad full of your favorite vegetables. It's easy, quick and unique.

1/4	cup plus 1 tablespoon all-purpose flour, *divided*
1	teaspoon salt
4	tilapia fillets (4 ounces *each*)
2	tablespoons plus 2 teaspoons butter, *divided*
1/3	cup reduced-sodium chicken broth
2	tablespoons white wine *or* additional reduced-sodium chicken broth
1-1/2	teaspoons lemon juice
1-1/2	teaspoons minced fresh parsley
1/4	cup sliced almonds, toasted
2	cups hot cooked rice

- In a shallow bowl, combine 1/4 cup flour and salt. Dip fillets in flour mixture. In a large nonstick skillet coated with cooking spray, cook fillets in 2 tablespoons butter over medium-high heat for 4-5 minutes on each side or until fish flakes easily with a fork. Remove and keep warm.

- In the same skillet, melt the remaining butter. Stir in the remaining flour until smooth; gradually add the broth, wine and lemon juice. Bring to a boil; cook and stir for 2 minutes or until thickened. Stir in parsley. Spoon sauce over fish; sprinkle with almonds. Serve with rice.

YIELD: 4 servings.

NUTRITION FACTS: 1 fillet with 1/2 cup rice and 4 teaspoons sauce equals 334 calories, 12 g fat (6 g saturated fat), 75 mg cholesterol, 586 mg sodium, 30 g carbohydrate, 1 g fiber, 26 g protein. **DIABETIC EXCHANGES:** 2 starch, 2 lean meat, 2 fat.

TILAPIA & LEMON SAUCE

334 CALORIES

makeover manicotti crepes

Christine Rukavena | MILWAUKEE, WISCONSIN

This made-lighter main dish will add a special touch to any event. Green pepper and garlic give it a fresh vegetable aroma.

1 can (28 ounces) whole tomatoes, undrained
1-1/2 cups water
1 can (8 ounces) tomato sauce
3 teaspoons sugar
1 teaspoon dried oregano
1/4 teaspoon celery salt

CREPES:
2 eggs
1 cup egg substitute
1-3/4 cups fat-free milk
1 teaspoon canola oil
1-1/2 cups all-purpose flour
1/4 teaspoon salt

FILLING:
3 slices whole wheat bread, cubed
1/2 cup fat-free milk
1/4 cup egg substitute
1 cup finely chopped green pepper

MAKEOVER MANICOTTI CREPES

319 CALORIES

3 tablespoons minced fresh parsley
2 garlic cloves, minced
1 teaspoon salt
1 teaspoon pepper
1 pound lean ground beef (90% lean)
1/2 pound Italian turkey sausage links, casings removed
1 cup (4 ounces) shredded part-skim mozzarella cheese
1/4 cup shredded Parmesan cheese

- For sauce, place tomatoes in a blender; cover and process until smooth. Transfer to a large saucepan; add the water, tomato sauce, sugar, oregano and celery salt. Bring to a boil. Reduce heat; gently simmer, uncovered, for 2 hours or until reduced to 4-1/2 cups, stirring occasionally.

- Meanwhile, for crepes, beat the eggs, egg substitute, milk and oil in a large bowl. Combine flour and salt; add egg mixture and stir until smooth. Cover and refrigerate for 1 hour.

- For filling, in a large bowl, soak bread in milk for 5 minutes. Stir in the egg substitute, green pepper, parsley, garlic, salt and pepper. Crumble beef and sausage over mixture; mix well. Stir in mozzarella. Cover and refrigerate until assembling.

- Coat an 8-in. nonstick skillet with cooking spray; heat. Stir crepe batter; pour 3 tablespoons into center of skillet. Lift and tilt pan to coat bottom evenly. Cook until top appears dry; turn and cook 15-20 seconds longer. Remove to a wire rack. Repeat with remaining batter, coating skillet with cooking spray as needed. When cool, stack the crepes with waxed paper or paper towels in between.

- Spread about 1/4 cup filling down the center of each crepe; roll up and place in a 13-in. x 9-in. baking dish and an 11-in. x 7-in. baking dish coated with cooking spray. Spoon sauce over top; sprinkle with Parmesan cheese. Cover and bake at 350° for 35-45 minutes or until a meat thermometer reads 165°.

YIELD: 10 servings.

NUTRITION FACTS: 2 filled crepes equals 319 calories, 10 g fat (4 g saturated fat), 91 mg cholesterol, 977 mg sodium, 30 g carbohydrate, 2 g fiber, 26 g protein.

291 CALORIES

TURKEY DIVAN

turkey divan

It looks and tastes decadent, but at just 291 calories per serving, this classic entree from our Test Kitchen isn't much of a splurge. Pair it with a salad and slice of whole grain bread for a complete meal.

1-1/2 cups water
16 fresh asparagus spears, trimmed
2 egg whites
1 egg
2 tablespoons fat-free milk
1-1/4 cups seasoned bread crumbs
1 package (17.6 ounces) turkey breast cutlets
1/4 cup butter, cubed
8 slices deli ham
8 slices reduced-fat Swiss cheese

- In a large skillet, bring water to a boil. Add asparagus; cover and boil for 3 minutes. Drain and pat dry.

- In a shallow bowl, beat the egg whites, egg and milk. Place bread crumbs in another shallow bowl. Dip turkey in egg mixture, then coat with crumbs.

- In a large skillet, cook turkey in butter in batches for 2-3 minutes on each side or until meat is no longer pink. Layer with a ham slice, two asparagus spears and cheese. Cover and cook for 1 minute or until cheese is melted. Transfer to a platter; keep warm.

YIELD: 8 servings.

NUTRITION FACTS: 1 serving equals 291 calories, 12 g fat (6 g saturated fat), 100 mg cholesterol, 595 mg sodium, 16 g carbohydrate, 1 g fiber, 31 g protein. DIABETIC EXCHANGES: 3 lean meat, 2 fat, 1 starch.

pizza joes

Connie Pettit | LOGAN, OHIO

If you're tired of the same old, boring sloppy joes, here's a tasty twist! These saucy, kid-friendly sandwiches have a definite pizza flavor that families will love, but be sure to serve them with a fork!

1 pound lean ground beef (90% lean)
1 medium onion, chopped
1/4 cup chopped green pepper
1 jar (14 ounces) pizza sauce
3 ounces sliced turkey pepperoni (about 50 slices), chopped
1/2 teaspoon dried basil
1/4 teaspoon dried oregano
6 hamburger buns, split
6 tablespoons shredded part-skim mozzarella cheese

- In a large nonstick skillet, cook the beef, onion and pepper over medium heat until meat is no longer pink. Drain if necessary. Stir in the pizza sauce, pepperoni and herbs. Bring to a boil. Reduce heat; cover and simmer for 10 minutes.

- Spoon 2/3 cup beef mixture onto each bun; sprinkle with cheese. Place on a baking sheet. Broil 3-4 in. from the heat for 1 minute or until cheese is melted. Replace tops.

YIELD: 6 servings.

NUTRITION FACTS: 1 sandwich equals 329 calories, 11 g fat (4 g saturated fat), 59 mg cholesterol, 825 mg sodium, 29 g carbohydrate, 3 g fiber, 26 g protein.

PIZZA JOES

329 CALORIES

292 CALORIES

BLACK BEAN VEGGIE ENCHILADAS

black bean veggie enchiladas

Nicole Barnett | AURORA, COLORADO

I created this recipe one night when we were in the mood for enchiladas but didn't want all the fat and calories of the traditional ones. I used ingredients I had on hand that day, and now this recipe is a surefire family favorite!

- 1 small onion, chopped
- 1 small green pepper, chopped
- 1/2 cup sliced fresh mushrooms
- 2 teaspoons olive oil
- 1 garlic clove, minced
- 1 can (15 ounces) black beans, rinsed and drained
- 3/4 cup frozen corn, thawed
- 1 can (4 ounces) chopped green chilies
- 2 tablespoons reduced-sodium taco seasoning
- 1 teaspoon dried cilantro flakes
- 6 whole wheat tortillas (8 inches), warmed
- 1/2 cup enchilada sauce
- 3/4 cup shredded reduced-fat Mexican cheese blend

- In a large skillet, saute the onion, green pepper and mushrooms in oil until crisp-tender. Add the garlic; cook 1 minute longer. Add the beans, corn, chilies, taco seasoning and cilantro; cook for 2-3 minutes or until heated through.

- Spoon 1/2 cup of the bean mixture down the center of each tortilla. Roll up and place seam side down in a greased 13-in. x 9-in. baking dish. Top with the enchilada sauce and cheese.

- Bake, uncovered, at 350° for 25-30 minutes or until heated through.

YIELD: 6 enchiladas.

NUTRITION FACTS: 1 enchilada equals 292 calories, 8 g fat (2 g saturated fat), 10 mg cholesterol, 759 mg sodium, 43 g carbohydrate, 6 g fiber, 13 g protein.

phyllo-wrapped halibut

Carrie Vazzano | ROLLING MEADOWS, ILLINOIS

I created this easy entree to convince my husband that seafood doesn't have to taste "fishy." He likes the flaky, phyllo wrapping as well as veggies hidden inside.

- 4 cups fresh baby spinach
- 3/4 cup chopped sweet red pepper
- 3/4 teaspoon salt-free lemon-pepper seasoning, *divided*
- 1/2 teaspoon lemon juice
- 6 sheets phyllo dough (14 inches x 9 inches)
- 2 tablespoons reduced-fat butter, melted, *divided*
- 2 halibut fillets (4 ounces *each*)
- 1/4 teaspoon salt
- 1/8 teaspoon pepper
- 1/4 cup shredded part-skim mozzarella cheese

- In a large nonstick skillet lightly coated with cooking spray, saute spinach and red pepper until tender. Add 1/2 teaspoon lemon-pepper and lemon juice. Remove from the heat; cool.

PHYLLO-WRAPPED HALIBUT

330 CALORIES

- Line a baking sheet with foil and coat the foil with cooking spray; set aside. Place one sheet of phyllo dough on a work surface; brush with butter. (Until ready to use, keep phyllo dough covered with plastic wrap and a damp towel to prevent it from drying out.) Layer remaining phyllo over first sheet, brushing each with butter. Cut stack in half widthwise.

- Place a halibut fillet in the center of each square; sprinkle with salt and pepper. Top with cheese and spinach mixture. Fold sides and bottom edge over fillet and roll up to enclose it; trim end of phyllo if necessary. Brush with remaining butter; sprinkle with remaining lemon-pepper.

- Place seam side down on prepared baking sheet. Bake at 375° for 20-25 minutes or until golden brown.

YIELD: 2 servings.

EDITOR'S NOTE: This recipe was tested with Land O'Lakes light stick butter.

NUTRITION FACTS: 1 serving equals 330 calories, 12 g fat (6 g saturated fat), 64 mg cholesterol, 676 mg sodium, 26 g carbohydrate, 4 g fiber, 33 g protein. **DIABETIC EXCHANGES:** 4 lean meat, 2 vegetable, 1 starch, 1 fat.

herbed turkey tetrazzini

Brigitte Garringer | COPPER CANYON, TEXAS

There are many versions of this old-fashioned casserole. Mine offers a little more zip due to the thyme and lemon peel. It's a nice way to use up any leftover turkey you might have.

6	cups uncooked egg noodles
1/3	cup sliced green onions
2	tablespoons olive oil
1	pound sliced fresh mushrooms
3	tablespoons minced fresh parsley
1	tablespoon minced fresh thyme *or* 1 teaspoon dried thyme
2	bay leaves
1	garlic clove, minced
2	teaspoons grated lemon peel
1/4	cup butter
1/4	cup all-purpose flour

326 CALORIES

HERBED TURKEY TETRAZZINI

2	cups chicken broth
1	egg yolk, beaten
1	cup milk
4	cups cubed cooked turkey
	Salt and pepper to taste
1/3	cup dry bread crumbs
1/3	cup grated Parmesan cheese
1/2	cup sliced almonds, toasted

- Cook noodles according to package directions. Meanwhile, in a Dutch oven, saute onions in oil for 3 minutes. Add the mushrooms, parsley, thyme and bay leaves. Cook until mushrooms are lightly browned. Add garlic; cook 1 minute longer. Discard bay leaves.

- Transfer mushroom mixture to a small bowl; stir in lemon peel and set aside. Drain noodles; set aside.

- In the Dutch oven, melt butter over medium heat. Stir in flour until smooth. Whisk in broth. Bring to a boil; cook and stir for 2 minutes or until thickened. Combine egg yolk and milk; stir into white sauce. Cook and stir 2 minutes longer.

- Stir in mushroom mixture and turkey; heat through. Fold in noodles. Season with salt and pepper.

- Spoon into a greased 13-in. x 9-in. baking dish. Toss bread crumbs and cheese; sprinkle over the top. Bake, uncovered, at 350° for 25-30 minutes or until lightly browned. Sprinkle with almonds.

YIELD: 12 servings.

NUTRITION FACTS: 1-1/3 cups equals 326 calories, 14 g fat (5 g saturated fat), 91 mg cholesterol, 296 mg sodium, 28 g carbohydrate, 2 g fiber, 22 g protein.

italian pasta casserole

Denise Rasmussen | SALINA, KANSAS

All the traditional flavors are found in this dish, reminiscent of lasagna. This is a zippy and hearty recipe that our family and guests really like.

2	cups uncooked spiral pasta
1/2	pound lean ground beef (90% lean)
1/2	pound Italian turkey sausage links, casings removed
1	small onion, finely chopped
1	garlic clove, minced
2	cans (14-1/2 ounces *each*) diced tomatoes, undrained
1/3	cup tomato paste
3/4	teaspoon Italian seasoning
1/2	teaspoon chili powder
1/4	teaspoon dried oregano
1/8	teaspoon salt
1/8	teaspoon garlic powder
1/8	teaspoon dried thyme
1/8	teaspoon pepper
2	ounces sliced turkey pepperoni
1	cup (4 ounces) shredded part-skim mozzarella cheese

- Cook pasta according to package directions. Meanwhile, crumble beef and sausage into a large skillet; add onion and garlic. Cook and stir over medium heat until meat is no longer pink; drain. Stir in the tomatoes, tomato paste and seasonings. Bring to a boil. Reduce heat; simmer, uncovered, for 5 minutes.

ITALIAN PASTA CASSEROLE

335 CALORIES

- Drain pasta; stir in meat mixture and pepperoni. Transfer half of pasta mixture to a 2-qt. baking dish coated with cooking spray. Sprinkle with half of cheese; repeat layers. Cover and bake at 350° for 20-25 minutes or until bubbly.

YIELD: 6 servings.

NUTRITION FACTS: 1 cup equals 335 calories, 11 g fat (4 g saturated fat), 64 mg cholesterol, 752 mg sodium, 33 g carbohydrate, 4 g fiber, 26 g protein. **DIABETIC EXCHANGES:** 2 starch, 2 lean meat, 1-1/2 fat.

low-cal shrimp rice casserole

318 CALORIES

Marie Roberts | LAKE CHARLES, LOUISIANA

I love the lighter version of my shrimp casserole. It has only half the calories of my original recipe.

1	pound uncooked medium shrimp, peeled and deveined
2	tablespoons butter, *divided*
12	ounces fresh mushrooms, sliced
1	large green pepper, chopped
1	medium onion, chopped
3	tablespoons all-purpose flour
3/4	teaspoon salt
1/8	teaspoon cayenne pepper
1-1/3	cups fat-free milk
3	cups cooked brown rice
1	cup (4 ounces) shredded reduced-fat cheddar cheese, *divided*

- In a large nonstick skillet, saute shrimp in 1 tablespoon butter for 2-3 minutes or until shrimp turn pink. Remove and set aside. In the same skillet, saute the mushrooms, green pepper and onion in remaining butter until tender. Stir in the flour, salt and cayenne. Gradually add milk until blended. Bring to a boil; cook and stir for 2 minutes or until thickened. Add the rice, 1/2 cup cheese and shrimp; stir until combined.

- Pour into a 1-1/2-qt. baking dish coated with cooking spray. Cover and bake at 325° for 30-35 minutes or until heated through. Sprinkle with remaining cheese; cover and let stand for 5 minutes or until cheese is melted.

YIELD: 6 servings.

327 CALORIES

BEEF AND WILD RICE MEDLEY

beef and wild rice medley

Janelle Christensen I BIG LAKE, MINNESOTA

A packaged rice mix speeds up preparation of this tasty entree. Cayenne pepper gives the beef a little kick, and an assortment of veggies adds color and crunch.

1/2	teaspoon garlic powder
1/2	teaspoon dried thyme
1/8	teaspoon cayenne pepper
1	pound beef top sirloin steak, cut into 3/4-inch cubes
1	tablespoon canola oil
1/4	cup sliced celery
1/4	cup julienned green pepper
2-1/4	cups water
1	package (6 ounces) long grain and wild rice mix
1	small tomato, chopped
2	tablespoons chopped green onion

• In a small bowl, combine the garlic powder, thyme and cayenne. Sprinkle over beef.

• In a large saucepan coated with cooking spray, cook beef in oil until no longer pink; drain. Stir in celery and green pepper; cook 2 minutes longer or until vegetables are crisp-tender. Stir in the water and rice mix with contents of seasoning packet.

• Bring to a boil. Reduce heat; cover and simmer for 23-28 minutes or until rice is tender. Stir in tomato; heat through. Sprinkle with onion.

YIELD: 4 servings.

329 CALORIES

de-lightful tuna casserole

Colleen Willey I HAMBURG, NEW YORK

This mild, homemade tuna casserole will truly satisfy your family's craving for comfort food without all the fat!

 classic

1	package (7 ounces) elbow macaroni
1	can (10-3/4 ounces) reduced-fat reduced-sodium condensed cream of mushroom soup, undiluted
1	cup sliced fresh mushrooms
1	cup (4 ounces) shredded reduced-fat cheddar cheese
1	cup fat-free milk
1	can (6 ounces) light water-packed tuna, drained and flaked
2	tablespoons diced pimientos
3	teaspoons dried minced onion
1	teaspoon ground mustard
1/4	teaspoon salt
1/3	cup crushed cornflakes

• Cook macaroni according to the package directions. Meanwhile, in a large bowl, combine the cream soup, mushrooms, cheddar cheese, milk, tuna, pimientos, onion, mustard and salt. Drain macaroni; add to tuna mixture and mix well.

• Transfer to a 2-qt. baking dish coated with cooking spray. Sprinkle with cornflakes. Bake, uncovered, at 350° for 25-30 minutes or until bubbly.

YIELD: 5 servings.

311 CALORIES

CRAB CAKES WITH FRESH LEMON

crab cakes with fresh lemon

Edie DeSpain | LOGAN, UTAH

Fresh lemons and lemon juice bring out all the great flavors in these crispy crab cakes. Be careful not to overcook, or they'll be dry instead of moist and delicate.

classic

- 2/3 cup yellow cornmeal
- 1/3 cup fat-free milk
- 1 small sweet red pepper, finely chopped
- 4 green onions, chopped
- 1 teaspoon canola oil
- 3 egg whites, lightly beaten
- 1/3 cup reduced-fat mayonnaise
- 1/4 cup all-purpose flour
- 1/4 cup minced fresh parsley
- 2 tablespoons lemon juice
- 1/4 teaspoon seafood seasoning
- 1/8 teaspoon cayenne pepper
- 4 pouches (3.53 ounces *each*) premium crabmeat, drained
- 1 cup frozen corn, thawed
- 8 lemon wedges

- In a large bowl, combine cornmeal and milk; set aside. In a large nonstick skillet, saute red pepper and onions in oil until tender. Remove from the heat.

- Add the egg whites, mayonnaise, flour, parsley, lemon juice, seafood seasoning and cayenne to the reserved cornmeal mixture; mix well. Fold in the crab, corn and red pepper mixture.

- Coat the same skillet with cooking spray; drop crab mixture by scant 1/2 cupfuls into the pan. Press into 3/4-in.-thick patties. Cook in batches over medium heat for 4-6 minutes on each side or until golden brown. Serve with lemon wedges.

YIELD: 4 servings.

NUTRITION FACTS: 2 crab cakes equals 311 calories, 9 g fat (1 g saturated fat), 67 mg cholesterol, 764 mg sodium, 43 g carbohydrate, 5 g fiber, 17 g protein. **DIABETIC EXCHANGES:** 3 starch, 2 lean meat, 1-1/2 fat.

307 CALORIES

saucy parmesan chicken

Bobby Taylor | MICHIGAN CITY, INDIANA

This recipe has been in my file for years. It makes a fast, tasty and moist chicken dish. Curry powder lends a unique flavor but can easily be omitted, if you prefer.

- 1/2 cup chopped onion
- 2 tablespoons butter
- 1 can (10-3/4 ounces) condensed tomato soup, undiluted
- 1/3 cup beer *or* nonalcoholic beer
- 1/2 teaspoon curry powder
- 1/2 teaspoon dried oregano
- 1/4 teaspoon salt
- 1/8 teaspoon pepper
- 6 boneless skinless chicken breast halves (7 ounces *each*)
- 1/4 cup grated Parmesan cheese

- In a large skillet, saute onion in butter until tender. Add the soup, beer, curry, oregano, salt and pepper; bring to a boil. Reduce heat; simmer, uncovered, for 8-10 minutes or until thickened, stirring occasionally.

- Place chicken in a greased 13-in. x 9-in. baking dish. Pour soup mixture over chicken. Bake, uncovered, at 375° for 24-28 minutes or until a meat thermometer reads 170°. Sprinkle with cheese.

YIELD: 6 servings.

NUTRITION FACTS: 1 chicken breast half equals 307 calories, 9 g fat (4 g saturated fat), 123 mg cholesterol, 568 mg sodium, 10 g carbohydrate, 1 g fiber, 42 g protein.

326 CALORIES

WEEKNIGHT CHICKEN POTPIE

weeknight chicken potpie

Lisa Sjursen-Darling I SCOTTSVILLE, NEW YORK

I have long days at work, so I really appreciate quick recipes. My husband enjoys this casserole and often makes it while I'm working.

classic

1	small onion, chopped
1	teaspoon canola oil
1-1/2	cups fat-free milk, *divided*
1/2	cup reduced-sodium chicken broth
3/4	teaspoon rubbed sage
1/8	teaspoon pepper
1/4	cup all-purpose flour
4	cups cubed cooked chicken breast
3	cups frozen chopped broccoli, thawed and drained
1-1/2	cups (6 ounces) shredded reduced-fat cheddar cheese
1	tube (11.3 ounces) refrigerated dinner rolls

- In a large nonstick saucepan, saute onion in oil until tender. Stir in 3/4 cup milk, broth, sage and pepper. In a small bowl, combine flour and remaining milk until smooth; gradually stir into onion mixture. Bring to a boil; cook and stir for 1-2 minutes or until thickened. Stir in the chicken, broccoli and cheese; heat through.

- Transfer to a 2-qt. baking dish coated with cooking spray. Separate rolls; arrange over chicken mixture. Bake, uncovered, at 350° for 25-30 minutes or until filling is bubbly and rolls are golden brown.

YIELD: 8 servings.

NUTRITION FACTS: 3/4 cup chicken mixture with 1 roll equals 326 calories, 9 g fat (4 g saturated fat), 70 mg cholesterol, 511 mg sodium, 28 g carbohydrate, 2 g fiber, 33 g protein. **DIABETIC EXCHANGES:** 4 lean meat, 2 starch.

tasty mozzarella chicken

Nancy Foust I STONEBORO, PENNSYLVANIA

This is a chicken recipe anyone will enjoy! The bubbly cheese is the perfect topping.

1	egg
2	tablespoons water
2/3	cup dry bread crumbs
1	envelope reduced-sodium onion soup mix
1/8	teaspoon pepper
6	boneless skinless chicken breast halves (5 ounces *each*)
1-1/2	cups spaghetti sauce
1	can (7 ounces) mushroom stems and pieces, drained
1	cup (4 ounces) shredded part-skim mozzarella cheese

- In a shallow bowl, beat egg and water. In another shallow bowl, combine the bread crumbs, soup mix and pepper. Dip chicken in egg mixture, then coat with crumb mixture.

- Place in a greased 13-in. x 9-in. baking dish. Bake, uncovered, at 400° for 22-25 minutes or until juices run clear.

- In a small bowl, combine spaghetti sauce and mushrooms; spoon over chicken. Sprinkle with cheese. Bake 5-7 minutes longer or until sauce is bubbly and cheese is melted.

YIELD: 6 servings.

NUTRITION FACTS: 1 chicken breast half equals 304 calories, 9 g fat (4 g saturated fat), 103 mg cholesterol, 792 mg sodium, 15 g carbohydrate, 2 g fiber, 37 g protein. **DIABETIC EXCHANGES:** 5 lean meat, 1 starch.

TASTY MOZZARELLA CHICKEN

304 CALORIES

chicken pasta dinner

Green beans add nice crunch and a bit of color to this tasty meal-in-one from our Test Kitchen.

- 4 **cups uncooked spiral pasta**
- 1/2 **pound fresh green beans, trimmed and cut into 1/4-inch pieces**
- 3/4 **pound boneless skinless chicken breasts, cut into 1/2-inch pieces**
- 3 **teaspoons olive oil,** *divided*
- 1 **jar (7 ounces) roasted sweet red peppers, drained**
- 1 **garlic clove, minced**
- 3/4 **cup reduced-sodium chicken broth**
- 3/4 **cup fat-free evaporated milk,** *divided*
- 1/4 **cup minced fresh basil** *or* **4 teaspoons dried basil**
- 1/2 **teaspoon salt**
- 1/4 **teaspoon pepper**
- 2 **teaspoons cornstarch**
- 5 **tablespoons shredded Parmesan cheese**

- Cook pasta according to package directions, adding green beans during the last 2 minutes. Meanwhile, in a large nonstick skillet, saute chicken in 2 teaspoons oil until no longer pink. Remove and keep warm. In the same pan, saute red peppers and garlic in remaining oil for 1 minute.

- Stir in the chicken broth, 1/2 cup milk, basil, salt and pepper. Bring to a boil. Reduce heat; simmer, uncovered, for 3 minutes or until slightly thickened. Remove from the heat; cool slightly. Transfer to a blender; cover and process until smooth. Return to the pan.

- Add chicken to the pepper mixture. Combine cornstarch and remaining milk until smooth; gradually stir into the chicken mixture. Bring to a boil; cook and stir for 2 minutes or until thickened.

- Drain pasta mixture; toss with the sauce. Sprinkle each serving with 1 tablespoon cheese.

YIELD: 5 servings.

NUTRITION FACTS: 1-1/4 cups equals 345 calories, 6 g fat (2 g saturated fat), 42 mg cholesterol, 625 mg sodium, 44 g carbohydrate, 3 g fiber, 25 g protein. **DIABETIC EXCHANGES:** 2-1/2 starch, 2 lean meat, 1 vegetable, 1/2 fat.

347 CALORIES

GINGERED BEEF STIR-FRY

gingered beef stir-fry

Sonja Blow | NIXA, MISSOURI

A friend who owns a bed-and-breakfast in Maryland shared this terrific family recipe with me. It's a delicious and different way to cook asparagus.

- 3 **tablespoons reduced-sodium soy sauce,** *divided*
- 1 **tablespoon sherry**
- 1/4 **teaspoon minced fresh gingerroot** *or* **dash ground ginger**
- 1/2 **pound beef flank steak, cut into thin strips**
- 1 **teaspoon cornstarch**
- 1/2 **cup beef broth**
- 1-1/2 **teaspoons hoisin sauce**
- 1/8 **teaspoon sugar**
- 2 **tablespoons canola oil,** *divided*
- 2 **pounds fresh asparagus, trimmed and cut into 1-inch pieces**
- 1 **garlic clove, minced**
- 3 **cups hot cooked rice**

- In a large resealable plastic bag, combine 2 tablespoons soy sauce, sherry and ginger; add the beef. Seal bag and turn to coat; refrigerate for 30 minutes.

- In a small bowl, combine the cornstarch, broth, hoisin sauce, sugar and remaining soy sauce until smooth; set mixture aside.

- In a large skillet or wok, stir-fry beef in 1 tablespoon oil until no longer pink. Remove and set aside. Stir-fry asparagus in remaining oil until crisp-tender. Add garlic; cook 1 minute longer.

- Stir cornstarch mixture and add to the pan. Bring to a boil; cook and stir for 2 minutes or until thickened. Return beef to the pan; heat through. Serve with rice.

YIELD: 4 servings.

NUTRITION FACTS: 1-1/4 cups stir-fry with 3/4 cup rice equals 347 calories, 12 g fat (2 g saturated fat), 27 mg cholesterol, 645 mg sodium, 41 g carbohydrate, 2 g fiber, 18 g protein. **DIABETIC EXCHANGES:** 2 starch, 2 fat, 1 lean meat, 1 vegetable.

pork burritos

320 CALORIES

Sharon Belmont I LINCOLN, NEBRASKA

I have been making this recipe for 20 years, changing it here and there until I came up with this delicious version, which I now serve. It's a favorite for company and family.

- 1 boneless pork sirloin roast (3 pounds)
- 1/4 cup reduced-sodium chicken broth
- 1 envelope reduced-sodium taco seasoning
- 1 tablespoon dried parsley flakes
- 2 garlic cloves, minced
- 1/2 teaspoon pepper
- 1/4 teaspoon salt
- 1 can (16 ounces) refried beans
- 1 can (4 ounces) chopped green chilies
- 14 flour tortillas (8 inches), warmed

Optional toppings: shredded lettuce, chopped tomatoes, chopped green pepper, guacamole, reduced-fat sour cream and shredded reduced-fat cheddar cheese

- Cut roast in half; place in a 4- or 5-qt. slow cooker. In a small bowl, combine the broth, taco seasoning, parsley, garlic, pepper and salt. Pour over roast. Cover and cook on low for 8-10 hours or until meat is very tender.

- Remove pork from the slow cooker; cool slightly. Shred with two forks; set aside. Skim fat from the liquid; stir in beans and chilies. Return pork to the slow cooker; heat through. Spoon 1/2 cup pork mixture down the center of each tortilla; add toppings of your choice. Fold sides and ends over filling and roll up.

YIELD: 14 servings.

NUTRITION FACTS: 1 burrito (calculated without optional toppings) equals 320 calories, 9 g fat (3 g saturated fat), 61 mg cholesterol, 606 mg sodium, 33 g carbohydrate, 2 g fiber, 26 g protein. **DIABETIC EXCHANGES:** 2 starch, 2 lean meat, 1 fat.

mock manicotti

Deanne Schwarting I NORTH ENGLISH, IOWA

I've always tried to get my children to eat vegetables. When my son sampled manicotti at a restaurant and liked it, I came up with this version. It was a hit!

- 3 cups (24 ounces) fat-free cottage cheese, drained
- 1 package (10 ounces) frozen chopped spinach, thawed and squeezed dry
- 1 package (8 ounces) reduced-fat cream cheese
- 1/2 cup reduced-fat sour cream
- 1 teaspoon garlic powder
- 1/8 teaspoon salt
- 1/8 teaspoon pepper
- 8 lasagna noodles, cooked, rinsed and drained
- 1 cup (4 ounces) shredded part-skim mozzarella cheese
- 1 cup meatless spaghetti sauce, optional

- In a large bowl, combine the first seven ingredients. Spread 1/2 cup over each noodle; roll up jelly-roll style. Place seam side down in an 11-in. x 7-in. baking dish coated with cooking spray. Sprinkle with mozzarella cheese.

- Cover and bake at 350° for 35 minutes. Uncover; drizzle with spaghetti sauce if desired. Bake 10 minutes longer or until heated through.

YIELD: 8 servings.

NUTRITION FACTS: 1 piece (calculated without spaghetti sauce) equals 287 calories, 10 g fat (7 g saturated fat), 37 mg cholesterol, 545 mg sodium, 26 g carbohydrate, 2 g fiber, 22 g protein. **DIABETIC EXCHANGES:** 2 lean meat, 1-1/2 starch, 1 fat.

MOCK MANICOTTI

287 CALORIES

263 CALORIES

PORK CHOPS WITH BLUE CHEESE SAUCE

pork chops with blue cheese sauce

Kathy Specht | CLINTON, MONTANA

These wonderful chops have an out-of-the-ordinary kick. The recipe makes a decadent, but quick and easy weeknight meal. Even if you aren't a blue cheese fan, you'll enjoy the mild-flavored sauce.

- 4 bone-in pork loin chops (7 ounces *each*)
- 1 teaspoon coarsely ground pepper

SAUCE:

- 1 green onion, finely chopped
- 1 garlic clove, minced
- 1 teaspoon butter
- 1 tablespoon all-purpose flour
- 2/3 cup fat-free milk
- 3 tablespoons crumbled blue cheese
- 1 tablespoon white wine *or* reduced-sodium chicken broth

- Sprinkle pork chops on both sides with pepper. Broil 3-4 in. from the heat for 4-6 minutes on each side or until a meat thermometer reads 160°.

- Meanwhile, in a small saucepan, saute onion and garlic in butter until tender. Sprinkle with the flour; stir until blended. Gradually add milk. Bring to a boil; cook and stir for 2 minutes or until thickened. Add cheese and wine; heat through. Serve sauce with chops.

YIELD: 4 servings.

NUTRITION FACTS: 1 pork chop with 3 tablespoons sauce equals 263 calories, 11 g fat (5 g saturated fat), 94 mg cholesterol, 176 mg sodium, 5 g carbohydrate, trace fiber, 33 g protein. **DIABETIC EXCHANGE:** 5 lean meat.

311 CALORIES

pasta pizza

Andrea Quick | COLUMBUS, OHIO

My family often requests this meatless main dish, a tempting cross between pizza and spaghetti.

- 8 ounces uncooked angel hair pasta
- 2 cups sliced fresh mushrooms
- 1/2 cup chopped green pepper
- 1/4 cup chopped onion
- 4 teaspoons olive oil, *divided*
- 1 can (15 ounces) pizza sauce
- 1/4 cup sliced ripe olives
- 1/2 cup shredded part-skim mozzarella cheese
- 1/4 teaspoon Italian seasoning

- Cook pasta according to package directions; drain.

- In a 10-in. ovenproof skillet, saute the mushrooms, green pepper and onion in 1 teaspoon oil until tender. Remove with a slotted spoon and keep warm. In the same skillet, heat remaining oil over medium-high. Spread pasta evenly in skillet to form a crust. Cook for 5-7 minutes or until lightly browned.

- Turn crust onto a large plate. Reduce heat to medium; slide crust back into skillet. Top with pizza sauce, sauteed vegetables, olives, cheese and Italian seasoning. Bake at 400° for 10-12 minutes or until cheese is melted.

YIELD: 4 servings.

NUTRITION FACTS: 1 serving equals 311 calories, 9 g fat (2 g saturated fat), 7 mg cholesterol, 376 mg sodium, 46 g carbohydrate, 4 g fiber, 14 g protein.

veggie-cheese stuffed shells

Sharon Delaney-Chronis | SOUTH MILWAUKEE, WISCONSIN

Need a great-tasting meatless dish you can count on? These pleasing pasta shells are packed with veggies, three kinds of cheese and wonderful flavor.

- 6 uncooked jumbo pasta shells
- 2/3 cup reduced-fat ricotta cheese
- 1/2 cup shredded part-skim mozzarella cheese, *divided*

1/4 cup shredded carrot

1/4 cup shredded zucchini

2 tablespoons grated Parmesan cheese

1/2 teaspoon dried parsley flakes

1/2 teaspoon dried oregano

1/8 teaspoon garlic powder

1/8 teaspoon pepper

3/4 cup meatless spaghetti sauce, *divided*

- Cook pasta according to package directions. Meanwhile, in a small bowl, combine the ricotta cheese, 1/4 cup mozzarella cheese, carrot, zucchini, Parmesan cheese, parsley, oregano, garlic powder and pepper.

- Spread 1/4 cup spaghetti sauce in a 3-cup baking dish coated with cooking spray. Drain shells; stuff with cheese mixture. Place in prepared baking dish. Top with remaining spaghetti sauce.

- Cover and bake at 350° for 25 minutes. Uncover; sprinkle with remaining mozzarella. Bake 10-15 minutes longer or until bubbly.

YIELD: 2 servings.

NUTRITION FACTS: 3 stuffed shells equals 326 calories, 10 g fat (6 g saturated fat), 40 mg cholesterol, 721 mg sodium, 37 g carbohydrate, 3 g fiber, 21 g protein. **DIABETIC EXCHANGES:** 2 medium-fat meat, 2 vegetable, 1-1/2 starch.

VEGGIE-CHEESE STUFFED SHELLS

326 CALORIES

317 CALORIES

MUSHROOM CHICKEN ALFREDO

mushroom chicken alfredo

Margery Bryan | MOSES LAKE, WASHINGTON

All you need is one skillet to make this creamy, delicious scaled-down dinner. It's an effortless way to dress up packaged noodles and sauce, plus clean-up is a breeze.

1/2 pound boneless skinless chicken breasts, cut into 2-inch cubes

1 tablespoon butter

1 cup sliced fresh mushrooms

1 small onion, sliced

1-3/4 cups water

1/2 cup 2% milk

1 package (4.4 ounces) quick-cooking noodles and Alfredo sauce mix

Minced fresh parsley, optional

- In a large nonstick skillet, cook the chicken in butter for 6 minutes or until meat is no longer pink. Remove and keep warm. In the same skillet, saute mushrooms and onion until tender.

- Stir in the water and milk; bring to a boil. Stir in contents of noodles and sauce mix; boil for 8 minutes or until the noodles are tender.

- Return chicken to the pan; heat through. Garnish with parsley if desired.

YIELD: 3 servings.

NUTRITION FACTS: 1-1/3 cups equals 317 calories, 11 g fat (6 g saturated fat), 105 mg cholesterol, 727 mg sodium, 30 g carbohydrate, 1 g fiber, 24 g protein. **DIABETIC EXCHANGES:** 2 starch, 2 lean meat, 1 fat.

pizza roll-up

Janice Christofferson | EAGLE RIVER, WISCONSIN

I live in the Northwoods, and this is a great, hearty dish for dinner. It's also good made with ground turkey or Italian sausage instead of ground beef.

- 1/2 **pound lean ground beef (90% lean)**
- 1 **tube (13.8 ounces) refrigerated pizza crust**
- 1 **package (10 ounces) frozen chopped spinach, thawed and squeezed dry**
- 1 **jar (7 ounces) roasted sweet red peppers, drained and sliced**
- 1 **cup (4 ounces) shredded part-skim mozzarella cheese**
- 1/2 **teaspoon onion powder**
- 1/2 **teaspoon pepper**
- 1/2 **cup loosely packed basil leaves**

Cooking spray

- 1 **tablespoon grated Parmesan cheese**
- 1 **can (8 ounces) pizza sauce, warmed**

- In a small nonstick skillet, cook beef over medium heat until no longer pink; drain.

- Unroll dough into one long rectangle; top with spinach, beef, roasted peppers and mozzarella cheese. Sprinkle with onion powder and pepper. Top with basil.

PIZZA ROLL-UP

316 CALORIES

274 CALORIES

ROMANO CHICKEN SUPREME

- Roll up jelly-roll style, starting with a short side; tuck ends under and pinch seam to seal. Place roll-up on a baking sheet coated with cooking spray; spritz top and sides with additional cooking spray. Sprinkle with Parmesan cheese.

- Bake at 375° for 25-30 minutes or until golden brown. Let stand for 5 minutes. Cut into scant 1-in. slices. Serve with pizza sauce.

YIELD: 6 servings.

NUTRITION FACTS: 2 slices with 2 tablespoons pizza sauce equals 316 calories, 8 g fat (3 g saturated fat), 30 mg cholesterol, 824 mg sodium, 37 g carbohydrate, 3 g fiber, 20 g protein.

romano chicken supreme

Anna Minegar | ZOLFO SPRINGS, FLORIDA

Plenty of Romano cheese and golden brown bread crumbs add fantastic flavor and crunch to this tender chicken-and-mushroom recipe.

- 6 **boneless skinless chicken breast halves (5 ounces *each*)**
- 1/4 **teaspoon salt**
- 1 **pound fresh mushrooms, chopped**
- 1 **tablespoon lemon juice**
- 1 **teaspoon dried basil**
- 3 **tablespoons butter**
- 2 **garlic cloves, minced**

1/2 cup reduced-sodium chicken broth

2 tablespoons orange juice

1 cup soft bread crumbs

1/3 cup grated Romano cheese

- In a large skillet coated with cooking spray, brown the chicken on both sides over medium heat. Transfer to a 13-in. x 9-in. baking dish coated with cooking spray; sprinkle with salt.

- In the same skillet, saute the mushrooms, lemon juice and basil in butter. Add garlic and cook for 1 minute or until tender. Stir in the broth and orange juice; bring to a boil. Reduce heat; simmer, uncovered, for 2-3 minutes or until heated through. Spoon over chicken; sprinkle with bread crumbs and cheese.

- Bake, uncovered, at 400° for 20-25 minutes or until a meat thermometer reads 170°.

YIELD: 6 servings.

NUTRITION FACTS: 1 chicken breast half with about 1/4 cup mushroom mixture equals 274 calories, 11 g fat (6 g saturated fat), 100 mg cholesterol, 413 mg sodium, 8 g carbohydrate, 1 g fiber, 34 g protein. **DIABETIC EXCHANGES:** 4 lean meat, 1 fat, 1/2 starch.

grilled snapper with caper sauce

Alaina Showalter | CLOVER, SOUTH CAROLINA

This recipe uses snapper, but if you prefer a different fish, consider mahi mahi. It is a delicious firm, mild fish that won't fall apart on the grill.

1/3 cup lime juice

1 jalapeno pepper, seeded

3 garlic cloves, peeled

1-1/4 teaspoons fresh thyme leaves *or* 1/4 teaspoon dried thyme

1 teaspoon salt

1 teaspoon pepper

4 red snapper fillets (6 ounces *each*)

SAUCE:

3 tablespoons lime juice

3 tablespoons olive oil

2 tablespoons water

2 teaspoons red wine vinegar

1/2 cup fresh cilantro leaves

1 shallot, peeled

1 tablespoon capers, drained

1-1/2 teaspoons chopped seeded jalapeno pepper

1 garlic clove, peeled and halved

1/4 teaspoon pepper

- In a food processor, combine the first six ingredients; cover and process until blended. Pour into a large resealable plastic bag. Add the fillets; seal bag and turn to coat. Refrigerate for 30 minutes.

- Drain and discard marinade. Using long-handled tongs, dip a paper towel in cooking oil and lightly coat the grill rack. Grill fillets, covered, over medium heat or broil 4 in. from the heat for 3-5 minutes on each side or until fish flakes easily with a fork.

- Meanwhile, combine the sauce ingredients in a small food processor. Cover and process until blended. Serve with the fish.

YIELD: 4 servings.

EDITOR'S NOTE: When cutting hot peppers, disposable gloves are recommended. Avoid touching your face.

NUTRITION FACTS: 1 fillet with 3 tablespoons sauce equals 272 calories, 12 g fat (2 g saturated fat), 60 mg cholesterol, 435 mg sodium, 5 g carbohydrate, 1 g fiber, 34 g protein. **DIABETIC EXCHANGES:** 5 lean meat, 2 fat.

GRILLED SNAPPER WITH CAPER SAUCE

272 CALORIES

beef stroganoff

338 CALORIES

Patty Rody | PUYALLUP, WASHINGTON

Creamy and comforting, you'll crave this hearty Beef Stroganoff no matter what the weather.

 classic

5 tablespoons all-purpose flour, *divided*
1/2 teaspoon salt
1 pound beef top sirloin steak, cut into thin strips
4 tablespoons butter, *divided*
1 cup sliced fresh mushrooms
1/2 cup chopped sweet onion
1 garlic clove, minced
1 tablespoon tomato paste
1-1/4 cups beef broth
1 cup (8 ounces) sour cream
2 tablespoons sherry *or* beef broth
Hot cooked egg noodles *or* brown rice

- In a large resealable plastic bag, combine 2 tablespoons flour and salt. Add beef, a few pieces at a time, and shake to coat. In a large skillet over medium-high heat, brown beef in 2 tablespoons butter. Add mushrooms and onion; cook and stir until vegetables are tender. Add garlic; cook 1 minute longer. Remove and keep warm.

- In the same skillet, melt remaining butter. Stir in tomato paste and remaining flour until smooth. Gradually add broth; bring to a boil. Cook and stir for 2 minutes or until thickened.

- Carefully return beef mixture to the pan. Add sour cream and sherry; heat through (do not boil). Serve with noodles or rice.

YIELD: 5 servings.

NUTRITION FACTS: 1 cup (calculated without noodles) equals 338 calories, 21 g fat (13 g saturated fat), 107 mg cholesterol, 581 mg sodium, 11 g carbohydrate, 1 g fiber, 21 g protein.

loaded mexican pizza

Mary Barker | KNOXVILLE, TENNESSEE

My husband, Steve, is a picky eater, but he actually looks forward to this zesty pizza. It's also one of those meals that tastes even better the next day.

1 can (15 ounces) black beans, rinsed and drained
1 medium red onion, chopped
1 small sweet yellow pepper, chopped
3 teaspoons chili powder
3/4 teaspoon ground cumin
3 medium tomatoes, chopped
1 jalapeno pepper, seeded and finely chopped
1 garlic clove, minced
1 prebaked 12-inch thin pizza crust
2 cups chopped fresh spinach
2 tablespoons minced fresh cilantro
Hot pepper sauce to taste
1/2 cup shredded reduced-fat cheddar cheese
1/2 cup shredded pepper Jack cheese

- In a small bowl, mash black beans; stir in the onion, yellow pepper, chili powder and cumin. In another bowl, combine the tomatoes, jalapeno and garlic.

- Place the crust on an ungreased 12-in. pizza pan; spread with bean mixture. Top with tomato mixture and spinach. Sprinkle with cilantro, hot pepper sauce and cheeses.

- Bake at 400° for 12-15 minutes or until cheese is melted.

YIELD: 6 slices.

EDITOR'S NOTE: When cutting hot peppers, disposable gloves are recommended. Avoid touching your face.

NUTRITION FACTS: 1 slice equals 297 calories, 9 g fat (4 g saturated fat), 17 mg cholesterol, 566 mg sodium, 41 g carbohydrate, 6 g fiber, 15 g protein. **DIABETIC EXCHANGES:** 2-1/2 starch, 1 lean meat, 1 vegetable.

LOADED MEXICAN PIZZA

297 CALORIES

TURKEY WITH CURRIED CREAM SAUCE

turkey with curried cream sauce

Lori Lockrey | SCARBOROUGH, ONTARIO

For a different turkey dish, try this delicious curry version. It comes together quickly and disappears fast.

- 2 tablespoons butter
- 2 tablespoons all-purpose flour
- 1/2 teaspoon curry powder
- 1 cup chicken broth
- 1/4 cup milk
- 1 small yellow summer squash, sliced
- 1 small zucchini, sliced
- 1/2 small onion, thinly sliced
- 2 teaspoons canola oil
- 2 cups cubed cooked turkey breast
- 1/2 teaspoon grated lemon peel
- Hot cooked rice
- 3 tablespoons chopped cashews

- In a small saucepan, melt butter; stir in flour and curry until smooth. Gradually add broth and milk. Bring to a boil; cook and stir for 1-2 minutes or until thickened. Remove from the heat; set aside.

- In a large skillet, saute the squash, zucchini and onion in oil until tender. Add the turkey, lemon peel and reserved sauce; heat through. Serve with rice. Sprinkle each serving with cashews.

YIELD: 3 servings.

NUTRITION FACTS: 1 cup (calculated without rice) equals 333 calories, 17 g fat (7 g saturated fat), 104 mg cholesterol, 502 mg sodium, 13 g carbohydrate, 2 g fiber, 33 g protein.

pizza lover's pie

Carol Gillespie | CHAMBERSBURG, PENNSYLVANIA

Love pizza? Then you'll love the tasty spin this recipe puts on it. Plus, it's easy to tailor for picky eaters.

- 1/4 pound bulk pork sausage
- 1/2 cup chopped green pepper
- 1/4 cup chopped onion
- 1 loaf (1 pound) frozen bread dough, thawed and halved
- 2 cups (8 ounces) shredded part-skim mozzarella cheese
- 1/2 cup grated Parmesan cheese
- 1 can (8 ounces) pizza sauce
- 8 slices pepperoni
- 1 can (4 ounces) mushroom stems and pieces, drained
- 1/4 teaspoon dried oregano

- In a large skillet, cook the sausage, pepper and onion over medium heat until meat is no longer pink; drain. Set aside.

- Roll half of dough into a 12-in. circle. Transfer to a greased 9-in. deep-dish pie plate. Layer with half of the mozzarella cheese, Parmesan cheese and pizza sauce. Top with the sausage mixture, pepperoni, mushrooms and 1/8 teaspoon oregano.

- Roll out remaining dough to fit top of pie. Place over filling; seal edges. Layer with remaining pizza sauce, cheeses and oregano.

- Bake at 400° for 18-22 minutes or until golden brown.

YIELD: 8 servings.

NUTRITION FACTS: 1 piece equals 305 calories, 12 g fat (5 g saturated fat), 27 mg cholesterol, 743 mg sodium, 32 g carbohydrate, 3 g fiber, 17 g protein. **DIABETIC EXCHANGES:** 2 starch, 2 medium-fat meat.

...ey scallopini

...arren | NORTH MANCHESTER, INDIANA

...ick recipe is easy to double for company. It's
g... ...erved with rice, pasta or veggies. A splash of
white wine and spicy mustard adds special flavor.

- 1/3 cup all-purpose flour
- 1/4 teaspoon dried rosemary, crushed
- 1/4 teaspoon dried thyme
- 1/8 teaspoon white pepper
- 1 package (17.6 ounces) turkey breast cutlets
- 4 teaspoons canola oil
- 1/4 cup white wine *or* reduced-sodium chicken broth
- 1/2 teaspoon cornstarch
- 1/3 cup reduced-sodium chicken broth
- 1/2 cup reduced-fat sour cream
- 1 teaspoon spicy brown mustard

Paprika, optional

- In a large resealable plastic bag, combine the flour, rosemary, thyme and pepper. Add the turkey; seal bag and shake to coat. In a large nonstick skillet coated with cooking spray, cook turkey in oil over medium heat for 2-4 minutes on each side or until no longer pink.

TURKEY SCALLOPINI

263 CALORIES

304 CALORIES

STIR-FRIED STEAK & VEGGIES

- Add wine to skillet; cook and stir for 30 seconds, stirring to loosen browned bits from pan. Combine cornstarch and broth until smooth; stir into skillet. Bring to a boil; cook and stir for 2 minutes or until slightly thickened. Add sour cream and mustard; heat through. Pour over turkey; sprinkle with paprika if desired.

YIELD: 4 servings.

NUTRITION FACTS: 4 ounces cooked turkey with about 2 tablespoons sauce equals 263 calories, 8 g fat (2 g saturated fat), 88 mg cholesterol, 194 mg sodium, 11 g carbohydrate, trace fiber, 34 g protein. DIABETIC EXCHANGES: 4 lean meat, 1 starch, 1 fat.

stir-fried steak & veggies

Vicky Priestley | ALUM CREEK, WEST VIRGINIA

Are you ready for this? Convenience products such as frozen vegetables combine with simple seasonings for a healthy meal you'll rave about. Best of all, it can be ready in under 30 minutes for busy weeknights!

- 1-1/2 cups uncooked instant brown rice
- 1 tablespoon cornstarch
- 1 tablespoon brown sugar
- 3/4 teaspoon ground ginger
- 1/2 teaspoon chili powder
- 1/4 teaspoon garlic powder
- 1/4 teaspoon pepper
- 1/2 cup cold water
- 1/4 cup reduced-sodium soy sauce

- 1 pound beef top sirloin steak, cut into 1/2-inch cubes
- 2 tablespoons canola oil, *divided*
- 1 package (16 ounces) frozen stir-fry vegetable blend, thawed

- Cook rice according to package directions. Meanwhile, in a small bowl, combine the cornstarch, brown sugar and seasonings. Stir in water and soy sauce until smooth; set aside.

- In a large nonstick skillet or wok coated with cooking spray, stir-fry beef in 1 tablespoon oil until no longer pink. Remove and keep warm. Stir-fry the vegetables in remaining oil until crisp-tender.

- Stir cornstarch mixture and add to the pan. Bring to a boil; cook and stir for 2 minutes or until thickened. Add beef; heat through. Serve with rice.

YIELD: 6 servings.

NUTRITION FACTS: 3/4 cup stir-fry with 1/2 cup rice equals 304 calories, 8 g fat (2 g saturated fat), 42 mg cholesterol, 470 mg sodium, 37 g carbohydrate, 3 g fiber, 19 g protein. **DIABETIC EXCHANGES:** 2 lean meat, 2 vegetable, 1-1/2 starch, 1 fat.

marvelous chicken enchiladas

Rebekah Sabo | ROCHESTER, NEW YORK

I love Mexican food, and this is one of my favorite dishes. Try using Monterey Jack cheese in place of the cheddar for a slightly milder flavor.

- 1 pound boneless skinless chicken breasts, cut into thin strips
- 4 teaspoons chili powder
- 2 teaspoons olive oil
- 2 tablespoons all-purpose flour
- 1-1/2 teaspoons ground coriander
- 1 teaspoon baking cocoa
- 1 cup fat-free milk
- 1 cup frozen corn, thawed
- 4 green onions, chopped
- 1 can (4 ounces) chopped green chilies, drained
- 1/2 teaspoon salt

classic

- 1/2 cup minced fresh cilantro, *divided*
- 6 whole wheat tortillas (8 inches)
- 1/2 cup salsa
- 1/2 cup tomato sauce
- 1/2 cup shredded reduced-fat cheddar cheese

- Sprinkle chicken with chili powder. In a large nonstick skillet coated with cooking spray, cook chicken in oil over medium heat until no longer pink. Sprinkle with flour, coriander and cocoa; stir until blended.

- Gradually stir in milk. Bring to a boil; cook and stir for 2 minutes or until thickened. Add the corn, onions, chilies and salt; cook and stir 2 minutes longer or until heated through. Remove from the heat. Stir in 1/4 cup cilantro.

- Spread 2/3 cup filling down the center of each tortilla. Roll up and place seam side down in a 13-in. x 9-in. baking dish coated with cooking spray.

- In a small bowl, combine the salsa, tomato sauce and remaining cilantro; pour over enchiladas. Sprinkle with cheddar cheese.

- Cover and bake at 375° for 25 minutes or until heated through.

YIELD: 6 enchiladas.

NUTRITION FACTS: 1 enchilada equals 270 calories, 7 g fat (2 g saturated fat), 49 mg cholesterol, 768 mg sodium, 35 g carbohydrate, 4 g fiber, 24 g protein. **DIABETIC EXCHANGES:** 2 starch, 2 lean meat, 1 fat.

MARVELOUS CHICKEN ENCHILADAS

270 CALORIES

apple-cherry pork chops

Doris Heath | FRANKLIN, NORTH CAROLINA

You'll never want pork chops any other way once you try this recipe! I season the juicy chops with a fragrant herb rub and serve them with a scrumptious sauce.

- 2 boneless pork loin chops (1/2 inch thick and 5 ounces *each*)
- 1/4 teaspoon dried thyme
- 1/8 teaspoon salt
- 1 tablespoon olive oil
- 2/3 cup apple juice
- 1 small apple, sliced
- 2 tablespoons dried cherries *or* cranberries
- 2 tablespoons chopped onion
- 1 teaspoon cornstarch
- 1 tablespoon cold water

- Sprinkle pork chops with thyme and salt. In a large skillet, cook pork in oil for 3-4 minutes on each side or until juices run clear. Remove and keep warm.

- In the same skillet, combine the apple juice, apple, cherries and onion. Bring to a boil. In a small bowl, combine cornstarch and water until smooth; stir into skillet. Cook and stir for 1-2 minutes or until thickened. Spoon over pork chops.

YIELD: 2 servings.

NUTRITION FACTS: 1 pork chop equals 350 calories, 15 g fat (4 g saturated fat), 68 mg cholesterol, 191 mg sodium, 25 g carbohydrate, 2 g fiber, 28 g protein.

APPLE-CHERRY PORK CHOPS

350 CALORIES

339 CALORIES hamburger corn bread casserole

Kathy Garrison | FORT WORTH, TEXAS

Welcome friends in from the cold with a comforting dish that all ages will love. A layer of corn bread makes this meal-in-one both filling and delicious.

- 1 pound lean ground beef (90% lean)
- 1 small onion, chopped
- 1 can (15 ounces) Ranch Style beans (pinto beans in seasoned tomato sauce)
- 1 can (14-1/2 ounces) diced tomatoes, undrained
- 1 teaspoon chili powder
- 1 teaspoon Worcestershire sauce

TOPPING:

- 1/2 cup all-purpose flour
- 1/2 cup cornmeal
- 2 tablespoons sugar
- 2 teaspoons baking powder
- 1/4 teaspoon salt
- 1 egg, beaten
- 1/2 cup fat-free milk
- 1 tablespoon canola oil

- In a large skillet, cook the beef and onion over medium heat until meat is no longer pink; drain. Add the beans, tomatoes, chili powder and Worcestershire sauce; bring to a boil. Reduce heat; simmer, uncovered, for 5 minutes.

- Transfer to an 11-in. x 7-in. baking dish coated with cooking spray. For topping, in a small bowl, combine the flour, cornmeal, sugar, baking powder and salt. Combine the egg, milk and oil; stir into dry ingredients just until moistened. Spoon over filling; gently spread to cover the top.

- Bake, uncovered, at 425° for 14-18 minutes or until the filling is bubbly and a toothpick inserted into the topping comes out clean. Let casserole stand for 5 minutes before cutting.

YIELD: 6 servings.

NUTRITION FACTS: 1 serving equals 339 calories, 10 g fat (3 g saturated fat), 73 mg cholesterol, 722 mg sodium, 38 g carbohydrate, 6 g fiber, 22 g protein. **DIABETIC EXCHANGES:** 3 lean meat, 2 starch, 1 vegetable, 1/2 fat.

LIGHT-BUT-HEARTY TUNA CASSEROLE

light-but-hearty tuna casserole

Heidi Carofano | BROOKLYN, NEW YORK

My boyfriend grew up loving his mother's tuna casserole and says he can't tell at all that this one is light! I make it at least once a month.

- 3 cups uncooked yolk-free noodles
- 1 can (10-3/4 ounces) reduced-fat reduced-sodium condensed cream of mushroom soup, undiluted
- 1/2 cup fat-free milk

classic

- 2 tablespoons reduced-fat mayonnaise
- 1/2 teaspoon ground mustard
- 1 can (5 ounces) white water-packed solid tuna
- 1 jar (6 ounces) sliced mushrooms, drained
- 1/4 cup chopped roasted sweet red pepper

TOPPING:

- 1/4 cup dry bread crumbs
- 1 tablespoon butter, melted
- 1/2 teaspoon paprika
- 1/4 teaspoon Italian seasoning
- 1/4 teaspoon pepper

- Cook noodles according to package directions.

- In a large bowl, combine the soup, milk, mayonnaise and mustard. Stir in the tuna, mushrooms and red pepper. Drain noodles; add to soup mixture and stir until blended. Transfer to an 8-in. square baking dish coated with cooking spray.

- Combine topping ingredients; sprinkle over casserole. Bake at 400° for 25-30 minutes or until bubbly.

YIELD: 4 servings.

dinners | 251-350 CALORIES

NUTRITION FACTS: 1-1/2 cups equals 322 calories, 9 g fat (3 g saturated fat), 32 mg cholesterol, 843 mg sodium, 39 g carbohydrate, 4 g fiber, 18 g protein.

lasagna corn carne

Mary Lou Wills | LA PLATA, MARYLAND

This recipe is a tasty spin on traditional lasagna.

- 1 pound lean ground beef (90% lean)
- 1 jar (16 ounces) salsa
- 1 can (16 ounces) kidney beans, rinsed and drained
- 1 can (14-3/4 ounces) cream-style corn
- 1 large onion, chopped
- 1 medium green pepper, chopped
- 1 celery rib, chopped
- 3 garlic cloves, minced
- 1 tablespoon minced fresh basil *or* 1 teaspoon dried basil
- 1 teaspoon salt
- 1 teaspoon chili powder
- 12 lasagna noodles, cooked and drained
- 2 cups (8 ounces) shredded part-skim mozzarella cheese
- 1/2 cup grated Parmesan cheese

- In a large skillet, cook beef over medium heat until no longer pink; drain. Add the salsa, beans, vegetables, garlic and seasonings. Bring to a boil. Reduce heat; cover and simmer for 15 minutes.

- Spread a fourth of the meat sauce in a greased 13-in. x 9-in. baking dish; top with four noodles. Repeat layers once. Top with half of the remaining sauce; sprinkle with half the cheeses. Layer with the remaining noodles, sauce and cheeses.

- Cover and bake at 350° for 30 minutes. Uncover; bake 15-20 minutes longer or until heated through. Let stand for 15 minutes before cutting.

YIELD: 12 servings.

NUTRITION FACTS: 1 piece equals 292 calories, 8 g fat (4 g saturated fat), 37 mg cholesterol, 674 mg sodium, 36 g carbohydrate, 4 g fiber, 20 g protein. **DIABETIC EXCHANGES:** 2-1/2 starch, 2 lean meat.

PITA BURGERS

garlic chicken penne

Anne Nock | AVON LAKE, OHIO

All it takes is four ingredients and 20 minutes to have this hearty dish ready for the table. Chicken, snap peas and pasta star in this medley, and the garlicky sauce ties it all together nicely.

> 8 ounces uncooked penne pasta
>
> 1-1/2 cups frozen sugar snap peas
>
> 1 package (1.6 ounces) garlic-herb pasta sauce mix
>
> 1 package (6 ounces) sliced cooked chicken

- In a large saucepan, cook pasta in boiling water for 6 minutes. Add peas; return to a boil. Cook for 4-5 minutes or until pasta is tender. Meanwhile, prepare sauce mix according to package directions.

- Drain pasta mixture; add chicken. Drizzle with sauce and toss to coat.

YIELD: 4 servings.

NUTRITION FACTS: 1-1/3 cups equals 429 calories, 12 g fat (6 g saturated fat), 62 mg cholesterol, 665 mg sodium, 54 g carbohydrate, 3 g fiber, 26 g protein.

GARLIC CHICKEN PENNE

pita burgers

Dorothy Wiedeman | EATON, COLORADO

This is a tasty variation on the traditional hamburger at backyard get-togethers. Similar to Greek gyros, the herbed ground beef patties are stuffed in pita bread with a yummy cucumber lettuce mixture.

> 1 small onion, chopped
>
> 1 garlic clove, minced
>
> 1 teaspoon dried oregano
>
> 3/4 teaspoon salt
>
> 1/2 teaspoon dried basil
>
> 1/4 teaspoon dried rosemary, crushed
>
> 1-1/2 pounds lean ground beef (90% lean)
>
> 2 cups shredded lettuce
>
> 1 medium cucumber, seeded and chopped
>
> 1 cup (8 ounces) reduced-fat plain yogurt
>
> 1 tablespoon sesame seeds, toasted
>
> 6 whole pita breads

- In a small bowl, combine the onion, garlic and seasonings; crumble beef over the mixture and mix well. Shape into six patties.

- Grill or broil for 5-7 minutes on each side or until a meat thermometer reads 160° and juices run clear.

- Meanwhile, in a small bowl, combine the lettuce, cucumber, yogurt and sesame seeds. Top each burger with lettuce mixture; serve on pita breads.

YIELD: 6 servings.

NUTRITION FACTS: 1 burger equals 409 calories, 12 g fat (5 g saturated fat), 44 mg cholesterol, 731 mg sodium, 40 g carbohydrate, 3 g fiber, 32 g protein.

dinners | 351-450 CALORIES

herbed pork and potatoes

Kate Collins | AUBURN, WASHINGTON

This recipe is wonderful because it's not only delicious, but the potatoes are a hot built-in side dish! We made it for our anniversary party, and our guests were more than impressed.

- 3 tablespoons minced fresh rosemary
- 2 tablespoons minced fresh marjoram
- 8 garlic cloves, minced
- 4 teaspoons minced fresh sage
- 4 teaspoons olive oil, *divided*
- 2 teaspoons salt
- 2 teaspoons pepper
- 1 boneless whole pork loin roast (3 pounds)
- 4 pounds medium red potatoes, quartered

- In a small bowl, combine the rosemary, marjoram, garlic, sage, 3 teaspoons oil, salt and pepper. Rub roast with 2 tablespoons herb mixture.

- In a Dutch oven over medium-high heat, brown roast in remaining oil on all sides. Place in a roasting pan coated with cooking spray. Toss potatoes with remaining herb mixture; arrange around roast.

- Cover and bake at 350° for 1 to 1-1/4 hours or until a meat thermometer reads 160°. Let stand for 10 minutes before slicing.

YIELD: 9 servings.

NUTRITION FACTS: 4 ounces cooked pork with 3/4 cup potatoes equals 358 calories, 9 g fat (3 g saturated fat), 75 mg cholesterol, 581 mg sodium, 34 g carbohydrate, 4 g fiber, 33 g protein. **DIABETIC EXCHANGES:** 4 lean meat, 2 starch, 1/2 fat.

HERBED PORK AND POTATOES

358 CALORIES

402 CALORIES

SWISS STEAK SUPPER

swiss steak supper

Kathleen Romaniuk | CHOMEDEY, QUEBEC

This satisfying slow-cooked dinner is a favorite. I keep peppered seasoned salt on hand to use instead of the seasoned salt and ground pepper.

- 1-1/2 pounds beef top round steak
- 1/2 teaspoon seasoned salt
- 1/4 teaspoon coarsely ground pepper
- 1 tablespoon canola oil
- 3 medium potatoes
- 1-1/2 cups fresh baby carrots
- 1 medium onion, sliced
- 1 can (14-1/2 ounces) Italian diced tomatoes
- 1 jar (12 ounces) home-style beef gravy
- 1 tablespoon minced fresh parsley

- Cut steak into six serving-size pieces; flatten to 1/4-in. thickness. Rub with seasoned salt and pepper. In a large skillet, brown beef in oil on both sides; drain.

- Cut each potato into eight wedges. In a 5-qt. slow cooker, layer the potatoes, carrots, beef and onion. Combine tomatoes and gravy; pour over the top.

- Cover and cook on low for 5-1/2 to 6 hours or until meat and vegetables are tender. Sprinkle with parsley.

YIELD: 6 servings.

NUTRITION FACTS: 1 serving equals 402 calories, 6 g fat (2 g saturated fat), 67 mg cholesterol, 822 mg sodium, 53 g carbohydrate, 5 g fiber, 33 g protein.

380 CALORIES

SANTA FE CHICKEN PITA PIZZAS

santa fe chicken pita pizzas

Athena Russell | FLORENCE, SOUTH CAROLINA

This recipe is quick and easy, and because you're making individual pizzas, each one can be altered to suit everyone's tastes.

  4   pita breads (6 inches)
1/2   cup refried black beans
1/2   cup salsa
  1   cup cubed cooked chicken breast
  2   tablespoons chopped green chilies
  2   tablespoons sliced ripe olives
3/4   cup shredded Colby-Monterey Jack cheese
1/2   cup reduced-fat sour cream
  1   green onion, chopped

- Place pita breads on an ungreased baking sheet; spread with beans. Top each with salsa, chicken, chilies, olives and cheese.

- Bake at 350° for 8-10 minutes or until cheese is melted. Serve with sour cream; sprinkle with onion.

YIELD: 4 servings.

NUTRITION FACTS: 1 pita pizza with 2 tablespoons sour cream equals 380 calories, 11 g fat (7 g saturated fat), 56 mg cholesterol, 796 mg sodium, 43 g carbohydrate, 4 g fiber, 24 g protein. **DIABETIC EXCHANGES:** 3 starch, 2 lean meat, 1 fat.

chili mac casserole

Janet Kanzler | YAKIMA, WASHINGTON

With wagon wheel pasta and popular Tex-Mex ingredients, this beefy main dish is a surefire family-pleaser. Simply add a mixed green salad with any light dressing you like for a complete dinner.

  1   cup uncooked wagon wheel pasta
  1   pound lean ground beef (90% lean)
1/2   cup chopped onion
1/2   cup chopped green pepper
  1   can (15 ounces) turkey chili with beans
  1   can (14-1/2 ounces) stewed tomatoes, undrained
  1   cup crushed baked tortilla chip scoops
  1   cup (4 ounces) shredded reduced-fat cheddar cheese, *divided*
1/4   cup uncooked instant rice
  1   teaspoon chili powder
1/4   teaspoon salt
1/8   teaspoon pepper

classic

- Cook pasta according to package directions. Meanwhile, in a large nonstick skillet, cook the beef, onion and green pepper over medium heat until meat is no longer pink; drain. Stir in the chili, tomatoes, chips, 1/2 cup cheese, rice, chili powder, salt and pepper. Drain pasta; add to beef mixture.

CHILI MAC CASSEROLE

358 CALORIES

- Transfer to a 2-qt. baking dish coated with cooking spray. Sprinkle with remaining cheese. Bake, uncovered, at 350° for 25-30 minutes or until cheese is melted.

YIELD: 6 servings.

NUTRITION FACTS: 1 cup equals 358 calories, 11 g fat (5 g saturated fat), 60 mg cholesterol, 847 mg sodium, 36 g carbohydrate, 4 g fiber, 28 g protein. **DIABETIC EXCHANGES:** 3 lean meat, 2 starch, 1 vegetable.

SLOW-COOKED SHREDDED PORK

slow-cooked shredded pork

Shirleymae Haefner | O'FALLON, MISSOURI

The tasty pork filling for these sandwiches requires very little work because it's prepared in the slow cooker. The mild sauce is appealing, too.

1	boneless whole pork loin roast (2 to 3 pounds)
1	large onion, thinly sliced
1	cup beer *or* nonalcoholic beer
1	cup chili sauce
2	tablespoons brown sugar
1	tablespoon prepared horseradish
8	sandwich rolls, split

- Place the roast in a 3-qt. slow cooker. Top with onion. Combine the beer, chili sauce, brown sugar and horseradish; pour over pork and onion. Cover and cook on low for 6 to 6-1/2 hours or until meat is very tender.

- Remove pork; shred with two forks. Return meat to cooking juices; heat through. Use a slotted spoon to serve on rolls.

YIELD: 8 servings.

NUTRITION FACTS: 1 sandwich equals 413 calories, 10 g fat (4 g saturated fat), 56 mg cholesterol, 847 mg sodium, 50 g carbohydrate, 2 g fiber, 29 g protein.

skillet pasta florentine

Kelly Turnbull | JUPITER, FLORIDA

Here's a great weeknight supper that's budget-friendly, healthy and liked by children. With such a thick, cheesy topping, who'd ever guess that it's light?

3	cups uncooked spiral pasta
1	egg, lightly beaten
2	cups (16 ounces) 2% cottage cheese
1-1/2	cups reduced-fat ricotta cheese
1	package (10 ounces) frozen chopped spinach, thawed and squeezed dry
1	cup (4 ounces) shredded part-skim mozzarella cheese, *divided*
1	teaspoon *each* dried parsley flakes, oregano and basil
1	jar (14 ounces) meatless spaghetti sauce
2	tablespoons grated Parmesan cheese

- Cook pasta according to package directions. Meanwhile, in a large bowl, combine the egg, cottage cheese, ricotta, spinach, 1/2 cup mozzarella and herbs.

- Drain pasta. Place half of sauce in a large skillet; layer with pasta and remaining sauce. Top with cheese mixture.

- Bring to a boil. Reduce heat; cover and cook for 25-30 minutes or until a thermometer reads 160°.

- Sprinkle with Parmesan cheese and remaining mozzarella cheese; cover and cook 5 minutes longer or until cheese is melted. Let stand for 5 minutes before serving.

YIELD: 6 servings.

NUTRITION FACTS: 1 serving equals 383 calories, 9 g fat (5 g saturated fat), 73 mg cholesterol, 775 mg sodium, 47 g carbohydrate, 4 g fiber, 27 g protein.

CHICKEN NOODLE CASSEROLE

tlapia with jasmine rice

Shirl Parsons | CAPE CARTERET, NORTH CAROLINA

This recipe for tender, full-flavored tilapia is to die for. Fragrant jasmine rice brings a special touch to the mouthwatering dish.

- 3/4 cup water
- 1/2 cup uncooked jasmine rice
- 1-1/2 teaspoons butter
- 1/4 teaspoon ground cumin
- 1/4 teaspoon seafood seasoning
- 1/4 teaspoon pepper
- 1/8 teaspoon salt
- 2 tilapia fillets (6 ounces *each*)
- 1/4 cup fat-free Italian salad dressing

- In a large saucepan, bring the water, rice and butter to a boil. Reduce heat; cover and simmer for 15-20 minutes or until liquid is absorbed and rice is tender.

- Combine the seasonings; sprinkle over fillets. Place salad dressing in a large skillet; cook over medium heat until heated through. Add fish; cook for 3-4 minutes on each side or until fish flakes easily with a fork. Serve with rice.

YIELD: 2 servings.

NUTRITION FACTS: 1 fillet with 3/4 cup rice equals 356 calories, 5 g fat (3 g saturated fat), 91 mg cholesterol, 743 mg sodium, 41 g carbohydrate, 1 g fiber, 35 g protein. **DIABETIC EXCHANGES:** 4 lean meat, 3 starch, 1/2 fat.

TILAPIA WITH JASMINE RICE

chicken noodle casserole

Sylvia McCrone | DANVILLE, ILLINOIS

This rich casserole is ideal comfort food for your family on a chilly night. Round out the menu with a favorite steamed vegetable for a hearty meal.

- 5 cups uncooked egg noodles
- 1 cup frozen peas
- 1 celery rib, chopped
- 1 medium carrot, chopped
- 4 cups cubed cooked chicken breast
- 1 can (14-3/4 ounces) cream-style corn
- 1 can (10-3/4 ounces) reduced-fat reduced-sodium condensed cream of chicken soup, undiluted
- 2 cups (8 ounces) shredded reduced-fat Colby-Monterey Jack cheese, *divided*
- 1 small onion, chopped
- 1/4 cup chopped green pepper
- 1/4 cup chopped sweet red pepper
- 1/4 teaspoon pepper

classic

- In a large saucepan, cook noodles according to package directions, adding the peas, celery and carrot during the last 5 minutes of cooking. Drain.

- Stir in the chicken, corn, soup, 1 cup cheese, onion, green and red peppers and pepper. Transfer mixture to a 13-in. x 9-in. baking dish coated with cooking spray.

- Cover and bake at 350° for 30 minutes. Sprinkle with remaining cheese; bake 10 minutes longer or until cheese is melted.

YIELD: 8 servings.

NUTRITION FACTS: 1-1/2 cups equals 367 calories, 9 g fat (5 g saturated fat), 92 mg cholesterol, 606 mg sodium, 37 g carbohydrate, 3 g fiber, 34 g protein. **DIABETIC EXCHANGES:** 4 lean meat, 2 starch, 1 vegetable.

creamed turkey on mashed potatoes

Here's a no-fuss classic from our Test Kitchen. The creamy turkey mixture blends perfectly with tasty mashed potatoes for a meal-in-one sensation.

- 1/2 cup chopped onion
- 2 tablespoons butter
- 2 tablespoons all-purpose flour
- 1/4 teaspoon salt
- 1/8 teaspoon white pepper
- 2 cups fat-free milk
- 2 cups cubed cooked turkey breast
- 1 cup frozen mixed vegetables
- 2 cups mashed potatoes (with added milk and butter)

- In a large saucepan, saute the onion in butter until tender. Sprinkle with the flour, salt and pepper. Stir in the milk until blended.

- Bring to a boil; cook and stir for 2 minutes or until thickened and bubbly. Add the turkey and vegetables; cover and simmer until heated through. Serve over mashed potatoes.

YIELD: 4 servings.

NUTRITION FACTS: 1 cup turkey mixture with 1/2 cup mashed potatoes equals 358 calories, 11 g fat (6 g saturated fat), 89 mg cholesterol, 628 mg sodium, 35 g carbohydrate, 4 g fiber, 29 g protein. **DIABETIC EXCHANGES:** 3 lean meat, 2 starch, 1-1/2 fat, 1/2 fat-free milk.

CREAMED TURKEY ON MASHED POTATOES

358 CALORIES

BEEF BARBECUE

414 CALORIES

beef barbecue

Karen Walker | STERLING, VIRGINIA

We like to keep our freezer stocked with plenty of beef roasts. When we're not in the mood for pot roast, I fix these satisfying sandwiches instead. The meat slow cooks in a juicy sauce while I'm at work. Then I just thinly slice it and serve it on rolls.

- 1 boneless beef chuck roast (3 pounds)
- 1 cup barbecue sauce
- 1/2 cup apricot preserves
- 1/3 cup chopped green *or* sweet red pepper
- 1 small onion, chopped
- 1 tablespoon Dijon mustard
- 2 teaspoons brown sugar
- 12 sandwich rolls, split

- Cut the roast into quarters; place in a greased 5-qt. slow cooker. In a bowl, combine barbecue sauce, preserves, green pepper, onion, mustard and brown sugar; pour over roast. Cover and cook on low for 6-8 hours or until meat is tender.

- Remove roast and thinly slice; return meat to slow cooker and stir gently. Cover and cook 20-30 minutes longer. Skim fat from sauce. Serve beef and sauce on rolls.

YIELD: 12 servings.

NUTRITION FACTS: 3 ounces cooked beef equals 414 calories, 14 g fat (5 g saturated fat), 74 mg cholesterol, 564 mg sodium, 43 g carbohydrate, 2 g fiber, 28 g protein.

JALAPENO-APRICOT PORK TENDERLOIN

378 CALORIES

jalapeno-apricot pork tenderloin

Amber Shea Ford | OVERLAND PARK, KANSAS

The perfect blend of spices is what sets this dish apart. I like to double the recipe and freeze the second tenderloin for later. The sweet-spicy glaze would also taste delicious over chicken.

- 2 teaspoons olive oil
- 1 garlic clove, minced
- 1 teaspoon dried oregano
- 1/2 teaspoon salt
- 1/2 teaspoon ground cumin
- 1/4 teaspoon ground coriander
- 1 pork tenderloin (3/4 pound)

GLAZE:

- 1/3 cup apricot preserves
- 1 tablespoon lime juice
- 1 tablespoon diced seeded jalapeno pepper
- 1/4 teaspoon ground cumin
- 1/8 teaspoon garlic salt

- In a large resealable plastic bag, combine the first six ingredients; add the pork. Seal bag and turn to coat; refrigerate for up to 2 hours. Drain and discard marinade.

- Place pork in an 11-in. x 7-in. baking dish coated with cooking spray. Bake, uncovered, at 400° for 15 minutes.

- In a small bowl, combine the glaze ingredients; spoon 1/4 cup over pork. Bake 5-10 minutes longer or until a meat thermometer reads 160°. Let stand for 5 minutes before slicing. Serve with remaining glaze.

YIELD: 2 servings.

EDITOR'S NOTE: When cutting hot peppers, disposable gloves are recommended. Avoid touching your face.

NUTRITION FACTS: 5 ounces cooked pork with 1/4 cup glaze equals 378 calories, 11 g fat (3 g saturated fat), 95 mg cholesterol, 818 mg sodium, 37 g carbohydrate, 1 g fiber, 35 g protein.

384 CALORIES

taco pasta shells

Anne Thomsen | WESTCHESTER, OHIO

Here's a kid-friendly dish so flavorful and fun, nobody will guess that it's also lower in fat. It's a great family supper for busy weeknights!

- 18 uncooked jumbo pasta shells
- 1-1/2 pounds lean ground beef (90% lean)
- 1 bottle (16 ounces) taco sauce, *divided*
- 3 ounces fat-free cream cheese, cubed
- 2 teaspoons chili powder
- 3/4 cup shredded reduced-fat Mexican cheese blend, *divided*
- 20 baked tortilla chip scoops, coarsely crushed

- Cook pasta according to package directions. Meanwhile, in a large nonstick skillet over medium heat, cook beef until no longer pink; drain. Add 1/2 cup taco sauce, cream cheese and chili powder; cook and stir until blended. Stir in 1/4 cup cheese blend.

- Drain pasta and rinse in cold water; stuff each shell with about 2 tablespoons beef mixture. Arrange in an 11-in. x 7-in. baking dish coated with cooking spray. Spoon remaining taco sauce over the top.

- Cover and bake at 350° for 20 minutes. Uncover; sprinkle with remaining cheese blend. Bake 5-10 minutes longer or until heated through and cheese is melted. Sprinkle with chips.

YIELD: 6 servings.

NUTRITION FACTS: 3 stuffed shells equals 384 calories, 13 g fat (5 g saturated fat), 67 mg cholesterol, 665 mg sodium, 33 g carbohydrate, 3 g fiber, 33 g protein.

360 CALORIES

MUSHROOM PORK RAGOUT

mushroom pork ragout

Connie McDowell I GREENWOOD, DELAWARE

Savory, slow-cooked pork is luscious draped in a delightful tomato gravy and served over noodles. It's a nice change from regular pork roast. I serve it with broccoli or green beans on the side.

- 1 pork tenderloin (3/4 pound)
- 1/8 teaspoon salt
- 1/8 teaspoon pepper
- 1 tablespoon cornstarch
- 3/4 cup canned crushed tomatoes, *divided*
- 1 tablespoon chopped sun-dried tomatoes (not packed in oil)
- 1-1/4 teaspoons dried savory
- 1-1/2 cups sliced fresh mushrooms
- 1/3 cup sliced onion
- 1-1/2 cups hot cooked egg noodles

- Rub pork with salt and pepper; cut in half. In a 1-1/2-qt. slow cooker, combine the cornstarch, 1/2 cup crushed tomatoes, sun-dried tomatoes and savory. Top with mushrooms, onion and pork. Pour remaining tomatoes over pork. Cover and cook on low for 3-4 hours or until meat is tender.

- Remove meat and cut into slices. Stir cooking juices until smooth; serve with pork and noodles.

YIELD: 2 servings.

NUTRITION FACTS: 5 ounces cooked pork and 3/4 cup gravy with 3/4 cup noodles equals 360 calories, 7 g fat (2 g saturated fat), 122 mg cholesterol, 309 mg sodium, 32 g carbohydrate, 3 g fiber, 40 g protein. DIABETIC EXCHANGES: 5 lean meat, 2 vegetable, 1 starch.

chicken fettuccine alfredo

LaDonna Reed I PONCA CITY, OKLAHOMA

This recipe is very creamy and tasty. You'll be surprised it's so light. A filling dish that's also good for you, this recipe mixes tender chunks of chicken with peas, noodles and a smooth sauce.

- 6 ounces uncooked fettuccine
- 1 pound boneless skinless chicken breasts, cubed
- 1 small onion, chopped
- 1/2 teaspoon salt
- 1/8 teaspoon cayenne pepper
- 1 tablespoon butter
- 4 garlic cloves, minced
- 4-1/2 teaspoons all-purpose flour
- 1-1/2 cups fat-free half-and-half
- 1 cup frozen peas, thawed
- 1/4 cup grated Parmesan cheese

classic

- Cook fettuccine according to package directions. Meanwhile, in a large skillet, saute the chicken, onion, salt and cayenne in butter until chicken is no longer pink. Add garlic; cook 1 minute longer. Stir in flour until blended.

- Gradually add the half-and-half, peas and cheese. Bring to a boil; cook and stir for 1-2 minutes or until thickened. Drain fettuccine; toss with chicken mixture.

YIELD: 4 servings.

NUTRITION FACTS: 1 cup equals 425 calories, 8 g fat (4 g saturated fat), 75 mg cholesterol, 577 mg sodium, 49 g carbohydrate, 4 g fiber, 36 g protein.

CHICKEN FETTUCCINE ALFREDO

425 CALORIES

BEEFY RED PEPPER PASTA

beefy red pepper pasta

Marge Werner | BROKEN ARROW, OKLAHOMA

Chock-full of veggies and gooey with cheese, this hearty one-dish-meal will warm the whole family right down to their toes! Pureed roasted red peppers add zing and color to the sauce.

- 1 jar (12 ounces) roasted sweet red peppers, drained
- 1 pound lean ground beef (90% lean)
- 1 small onion, chopped
- 1 can (14-1/2 ounces) diced tomatoes, undrained
- 2 garlic cloves, minced
- 1 teaspoon dried oregano
- 1 teaspoon dried basil
- 3/4 teaspoon salt
- 8 ounces uncooked ziti *or* small tube pasta
- 1-1/2 cups cut fresh green beans
- 1-1/2 cups (6 ounces) shredded part-skim mozzarella cheese

- Place peppers in a food processor; cover and process until smooth. In a large skillet, cook beef and onion until meat is no longer pink; drain. Stir in the pepper puree, tomatoes, garlic, oregano, basil and salt. Bring to a boil. Reduce heat; simmer, uncovered, for 15 minutes.

- Meanwhile, in a Dutch oven, cook pasta according to package directions, adding green beans during the last 5 minutes of cooking. Cook until pasta and green beans are tender; drain. Return to the pan; stir in meat sauce. Sprinkle with cheese; stir until melted.

YIELD: 6 servings.

NUTRITION FACTS: 1-2/3 cups equals 362 calories, 11 g fat (5 g saturated fat), 53 mg cholesterol, 739 mg sodium, 38 g carbohydrate, 4 g fiber, 28 g protein. **DIABETIC EXCHANGES:** 3 lean meat, 2 starch, 1 vegetable.

chicken hot dish

Amber Dudley | NEW PRAGUE, MINNESOTA

You won't believe how easy this chicken recipe is to make! By simply layering a variety of delicious ingredients, you'll create a meal everyone will enjoy.

- 1 package (26 ounces) frozen shredded hash brown potatoes, thawed
- 1 package (24 ounces) frozen California-blend vegetables
- 3 cups cubed cooked chicken
- 1 can (10-3/4 ounces) reduced-fat reduced-sodium condensed cream of chicken soup, undiluted
- 1 can (10-3/4 ounces) reduced-fat reduced-sodium condensed cream of mushroom soup, undiluted
- 1 cup reduced-sodium chicken broth
- 3/4 cup french-fried onions

- In a greased 13-in. x 9-in. baking dish, layer the potatoes, vegetables and chicken. In a large bowl, combine soups and broth; pour over chicken (dish will be full).

- Cover and bake at 375° for 1 hour. Uncover; sprinkle with french-fried onions. Bake 10 minutes longer or until heated through.

YIELD: 6 servings.

NUTRITION FACTS: 1 serving equals 374 calories, 11 g fat (3 g saturated fat), 68 mg cholesterol, 660 mg sodium, 39 g carbohydrate, 5 g fiber, 28 g protein. **DIABETIC EXCHANGES:** 3 lean meat, 2 starch, 1 vegetable.

pot roast with vegetables

Cheryl Rihn | BLOOMER, WISCONSIN

My mother prepared this pot roast at least once a week when I was a child, and I still love it!

- 1 beef sirloin tip roast (3 pounds)
- 2 tablespoons canola oil
- 4 large potatoes, peeled and quartered
- 4 large carrots, cut into 2-inch pieces
- 1 large onion, cut into wedges
- 2 cups water
- 1 teaspoon beef bouillon granules

classic

1/2 teaspoon salt
1/4 teaspoon pepper
  3 tablespoons cornstarch
  3 tablespoons cold water

- In a pressure cooker, brown roast in oil on all sides. Add potatoes, carrots, onion and water. Close cover securely; place pressure regulator on vent pipe. Bring cooker to full pressure over high heat. Reduce heat to medium-high; cook for 40 minutes. (Pressure regulator should maintain a slow steady rocking motion; adjust heat if needed.)

- Remove from the heat; allow pressure to drop on its own. Remove meat and vegetables; keep warm. Bring cooking juices in pressure cooker to a boil. Add bouillon, salt and pepper.

- Combine cornstarch and cold water until smooth; stir into juices. Bring to a boil; cook and stir for 2 minutes or until thickened. Serve with roast and vegetables.

YIELD: 8 servings.

EDITOR'S NOTE: This recipe was tested at 13 pounds of pressure (psi).

NUTRITION FACTS: 1 serving equals 417 calories, 11 g fat (3 g saturated fat), 90 mg cholesterol, 343 mg sodium, 41 g carbohydrate, 4 g fiber, 36 g protein.

POT ROAST WITH VEGETABLES

saucy tarragon chicken

379 CALORIES

Mary Steiner | WEST BEND, WISCONSIN
This delightful golden chicken dish features plenty of mushroom gravy and boasts a mild, satisfying taste with just a hint of lemon and tarragon.

  3 cups uncooked egg noodles
  4 boneless skinless chicken breast halves (4 ounces *each*)
3/4 teaspoon dried tarragon
3/4 teaspoon lemon-pepper seasoning
  1 tablespoon butter
  2 cups sliced fresh mushrooms
  4 garlic cloves, minced
  1 can (14-1/2 ounces) reduced-sodium chicken broth, *divided*
  3 tablespoons sherry *or* additional reduced-sodium chicken broth
  3 tablespoons all-purpose flour
1/4 cup reduced-fat sour cream

- Cook the noodles according to the package directions. Meanwhile, sprinkle chicken with tarragon and lemon-pepper. In a large nonstick skillet over medium-high heat, brown chicken in butter on both sides. Remove and keep warm.

- In the same skillet, saute mushrooms until tender. Add garlic; cook 1 minute longer. Add 1 cup broth and sherry, stirring to loosen browned bits from pan.

- Return the chicken to the pan; bring to a boil. Reduce heat; simmer, uncovered, for 7-10 minutes or until a meat thermometer reads 170°. Remove the chicken and keep warm.

- Combine flour and remaining broth until smooth; stir into pan juices. Bring to a boil; cook and stir for 1-2 minutes or until thickened. Remove from the heat; stir in sour cream. Drain noodles; serve with chicken and sauce.

YIELD: 4 servings.

NUTRITION FACTS: 1 chicken breast half with 1/4 cup sauce and 3/4 cup noodles equals 379 calories, 9 g fat (4 g saturated fat), 116 mg cholesterol, 454 mg sodium, 39 g carbohydrate, 2 g fiber, 33 g protein. **DIABETIC EXCHANGES:** 3 lean meat, 2-1/2 starch.

...le-spiced pork

...Murray | ALLENSTOWN, NEW HAMPSHIRE

This sweet and savory combination serves up the flavors of fall. I've passed this recipe on many times. It also works well with ground pork or cubed leftover pork roast.

- 2 cups uncooked yolk-free noodles
- 1 pork tenderloin (1 pound), halved lengthwise and cut into 1/2-inch slices
- 1/4 cup chopped celery
- 2 tablespoons chopped onion
- 1 tablespoon canola oil
- 2 medium tart apples, chopped
- 1/3 cup raisins
- 1 tablespoon brown sugar
- 1/2 teaspoon seasoned salt
- 1/4 to 1/2 teaspoon ground cinnamon
- 4-1/2 teaspoons cornstarch
- 1 can (14-1/2 ounces) reduced-sodium beef broth
- 2 tablespoons chopped walnuts

- Cook noodles according to package directions; drain. Meanwhile, in a large skillet, brown pork with celery and onion in oil; drain. Add the apples, raisins, brown sugar, seasoned salt and cinnamon. Cook and stir over medium heat for 8-10 minutes or until pork is no longer pink and vegetables are tender.

- In a small bowl, combine cornstarch and broth until smooth; gradually add to the pork mixture. Bring to a boil; cook and stir for 2 minutes or until thickened. Serve with noodles. Sprinkle with walnuts.

YIELD: 4 servings.

NUTRITION FACTS: 1 cup spiced pork with 1/2 cup noodles equals 376 calories, 10 g fat (2 g saturated fat), 65 mg cholesterol, 444 mg sodium, 43 g carbohydrate, 4 g fiber, 28 g protein. **DIABETIC EXCHANGES:** 3 lean meat, 1-1/2 starch, 1 fruit, 1/2 fat.

353 CALORIES makeover sloppy joe mac and cheese

Our home economists decreased the butter and replaced the half-and-half with milk to cut a whopping 658 calories and more than half the fat from this casserole. Even though the cholesterol was reduced by 75% and the sodium by 40%, this dish offers all the heartwarming comfort of the original submission.

- 1 package (16 ounces) elbow macaroni
- 3/4 pound lean ground turkey
- 1/2 cup finely chopped celery
- 1/2 cup shredded carrot
- 1 can (14-1/2 ounces) diced tomatoes, undrained
- 1 can (6 ounces) tomato paste
- 1/2 cup water
- 1 envelope sloppy joe mix
- 1 small onion, finely chopped
- 1 tablespoon butter
- 1/3 cup all-purpose flour
- 1 teaspoon ground mustard
- 3/4 teaspoon salt
- 1/4 teaspoon pepper
- 4 cups 2% milk
- 1 tablespoon Worcestershire sauce
- 8 ounces reduced-fat process cheese (Velveeta), cubed
- 2 cups (8 ounces) shredded cheddar cheese, *divided*

APPLE-SPICED PORK

376 CALORIES

dinners | 351-450 CALORIES

- Cook macaroni according to the package directions. Meanwhile, in a large nonstick skillet, cook the turkey, celery and carrot over medium heat until meat is no longer pink and vegetables are tender; drain. Add the tomatoes, tomato paste, water and sloppy joe mix. Bring to a boil. Reduce heat; cover and simmer for 10 minutes, stirring occasionally.

- Drain macaroni; set aside. In a large saucepan, saute onion in butter until tender. Stir in the flour, mustard, salt and pepper until smooth. Gradually add milk and Worcestershire sauce. Bring to a boil; cook and stir for 1-2 minutes or until thickened. Remove from the heat. Stir in the process cheese until melted. Add macaroni and 1 cup cheddar cheese; mix well.

- Spread two-thirds of the macaroni mixture in a 13-in. x 9-in. baking dish coated with cooking spray. Spread turkey mixture to within 2 in. of edges. Spoon remaining macaroni mixture around edges of pan. Cover and bake at 375° for 30-35 minutes or until bubbly. Uncover; sprinkle with remaining cheddar cheese. Cover and let stand until cheese is melted.

YIELD: 10 servings.

NUTRITION FACTS: 1 cup equals 353 calories, 12 g fat (7 g saturated fat), 54 mg cholesterol, 877 mg sodium, 42 g carbohydrate, 3 g fiber, 20 g protein.

sweet and sour chicken

Lori Burtenshaw | TERRETON, IDAHO

I first tasted this yummy dish at our friends' home. I immediately asked for the recipe, and we've enjoyed it ever since. We call it "favorite chicken" at our house!

- 1 tablespoon plus 2 teaspoons reduced-sodium soy sauce, *divided*
- 1 tablespoon sherry *or* reduced-sodium chicken broth
- 1/2 teaspoon salt
- 1/2 teaspoon garlic powder
- 1/2 teaspoon ground ginger
- 1 pound boneless skinless chicken breasts, cut into 1-inch cubes
- 1 can (20 ounces) unsweetened pineapple chunks
- 2 tablespoons plus 1/3 cup cornstarch, *divided*

428 CALORIES

SWEET AND SOUR CHICKEN

- 2 tablespoons sugar
- 1/4 cup cider vinegar
- 1/4 cup ketchup
- 1 tablespoon canola oil
- 2 cups hot cooked rice

- In a large resealable plastic bag, combine 1 tablespoon soy sauce, sherry, salt, garlic powder and ginger; add the chicken. Seal bag and turn to coat; refrigerate for 30 minutes.

- Drain pineapple, reserving juice; set pineapple aside. Add enough water to juice to measure 1 cup. In a small bowl, combine 2 tablespoons cornstarch, sugar and pineapple juice mixture until smooth; stir in the vinegar, ketchup and remaining soy sauce. Set aside.

- Drain chicken and discard marinade. Place remaining cornstarch in a large resealable plastic bag. Add chicken, a few pieces at a time, and shake to coat. In a large nonstick skillet or wok coated with cooking spray, stir-fry chicken in oil until no longer pink. Remove and keep warm.

- Stir pineapple juice mixture and add to the pan. Bring to a boil; cook and stir for 2 minutes or until thickened. Add chicken and reserved pineapple; heat through. Serve with rice.

YIELD: 4 servings.

NUTRITION FACTS: 1 cup chicken mixture with 1/2 cup rice equals 428 calories, 6 g fat (1 g saturated fat), 63 mg cholesterol, 571 mg sodium, 65 g carbohydrate, 2 g fiber, 26 g protein.

373 CALORIES

TORTELLINI WITH SALMON-RICOTTA SAUCE

tortellini with salmon-ricotta sauce

Beth Dauenhauer I PUEBLO, COLORADO

I like to serve this with a colorful vegetable, such as a tomato salad or peas and carrots. It's equally good with canned salmon or tuna, too.

- 1 package (9 ounces) refrigerated cheese tortellini
- 2 green onions, sliced
- 1 teaspoon butter
- 2 garlic cloves, minced
- 1 teaspoon cornstarch
- 1 cup fat-free milk
- 1/2 cup shredded part-skim mozzarella cheese
- 1 cup fat-free ricotta cheese
- 1 pouch (7.1 ounces) boneless skinless pink salmon
- 2 tablespoons snipped fresh dill *or* 2 teaspoons dill weed
- 1-1/2 teaspoons grated lemon peel
- 1-1/2 teaspoons lemon juice
- 1/4 teaspoon salt

- Cook tortellini according to the package directions. Meanwhile, in a large saucepan, saute onions in butter until tender. Add garlic; cook 1 minute longer. Combine cornstarch and milk until smooth; gradually stir into the pan. Bring to a boil; cook and stir for 2 minutes or until slightly thickened.

- Stir in mozzarella cheese until melted. Stir in the ricotta cheese, salmon, dill, lemon peel, lemon juice and salt.

- Drain tortellini; add to ricotta sauce. Cook and stir until heated through.

YIELD: 4 servings.

NUTRITION FACTS: 1 cup equals 373 calories, 11 g fat (6 g saturated fat), 67 mg cholesterol, 797 mg sodium, 40 g carbohydrate, 2 g fiber, 28 g protein. **DIABETIC EXCHANGES:** 3 lean meat, 2-1/2 starch, 1 fat.

paprika beef stroganoff

Lara Taylor I VIRGINIA BEACH, VIRGINIA

I am a busy home-schooling mother of two. I love this recipe because everyone looks forward to it, and I can let it simmer while I do other things. It fills my home with a delightful aroma.

- 2 pounds beef top round steak, cut into thin strips
- 1 tablespoon plus 2 teaspoons canola oil, *divided*
- 1 large onion, sliced
- 1 large green pepper, cut into strips
- 1/2 pound sliced fresh mushrooms
- 1-1/4 cups reduced-sodium beef broth, *divided*

PAPRIKA BEEF STROGANOFF

414 CALORIES

1 can (8 ounces) tomato sauce

3/4 cup sherry *or* additional reduced-sodium beef broth

2 tablespoons Worcestershire sauce

2 tablespoons prepared mustard

2 teaspoons paprika

1 bay leaf

1/2 teaspoon dried thyme

1/4 teaspoon pepper

1 package (12 ounces) yolk-free noodles

3 tablespoons all-purpose flour

1 cup (8 ounces) reduced-fat sour cream

- In a large nonstick skillet coated with cooking spray, cook beef in 1 tablespoon oil until no longer pink; drain and set aside.

- In the same skillet, saute onion and green pepper in remaining oil for 1 minute. Stir in mushrooms; cook for 3-4 minutes or until tender. Stir in 1 cup broth, tomato sauce, sherry, Worcestershire sauce, mustard, paprika, bay leaf, thyme and pepper. Return beef to the pan; bring to a boil. Reduce heat; cover and simmer for 40-50 minutes or until meat is tender.

- Cook the noodles according to the package directions. Meanwhile, combine flour and remaining broth until smooth; gradually stir into beef mixture. Bring to a boil; cook and stir for 2 minutes or until thickened. Discard bay leaf. Remove from the heat; stir in sour cream until blended. Drain noodles; serve with stroganoff.

YIELD: 8 servings.

NUTRITION FACTS: 3/4 cup stroganoff with 1 cup noodles equals 414 calories, 10 g fat (3 g saturated fat), 74 mg cholesterol, 360 mg sodium, 42 g carbohydrate, 4 g fiber, 36 g protein.

chinese pork 'n' noodles

Jennifer Enzer | MANCHESTER, MICHIGAN

I based the recipe for these noodles on a similar dish I found in a magazine. I changed a few things around and my husband and I loved it. It's just as good when the pork is replaced with seafood.

398 CALORIES

CHINESE PORK 'N' NOODLES

6 ounces uncooked angel hair pasta

3 tablespoons hoisin sauce

2 tablespoons reduced-sodium soy sauce

2 teaspoons sesame oil

1 pork tenderloin (1 pound), thinly sliced and halved

3 teaspoons canola oil, *divided*

3/4 cup julienned sweet red pepper

3/4 cup halved fresh snow peas

1/2 cup sliced onion

1 cup sliced cabbage

1/4 cup minced fresh cilantro

- Cook pasta according to package directions. Meanwhile, in a small bowl, combine the hoisin sauce, soy sauce and sesame oil; set aside.

- In a large nonstick skillet or wok, stir-fry pork in 2 teaspoons canola oil for 3 minutes or until no longer pink. Remove and keep warm. In the same skillet, stir-fry the red pepper, peas and onion in remaining oil for 3 minutes. Add cabbage; stir-fry 2 minutes longer or until vegetables are crisp-tender.

- Stir reserved hoisin sauce mixture and stir into skillet. Return pork to the pan; heat through. Drain pasta and add to skillet; toss to coat. Sprinkle each serving with 1 tablespoon cilantro.

YIELD: 4 servings.

NUTRITION FACTS: 1-1/2 cups equals 398 calories, 11 g fat (2 g saturated fat), 64 mg cholesterol, 550 mg sodium, 43 g carbohydrate, 3 g fiber, 30 g protein. **DIABETIC EXCHANGES:** 3 lean meat, 2-1/2 starch, 1 vegetable, 1 fat.

side dishes

Counting calories doesn't mean settling for carrot sticks when it comes to rounding out meals. Dig into classics such as scalloped potatoes, cheese fries and even fettuccine! Stick to a 500-calorie dinner by pairing these side dishes with entrees from pages 162 to 239.

252

261

243

The first section in this chapter offers items that make it a breeze to plan calorie-smart meals. Later in the chapter, you'll find more substantial side dishes. Creamy Spinach Casserole (p. 265), Mushroom Rice (p. 266) and Zucchini Pasta (p. 267) would even make great meatless entrees!

potato vegetable medley

Joann Jensen | LOWELL, INDIANA

Mom made this easy side with fresh vegetables from our garden. Knowing that us kids helped plant, nurture and pick the veggies made it even tastier!

- 6 small red potatoes, quartered
- 16 baby carrots, halved lengthwise
- 1 small onion, cut into wedges
- 1/2 cup chicken broth
- 1-1/4 teaspoons seasoned salt, *divided*
- 2 medium zucchini, chopped
- 2 tablespoons minced fresh parsley

- In a greased 2-qt. baking dish, combine the potatoes, carrots, onion, broth and 1 teaspoon seasoned salt.

- Cover and bake at 400° for 30 minutes. Stir in zucchini and remaining seasoned salt. Bake 10-15 minutes longer or until vegetables are tender. Sprinkle with parsley.

YIELD: 6 servings.

NUTRITION FACTS: 3/4 cup equals 59 calories, trace fat (trace saturated fat), trace cholesterol, 424 mg sodium, 13 g carbohydrate, 2 g fiber, 2 g protein. **DIABETIC EXCHANGES:** 1 vegetable, 1/2 starch.

POTATO VEGETABLE MEDLEY

59 CALORIES

80 CALORIES

GREEK-STYLE SQUASH

greek-style squash

Betty Washburn | RENO, NEVADA

This is a great way to use up summer squash! You can almost taste the sunshine in this colorful and quick vegetable dish. Best of all, the foil packets make for carefree cleanup.

- 2 small yellow summer squash, thinly sliced
- 2 small zucchini, thinly sliced
- 1 medium tomato, seeded and chopped
- 1/4 cup pitted ripe olives
- 2 tablespoons chopped green onion
- 2 teaspoons olive oil
- 1 teaspoon lemon juice
- 3/4 teaspoon garlic salt
- 1/4 teaspoon dried oregano
- 1/8 teaspoon pepper
- 2 tablespoons grated Parmesan cheese

- Place the yellow squash, zucchini, tomato, olives and onion on a double thickness of heavy-duty foil (about 17 in. x 18 in.). Combine the oil, lemon juice, garlic salt, oregano and pepper; pour over vegetables. Fold foil around mixture and seal tightly.

- Grill, covered, over medium heat for 30-35 minutes or until vegetables are tender. Open foil carefully to allow steam to escape. Transfer vegetables to a serving bowl. Sprinkle with cheese.

YIELD: 4 servings.

NUTRITION FACTS: 3/4 cup equals 80 calories, 5 g fat (1 g saturated fat), 2 mg cholesterol, 479 mg sodium, 8 g carbohydrate, 3 g fiber, 4 g protein. **DIABETIC EXCHANGES:** 2 vegetable, 1/2 fat.

grilled broccoli & cauliflower

Tara Delgado | WAUSEON, OHIO

This is a great side to just about any meat. For a variation, add one large baking potato, or mix in asparagus for a veggie extravaganza!

- 1 cup fresh broccoli florets
- 1 cup fresh cauliflowerets
- 1 small onion, cut into wedges

Refrigerated butter-flavored spray

- 1/4 teaspoon garlic salt
- 1/8 teaspoon paprika
- 1/8 teaspoon pepper

- In a large bowl, combine the broccoli, cauliflower and onion; spritz with butter-flavored spray. Sprinkle with the garlic salt, paprika and pepper; toss to coat. Place vegetables on a double thickness of heavy-duty foil (about 18-in. x 12-in.); fold foil around vegetables and seal tightly.

- Grill, covered, over medium heat for 10-15 minutes or until vegetables are tender. Open foil carefully to allow steam to escape.

YIELD: 2 servings.

NUTRITION FACTS: 1 cup equals 47 calories, 1 g fat (trace saturated fat), 0 cholesterol, 262 mg sodium, 8 g carbohydrate, 3 g fiber, 2 g protein. **DIABETIC EXCHANGE:** 2 vegetable.

GRILLED BROCCOLI & CAULIFLOWER

47 CALORIES

98 CALORIES

ZIPPY GREEN BEANS

zippy green beans

Suzanne McKinley | LYONS, GEORGIA

A sweet-and-sour sauce makes these fresh green beans special. The tangy treatment for this everyday vegetable dresses them up nicely, so they work with most any meal.

- 4 cups fresh *or* frozen green beans, cut into 2-inch pieces
- 2 bacon strips, diced
- 1 medium onion, thinly sliced
- 1/2 cup white wine *or* apple juice
- 3 tablespoons sugar
- 3 tablespoons tarragon vinegar
- 1/4 teaspoon salt
- 2 teaspoons cornstarch
- 1 tablespoon cold water

classic

- Place beans in a saucepan and cover with water; bring to a boil. Cook, uncovered, for 8-10 minutes or until crisp-tender.

- Meanwhile, in a large nonstick skillet, cook bacon over medium heat until crisp. Remove with a slotted spoon to paper towels. Drain, reserving 1 teaspoon drippings. In the same skillet, saute onion until tender. Stir in the wine, sugar, vinegar and salt.

- Combine cornstarch and cold water until smooth; add to the skillet. Bring to a boil; cook and stir for 2 minutes or until thickened. Drain beans; top with onion mixture. Sprinkle with bacon; toss to coat.

YIELD: 6 servings.

NUTRITION FACTS: 3/4 cup equals 98 calories, 2 g fat (1 g saturated fat), 3 mg cholesterol, 140 mg sodium, 16 g carbohydrate, 3 g fiber, 2 g protein. **DIABETIC EXCHANGES:** 2 vegetable, 1/2 starch.

76 CALORIES

SAVORY BRUSSELS SPROUTS

basil cherry tomatoes

Melissa Stevens I ELK RIVER, MINNESOTA

These tomatoes are a quick, delicious side dish and add Italian flair to any dinner. Basil and olive oil are simple additions to sweet cherry tomatoes, but the flavors are wonderful together.

- 3 pints cherry tomatoes, halved
- 1/2 cup chopped fresh basil
- 1-1/2 teaspoons olive oil

Salt and pepper to taste

Lettuce leaves, optional

- In a large bowl, combine the tomatoes, basil, oil, salt and pepper. Cover and refrigerate until serving. Serve on lettuce if desired.

YIELD: 6 servings.

NUTRITION FACTS: 1 serving (calculated without salt) equals 42 calories, 2 g fat (trace saturated fat), 0 cholesterol, 14 mg sodium, 7 g carbohydrate, 2 g fiber, 1 g protein. **DIABETIC EXCHANGE:** 1 vegetable.

BASIL CHERRY TOMATOES

42 CALORIES

savory brussels sprouts

Paula Michaud I WATERBURY, CONNECTICUT

This is a family favorite that's fast and easy! Brussels sprouts are treated to a creamy, guilt-free sauce in this delicious recipe.

- 1 pound fresh brussels sprouts

DIJON MUSTARD SAUCE:

- 1/2 cup fat-free plain yogurt
- 1 tablespoon reduced-fat mayonnaise
- 1-1/2 teaspoons Dijon mustard
- 1/4 teaspoon celery seed

- Cut an "X" in the core of each brussels sprout. Place in a steamer basket; place in a large saucepan over 1 in. of water. Bring to a boil; cover and steam for 8-11 minutes or until tender.

- Meanwhile, in a small saucepan, combine the yogurt, mayonnaise, mustard and celery seed. Cook and stir just until heated through. Serve with brussels sprouts.

YIELD: 4 servings.

NUTRITION FACTS: 3/4 cup brussels sprouts with 2 tablespoons sauce equals 76 calories, 2 g fat (trace saturated fat), 2 mg cholesterol, 120 mg sodium, 13 g carbohydrate, 4 g fiber, 5 g protein. **DIABETIC EXCHANGE:** 2 vegetable.

spiced glazed carrots

Nancy Zimmerman | CAPE MAY COURT HOUSE, NEW JERSEY

Packed with beta-carotene, these carrots flavored with honey, apple juice and cinnamon are hard to turn down. They boast a little kick that brings big flavor to your table!

- 1 pound fresh carrots, cut into 1/2-in. slices
- 3/4 cup unsweetened apple juice
- 1 cinnamon stick (3 inches)
- 3/4 teaspoon ground cumin
- 1/2 teaspoon ground ginger
- 1/4 teaspoon ground coriander
- **Dash cayenne pepper**
- 2 teaspoons lemon juice
- 2 teaspoons honey

- In a large nonstick skillet coated with cooking spray, combine the first seven ingredients. Bring to a boil. Reduce heat; cover and simmer for 5-8 minutes or until carrots are crisp-tender.

SPICED GLAZED CARROTS

83 CALORIES

- Discard cinnamon stick. Add lemon juice and honey to carrots. Bring to a boil; cook, uncovered, for 2 minutes or until sauce is thickened.

YIELD: 4 servings.

NUTRITION FACTS: 2/3 cup equals 83 calories, trace fat (trace saturated fat), 0 cholesterol, 81 mg sodium, 20 g carbohydrate, 3 g fiber, 1 g protein. **DIABETIC EXCHANGE:** 1 starch.

76 CALORIES

BROCCOLI WITH LEMON SAUCE

broccoli with lemon sauce

Barbara Frasier | FYFFE, ALABAMA

Enjoy this refreshing, delicious alternative to traditional cheese and broccoli. The lemon sauce is great over cauliflower, too!

- 3 pounds fresh broccoli spears
- 1 cup chicken broth
- 1 tablespoon butter
- 4-1/2 teaspoons cornstarch
- 1/4 cup cold water
- 2 egg yolks, lightly beaten
- 3 tablespoons lemon juice
- 2 tablespoons grated lemon peel

- Place broccoli in a large saucepan; add 1 in. of water. Bring to a boil. Reduce heat; cover and cook for 5-8 minutes or until crisp-tender.

- Meanwhile, in a small heavy saucepan, heat broth and butter until butter is melted. Combine cornstarch and water until smooth; stir into broth mixture. Bring to a boil; cook and stir for 2 minutes or until thickened and bubbly.

- Remove from the heat. Stir a small amount of hot mixture into egg yolks; return all to the pan, stirring constantly. Bring to a gentle boil; cook and stir 2 minutes longer. Remove from the heat. Gently stir in lemon juice and peel. Drain broccoli; serve with sauce.

YIELD: 10 servings (1-1/4 cups sauce).

NUTRITION FACTS: 3/4 cup broccoli with 2 tablespoons sauce equals 76 calories, 3 g fat (1 g saturated fat), 44 mg cholesterol, 164 mg sodium, 12 g carbohydrate, 5 g fiber, 4 g protein. **DIABETIC EXCHANGES:** 2 vegetable, 1/2 fat.

51 CALORIES

COLORFUL VEGGIE SAUTE

colorful veggie saute

Pamela Stewart | BELCHER, KENTUCKY

A low-fat meal doesn't skimp on flavor with this tasty saute on its side. The medley of squash and other garden-fresh ingredients is brightened by the hearty steak seasoning.

- 1 small zucchini, sliced
- 1 yellow summer squash, sliced
- 1 small onion, halved and sliced
- 1 cup sliced fresh mushrooms
- 1 small green pepper, julienned
- 1/2 cup thinly sliced fresh carrots
- 1 tablespoon butter
- 3 cups coarsely chopped fresh spinach
- 1/2 teaspoon steak seasoning
- 1/4 teaspoon garlic salt

- In a large skillet, saute the zucchini, yellow squash, onion, mushrooms, green pepper and carrots in butter until crisp-tender.

- Add the spinach, steak seasoning and garlic salt; saute 3-4 minutes longer or just until spinach is wilted.

YIELD: 5 servings.

EDITOR'S NOTE: This recipe was tested with McCormick's Montreal Steak Seasoning. Look for it in the spice aisle.

NUTRITION FACTS: 3/4 cup equals 51 calories, 3 g fat (2 g saturated fat), 6 mg cholesterol, 202 mg sodium, 7 g carbohydrate, 2 g fiber, 2 g protein. **DIABETIC EXCHANGES:** 1 vegetable, 1/2 fat.

Here are some typical side dishes and the amount of calories in them so you can determine how to stay within your goal of a 500-calorie dinner.

- **1 serving bow-tie pasta,** 200 calories
- **1/2 cup cooked long-grain white rice,** 103 calories
- **1 cup cooked egg noodles,** 221 calories

- **1 cup cooked spaghetti,** 182 calories
- **1 cup cooked whole wheat spaghetti,** 176 calories
- **1/2 cup canned corn,** 83 calories

- **1/2 cup canned fat-free refried beans,** 90 calories
- **1 small baked sweet potato,** 128 calories
- **1/2 cup canned peas,** 59 calories

For the calorie counts of other side items, see the Free Foods Chart on page 43 and the Smart Snacks List on page 67.
For additional calorie calculations, check the Nutrition Facts labels on food packages.

85 CALORIES

COLORFUL ZUCCHINI SPEARS

colorful zucchini spears

Jan Caldwell | SHINGLE SPRINGS, CALIFORNIA

A bit of bacon lends hearty flavor to this colorful side dish, while low-fat cheese helps keep the calories in check.

- 1 bacon strip, cut into 1-inch pieces
- 1 medium zucchini
- 1/8 teaspoon salt
- 1/8 teaspoon dried oregano
- 1/8 teaspoon garlic powder
- 1/8 teaspoon pepper
- 1 plum tomato, halved and sliced
- 1/4 cup sliced onion
- 1/4 cup shredded reduced-fat sharp cheddar cheese

- In a small nonstick skillet, cook bacon over medium heat until cooked but not crisp. Using a slotted spoon, remove bacon to paper towels to drain. Cut zucchini in half widthwise; cut halves lengthwise into quarters. Place in an ungreased shallow 1-qt. baking dish.

- Combine the salt, oregano, garlic powder and pepper; sprinkle half over the zucchini. Top with tomato, onion, remaining seasonings and bacon. Bake, uncovered, at 350° for 15 minutes. Sprinkle with cheese; bake 5-10 minutes longer or until zucchini is tender.

YIELD: 2 servings.

NUTRITION FACTS: 1 cup equals 85 calories, 5 g fat (3 g saturated fat), 13 mg cholesterol, 202 mg sodium, 6 g carbohydrate, 2 g fiber, 6 g protein. **DIABETIC EXCHANGES:** 1 medium-fat meat, 1 vegetable.

steamed kale

Mary Bilyeu | ANN ARBOR, MICHIGAN

You'll find a wonderful accompaniment to most any entree with good-for-you kale, which is packed with vitamins. I use garlic, red pepper and balsamic vinegar to keep my family coming back for more!

- 1 bunch kale
- 1 tablespoon olive oil
- 3 garlic cloves, minced
- 2/3 cup water
- 1/4 teaspoon salt
- 1/8 teaspoon crushed red pepper flakes
- 1 tablespoon balsamic vinegar

- Trim kale, discarding the thick ribs and stems. Chop leaves. In a Dutch oven, saute kale leaves in oil until wilted. Add garlic; cook 1 minute longer.

- Stir in the water, salt and pepper flakes. Bring to a boil. Reduce heat; cover and simmer for 20-25 minutes or until the kale is tender. Remove from the heat; stir in the vinegar.

YIELD: 4 servings.

NUTRITION FACTS: 3/4 cup equals 61 calories, 4 g fat (1 g saturated fat), 0 cholesterol, 171 mg sodium, 6 g carbohydrate, 1 g fiber, 2 g protein. **DIABETIC EXCHANGES:** 1 vegetable, 1/2 fat.

STEAMED KALE

61 CALORIES

61 CALORIES

GRILLED GARDEN VEGGIES

grilled garden veggies

Holly Wilhelm | SIOUX FALLS, SOUTH DAKOTA

This is a great recipe because you can use whatever vegetables you have on hand. It tastes great with a combination of any of them!

- 2 tablespoons olive oil, *divided*
- 1 small onion, chopped
- 2 garlic cloves, minced
- 1 teaspoon dried rosemary, crushed, *divided*
- 2 small zucchini, sliced
- 2 small yellow summer squash, sliced
- 1/2 pound medium fresh mushrooms, quartered
- 1 large tomato, diced
- 3/4 teaspoon salt
- 1/4 teaspoon pepper

- Drizzle 1 tablespoon oil over a double thickness of heavy-duty foil (about 24 in. x 12 in.). Combine the onion, garlic and 1/2 teaspoon rosemary; spoon over foil. Top with zucchini, yellow squash, mushrooms and tomato; drizzle with the remaining oil. Sprinkle with salt, pepper and remaining rosemary.

- Fold foil around vegetables and seal tightly. Grill, covered, over medium heat for 15-20 minutes or until tender. Open foil carefully to allow steam to escape.

YIELD: 8 servings.

NUTRITION FACTS: 1 serving (3/4 cup) equals 61 calories, 4 g fat (1 g saturated fat), 0 cholesterol, 227 mg sodium, 6 g carbohydrate, 2 g fiber, 2 g protein. **DIABETIC EXCHANGES:** 1 vegetable, 1/2 fat.

warm garlicky grape tomatoes

Rose Gulledge | CROFTON, MARYLAND

This is one of our favorite quick ways to use up a large crop of grape tomatoes (or to remedy an overzealous tomato shopper)!

- 2 cups grape tomatoes
- 3 garlic cloves, minced
- 1-1/2 teaspoons minced fresh basil
- 1/2 teaspoon salt-free garlic seasoning blend
- 1/4 teaspoon salt
- 1/8 teaspoon pepper
- 1 teaspoon olive oil, *divided*
- 1/4 cup soft whole wheat bread crumbs
- 1/4 cup crumbled feta cheese

- In a small bowl, combine the tomatoes, garlic, basil, seasoning blend, salt and pepper. Add 1/2 teaspoon oil; toss to coat. Transfer to a 3-cup baking dish coated with cooking spray.

- Bake at 425° for 15 minutes. Combine bread crumbs and remaining oil; sprinkle over the top. Sprinkle with cheese. Bake 5-10 minutes longer or until cheese is softened and tomatoes are tender.

YIELD: 4 servings.

NUTRITION FACTS: 1/2 cup equals 64 calories, 3 g fat (1 g saturated fat), 4 mg cholesterol, 259 mg sodium, 8 g carbohydrate, 2 g fiber, 3 g protein. **DIABETIC EXCHANGES:** 1 vegetable, 1/2 fat.

WARM GARLICKY GRAPE TOMATOES

64 CALORIES

bravo broccoli

Here's a fast, delicious way to dress up crisp-tender broccoli from our Test Kitchen! Just toss with a simple sweet-sour mixture that gets a slight kick from crushed red pepper flakes.

- 1 **bunch broccoli, cut into florets**
- 1 **tablespoon butter, melted**
- 1 **tablespoon rice vinegar**
- 1-1/2 **teaspoons brown sugar**
- 1/4 **teaspoon salt**
- 1/4 **teaspoon crushed red pepper flakes**
- 1/8 **teaspoon garlic powder**

- Place broccoli in a steamer basket; place in a large saucepan over 1 in. of water. Bring to a boil; cover and steam for 3-4 minutes or until tender. Transfer to a large bowl.

- Combine the remaining ingredients; drizzle over broccoli and gently toss to coat.

YIELD: 4 servings.

NUTRITION FACTS: 3/4 cup equals 78 calories, 3 g fat (2 g saturated fat), 8 mg cholesterol, 210 mg sodium, 10 g carbohydrate, 5 g fiber, 5 g protein. **DIABETIC EXCHANGES:** 2 vegetable, 1/2 fat.

BRAVO BROCCOLI

DIJON GREEN BEANS

dijon green beans

Jannine Fisk | MALDEN, MASSACHUSETTS
I love this recipe because it combines the freshness of garden green beans with a warm and tangy dressing. It's a wonderful, quick and easy side dish.

- 1-1/2 **pounds fresh green beans, trimmed**
- 2 **tablespoons red wine vinegar**
- 2 **tablespoons olive oil**
- 2 **teaspoons Dijon mustard**
- 1/2 **teaspoon salt**
- 1/4 **teaspoon pepper**
- 1 **cup grape tomatoes, halved**
- 1/2 **small red onion, sliced**
- 2 **tablespoons grated Parmesan cheese**

- Place beans in a large saucepan and cover with water. Bring to a boil. Cook, uncovered, for 8-10 minutes or until crisp-tender.

- Meanwhile, for dressing, whisk the vinegar, oil, mustard, salt and pepper in a small bowl. Drain beans; place in a large bowl. Add tomatoes and onion. Drizzle with dressing and toss to coat. Sprinkle with Parmesan cheese.

YIELD: 10 servings.

NUTRITION FACTS: 3/4 cup equals 54 calories, 3 g fat (1 g saturated fat), 1 mg cholesterol, 167 mg sodium, 6 g carbohydrate, 2 g fiber, 2 g protein. **DIABETIC EXCHANGES:** 1 vegetable, 1/2 fat.

zucchini parmesan

81 CALORIES

Sandi Guettler | BAY CITY, MICHIGAN

You'll knock their socks off with this easy-to-prep side that's absolutely delicious. My favorite time to make it is when the zucchini is fresh out of the garden.

- 1/2 to 1 teaspoon minced garlic
- 1 tablespoon olive oil
- 4 medium zucchini, cut into 1/4-inch slices
- 1 can (14-1/2 ounces) Italian diced tomatoes, undrained
- 1 teaspoon seasoned salt
- 1/4 teaspoon pepper
- 1/4 cup grated Parmesan cheese

- In a large skillet, saute garlic in oil. Add zucchini; cook and stir for 4-5 minutes or until crisp-tender.

- Stir in the tomatoes, seasoned salt and pepper. Simmer, uncovered, for 9-10 minutes or until liquid is absorbed and mixture is heated through. Sprinkle with Parmesan cheese. Serve with a slotted spoon.

YIELD: 6 servings.

NUTRITION FACTS: 1/2 cup equals 81 calories, 3 g fat (1 g saturated fat), 3 mg cholesterol, 581 mg sodium, 10 g carbohydrate, 2 g fiber, 3 g protein. **DIABETIC EXCHANGES:** 2 vegetable, 1/2 fat.

lemon garlic mushrooms

Diane Hixon | NICEVILLE, FLORIDA

I baste whole mushrooms with a lemony sauce to prepare this simple side dish. Using skewers or a grill basket makes it easy to turn the mushrooms.

- 1/4 cup lemon juice
- 3 tablespoons minced fresh parsley
- 2 tablespoons olive oil
- 3 garlic cloves, minced

Pepper to taste

- 1 pound large fresh mushrooms

- In a small bowl, combine the first five ingredients; set aside. Grill mushrooms, covered, over medium-hot heat

96 CALORIES

LEMON GARLIC MUSHROOMS

for 5 minutes. Brush generously with lemon mixture. Turn mushrooms; grill 5-8 minutes longer or until tender. Brush with remaining lemon mixture before serving.

YIELD: 4 servings.

NUTRITION FACTS: 1 serving equals 96 calories, 7 mg sodium, 0 cholesterol, 8 g carbohydrate, 3 g protein, 7 g fat, 2 g fiber. **DIABETIC EXCHANGES:** 1-1/2 fat, 1 vegetable.

italian vegetable medley

79 CALORIES

Margaret Wilson | SUN CITY, CALIFORNIA

Round out a variety of menus with this idea that lends a delicious pop of color. If you have them, use leftover veggies. People are always surprised at how very easy this dish is!

- 1 package (16 ounces) broccoli stir-fry vegetables
- 1 tablespoon butter
- 2 tablespoons grated Parmesan cheese
- 1 tablespoon seasoned bread crumbs
- 1/8 teaspoon garlic powder
- 1/8 teaspoon seasoned salt
- 1/8 teaspoon pepper

- Microwave vegetables according to package directions; drain. Stir in butter. Meanwhile, in a small bowl, combine the cheese, bread crumbs, garlic powder, salt and pepper; sprinkle over vegetables.

YIELD: 4 servings.

NUTRITION FACTS: 3/4 cup equals 79 calories, 4 g fat (2 g saturated fat), 10 mg cholesterol, 174 mg sodium, 7 g carbohydrate, 2 g fiber, 2 g protein. **DIABETIC EXCHANGES:** 1 vegetable, 1/2 fat.

62 CALORIES

RED CABBAGE WITH APPLES

red cabbage with apples

Michelle Dougherty | LEWISTON, IDAHO

Looking for a tasty, lower-in-sodium alternative to sauerkraut to serve with pork entrees? Try this colorful side dish with the slightly sweet flavor of apples.

> 3 cups shredded red cabbage
>
> 1 medium apple, peeled and thinly sliced
>
> 1 small onion, halved and sliced
>
> 2 tablespoons water
>
> 2 tablespoons thawed apple juice concentrate
>
> 1/2 teaspoon chicken bouillon granules
>
> 1/4 teaspoon salt
>
> 1/4 teaspoon caraway seeds
>
> 1 tablespoon red wine vinegar

- In a large saucepan, combine the first eight ingredients. Bring to a boil. Reduce heat; cover and simmer for 10-15 minutes or until cabbage is tender. Stir in vinegar.

YIELD: 4 servings.

NUTRITION FACTS: 1/2 cup equals 62 calories, trace fat (trace saturated fat), trace cholesterol, 261 mg sodium, 15 g carbohydrate, 2 g fiber, 1 g protein. **DIABETIC EXCHANGES:** 1 vegetable, 1/2 fruit.

grilled hash browns

Kelly Chastain | BEDFORD, INDIANA

Since my husband and I love to grill meats, we're always looking for easy side dishes that cook on the grill, too. So I came up with this simple, tasty recipe for hash browns.

> 3-1/2 cups frozen cubed hash brown potatoes, thawed
>
> 1 small onion, chopped
>
> 1 tablespoon beef bouillon granules

Dash seasoned salt

Dash pepper

> 1 tablespoon butter, melted

- Place potatoes on a piece of heavy-duty foil (about 20 in. x 18 in.) coated with cooking spray. Sprinkle with onion, bouillon, seasoned salt and pepper; drizzle with butter.

- Fold foil around potatoes and seal tightly. Grill, covered, over indirect medium heat for 10-15 minutes or until potatoes are tender, turning once.

YIELD: 4 servings.

NUTRITION FACTS: 3/4 cup equals 89 calories, 3 g fat (2 g saturated fat), 8 mg cholesterol, 652 mg sodium, 14 g carbohydrate, 1 g fiber, 2 g protein.

GRILLED HASH BROWNS

89 CALORIES

90 CALORIES

GARLIC OREGANO ZUCCHINI

garlic oregano zucchini

Teresa Kraus | CORTEZ, COLORADO

I've found that this flavorful side dish complements almost any main course, from chicken to fish. If you like, use half yellow summer squash with the zucchini for a colorful variation.

- 1 teaspoon minced garlic
- 2 tablespoons canola oil
- 4 medium zucchini, sliced
- 1 teaspoon dried oregano
- 1/2 teaspoon salt
- 1/8 teaspoon pepper

- In a large skillet, cook and stir the garlic in oil over medium heat for 1 minute. Add the zucchini, oregano, salt and pepper. Cook and stir for 4-6 minutes or until zucchini is crisp-tender.

YIELD: 4 servings.

NUTRITION FACTS: 1 cup equals 90 calories, 7 g fat (1 g saturated fat), 0 cholesterol, 301 mg sodium, 6 g carbohydrate, 3 g fiber, 2 g protein. **DIABETIC EXCHANGES:** 1-1/2 fat, 1 vegetable.

tomato corn salad

Mary Relyea | CANASTOTA, NEW YORK

The lightly dressed salad and the colorful presentation in the tomato shell make this a great summer side dish that is sure to please your guests. The basil flavor is compatible with all the ingredients and the salad is especially tasty with a barbecue entree.

- 4 medium tomatoes
- 1 large ear sweet corn, husk removed
- 1/4 cup chopped red onion
- 1/4 cup loosely packed fresh basil leaves, chopped
- 2 teaspoons olive oil
- 1-1/2 teaspoons balsamic *or* white wine vinegar
- 1/4 teaspoon garlic salt
- 1/4 teaspoon pepper

- Cut a thin slice off the top of each tomato. Scoop out pulp, leaving 1/2-in. shells. Seed and chop enough of the pulp to equal 1 cup (discard any remaining pulp or save for another use). Place chopped tomato and tomato cups, inverted, on paper towels to drain.

- In a large saucepan, cook corn in boiling water for 3-5 minutes or until tender. Drain and immediately place corn in ice water; drain. Cut corn off cob.

- In a small bowl, combine the corn, chopped tomato, onion and basil. In another bowl, whisk the oil, vinegar, garlic salt and pepper. Pour over corn mixture and toss to coat. Cover and refrigerate for 30 minutes. Spoon into tomato cups.

YIELD: 4 servings.

NUTRITION FACTS: 1 stuffed tomato equals 84 calories, 3 g fat (trace saturated fat), 0 cholesterol, 127 mg sodium, 14 g carbohydrate, 3 g fiber, 3 g protein. **DIABETIC EXCHANGES:** 1 vegetable, 1/2 starch, 1/2 fat.

TOMATO CORN SALAD

84 CALORIES

101-200 calories

roasted potatoes with thyme and gorgonzola

Virginia Sturm | SAN FRANCISCO, CALIFORNIA

Creamy Gorgonzola cheese turns this basic potato recipe into a savory and spectacular side! Try this recipe with all your favorite entrees.

1/2	**pound small red potatoes, halved**
1-1/2	**teaspoons olive oil**
1-1/2	**teaspoons minced fresh thyme** *or* **1/2 teaspoon dried thyme**
1/8	**teaspoon salt**
1/8	**teaspoon pepper**
3	**tablespoons crumbled Gorgonzola cheese**

- In a large bowl, combine the first five ingredients. Arrange in a greased 15-in. x 10-in. x 1-in. baking pan.

- Bake, uncovered, at 425° for 20-25 minutes or until potatoes are tender, stirring once. Sprinkle with cheese.

YIELD: 2 servings.

NUTRITION FACTS: 2/3 cup equals 150 calories, 7 g fat (3 g saturated fat), 9 mg cholesterol, 297 mg sodium, 19 g carbohydrate, 2 g fiber, 4 g protein. **DIABETIC EXCHANGES:** 1 starch, 1 fat.

ROASTED POTATOES WITH THYME AND GORGONZOLA

150 CALORIES

130 CALORIES

CORN 'N' RED PEPPER MEDLEY

corn 'n' red pepper medley

Lillian Julow | GAINESVILLE, FLORIDA

This fresh-tasting side dish is a fun treatment for corn. It's pretty, comes together quickly on the stovetop and goes well with just about any main course.

2	**cups fresh corn**
1	**tablespoon olive oil**
2	**large sweet red peppers, chopped**
1/2	**cup chopped onion**
1	**garlic clove, minced**
1/4	**cup minced fresh parsley**
1/2	**teaspoon chili powder**
1/2	**teaspoon salt**
1/4	**teaspoon pepper**

- In a large nonstick skillet, cook corn in oil for 2 minutes. Add the red peppers, onion and garlic; cook and stir for 4-6 minutes or until the red peppers are crisp-tender. Stir in the parsley, chili powder, salt and pepper; cook 1-2 minutes longer.

YIELD: 4 servings.

NUTRITION FACTS: 3/4 cup equals 130 calories, 5 g fat (1 g saturated fat), 0 cholesterol, 314 mg sodium, 22 g carbohydrate, 4 g fiber, 4 g protein. **DIABETIC EXCHANGES:** 1 starch, 1 vegetable, 1 fat.

creamed peas and carrots

Gayleen Grote | BATTLEVIEW, NORTH DAKOTA

Creamy sauce with a simple salt and pepper seasoning nicely complements peas and carrots in this colorful side dish.

- 4 medium carrots, sliced
- 2 cups frozen peas
- 1 tablespoon cornstarch
- 1/4 teaspoon salt
- 1/8 teaspoon pepper
- 1/2 cup heavy whipping cream

classic

- Place carrots in a large saucepan; add 1 in. of water. Bring to a boil. Reduce heat; cover and simmer for 10 minutes.

- Add peas; return to a boil. Reduce heat; cover and simmer 5-10 minutes longer or until vegetables are tender. Drain, reserving 1/2 cup cooking liquid. Return vegetables and reserved liquid to the pan.

- In a small bowl, combine the cornstarch, salt, pepper and cream until smooth. Stir into vegetables. Bring to a boil; cook and stir for 1-2 minutes or until thickened.

YIELD: 4 servings.

NUTRITION FACTS: 2/3 cup equals 191 calories, 11 g fat (7 g saturated fat), 41 mg cholesterol, 282 mg sodium, 18 g carbohydrate, 5 g fiber, 5 g protein.

CREAMED PEAS AND CARROTS

191 CALORIES

GARDEN PRIMAVERA FETTUCCINE

165 CALORIES

garden primavera fettuccine

Tammy Perrault | LANCASTER, OHIO

I created this side while trying to make broccoli Alfredo. I kept adding fresh vegetables, and the result was this creamy pasta dish!

- 1 package (12 ounces) fettuccine
- 1 cup fresh cauliflowerets
- 1 cup fresh broccoli florets
- 1/2 cup julienned carrot
- 1 small sweet red pepper, julienned
- 1/2 small yellow summer squash, sliced
- 1/2 small zucchini, sliced
- 1 cup Alfredo sauce from a jar
- 1 teaspoon dried basil

Shredded Parmesan cheese, optional

classic

- In a large saucepan, cook fettuccine according to package directions, adding vegetables during the last 4 minutes. Drain and return to the pan.

- Add Alfredo sauce and basil; toss to coat. Cook over low heat for 1-2 minutes or until heated through. Sprinkle with cheese if desired.

YIELD: 10 servings.

NUTRITION FACTS: 3/4 cup (calculated without cheese) equals 165 calories, 3 g fat (2 g saturated fat), 7 mg cholesterol, 121 mg sodium, 28 g carbohydrate, 3 g fiber, 7 g protein. **DIABETIC EXCHANGES:** 2 starch, 1/2 fat.

creamed kohlrabi

Lorraine Foss | PUYALLUP, WASHINGTON

This might look like potato salad, but it's actually kohlrabi cubes covered in a white, velvety sauce and accented with chives. Kohlrabi is a favorite vegetable of mine.

- 4 cups cubed peeled kohlrabies (about 6 medium)
- 2 tablespoons butter
- 2 tablespoons all-purpose flour
- 2 cups whole milk
- 1/2 teaspoon salt
- 1/4 teaspoon pepper

Dash paprika

- 1 egg yolk, beaten

Minced chives and additional paprika

- Place kohlrabies in a large saucepan; add 1 in. of water. Bring to a boil. Reduce heat; cover and simmer for 6-8 minutes or until crisp-tender.

- Meanwhile, in a small saucepan, melt butter. Stir in flour until smooth; gradually add milk. Bring to a boil. Stir in the salt, pepper and paprika. Gradually stir a small amount of hot mixture into egg yolk; return all to the pan, stirring constantly. Bring to a gentle boil; cook and stir for 2 minutes.

CREAMED KOHLRABI

- Drain kohlrabies and place in a serving bowl; add sauce and stir to coat. Sprinkle with chives and additional paprika.

YIELD: 6 servings.

NUTRITION FACTS: 2/3 cup equals 125 calories, 7 g fat (4 g saturated fat), 52 mg cholesterol, 276 mg sodium, 11 g carbohydrate, 3 g fiber, 5 g protein. **DIABETIC EXCHANGES:** 1-1/2 fat, 1 vegetable, 1/2 starch.

ONION AU GRATIN

onion au gratin

Carol Slocum | MECHANICVILLE, NEW YORK

Even if you're not an onion-lover, you'll like this simple side-dish casserole. With just 10 minutes of prep, it's easy to whip up.

- 1 cup thinly sliced sweet onion
- 2/3 cup condensed broccoli cheese soup, undiluted
- 1 cup stuffing mix
- 1/2 cup water
- 1 tablespoon butter, melted

- In a small bowl, combine onion and soup. Transfer to a 1-qt. baking dish coated with cooking spray. In a small bowl, combine the stuffing mix, water and butter. Let stand for 5 minutes. Spoon over onion.

- Bake, uncovered, at 350° for 25-30 minutes or until onion is tender and stuffing is browned.

YIELD: 2 cups.

NUTRITION FACTS: 2/3 cup equals 179 calories, 8 g fat (3 g saturated fat), 12 mg cholesterol, 700 mg sodium, 23 g carbohydrate, 1 g fiber, 4 g protein.

corn and broccoli in cheese sauce

Joyce Johnson | UNIONTOWN, OHIO

This dish is a standby. My daughter likes to add leftover ham to it. Save room in the oven by making this savory side in your slow cooker.

   1 package (16 ounces) frozen corn, thawed

   1 package (16 ounces) frozen broccoli florets, thawed

   4 ounces reduced-fat process cheese (Velveeta), cubed

1/2 cup shredded cheddar cheese

   1 can (10-1/4 ounces) reduced-fat reduced-sodium condensed cream of chicken soup, undiluted

1/4 cup fat-free milk

- In a 4-qt. slow cooker, combine the corn, broccoli and cheeses. In a small bowl, combine soup and milk; pour over vegetable mixture. Cover and cook on low for 3-4 hours or until heated through. Stir before serving.

YIELD: 8 servings.

NUTRITION FACTS: 3/4 cup equals 148 calories, 5 g fat (3 g saturated fat), 16 mg cholesterol, 409 mg sodium, 21 g carbohydrate, 3 g fiber, 8 g protein. **DIABETIC EXCHANGES:** 1 starch, 1 medium-fat meat.

CORN AND BROCCOLI IN CHEESE SAUCE

148 CALORIES

121 CALORIES

SPICED POLENTA STEAK FRIES

spiced polenta steak fries

Adults and kids alike will delight in these healthy steak-fry-stand-ins with a subtly crisp and spicy exterior and a creamy, sweet interior. Our Test Kitchen added dried seasonings to make them yummy!

   1 tube (1 pound) polenta

   1 tablespoon olive oil

1/4 teaspoon onion powder

1/4 teaspoon garlic powder

1/4 teaspoon chili powder

1/8 teaspoon paprika

1/8 teaspoon pepper

- Cut polenta in half widthwise; cut each portion in half lengthwise. Cut each section into eight strips. Arrange strips in a single layer in a 15-in. x 10-in. x 1-in. baking pan coated with cooking spray.

- Combine the oil and seasonings; drizzle over polenta strips and gently toss to coat. Bake at 425° for 7-10 minutes on each side or until golden brown.

YIELD: 4 servings.

NUTRITION FACTS: 8 fries equals 121 calories, 3 g fat (trace saturated fat), 0 cholesterol, 383 mg sodium, 20 g carbohydrate, 1 g fiber, 2 g protein. **DIABETIC EXCHANGES:** 1 starch, 1/2 fat.

159 CALORIES

CHIVE 'N' GARLIC CORN

chive 'n' garlic corn

Our home economists created this fresh-tasting corn side dish as a great way to dress up frozen corn. It uses only a few ingredients and cooks in a flash.

- 1 package (16 ounces) frozen corn, thawed
- 1/2 cup finely chopped onion
- 2 tablespoons butter
- 1/4 cup minced chives
- 1/2 teaspoon minced garlic
- 1/8 teaspoon salt

Pepper to taste

- In a large skillet, saute corn and onion in butter for 5-7 minutes or until tender. Stir in the chives, garlic, salt and pepper.

YIELD: 4 servings.

NUTRITION FACTS: 1/2 cup equals 159 calories, 7 g fat (4 g saturated fat), 15 mg cholesterol, 136 mg sodium, 26 g carbohydrate, 3 g fiber, 4 g protein. DIABETIC EXCHANGES: 1-1/2 starch, 1-1/2 fat.

never-fail scalloped potatoes

Agnes Ward | STRATFORD, ONTARIO
Take the chill off any blustery day and make something special to accompany meaty entrees. This creamy, stick-to-the-ribs, potato-and-onion side dish is one you'll turn to often.

- 2 tablespoons butter
- 3 tablespoons all-purpose flour *classic*
- 1 teaspoon salt
- 1/4 teaspoon pepper
- 1-1/2 cups fat-free milk
- 1/2 cup shredded reduced-fat cheddar cheese
- 1-3/4 pounds potatoes, peeled and thinly sliced (about 5 medium)
- 1 medium onion, halved and thinly sliced

- In a small nonstick skillet, melt butter. Stir in the flour, salt and pepper until smooth; gradually add the milk. Bring to a boil. Cook and stir for 2 minutes or until thickened. Remove from the heat; stir in cheese until blended.

- Place half of the potatoes in a 1-1/2-qt. baking dish coated with cooking spray; layer with half of the onion and cheese sauce. Repeat layers.

- Cover and bake at 350° for 50 minutes. Uncover; bake 10-15 minutes longer or until bubbly and potatoes are tender.

YIELD: 6 servings.

NUTRITION FACTS: 3/4 cup equals 196 calories, 6 g fat (4 g saturated fat), 18 mg cholesterol, 530 mg sodium, 29 g carbohydrate, 3 g fiber, 7 g protein. DIABETIC EXCHANGES: 2 starch, 1 fat.

NEVER-FAIL SCALLOPED POTATOES

196 CALORIES

154 CALORIES

SWEET PEPPER WILD RICE SALAD

• Drain wild rice if necessary; stir into vegetable mixture. Stir in white rice. Sprinkle with salt and pepper. Drizzle with lemon juice and remaining oil; toss to coat. Serve warm or at room temperature.

YIELD: 8 servings.

NUTRITION FACTS: 3/4 cup equals 154 calories, 4 g fat (1 g saturated fat), 0 cholesterol, 287 mg sodium, 26 g carbohydrate, 2 g fiber, 4 g protein. **DIABETIC EXCHANGES:** 1-1/2 starch, 1 fat.

sweet pepper wild rice salad

Sherryl Ludlow | ROLLA, MISSOURI

This wild rice salad is packed with health and fun flavors in every bite.

- 1/2 cup uncooked wild rice
- 1 can (14-1/2 ounces) reduced-sodium chicken broth *or* vegetable broth, *divided*
- 1-1/4 cups water, *divided*
- 3/4 cup uncooked long grain rice
- 1 medium sweet red pepper, chopped
- 1 medium sweet yellow pepper, chopped
- 1 medium zucchini, chopped
- 2 tablespoons olive oil, *divided*
- 4 green onions, chopped
- 1/2 teaspoon salt
- 1/4 teaspoon pepper
- 2 tablespoons lemon juice

• In a small saucepan, combine the wild rice, 1 cup broth and 1/2 cup water. Bring to a boil. Reduce heat; cover and simmer for 50-60 minutes or until rice is tender.

• Meanwhile, in a large saucepan, combine the long grain rice and remaining broth and water. Bring to a boil. Reduce heat; cover and simmer for 15-18 minutes or until rice is tender.

• In a large nonstick skillet, saute the peppers and zucchini in 1 tablespoon oil for 3 minutes. Add onions; saute 1-2 minutes longer or until vegetables are tender. Transfer to a large bowl.

in-a-flash beans

Linda Coleman | CEDAR RAPIDS, IOWA

No one will guess this recipe begins in a can. Chopped onions and green pepper lend a little crunch while barbecue sauce brings lots of home-cooked flavor.

- 1 can (15-3/4 ounces) pork and beans
- 1/2 cup barbecue sauce
- 1/2 cup chopped onion
- 1/4 cup chopped green pepper, optional

classic

• In a large saucepan, combine the beans, barbecue sauce, onion and green pepper if desired. Cook and stir over medium heat until heated through.

YIELD: 4 servings.

NUTRITION FACTS: 2/3 cup equals 129 calories, 2 g fat (trace saturated fat), 0 cholesterol, 647 mg sodium, 26 g carbohydrate, 6 g fiber, 6 g protein.

IN-A-FLASH BEANS

129 CALORIES

tortilla dressing

Dorothy Bray | ADKINS, TEXAS

This is not your typical stuffing. Tortillas, jalapenos, chili powder and cilantro lend to its southwestern flavor.

167 CALORIES

SEASONED BAKED POTATOES

- 8 corn tortillas (6 inches), cut into 1/4-inch strips
- 1/4 cup canola oil
- 8 flour tortillas (6 inches), cut into 1/4-inch strips
- 1 cup crushed corn bread stuffing
- 1 small onion, finely chopped
- 1/3 cup finely chopped sweet red pepper
- 1 jalapeno pepper, seeded and chopped
- 1 tablespoon minced fresh cilantro
- 1 tablespoon chili powder
- 1 teaspoon minced fresh sage *or* 1/4 teaspoon dried sage leaves
- 1/2 teaspoon ground coriander
- 1/2 teaspoon ground cumin
- 1/4 teaspoon salt
- 1 egg, lightly beaten
- 1 cup chicken broth

- In a large skillet, saute corn tortilla strips in oil in batches for 1 minute or until golden brown. Drain on paper towels.

- In a large bowl, combine the corn tortilla strips, flour tortilla strips, stuffing, onion, red pepper, jalapeno,

cilantro, chili powder, sage, coriander, cumin and salt. Stir in egg and broth.

- Transfer to a greased 13-in. x 9-in. baking dish. Cover and bake at 325° for 35-45 minutes or until a thermometer reads 160°. This dressing is best served as a side dish, rather than stuffed into poultry.

YIELD: 9 cups.

EDITOR'S NOTE: When cutting hot peppers, disposable gloves are recommended. Avoid touching your face.

NUTRITION FACTS: 3/4 cup equals 171 calories, 8 g fat (1 g saturated fat), 18 mg cholesterol, 370 mg sodium, 22 g carbohydrate, 2 g fiber, 4 g protein. **DIABETIC EXCHANGES:** 1-1/2 starch, 1 fat.

seasoned baked potatoes

Ruth Andrewson | LEAVENWORTH, WASHINGTON

My friends still remember these crisp, delicious potatoes brushed with basil, garlic and onion salt that I used to make. Now they can pass my recipe on to their friends.

- 4 medium baking potatoes
- 1 tablespoon olive oil
- 1-1/2 teaspoons dried basil
- 1/2 teaspoon onion salt
- 1/2 teaspoon garlic powder

classic

- Scrub potatoes and cut in half lengthwise; place cut side up on an ungreased baking sheet. Brush with oil. Sprinkle with basil, onion salt and garlic powder. Bake at 400° for 35-40 minutes or until tender.

YIELD: 4 servings.

NUTRITION FACTS: 2 potato halves equals 167 calories, 4 g fat (1 g saturated fat), 0 cholesterol, 237 mg sodium, 31 g carbohydrate, 3 g fiber, 4 g protein. **DIABETIC EXCHANGES:** 2 starch, 1/2 fat.

TORTILLA DRESSING

171 CALORIES

side dishes | 101-200 CALORIES

vegetable rice skillet

Arlene Lee | HOLLAND, MANITOBA

This is a favorite vegetable casserole of ours. It's very filling served over rice, and the cheese gives the veggies extra flavor. Great warmed up the next day if any is left!

1	medium onion, chopped
1	tablespoon butter
2	medium carrots, sliced
1-1/2	cups cauliflowerets
1-1/2	cups broccoli florets
1	cup uncooked long grain rice
2	garlic cloves, minced
1-1/2	cups reduced-sodium chicken broth
1	cup (4 ounces) shredded reduced-fat cheddar cheese
1	tablespoon minced fresh parsley
3/4	teaspoon salt
1/4	teaspoon pepper

- In a large nonstick skillet over medium heat, cook onion in butter until tender. Add carrots; cook 5 minutes longer. Stir in the cauliflower, broccoli, rice and garlic. Add broth; bring mixture to a boil.

VEGETABLE RICE SKILLET

164 CALORIES

- Reduce heat; cover and simmer for 20-25 minutes or until rice is tender. Remove from the heat; stir in the cheese, parsley, salt and pepper.

YIELD: 8 servings.

NUTRITION FACTS: 3/4 cup equals 164 calories, 5 g fat (3 g saturated fat), 14 mg cholesterol, 459 mg sodium, 24 g carbohydrate, 2 g fiber, 7 g protein. **DIABETIC EXCHANGES:** 1 starch, 1 vegetable, 1 fat.

189 CALORIES

SWEET POTATO BANANA BAKE

sweet potato banana bake

Susan McCartney | ONALASKA, WISCONSIN

This yummy casserole makes what's good for you taste good, too! Pairing bananas with sweet potatoes unites two power foods into a change-of-pace side dish. Try it with roasted poultry.

2	cups mashed sweet potatoes
1	cup mashed ripe bananas (2 to 3 medium)
1/2	cup reduced-fat sour cream
1	egg, lightly beaten
3/4	teaspoon curry powder
1/2	teaspoon salt

- In a large bowl, combine all ingredients until smooth. Transfer to a 1-qt. baking dish coated with cooking spray.

- Cover and bake at 350° for 30-35 minutes or until a thermometer inserted near the center reads 160°.

YIELD: 6 servings.

NUTRITION FACTS: 1/2 cup equals 189 calories, 3 g fat (2 g saturated fat), 42 mg cholesterol, 235 mg sodium, 37 g carbohydrate, 3 g fiber, 5 g protein.

168 CALORIES

THAI-STYLE GREEN BEANS

thai-style green beans

Candy McMenamin | LEXINGTON, SOUTH CAROLINA

Two for Thai, anyone? Peanut butter, soy and hoisin sauce flavor this quick and fabulous bean dish.

- 1 tablespoon reduced-sodium soy sauce
- 1 tablespoon hoisin sauce
- 1 tablespoon creamy peanut butter
- 1/8 teaspoon crushed red pepper flakes
- 1 tablespoon chopped shallot
- 1 teaspoon minced fresh gingerroot
- 1 tablespoon canola oil
- 1/2 pound fresh green beans, trimmed

Minced fresh cilantro and chopped dry roasted peanuts, optional

- In a small bowl, combine the soy sauce, hoisin sauce, peanut butter and red pepper flakes; set aside.

- In a small skillet, saute shallot and ginger in oil over medium heat for 2 minutes or until crisp-tender. Add green beans; cook and stir for 3 minutes or until crisp-tender. Add reserved sauce; toss to coat. Sprinkle with cilantro and peanuts if desired.

YIELD: 2 servings.

NUTRITION FACTS: 1 serving (calculated without peanuts) equals 168 calories, 12 g fat (1 g saturated fat), trace cholesterol, 476 mg sodium, 14 g carbohydrate, 4 g fiber, 5 g protein.

savory & saucy baked beans

A.G. Strickland | MARIETTA, GEORGIA

Dress up canned baked beans in a jiffy...with green pepper, celery and canned tomatoes. With just a hint of sweetness and a touch of garlic, these beans are a natural for potlucks.

- 1/2 cup chopped onion
- 1/2 cup chopped green pepper
- 1/2 cup chopped celery
- 1 can (28 ounces) vegetarian baked beans
- 1 can (14-1/2 ounces) diced tomatoes, drained
- 1/2 teaspoon pepper
- 1/4 teaspoon salt
- 1/4 teaspoon garlic powder

classic

- In a large saucepan coated with cooking spray, cook the onion, green pepper and celery for 3 minutes or until tender. Stir in beans, tomatoes, pepper, salt and garlic powder. Bring to a boil. Reduce heat; simmer, uncovered, for 10-15 minutes.

YIELD: 6 servings.

NUTRITION FACTS: 3/4 cup equals 148 calories, 1 g fat (trace saturated fat), 0 cholesterol, 648 mg sodium, 34 g carbohydrate, 7 g fiber, 7 g protein.

SAVORY & SAUCY BAKED BEANS

148 CALORIES

DOUBLE CORN DRESSING

double corn dressing

Berliene Grosh | LAKELAND, FLORIDA
I have served this delicious dressing, made with a dry stuffing mix, over the years to family and friends, and it always receives compliments. It goes great with pork or poultry.

- 1 package (12 ounces) unseasoned stuffing cubes
- 1 medium onion, finely chopped
- 1/2 *each* medium green, sweet yellow and red pepper, chopped
- 1 teaspoon garlic powder
- 1/2 teaspoon salt
- 1/4 teaspoon pepper
- 3 eggs, lightly beaten
- 1 can (15-1/4 ounces) whole kernel corn, drained
- 1 can (14-3/4 ounces) cream-style corn
- 1/2 cup butter, melted
- 1/2 to 1 cup chicken broth

- In a large bowl, combine the stuffing, onion, sweet peppers and seasonings. Add the eggs, corn and butter; toss to coat. Stir in enough broth to achieve desired moistness.

- Spoon into a 3-qt. baking dish coated with cooking spray. Cover and bake at 350° for 25 minutes or until a thermometer reads 160°. Uncover; bake 15-20 minutes longer or until golden brown.

YIELD: 16 servings.

NUTRITION FACTS: 3/4 cup equals 190 calories, 8 g fat (4 g saturated fat), 55 mg cholesterol, 485 mg sodium, 26 g carbohydrate, 2 g fiber, 5 g protein. **DIABETIC EXCHANGES:** 2 starch, 1-1/2 fat.

cheese fries

Melissa Tatum | GREENSBORO, NORTH CAROLINA
I came up with this recipe after my daughter had cheese fries at a restaurant and couldn't stop talking about them. She loves that I can fix them so quickly at home. Plus, the frozen fry packets can be refrigerated and reheated.

- 1 package (28 ounces) frozen steak fries
- 1 can (10-3/4 ounces) condensed cheddar cheese soup, undiluted
- 1/4 cup 2% milk
- 1/2 teaspoon garlic powder
- 1/4 teaspoon onion powder

Paprika

classic

- Arrange the steak fries in a single layer in two greased 15-in. x 10-in. x 1-in. baking pans. Bake at 450° for 15-18 minutes or until tender and golden brown.

- Meanwhile, in a small saucepan, combine the soup, milk, garlic powder and onion powder; heat through. Drizzle over fries; sprinkle with paprika.

YIELD: 8-10 servings.

NUTRITION FACTS: 1 serving equals 129 calories, 5 g fat (2 g saturated fat), 5 mg cholesterol, 255 mg sodium, 20 g carbohydrate, 2 g fiber, 3 g protein. **DIABETIC EXCHANGES:** 1 starch, 1 fat.

CHEESE FRIES

nutty vegetable rice

Kathy Rairigh | MILFORD, INDIANA

This is a nutritious and delicious recipe that my family and guests love. We enjoy it as a side dish to grilled meats.

- 2/3 cup water
- 1/2 teaspoon chicken bouillon granules
- 1/8 teaspoon salt

Dash pepper

- 1/4 cup uncooked long grain rice
- 3/4 cup sliced fresh mushrooms
- 1 medium carrot, shredded
- 1/4 cup minced fresh parsley
- 1 green onion, thinly sliced
- 2 tablespoons chopped pecans, toasted

- In a small saucepan, bring the water, bouillon, salt and pepper to a boil. Stir in rice. Reduce heat; cover and simmer for 15 minutes.

- Stir in the mushrooms, carrot, parsley and onion. Cover and cook for 5-10 minutes or until rice is tender and vegetables are crisp-tender. Sprinkle with pecans.

YIELD: 2 servings.

NUTRITION FACTS: 3/4 cup equals 162 calories, 6 g fat (1 g saturated fat), trace cholesterol, 386 mg sodium, 25 g carbohydrate, 3 g fiber, 4 g protein. **DIABETIC EXCHANGES:** 1 starch, 1 vegetable, 1 fat.

NUTTY VEGETABLE RICE

162 CALORIES

HERBED TWICE-BAKED POTATOES

150 CALORIES

herbed twice-baked potatoes

Ruth Andrewson | LEAVENWORTH, WASHINGTON

Light cream cheese, garlic powder and butter make these classic potatoes irresistible. Replace the basil with parsley if you'd like, or mix in your favorite seasoning blend.

- 2 medium baking potatoes
- 1-1/2 ounces reduced-fat cream cheese, cubed
- 1 tablespoon minced chives
- 1/4 teaspoon salt
- 1/4 teaspoon dried basil

Dash cayenne pepper

- 3 tablespoons fat-free milk
- 3 teaspoons butter, melted, *divided*

Dash garlic powder

Dash paprika

classic

- Scrub and pierce potatoes. Bake at 375° for 1 hour or until tender. Cool for 10 minutes. Cut potatoes in half. Scoop out pulp, leaving a thin shell.

- In a large bowl, mash pulp with the cream cheese, chives, salt, basil and cayenne. Add milk and 1-1/2 teaspoons butter; mash. Spoon into potato shells. Drizzle with remaining butter; sprinkle with garlic powder and paprika.

- Place on an ungreased baking sheet. Bake for 15-20 minutes or until heated through.

YIELD: 4 servings.

NUTRITION FACTS: 1 potato half equals 150 calories, 5 g fat (3 g saturated fat), 15 mg cholesterol, 234 mg sodium, 23 g carbohydrate, 2 g fiber, 4 g protein. **DIABETIC EXCHANGES:** 1-1/2 starch, 1 fat.

bulgur wheat salad

Millie McDonough | HOMELAND, CALIFORNIA

Fresh seasonings jazz up bulgur in this bright and simple side. Combined with ripe tomatoes and green onions, this scrumptious dish is a winner.

- 1 cup bulgur
- 1 cup boiling water
- 2 tablespoons lemon juice
- 2 tablespoons olive oil
- 1 garlic clove, minced
- 1/2 teaspoon salt
- 1/2 cup minced fresh parsley
- 2 medium tomatoes, chopped
- 4 green onions, chopped

- Place bulgur in a large bowl; stir in water. Cover and let stand for 30 minutes or until liquid is absorbed.

- In a small bowl, whisk the lemon juice, oil, garlic and salt. Stir into bulgur. Add parsley.

- Cover and refrigerate for at least 1 hour. Just before serving, stir in the tomatoes and onions.

YIELD: 6 servings.

NUTRITION FACTS: 2/3 cup equals 137 calories, 5 g fat (1 g saturated fat), 0 cholesterol, 210 mg sodium, 22 g carbohydrate, 5 g fiber, 4 g protein. **DIABETIC EXCHANGES:** 1-1/2 starch, 1 fat.

BULGUR WHEAT SALAD

137 CALORIES

155 CALORIES

TEXAS BARLEY SALAD

texas barley salad

Marilyn Sonnenberg | EDMONTON, ALBERTA

I got this recipe from a cook in Mexico while I was there on a mission trip. I've been making it ever since.

- 1 cup reduced-sodium chicken broth *or* vegetable broth
- 1/2 cup quick-cooking barley
- 1 medium tomato, seeded and chopped
- 3/4 cup frozen corn, thawed
- 1/2 cup chopped sweet red pepper
- 1/4 cup chopped seeded peeled cucumber
- 2 green onions, thinly sliced
- 2 tablespoons canola oil
- 4 teaspoons cider vinegar
- 1 garlic clove, minced
- 1/4 teaspoon salt
- 1/4 teaspoon pepper
- 1/4 teaspoon ground cumin
- 1/4 teaspoon chili powder

- In a small saucepan, bring broth to a boil. Stir in barley. Reduce heat; cover and simmer for 10-12 minutes or until tender. Cool.

- In a large bowl, combine the tomato, corn, red pepper, cucumber, onions and barley.

- In a small bowl, whisk the remaining ingredients. Pour over barley mixture and toss to coat. Cover and refrigerate for at least 1 hour.

YIELD: 5 servings.

NUTRITION FACTS: 3/4 cup equals 155 calories, 6 g fat (1 g saturated fat), 0 cholesterol, 251 mg sodium, 22 g carbohydrate, 5 g fiber, 4 g protein. **DIABETIC EXCHANGES:** 1-1/2 starch, 1 fat.

201-250 calories

208 CALORIES

RICE-STUFFED RED PEPPER

oven fries

Heather Byers | **PITTSBURGH, PENNSYLVANIA**

I jazz up my fries with paprika and garlic powder. Something about the combination of spices packs a heck of a punch. Everyone loves them.

classic

- 4 **medium potatoes**
- 1 **tablespoon olive oil**
- 2-1/2 **teaspoons paprika**
- 3/4 **teaspoon salt**
- 3/4 **teaspoon garlic powder**

- Cut each potato into 12 wedges. In a large bowl, combine the oil, paprika, salt and garlic powder. Add potatoes; toss to coat.

- Transfer to a 15-in. x 10-in. x 1-in. baking pan coated with cooking spray. Bake at 400° for 40-45 minutes or until tender, turning once.

YIELD: 4 servings.

NUTRITION FACTS: 12 potato wedges equals 204 calories, 4 g fat (1 g saturated fat), 0 cholesterol, 456 mg sodium, 39 g carbohydrate, 4 g fiber, 5 g protein.

OVEN FRIES

204 CALORIES

rice-stuffed red pepper

Mary Cloninger | **KENNEWICK, WASHINGTON**

Cooking for two is effortless when you have a recipe like this one. It's a favorite of mine and my husband's. You can use any color bell pepper you want, but red is so pretty.

- 1 **medium sweet red pepper**
- 1/2 **cup chopped fresh mushrooms**
- 1/2 **cup chopped onion**
- 1 **small garlic clove, minced**
- 2 **teaspoons butter**
- 1 **cup cooked rice**
- 1/4 **teaspoon salt**
- 1/8 **teaspoon pepper**
- 1/4 **cup crumbled feta cheese**
- 1/2 **teaspoon dried basil**

- Cut red pepper in half lengthwise and remove seeds. In a large saucepan, cook pepper halves in boiling water for 4-6 minutes or until crisp-tender. Drain and rinse in cold water; set aside.

- In a small skillet, saute the mushrooms, onion and garlic in butter until tender. Stir in the rice, salt and pepper. Spoon into pepper halves. Combine feta cheese and basil; sprinkle over filling.

- Place in two small baking dishes coated with cooking spray. Bake, uncovered, at 350° for 30-35 minutes or until heated through and cheese is lightly browned.

YIELD: 2 servings.

NUTRITION FACTS: 1/2 pepper equals 208 calories, 7 g fat (4 g saturated fat), 18 mg cholesterol, 473 mg sodium, 31 g carbohydrate, 3 g fiber, 6 g protein. **DIABETIC EXCHANGES:** 2 starch, 1 fat.

creamy spinach casserole

Annette Marie Young | WEST LAFAYETTE, INDIANA

Rich and comforting, this savory spinach casserole will be a welcome addition to the table. You'll love the short prep time and decadent taste.

- 2 cans (10-3/4 ounces *each*) reduced-fat reduced-sodium condensed cream of chicken soup, undiluted
- 1 package (8 ounces) reduced-fat cream cheese, cubed
- 1/2 cup fat-free milk
- 1/2 cup grated Parmesan cheese
- 4 cups herb seasoned stuffing cubes
- 2 packages (10 ounces *each*) frozen chopped spinach, thawed and squeezed dry

- In a large bowl, beat the soup, cream cheese, milk and Parmesan cheese until blended. Stir in stuffing cubes and spinach.

- Spoon into a 2-qt. baking dish coated with cooking spray. Bake, uncovered, at 350° for 35-40 minutes or until heated through.

YIELD: 10 servings.

NUTRITION FACTS: 2/3 cup equals 205 calories, 8 g fat (4 g saturated fat), 25 mg cholesterol, 723 mg sodium, 25 g carbohydrate, 3 g fiber, 9 g protein.

CREAMY SPINACH CASSEROLE

205 CALORIES

216 CALORIES

MICROWAVE ACORN SQUASH

microwave acorn squash

Kara de la Vega | SANTA ROSA, CALIFORNIA

You'll love this sinfully good side dish that works with just about any meal. With brown sugar, butter and honey, what's not to love? Someone even said it's so good it tastes like candy. We think kids will agree.

- 2 medium acorn squash
- 1/4 cup packed brown sugar
- 2 tablespoons butter
- 4 teaspoons honey
- 1/4 teaspoon salt
- 1/4 teaspoon pepper

classic

- Cut squash in half; discard seeds. Place squash cut side down in a microwave-safe dish. Cover and microwave on high for 10-12 minutes or until tender.

- Turn squash cut side up. Fill centers of squash with brown sugar, butter and honey; sprinkle with salt and pepper. Cover and microwave on high for 2-3 minutes or until heated through.

YIELD: 4 servings.

EDITOR'S NOTE: This recipe was tested in a 1,100-watt microwave.

NUTRITION FACTS: 1 squash half equals 216 calories, 6 g fat (4 g saturated fat), 15 mg cholesterol, 200 mg sodium, 43 g carbohydrate, 3 g fiber, 2 g protein.

shroom rice

McCaw | NASHVILLE, TENNESSEE

count on having any leftovers with this delicious, simple dish. A friend gave me the recipe more than a decade ago, and it's been a family favorite ever since.

- 1 small onion, finely chopped
- 1 celery rib, chopped
- 1/2 cup chopped celery leaves
- 2 tablespoons butter
- 1 pound sliced fresh mushrooms
- 3 cups uncooked instant rice
- 3 cups water
- 4 teaspoons Greek seasoning
- 1/2 cup chopped pecans, toasted

- In a large nonstick skillet coated with cooking spray, saute the onion, celery and celery leaves in butter for 4 minutes. Add mushrooms; cook 4 minutes longer.

- Add rice; cook for 4-5 minutes or until lightly browned. Stir in the water and Greek seasoning. Bring to a boil. Remove from the heat; cover and let stand for 5 minutes. Fluff with a fork. Sprinkle with pecans.

YIELD: 8 servings.

NUTRITION FACTS: 1 cup equals 232 calories, 9 g fat (2 g saturated fat), 8 mg cholesterol, 529 mg sodium, 35 g carbohydrate, 2 g fiber, 5 g protein. **DIABETIC EXCHANGES:** 2 starch, 1-1/2 fat, 1 vegetable.

MUSHROOM RICE

232 CALORIES

226 CALORIES

VEGGIE BEAN CASSEROLE

veggie bean casserole

LaRue Ritchie | BELLEVUE, ALBERTA

This salad freezes and reheats well, so I'll sometimes double the recipe. The colorful combination of carrots, corn, beans and tomatoes makes a suitable meatless main dish, too.

- 2 medium carrots, diced
- 2 celery ribs, chopped
- 1 large onion, chopped
- 1 medium green pepper, chopped
- 2 tablespoons canola oil
- 3 garlic cloves, minced
- 2 tablespoons chili powder
- 1/2 teaspoon ground cumin
- 1 can (28 ounces) diced tomatoes, undrained
- 2 cups frozen corn
- 1 can (16 ounces) kidney beans, rinsed and drained
- 1 can (15 ounces) garbanzo beans *or* chickpeas, rinsed and drained
- 1 can (15 ounces) tomato sauce
- 2 tablespoons picante sauce

- In a large Dutch oven, saute the carrots, celery, onion, green pepper in oil for 5 minutes. Add the garlic, chili powder and cumin; cook 1 minute longer. Stir in the remaining ingredients; bring to a boil.

- Cover and bake at 350° for 45-50 minutes or until thickened and vegetables are tender.

YIELD: 8 servings.

NUTRITION FACTS: 1 cup equals 226 calories, 5 g fat (1 g saturated fat), 0 cholesterol, 582 mg sodium, 39 g carbohydrate, 10 g fiber, 9 g protein.

zucchini pasta

Maria Regakis I SOMERVILLE, MASSACHUSETTS

The taste of this rich and creamy dish will have people convinced it's not low fat, but it is! Garlicky and fresh flavored, this will be a hit.

- 8 ounces uncooked linguine
- 4 cups coarsely shredded zucchini (about 3 medium)
- 4 teaspoons olive oil
- 2 garlic cloves, thinly sliced
- 1/4 cup fat-free plain yogurt
- 3/4 cup shredded reduced-fat cheddar cheese
- 3/4 teaspoon salt
- 1/4 teaspoon pepper

- Cook linguine according to package directions. In a sieve or colander, drain the zucchini, squeezing to remove excess liquid. Pat dry.

- In a large nonstick skillet, saute zucchini in oil for 2 minutes. Add garlic; saute 1-2 minutes longer or until zucchini is tender. Transfer to a large bowl. Add the yogurt, cheese, salt and pepper. Drain linguine; add to zucchini mixture and toss to coat.

YIELD: 6 servings.

NUTRITION FACTS: 3/4 cup equals 219 calories, 7 g fat (3 g saturated fat), 10 mg cholesterol, 395 mg sodium, 32 g carbohydrate, 2 g fiber, 10 g protein. **DIABETIC EXCHANGES:** 1-1/2 starch, 1-1/2 fat, 1 vegetable.

ZUCCHINI PASTA

219 CALORIES

ROSEMARY RICE

250 CALORIES

rosemary rice

Connie Regalado I EL PASO, TEXAS

This quick dish is a favorite with my family. It's low in fat because it gets flavor from herbs, not butter.

- 1/4 cup chopped onion
- 1 garlic clove, minced
- 1 tablespoon olive oil
- 1 can (14-1/2 ounces) reduced-sodium chicken broth *or* vegetable broth
- 1/4 cup water
- 1 cup uncooked long grain rice
- 1 tablespoon minced fresh rosemary *or* 1 teaspoon dried rosemary, crushed
- 1/4 teaspoon pepper
- 1/4 cup shredded Parmesan cheese

- In a saucepan, saute onion and garlic in oil until tender. Add broth and water. Stir in the rice, rosemary and pepper. Bring to a boil. Reduce heat; cover and simmer for 15-18 minutes or until rice is tender. Remove from the heat; stir in Parmesan cheese.

YIELD: 4 servings.

NUTRITION FACTS: 3/4 cup equals 250 calories, 5 g fat (1 g saturated fat), 4 mg cholesterol, 367 mg sodium, 42 g carbohydrate, 1 g fiber, 7 g protein.

desserts

There's always room for dessert…particularly classics such as chocolate cupcakes, apple strudel and lemon pie. When preparing supper, remember to set a few calories aside so you can treat yourself to a sweet nibble and land within the 500-calorie guideline for dinner.

282

272

277

Looking for a snack between meals? Consider the lower-calorie options at the start of this chapter. When you'd like to cap off a meal with something a bit more impressive, see the desserts toward the end of the section. Regardless, you're sure to find a bite to tickle your sweet tooth!

strawberry banana delight

Mary Blackledge I NORTH PLATTE, NEBRASKA
With a classic pairing of fruit flavors, this whipped gelatin is always light and refreshing.

> 1 package (.3 ounce) sugar-free strawberry gelatin
> 1 cup boiling water
> 6 ice cubes
> 2 medium ripe bananas, cut into chunks
> 4 tablespoons whipped topping
> 4 fresh strawberries

- In a small bowl, dissolve gelatin in boiling water; cool for 10 minutes. Add enough water to ice cubes to measure 1 cup. In a blender, combine gelatin and ice mixture; cover and process for 1 minute or until ice cubes are dissolved. Add bananas; process 1-2 minutes longer or until blended.

- Pour into four dessert dishes. Refrigerate for at least 30 minutes or until set. Garnish each with 1 tablespoon whipped topping and a strawberry.

YIELD: 4 servings.

NUTRITION FACTS: 1 cup equals 78 calories, 1 g fat (1 g saturated fat), 0 cholesterol, 48 mg sodium, 16 g carbohydrate, 2 g fiber, 2 g protein. **DIABETIC EXCHANGE:** 1 fruit.

STRAWBERRY BANANA DELIGHT

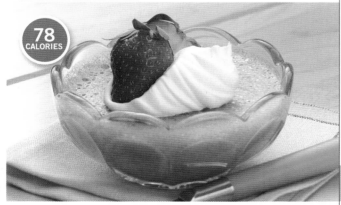

78 CALORIES

58 CALORIES

COCOA MINT TRUFFLES

cocoa mint truffles

These tender chocolate truffles will be a hit at your next get-together. Our home economists gave them rich, minty flavor on the inside, and a powdered cocoa layer on the outside. They're decadent, but oh-so-simple to prepare.

> 3/4 cup semisweet chocolate chips
> 6 mint Andes candies
> 3/4 cup whipped topping
> 2 tablespoons baking cocoa
> 1/8 teaspoon instant coffee granules

classic

- In a small saucepan, melt chocolate chips and candies over low heat. Transfer to a small bowl and cool to lukewarm, about 7 minutes. Beat in whipped topping. Place in the freezer for 15 minutes or until firm enough to form into balls.

- In a small bowl, combine cocoa and coffee granules. Shape chocolate mixture into 1-in. balls; roll in cocoa mixture. Store in an airtight container in the refrigerator.

YIELD: 16 servings.

NUTRITION FACTS: 1 serving (1 each) equals 58 calories, 4 g fat (2 g saturated fat), 0 cholesterol, 2 mg sodium, 7 g carbohydrate, 1 g fiber, 1 g protein.

92 CALORIES

CHUNKY FRUIT AND NUT FUDGE

chunky fruit and nut fudge

Allene Bary-Cooper | WICHITA FALLS, TEXAS

Variations on this fudge recipe are endless, but this version is my favorite. Besides five types of chips, it includes everything from dried fruit to nuts. Every bite is packed with flavor and crunch.

classic

- 1 package (11 ounces) dried cherries
- 1 cup dried cranberries
- 1-1/2 teaspoons plus 3/4 cup butter, softened, *divided*
- 1 can (14 ounces) sweetened condensed milk
- 1 package (12 ounces) miniature semisweet chocolate chips
- 1 package (11-1/2 ounces) milk chocolate chips
- 1 package (10 to 11 ounces) butterscotch chips
- 1 package (10 ounces) peanut butter chips
- 3 tablespoons heavy whipping cream
- 1 jar (7 ounces) marshmallow creme
- 1/2 teaspoon almond *or* rum extract
- 1-1/2 cups unsalted cashew halves
- 1 package (11-1/2 ounces) semisweet chocolate chunks

- In a large bowl, combine cherries and cranberries. Add enough warm water to cover; set aside. Line a 15-in. x 10-in. x 1-in. pan with foil and grease the foil with 1-1/2 teaspoons butter; set aside.

- In a large heavy saucepan, melt remaining butter. Stir in the milk, chips and cream. Cook and stir over low heat for 15-20 minutes or until chips are melted and mixture is smooth and blended (mixture will first appear separated, but continue stirring until fully blended). Remove from the heat; stir in marshmallow creme and extract.

- Drain the cherries and cranberries; pat dry with paper towels. Stir the fruit, cashews and chocolate chunks into chocolate mixture. Spread into prepared pan. Let stand at room temperature until set.

- Using foil, lift fudge out of pan. Discard foil; cut fudge into 1-in. squares.

YIELD: 6-3/4 pounds.

NUTRITION FACTS: 1 piece equals 92 calories, 5 g fat (3 g saturated fat), 4 mg cholesterol, 23 mg sodium, 12 g carbohydrate, 1 g fiber, 1 g protein.

79 CALORIES

trail mix clusters

Alina Niemi | HONOLULU, HAWAII

These homemade snacks make wonderful gifts because they look and taste like they came from an expensive chocolate shop. The dried fruit and nuts are heart-healthy and full of fiber.

- 2 cups (12 ounces) semisweet chocolate chips
- 1/2 cup unsalted sunflower kernels
- 1/2 cup salted pumpkin seeds *or* pepitas
- 1/2 cup coarsely chopped cashews
- 1/2 cup coarsely chopped pecans
- 1/4 cup flaked coconut
- 1/4 cup finely chopped dried apricots
- 1/4 cup dried cranberries
- 1/4 cup dried cherries *or* blueberries

- In a large microwave-safe bowl, melt chocolate chips; stir until smooth. Stir in the remaining ingredients.

- Drop by tablespoonfuls onto waxed paper-lined baking sheets. Refrigerate until firm. Store in the refrigerator.

YIELD: 4 dozen.

NUTRITION FACTS: 1 piece equals 79 calories, 6 g fat (2 g saturated fat), 0 cholesterol, 26 mg sodium, 8 g carbohydrate, 1 g fiber, 2 g protein. **DIABETIC EXCHANGES:** 1 fat, 1/2 starch.

96 CALORIES

JELLIED CHAMPAGNE DESSERT

jelled champagne dessert

Our home economists fashioned this refreshing dessert to look like a glass of bubbling champagne, making it perfect for New Year's Eve or any extra-special occasion.

- 1 **tablespoon unflavored gelatin**
- 2 **cups cold white grape juice,** *divided*
- 2 **tablespoons sugar**
- 2 **cups Champagne** *or* **club soda**
- 8 **fresh strawberries, hulled**

- In a small saucepan, sprinkle gelatin over 1 cup cold grape juice; let stand for 1 minute. Heat over low heat, stirring until gelatin is completely dissolved. Stir in sugar. Remove from the heat; stir in remaining grape juice. Cool to room temperature.

- Transfer gelatin mixture to a large bowl. Slowly stir in Champagne. Pour half of the mixture into eight Champagne or parfait glasses. Add one strawberry to each glass. Chill glasses and remaining gelatin mixture until almost set, about 1 hour.

- Place the reserved gelatin mixture in a blender; cover and process until foamy. Pour into glasses. Chill for 3 hours or until set.

YIELD: 8 servings.

NUTRITION FACTS: 1/2 cup equals 96 calories, trace fat (trace saturated fat), 0 cholesterol, 9 mg sodium, 13 g carbohydrate, trace fiber, 1 g protein. **DIABETIC EXCHANGE:** 1 starch.

raisin pound cake

LuEllen Spaulding I CARO, MICHIGAN

Yellow cake mix, applesauce and raisins make this moist, spiced loaf a no-fuss favorite. I turn to this recipe when unexpected guests drop by because I usually have the ingredients in the cupboard. For a special occasion, top slices with fresh fruit.

- 1 **package (18-1/4 ounces) yellow cake mix**
- 1 **cup applesauce**
- 1/2 **cup water**
- 1/4 **cup canola oil**
- 3 **eggs**
- 1/2 **teaspoon ground cinnamon**
- 1/4 **teaspoon ground nutmeg**
- 1/4 **teaspoon ground allspice**
- 1/2 **cup raisins**

classic

- In a bowl, combine dry cake mix, applesauce, water, oil, eggs, cinnamon, nutmeg and allspice. Beat on medium speed for 2 minutes. Stir in raisins. Pour into two greased 8-in. x 4-in. loaf pans.

- Bake at 350° for 45-50 minutes or until a toothpick inserted near the center comes out clean. Cool for 5-10 minutes before removing from pans to wire racks.

YIELD: 2 loaves.

NUTRITION FACTS: 1 slice equals 100 calories, 4 g fat (1 g saturated fat), 20 mg cholesterol, 108 mg sodium, 16 g carbohydrate, 1 g fiber, 1 g protein. **DIABETIC EXCHANGES:** 1 starch, 1 fat.

RAISIN POUND CAKE

100 CALORIES

mini apple strudels

Our Test Kitchen staff relied on sheets of phyllo dough to surround tender slices of apple in this clever play on strudel. Walnuts and cinnamon enhance the traditional apple pie flavor.

1-1/2	cups chopped peeled tart apples
2	tablespoons plus 2 teaspoons sugar
2	tablespoons chopped walnuts
1	tablespoon all-purpose flour
1/4	teaspoon ground cinnamon
6	sheets phyllo dough (14 inches x 9 inches)

Butter-flavored cooking spray

Confectioners' sugar, optional

- In a small bowl, combine the apples, sugar, walnuts, flour and cinnamon. Set aside.

- Place one sheet of phyllo dough on a work surface (keep remaining dough covered with plastic wrap and a damp towel to prevent it from drying out). Spray with butter-flavored spray.

- Fold in half widthwise; spray again with butter-flavored spray. Spoon a scant 1/3 cup filling onto phyllo about 2 in. from a short side. Fold side and edges over filling and roll up. Place seam side down on a baking sheet coated with cooking spray. Repeat.

- With a sharp knife, cut diagonal slits in tops of strudels. Spray strudels with butter-flavored spray. Bake at 350° for 20-22 minutes or until golden brown. Sprinkle with confectioners' sugar if desired.

YIELD: 6 servings.

NUTRITION FACTS: 1 strudel equals 100 calories, 3 g fat (trace saturated fat), 0 cholesterol, 45 mg sodium, 17 g carbohydrate, 1 g fiber, 2 g protein. **DIABETIC EXCHANGES:** 1 starch, 1/2 fat.

MINI APPLE STRUDELS

peanut butter granola mini bars

Vivian Levine | SUMMERFIELD, FLORIDA

Kids will flip over this delicious sweet snack! With honey, peanut butter, brown sugar and two types of chips, what's not to love?

1/2	cup reduced-fat creamy peanut butter
1/3	cup honey
1	egg
2	tablespoons canola oil
1	teaspoon vanilla extract
3-1/2	cups old-fashioned oats
1/2	cup packed brown sugar
3/4	teaspoon salt
1/3	cup peanut butter chips
1/3	cup miniature semisweet chocolate chips

- In a large bowl, beat the peanut butter, honey, egg, oil and vanilla until blended. Combine the oats, brown sugar and salt; add to the peanut butter mixture and mix well. Stir in chips. (Batter will be sticky.)

- Transfer mixture to a 13-in. x 9-in. baking dish coated with cooking spray. Bake at 350° for 12-15 minutes or until set and edges are lightly browned. Cool on a wire rack. Cut into bars.

YIELD: 3 dozen.

NUTRITION FACTS: 1 piece equals 93 calories, 4 g fat (1 g saturated fat), 6 mg cholesterol, 76 mg sodium, 14 g carbohydrate, 1 g fiber, 3 g protein. **DIABETIC EXCHANGES:** 1 starch, 1 fat.

blueberry angel cupcakes

Kathy Kittell | LENEXA, KANSAS

Like angel food cake, these yummy cupcakes don't last long at my house. They're so light and airy that they melt in your mouth.

- 11 egg whites
- 1 cup plus 2 tablespoons cake flour
- 1-1/2 cups sugar, *divided*
- 1-1/4 teaspoons cream of tartar
- 1 teaspoon vanilla extract
- 1/2 teaspoon salt
- 1-1/2 cups fresh *or* frozen blueberries
- 1 teaspoon grated lemon peel

GLAZE:
- 1 cup confectioners' sugar
- 3 tablespoons lemon juice

- Place egg whites in a large bowl; let stand at room temperature for 30 minutes. Sift together flour and 1/2 cup sugar three times; set aside.

- Add cream of tartar, vanilla and salt to egg whites; beat on medium speed until soft peaks form. Gradually add

76 CALORIES

BLUEBERRY ANGEL CUPCAKES

sugar, about 2 tablespoons at a time, beating on high until stiff glossy peaks form and sugar is dissolved. Gradually fold in flour mixture, about 1/2 cup at a time. Fold in blueberries and lemon peel.

- Fill paper-lined muffin cups three-fourths full. Bake at 375° for 14-17 minutes or until cupcakes spring back when lightly touched. Immediately remove from pans to wire racks to cool completely.

- In a small bowl, whisk confectioners' sugar and lemon juice until smooth. Brush over cupcakes. Let stand until set.

YIELD: 2-1/2 dozen.

EDITOR'S NOTE: If using frozen blueberries, use without thawing to avoid discoloring the batter.

NUTRITION FACTS: 1 cupcake equals 76 calories, trace fat (trace saturated fat), 0 cholesterol, 60 mg sodium, 18 g carbohydrate, trace fiber, 2 g protein. **DIABETIC EXCHANGE:** 1 starch.

Need an easy treat? Try these effortless bites!

- **For a truly no-fuss yet completely refreshing dessert, I simply mix left-over cooked white rice with sliced bananas and a can of undrained crushed pineapple.**
Sharon E., Rockwell, Iowa

- **My husband and I both have diabetes, so I'm always on the lookout for delicious desserts that don't contain a lot of sugar and fat. For a sweet treat, I simply spoon a can of light apricot halves (including the syrup) into parfait glasses. Then I top them with sugar-free instant vanilla pudding prepared with fat-free milk. I chill the parfaits until they are set,** and I top them with maraschino cherries for a pretty presentation.
Evelyn K., Elizabeth City North Carolina

- **I freeze banana slices, set them in a bowl and top them with fat-free whipped topping or vanilla yogurt. Then, I drizzle them with chocolate syrup for a sweet treat that is low in fat and calories. I also like to fix sugar-free pudding with fat-free milk. After it chills, I top a serving with a small amount of crumbled graham crackers and chocolate jimmies or sprinkles.**
Suzanne R., Grand Rapids, Michigan

- **Pour your GrapeNuts cereal into dessert bowls and add your favorite low-fat pudding. In 2 hours, the cereal forms a crunchy crust!**
Diana D., Rockland, Maine

- **I create quick desserts using left-over angel food cake. I crumble up the cake and put the crumbs in a pie pan. I top the cake with reduced-calorie vanilla ice cream and spread on a thin layer of strawberry jam. I then top the jam with a drizzle of chocolate or butterscotch ice cream topping, cover and set it in the freezer until solid.**
Karen G., Somerset, Kentucky

GINGER CREAM COOKIES

ginger cream cookies

Suvilla Jordan | KERSEY, PENNSYLVANIA

This great tasting ginger cookie truly lives up to its name; it is perfectly cake-like and the spices really blend together well. The cookie captures the flavor of the holiday season wonderfully.

1/2	cup molasses
1/4	cup sugar blend
1/4	cup canola oil
1	egg
1	teaspoon vanilla extract
2	cups all-purpose flour
1-1/2	teaspoons ground cinnamon
1	teaspoon baking soda
1	teaspoon ground ginger
3/4	teaspoon ground cloves
3/4	teaspoon ground nutmeg

- In a large bowl, beat the molasses, sugar blend, oil, egg and vanilla until well blended. Combine the remaining ingredients; gradually add to molasses mixture and mix well.

- Drop by rounded teaspoonfuls 2 in. apart onto baking sheets lightly coated with cooking spray.

- Bake at 350° for 8-10 minutes or until edges are lightly browned. Remove to wire racks.

YIELD: 3 dozen.

EDITOR'S NOTE: This recipe was tested with Splenda sugar blend.

NUTRITION FACTS: 1 cookie equals 60 calories, 2 g fat (trace saturated fat), 6 mg cholesterol, 39 mg sodium, 10 g carbohydrate, trace fiber, 1 g protein. **DIABETIC EXCHANGES:** 1/2 starch, 1/2 fat.

broiled pineapple dessert

For that "little something" sweet after a filling meal, try this scrumptious, cinnamon-sprinkled dessert from our Test Kitchen. It couldn't be much easier, and it makes a great change-of-pace sweet.

1	can (8 ounces) unsweetened sliced pineapple, drained and patted dry
2	teaspoons brown sugar
1/4	teaspoon ground cinnamon
1/4	cup miniature marshmallows

- In an ungreased 9-in. square baking pan, overlap pineapple in two stacks of two slices each. Combine brown sugar and cinnamon; sprinkle over pineapple.

- Broil 4-6 in. from the heat for 1 to 1-1/2 minutes or until sugar is melted. Top with marshmallows; broil 1 to 1-1/2 minutes longer or until marshmallows are golden brown.

YIELD: 2 servings.

NUTRITION FACTS: 1 serving equals 98 calories, trace fat (trace saturated fat), 0 cholesterol, 15 mg sodium, 25 g carbohydrate, 1 g fiber, trace protein. **DIABETIC EXCHANGES:** 1 fruit, 1/2 starch.

BROILED PINEAPPLE DESSERT

Grocery List

CHOCOLATE PUDDING SANDWICHES

chocolate pudding sandwiches

Jan Thomas | RICHMOND, VIRGINIA

These frozen cookie sandwiches are a favorite dessert and after-school snack for my kids...and even my diabetic husband who enjoys one now and then.

1-1/2 cups cold fat-free milk
   1 package (1.4 ounces) sugar-free instant chocolate pudding mix
   1 carton (8 ounces) frozen reduced-fat whipped topping, thawed
   1 cup miniature marshmallows
   2 packages (9 ounces *each*) chocolate wafers

- In a large bowl, whisk milk and pudding mix for 2 minutes; let stand for 2 minutes or until slightly thickened. Fold in whipped topping, then marshmallows.

- For each sandwich, spread about 2 tablespoons of the pudding mixture on the bottom of a chocolate wafer; top each with another wafer. Stack the sandwiches in an airtight container.

- Freeze until firm, about 3 hours. Remove from the freezer 5 minutes before serving.

YIELD: 43 sandwiches.

NUTRITION FACTS: 1 sandwich equals 73 calories, 2 g fat (1 g saturated fat), 1 mg cholesterol, 114 mg sodium, 12 g carbohydrate, 0.55 g fiber, 1 g protein. **DIABETIC EXCHANGES:** 1 starch.

pumpkin mousse

Patricia Sidloskas | ANNISTON, ALABAMA

Folks will never guess a dessert as creamy and delicious as this butterscotch-pumpkin blend could be so low in fat and calories!

1-1/2 cups cold fat-free milk
   1 package (1 ounce) sugar-free instant butterscotch pudding mix
   1/2 cup canned pumpkin
   1/2 teaspoon ground cinnamon
   1/4 teaspoon ground ginger
   1/4 teaspoon ground allspice
   1 cup fat-free whipped topping, *divided*

- In a large bowl, whisk milk and pudding mix for 2 minutes. Let stand for 2 minutes or until soft-set. Combine the pumpkin, cinnamon, ginger and allspice; fold into pudding. Fold in 1/2 cup whipped topping.

- Transfer to individual serving dishes. Refrigerate until serving. Garnish with remaining whipped topping.

YIELD: 4 servings.

NUTRITION FACTS: 2/3 cup mousse with 2 tablespoons whipped topping equals 96 calories, trace fat (trace saturated fat), 2 mg cholesterol, 360 mg sodium, 18 g carbohydrate, 1 g fiber, 4 g protein. **DIABETIC EXCHANGES:** 1/2 starch, 1/2 fat-free milk.

PUMPKIN MOUSSE

frozen fruit pops

60 CALORIES

June Dickenson | PHILIPPI, WEST VIRGINIA

My grandson and I made Frozen Fruit Pops for company, and everyone loved them.

classic

2-1/4 cups (18 ounces) raspberry yogurt
2 tablespoons lemon juice
2 medium ripe bananas, cut into chunks
12 Popsicle molds *or* paper cups (3 ounces *each*) and Popsicle sticks

- In a blender, combine the yogurt, lemon juice and bananas; cover and process for 45 seconds or until smooth. Stir if necessary.

- Fill molds or cups with 1/4 cup yogurt mixture; top with holders or insert sticks into cups. Freeze.

YIELD: 1 dozen.

NUTRITION FACTS: 1 fruit pop equals 60 calories, 1 g fat (trace saturated fat), 2 mg cholesterol, 23 mg sodium, 13 g carbohydrate, 1 g fiber, 2 g protein. **DIABETIC EXCHANGE:** 1 starch.

lemon pudding cups

84 CALORIES

Dolly Jones | HIGHLAND, INDIANA

This make-ahead recipe is a staple from my mother's church cookbook. The combination of sherbet and gelatin is light and lemony. The creamy cups are attractive enough for guests.

1 package (.3 ounce) sugar-free lemon gelatin
2 cups boiling water
1 pint lemon sherbet, softened
1 tablespoon lemon juice
1 tablespoon grated lemon peel
6 tablespoons reduced-fat whipped topping

- In a large bowl, dissolve gelatin in boiling water. Slowly stir in the sherbet, lemon juice and lemon peel. Pour into six dessert cups. Cover and refrigerate overnight. Garnish with whipped topping.

YIELD: 6 servings.

NUTRITION FACTS: 1/2 cup with 1 tablespoon whipped topping equals 84 calories, 1 g fat (1 g saturated fat), 3 mg cholesterol, 56 mg sodium, 16 g carbohydrate, 0.55 g fiber, 1 g protein. **DIABETIC EXCHANGE:** 1 starch.

cookie fruit baskets

Theresa Lieber | NORTH FORT MYERS, FLORIDA

When visiting a friend, I helped organize her recipe collection into scrapbooks. When I found this recipe, I asked to copy it. I served the elegant dessert at my bridge club luncheon and received rave reviews. Fill these five-ingredient cookie cups with any flavor of ice cream, frozen yogurt or sorbet.

1/4 cup butter
1/4 cup packed brown sugar
1/4 cup light corn syrup
3-1/2 tablespoons all-purpose flour
1/2 cup ground pecans
1/2 teaspoon vanilla extract
Vanilla ice cream and fresh berries

- In a small saucepan, melt butter over low heat. Stir in brown sugar and corn syrup; cook and stir until mixture comes to a boil. Remove from the heat. Stir in flour. Fold in pecans and vanilla.

- Drop by tablespoonfuls 3 in. apart onto parchment paper-lined baking sheets. Bake at 325° for 8-10 minutes or until golden brown.

- Cool for 30-60 seconds; peel cookies off paper. Immediately drape over inverted 6-oz. custard cups; cool completely. Scoop ice cream into baskets; top with berries.

YIELD: 12 servings.

NUTRITION FACTS: 1 cookie fruit basket (calculated without ice cream or berries) equals 100 calories, 6 g fat (3 g saturated fat), 10 mg cholesterol, 49 mg sodium, 12 g carbohydrate, trace fiber, 1 g protein. **DIABETIC EXCHANGES:** 1 starch, 1 fat.

COOKIE FRUIT BASKETS

100 CALORIES

77 CALORIES soft honey cookies

Rochelle Friedman | BROOKLYN, NEW YORK

This old-fashioned cookie has a pleasant honey-cinnamon flavor and a tender texture that resembles cake. It has been a family favorite for years, and I'm always happy to share the recipe.

- 1/4 cup sugar
- 2 tablespoons canola oil
- 1 egg
- 3 tablespoons honey
- 3/4 teaspoon vanilla extract
- 1 cup plus 2 tablespoons all-purpose flour
- 1/4 teaspoon baking powder
- 1/4 teaspoon ground cinnamon
- 1/8 teaspoon salt

- In a small bowl, beat sugar and oil until blended. Beat in egg; beat in honey and vanilla. Combine the flour, baking powder, cinnamon and salt; gradually add to sugar mixture and mix well (dough will be stiff). Cover and refrigerate for at least 2 hours.

- Drop dough by tablespoonfuls 2 in. apart onto a greased baking sheet. Bake at 350° for 8-10 minutes or until bottoms are lightly browned. Cool for 1 minute before removing from pan to a wire rack. Store cookies in an airtight container.

YIELD: 16 cookies.

NUTRITION FACTS: 1 cookie equals 77 calories, 2 g fat (trace saturated fat), 13 mg cholesterol, 29 mg sodium, 13 g carbohydrate, trace fiber, 1 g protein. **DIABETIC EXCHANGE:** 1 starch.

chocolate-dipped phyllo sticks

Our Test Kitchen staff gave from-scratch cookies a head start with convenient phyllo dough. The attractive sticks add an elegant look to any dessert table or even a holiday cookie tray.

- 4 sheets phyllo dough (14 inches x 9 inches)
- 2 tablespoons butter, melted
- 1 tablespoon sugar

CHOCOLATE-DIPPED PHYLLO STICKS

- 1/4 teaspoon ground cinnamon
- 2 ounces semisweet chocolate, finely chopped
- 1/2 teaspoon shortening
- 1/2 ounce white baking chocolate, melted

- Place one sheet of phyllo dough on a work surface; brush with butter. Cover with a second sheet of phyllo; brush with butter. (Keep remaining phyllo dough covered with plastic wrap and a damp towel to prevent it from drying out.) Cut phyllo in half lengthwise. Cut each half into five 4-1/2-in. x 2-3/4-in. rectangles. Tightly roll each rectangle from one long side, forming a 4-1/2-in.-long stick. Combine sugar and cinnamon. Coat sticks with cooking spray; sprinkle with cinnamon-sugar.

- Place on an ungreased baking sheet. Bake at 425° for 3-5 minutes or until lightly browned. Remove to a wire rack to cool. Repeat with remaining phyllo dough, butter and cinnamon-sugar.

- In a microwave, melt the semisweet chocolate and shortening; stir until smooth. Dip top half of phyllo sticks in chocolate; allow extra to drip off. Place on waxed paper; let stand until set. Drizzle with white chocolate.

YIELD: 20 sticks.

NUTRITION FACTS: 2 sticks equals 75 calories, 5 g fat (3 g saturated fat), 6 mg cholesterol, 43 mg sodium, 8 g carbohydrate, 1 g fiber, 1 g protein. **DIABETIC EXCHANGES:** 1 fat, 1/2 starch.

101-150 calories

frozen chocolate delight

Debbie Johnson | CENTERTOWN, MISSOURI

My daughter shared this chocolaty treat with me, and we both think it's a hit. I took it to an office party, and no one could believe this rich dessert was light.

- 3/4 **cup cold fat-free milk**
- 1 **package (1.4 ounces) sugar-free instant chocolate pudding mix**
- 2 **cups fat-free vanilla frozen yogurt, softened**
- 1/4 **cup reduced-fat chunky peanut butter**
- 2 **cups plus 2 tablespoons fat-free whipped topping,** *divided*

- In a large bowl, whisk milk and pudding mix for 2 minutes. Stir in the frozen yogurt and peanut butter until blended. Fold in 1 cup whipped topping. Transfer to an 8-in. square dish coated with cooking spray. Cover and freeze until firm.

- Remove from the freezer 10 minutes before serving. Cut into nine squares. Garnish each with 2 tablespoons whipped topping.

YIELD: 9 servings.

NUTRITION FACTS: 1 piece equals 134 calories, 3 g fat (1 g saturated fat), 1 mg cholesterol, 230 mg sodium, 22 g carbohydrate, 1 g fiber, 5 g protein. **DIABETIC EXCHANGES:** 1-1/2 starch, 1/2 fat.

FROZEN CHOCOLATE DELIGHT

134 CALORIES

146 CALORIES

SIMPLE LEMON PIE

simple lemon pie

Frances VanFossan | WARREN, MICHIGAN

Lemon meringue pie is one of my favorites, and this yummy, sweet-tart version is so good that no one will suspect that it's low in calories. Plus, a slice is a good option for anyone with diabetes.

- 1 **package (.8 ounce) sugar-free cook-and-serve vanilla pudding mix**
- 1 **package (.3 ounce) sugar-free lemon gelatin**
- 2-1/3 **cups water**
- 1/3 **cup lemon juice**
- 1 **reduced-fat graham cracker crust (8 inches)**
- 1-1/2 **cups reduced-fat whipped topping**

classic

- In a small saucepan, combine pudding mix and gelatin. Add water and lemon juice; stir until smooth. Cook and stir over medium heat until mixture comes to a boil. Cook and stir 1-2 minutes longer or until thickened.

- Remove from the heat; cool slightly. Pour into crust. Cover and refrigerate for 6 hours or overnight. Spread with whipped topping.

YIELD: 8 servings.

NUTRITION FACTS: 1 piece equals 146 calories, 5 g fat (3 g saturated fat), 0 cholesterol, 174 mg sodium, 22 g carbohydrate, trace fiber, 2 g protein. **DIABETIC EXCHANGES:** 1-1/2 starch, 1 fat.

frozen peach yogurt

Gaudrey_Georgia | TASTE OF HOME ONLINE COMMUNITY
With its fresh and sweet flavor, you'll be glad that
each bite of this cool and creamy treat delivers bone-
building benefits!

    4 **medium peaches, peeled and sliced**
    1 **envelope unflavored gelatin**
    1 **cup fat-free milk**
  1/2 **cup sugar**
Dash salt
 2-1/2 **cups vanilla yogurt**
    2 **teaspoons vanilla extract**

- Place peaches in a blender. Cover and process until
blended; set aside. In a small saucepan, sprinkle gelatin
over milk; let stand for 1 minute. Heat over low heat,
stirring until gelatin is completely dissolved. Remove
from the heat; stir in sugar and salt until sugar dissolves.
Add the yogurt, vanilla and reserved peaches.

FROZEN PEACH YOGURT

149 CALORIES

- Fill cylinder of ice cream freezer two-thirds full;
according to the manufacturer's directions. Whe
cream is frozen, transfer to a freezer container;
for 2-4 hours before serving.

YIELD: 6 cups.

NUTRITION FACTS: 3/4 cup equals 149 calories, 1 g fat (1 g saturated fat), 4 mg cholesterol, 83 mg sodium, 29 g carbohydrate,
1 g fiber, 6 g protein. **DIABETIC EXCHANGES:** 1 starch, 1/2 fruit,
1/2 reduced-fat milk.

120 CALORIES

macaroon kisses

Lee Roberts | RACINE, WISCONSIN
These irresistible cookies are sure to delight the
coconut and chocolate lover in everyone.

  1/3 **cup butter, softened**
    1 **package (3 ounces) cream cheese, softened**
  3/4 **cup sugar**
    1 **egg yolk**
    2 **teaspoons almond extract**
1-1/2 **cups all-purpose flour**
    2 **teaspoons baking powder**
  1/2 **teaspoon salt**
    5 **cups flaked coconut,** *divided*
  48 **milk chocolate kisses**
Coarse sugar

- In a large bowl, cream the butter, cream cheese and sugar
until light and fluffy. Beat in egg yolk and extract. Combine
the flour, baking powder and salt; gradually add to creamed
mixture and mix well. Stir in 3 cups coconut. Cover and
refrigerate for 1 hour or until dough is easy to handle.

- Roll into 1-in. balls and roll in the remaining coconut.
Place 2 in. apart on ungreased baking sheets.

- Bake at 350° for 10-12 minutes or until lightly browned.
Immediately press a chocolate kiss into the center of
each cookie; sprinkle with coarse sugar. Cool on pan for
2-3 minutes or until chocolate is softened. Remove to
wire racks to cool completely.

YIELD: 4 dozen.

NUTRITION FACTS: 1 cookie equals 120 calories, 7 g fat (5 g
saturated fat), 11 mg cholesterol, 85 mg sodium, 14 g carbohydrate, 1 g fiber, 1 g protein.

rocky road treat

Karen Grant | TULARE, CALIFORNIA

On a hot day, these sweet frozen pops are simple to prepare and guaranteed to bring out the kid in anyone. You won't be able to resist the chocolate and peanut topping!

> 1 package (3.4 ounces) cook-and-serve chocolate pudding mix
> 2-1/2 cups whole milk
> 1/2 cup chopped peanuts
> 1/2 cup miniature semisweet chocolate chips
> 12 disposable plastic cups (3 ounces *each*)
> 1/2 cup marshmallow creme
> 12 Popsicle sticks

- In a large microwave-safe bowl, combine pudding mix and milk. Microwave, uncovered, on high for 4-6 minutes or until bubbly and slightly thickened, stirring every 2 minutes. Cool for 20 minutes, stirring often.

- Meanwhile, combine the peanuts and chocolate chips; place about 2 tablespoons in each plastic cup. Stir marshmallow creme into pudding; spoon into cups. Insert Popsicle sticks; freeze.

YIELD: 12 servings.

EDITOR'S NOTE: This recipe was tested in a 1,100-watt microwave.

NUTRITION FACTS: 1 Popsicle equals 145 calories, 7 g fat (3 g saturated fat), 7 mg cholesterol, 89 mg sodium, 19 g carbohydrate, 1 g fiber, 4 g protein. **DIABETIC EXCHANGES:** 1 starch, 1 fat.

ROCKY ROAD TREAT

145 CALORIES

130 CALORIES

HEAVENLY SURPRISE MINI CUPCAKES

heavenly surprise mini cupcakes

Jorun Meierding | MANKATO, MINNESOTA

My grandmother was an accomplished baker, and this was one of the many special treats she liked to make. It's fun to bite into these dense chocolate cupcakes and discover a surprise inside.

classic

FILLING:

> 1 package (8 ounces) cream cheese, softened
> 1/3 cup sugar
> 1 egg
> 1/8 teaspoon salt
> 1 cup flaked coconut
> 1 cup finely chopped walnuts
> 1 cup (6 ounces) miniature semisweet chocolate chips

BATTER:

> 2 cups sugar
> 1-1/2 cups water
> 3/4 cup canola oil
> 2 eggs
> 2 teaspoons vanilla extract
> 1 teaspoon white vinegar
> 3 cups all-purpose flour
> 1/2 cup baking cocoa
> 1 teaspoon baking soda
> 1 teaspoon salt

FROSTING

1-1/3 cups semisweet chocolate chips

1/2 cup heavy whipping cream

- For filling, in a small bowl, beat cream cheese and sugar until light and fluffy. Add egg and salt; mix well. Stir in the coconut, walnuts and chocolate chips. Set aside.

- For batter, in a large bowl, beat the sugar, water, oil, eggs, vanilla and vinegar until well blended. Combine the flour, cocoa, baking soda and salt; gradually beat into oil mixture until blended.

- Fill paper-lined miniature muffin cups one-third full with batter. Drop filling by teaspoonfuls into each. Top with additional batter, filling muffin cups three-fourths full.

- Bake at 350° for 12-15 minutes or until a toothpick inserted in the cake portion of a cupcake comes out clean. Cool for 10 minutes before removing from pans to wire racks to cool completely.

- For frosting, in a small saucepan, melt chocolate chips with cream over low heat; stir until blended. Remove from the heat. Cool to room temperature. Frost cupcakes. Refrigerate leftovers.

YIELD: 6 dozen.

EDITOR'S NOTE: Cupcakes may also be baked in 30 paper-lined muffin cups for 20-25 minutes.

NUTRITION FACTS: 1 cupcake equals 130 calories, 7 g fat (3 g saturated fat), 15 mg cholesterol, 71 mg sodium, 15 g carbohydrate, 1 g fiber, 2 g protein. **DIABETIC EXCHANGES:** 1 starch, 1 fat.

tortilla dessert cups

Susan Miller | WAKEMAN, OHIO

These creamy bites taste so yummy, no one will ever guess they're low in anything!

3 tablespoons sugar

2 teaspoons ground cinnamon

10 flour tortillas (6 inches)

1 package (8 ounces) reduced-fat cream cheese

1 cup cold fat-free milk

1 package (1 ounce) sugar-free instant white chocolate *or* vanilla pudding mix

2 cups reduced-fat whipped topping

1/4 cup milk chocolate chips, melted

- In a small bowl, combine sugar and cinnamon. Coat one side of each tortilla with cooking spray; sprinkle with cinnamon-sugar. Turn tortillas over; repeat on the other side. Cut each tortilla into four wedges.

- For each dessert cup, place round edge of one tortilla wedge in the bottom of a muffin cup, shaping sides to fit cup. Place a second tortilla wedge in muffin cup, allowing bottom and sides to overlap. Bake at 350° for 10 minutes or until crisp and lightly browned. Cool completely in pan.

- Meanwhile, for filling, in a small bowl, beat cream cheese until smooth. In another bowl, whisk milk and pudding mix for 2 minutes. Let stand for 2 minutes or until soft-set. Beat in cream cheese on low until smooth. Fold in whipped topping. Cover and refrigerate for 1 hour.

- Carefully remove cups from pan. Pipe or spoon about 3 tablespoons filling into each cup. Drizzle or pipe with melted chocolate. Refrigerate for 5 minutes or until chocolate is set. Store in the refrigerator.

YIELD: 20 servings.

NUTRITION FACTS: 1 dessert cup equals 130 calories, 4 g fat (2 g saturated fat), 5 mg cholesterol, 178 mg sodium, 19 g carbohydrate, trace fiber, 4 g protein. **DIABETIC EXCHANGES:** 1 starch, 1 fat.

TORTILLA DESSERT CUPS

130 CALORIES

146 CALORIES

CHOCOLATE PEANUT BUTTER PARFAITS

chocolate peanut butter parfaits

Pat Soloman | CASPER, WYOMING

When a friend gave me this recipe I knew it was a keeper. It meets all my requirements; it's easy, low calorie, low fat and has a pretty presentation! You absolutely won't believe that this dessert is light.

- 2 tablespoons reduced-fat chunky peanut butter
- 2 tablespoons plus 2 cups cold fat-free milk, *divided*
- 1 cup plus 6 tablespoons reduced-fat whipped topping, *divided*
- 1 package (1.4 ounces) sugar-free instant chocolate fudge pudding mix
- 3 tablespoons finely chopped salted peanuts

- In a small bowl, combine peanut butter and 2 tablespoons milk. Fold in 1 cup whipped topping; set aside. In another small bowl, whisk remaining milk with the pudding mix for 2 minutes. Let stand for 2 minutes or until soft-set.

- Spoon half of the pudding into six parfait glasses or dessert dishes. Layer with reserved peanut butter mixture and remaining pudding. Refrigerate for at least 1 hour. Refrigerate remaining whipped topping.

- Just before serving, garnish each parfait with 1 tablespoon whipped topping and 1-1/2 teaspoons peanuts.

YIELD: 6 servings.

NUTRITION FACTS: 1 parfait equals 146 calories, 6 g fat (3 g saturated fat), 2 mg cholesterol, 300 mg sodium, 16 g carbohydrate, 1 g fiber, 6 g protein. **DIABETIC EXCHANGES:** 1 fat, 1/2 starch, 1/2 fat-free milk.

125 CALORIES

pumpkin chiffon dessert

Lynn Baker | OSMOND, NEBRASKA

This dessert is the perfect ending to a family dinner.

- 1 cup finely crushed gingersnaps (about 24)
- 3 tablespoons butter, melted
- 2 envelopes unflavored gelatin
- 1/2 cup fat-free milk
- 1/2 cup sugar
- 1 can (15 ounces) solid-pack pumpkin
- 1/2 teaspoon salt
- 1/2 teaspoon ground cinnamon
- 1/4 teaspoon ground ginger
- 1/4 teaspoon ground cloves
- 1 carton (8 ounces) frozen fat-free whipped topping, thawed

Additional whipped topping, optional

- In a small bowl, combine cookie crumbs and butter. Press onto the bottom of a greased 9-in. springform pan; set aside.

- In a large saucepan, combine gelatin and milk; let stand for 5 minutes. Heat milk mixture to just below boiling; remove from the heat. Stir in sugar until dissolved. Add the pumpkin, salt, cinnamon, ginger and cloves; mix well. Fold in whipped topping. Pour over crust. Refrigerate until set, about 3 hours.

- Remove sides of pan just before serving. Garnish with additional whipped topping if desired.

YIELD: 16 servings.

NUTRITION FACTS: 1 slice equals 125 calories, 3 g fat (2 g saturated fat), 6 mg cholesterol, 172 mg sodium, 22 g carbohydrate, 1 g fiber, 2 g protein. **DIABETIC EXCHANGES:** 1-1/2 starch, 1/2 fat.

chewy oatmeal raisin cookies

Trina Boitnott | BOONES MILL, VIRGINIA

Even picky preschoolers like my son devour these wholesome treats sprinkled with cinnamon and packed with raisins. Washed down with a glass of milk, the cookies are also great as an on-the-go breakfast.

- 1/3 **cup canola oil**
- 1/3 **cup packed brown sugar**
- 2 **tablespoons sugar**
- 3 **tablespoons water**
- 1 **egg white**
- 3/4 **teaspoon vanilla extract**
- 1/3 **cup all-purpose flour**
- 1/3 **cup whole wheat flour**
- 2 **teaspoons ground cinnamon**
- 1/2 **teaspoon baking soda**
- 1/4 **teaspoon salt**
- 2 **cups old-fashioned oats**
- 1/2 **cup raisins**

- In a large bowl, combine the oil, sugars, water, egg white and vanilla. Combine the flours, cinnamon, baking soda and salt; gradually add to sugar mixture and mix well. Stir in oats and raisins.

- Drop by scant 1/4 cupfuls onto baking sheets coated with cooking spray; flatten slightly with the back of a spoon. Bake

CHEWY OATMEAL RAISIN COOKIES

at 350° for 10-12 minutes or until golden brown. Cool for 1 minute before removing from pans to wire racks.

YIELD: 15 cookies.

NUTRITION FACTS: 1 cookie equals 144 calories, 6 g fat (1 g saturated fat), 0 cholesterol, 88 mg sodium, 22 g carbohydrate, 2 g fiber, 3 g protein. **DIABETIC EXCHANGES:** 1-1/2 starch, 1 fat.

old-fashioned molasses cake

148 CALORIES

Deanne Bagley | BATH, NEW YORK

This old-time spice cake is lower in fat but big on flavor. Serve it warm for breakfast on a frosty morning or have a square with hot cider on a snowy afternoon. It's a great cold-weather treat.

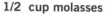

- 2 **tablespoons reduced-fat butter, softened**
- 1/4 **cup sugar**
- 1 **egg**
- 1/2 **cup molasses**
- 1 **cup all-purpose flour**
- 1 **teaspoon baking soda**
- 1/4 **teaspoon ground ginger**
- 1/4 **teaspoon ground cinnamon**
- 1/8 **teaspoon salt**
- 1/2 **cup hot water**
- 9 **tablespoons fat-free whipped topping**

- In a small bowl, beat butter and sugar until crumbly, about 2 minutes. Beat in egg and molasses. Combine the flour, baking soda, ginger, cinnamon and salt; add to butter mixture alternately with water and mix well.

- Transfer to a 9-in. square baking pan coated with cooking spray. Bake at 350° for 25-30 minutes or until a toothpick inserted near the center comes out clean. Cool on a wire rack. Cut cake into squares; garnish with whipped topping.

YIELD: 9 servings.

EDITOR'S NOTE: This recipe was tested with Land O'Lakes light stick butter.

NUTRITION FACTS: 1 piece with 1 tablespoon whipped topping equals 148 calories, 2 g fat (1 g saturated fat), 28 mg cholesterol, 205 mg sodium, 30 g carbohydrate, trace fiber, 2 g protein. **DIABETIC EXCHANGES:** 2 starch, 1/2 fat.

142 CALORIES

BERRIES IN A NEST

berries in a nest

Iola Egle | BELLA VISTA, ARKANSAS

This medley of fresh berries with sugar, pepper and balsamic vinegar makes a fun summer salad when served on lettuce. Or for an impressive dinner finale, serve this refreshing treat in phyllo cups.

- 4 **cups halved fresh strawberries**
- 1 **cup fresh blackberries**
- 1 **cup fresh raspberries**
- 1/3 **cup sugar**
- 3 **tablespoons balsamic vinegar**
- 1/4 to 1/2 **teaspoon coarsely ground pepper**

PHYLLO NESTS:

- 8 **sheets phyllo dough (14 inches x 9 inches)**

Cooking spray

- 2 **teaspoons sugar**
- 1/4 **teaspoon ground cinnamon**

- In a large bowl, combine the strawberries, blackberries and raspberries. Sprinkle with sugar; gently toss to coat. Let stand for 20 minutes. Pour vinegar over berries; sprinkle with pepper. Gently toss to coat. Cover and refrigerate for 2 hours.

- For phyllo nests, coat giant nonstick muffin cups with a cooking spray; set aside. Unroll phyllo dough sheets;

remove one sheet. (While assembling, keep remaining dough covered with plastic wrap and a damp cloth.)

- For each nest, cut one sheet in half lengthwise and cut in thirds widthwise. Stack three sections and place in a prepared cup; spray with cooking spray. Stack remaining three sections and place in cup, alternating points. Spray with cooking spray. Combine the sugar and cinnamon; sprinkle about 1/4 teaspoon cinnamon-sugar over dough. Repeat with remaining sheets of dough.

- Bake at 375° for 7-8 minutes or until golden brown. Cool for 5 minutes before carefully removing to a wire rack to cool completely.

- Using a slotted spoon, fill each nest with about 3/4 cup berry mixture. Drizzle with a small amount of juice. Serve immediately.

YIELD: 8 servings.

NUTRITION FACTS: One filled nest equals 142 calories, 1 g fat (0.55 g saturated fat), 0 cholesterol, 92 mg sodium, 33 g carbohydrate, 4 g fiber, 3 g protein. **DIABETIC EXCHANGES:** 1 fruit, 1 starch.

108 CALORIES

coconut macaroons

Penny Ann Habeck | SHAWANO, WISCONSIN

These cookies are my husband's favorite, so I always have to make a few batches if I plan to give any away as gifts.

- 1-1/3 **cups flaked coconut**
- 1/3 **cup sugar**
- 2 **tablespoons all-purpose flour**
- 1/8 **teaspoon salt**
- 2 **egg whites**
- 1/2 **teaspoon vanilla extract**

- In a small bowl, combine the coconut, sugar, flour and salt. Stir in egg whites and vanilla; mix well.

- Drop by rounded teaspoonfuls onto greased baking sheets. Bake at 325° for 18-20 minutes or until golden brown. Cool on a wire rack.

YIELD: about 1-1/2 dozen.

NUTRITION FACTS: 2 macaroons equals 108 calories, 5 g fat (4 g saturated fat), 0 cholesterol, 81 mg sodium, 15 g carbohydrate, 1 g fiber, 1 g protein. **DIABETIC EXCHANGES:** 1 starch, 1 fat.

cinnamon peach enchiladas

Irene Glembotskaya | BROOKLYN, NEW YORK

These sweet enchiladas are a pleasant change from traditional peach pie and are a whole lot easier. Simply fill warmed tortillas with the cinnamon-peach mixture, and wait for the compliments!

> 4 cups sliced peeled fresh peaches
>
> 1/3 cup sugar
>
> 1 teaspoon ground cinnamon
>
> 4 flour tortillas (8 inches)
>
> **Butter-flavored cooking spray**

- In a large bowl, combine the peaches, sugar and cinnamon; let stand for 5 minutes. Spritz tortillas with butter-flavored spray.

- In a nonstick skillet, cook tortillas over medium heat until warmed and lightly browned on both sides. Fill each with about 3/4 cup peaches and roll up. Cut in half to serve.

YIELD: 8 servings.

NUTRITION FACTS: 1/2 enchilada equals 143 calories, 2 g fat (trace saturated fat), 0 cholesterol, 125 mg sodium, 31 g carbohydrate, 2 g fiber, 3 g protein. **DIABETIC EXCHANGES:** 1-1/2 starch, 1/2 fruit.

CINNAMON PEACH ENCHILADAS

143 CALORIES

BUTTERSCOTCH BLISS LAYERED DESSERT

136 CALORIES

butterscotch bliss layered dessert

Janice Vernon | LAS CRUCES, NEW MEXICO

Four easy layers come together for a fantastic treat that's perfect for cooling down summer nights. Take this to a gathering, and we bet you'll bring home an empty dish!

> 1-1/2 cups graham cracker crumbs
>
> **Sugar substitute equivalent to 1/2 cup sugar,** *divided*
>
> 6 tablespoons butter, melted
>
> 2 packages (8 ounces *each*) reduced-fat cream cheese
>
> 3 cups cold fat-free milk, *divided*
>
> 2 packages (1 ounce *each*) sugar-free instant butterscotch pudding mix
>
> 1 carton (8 ounces) frozen reduced-fat whipped topping, thawed
>
> 1/2 teaspoon rum extract

- In a small bowl, combine the cracker crumbs, 1/4 cup sugar substitute and butter. Press into a 13-in. x 9-in. dish coated with cooking spray.

- In a small bowl, beat the cream cheese, 1/4 cup milk and remaining sugar substitute until smooth. Spread over crust.

- In another bowl, whisk remaining milk with the pudding mix for 2 minutes. Let stand for 2 minutes or until soft-set. Gently spread over cream cheese layer. Combine whipped topping and extract; spread over the top. Refrigerate for at least 4 hours.

YIELD: 24 servings.

EDITOR'S NOTE: This recipe was tested with Splenda no-calorie sweetener.

NUTRITION FACTS: 1 piece equals 136 calories, 8 g fat (6 g saturated fat), 21 mg cholesterol, 245 mg sodium, 12 g carbohydrate, trace fiber, 3 g protein. **DIABETIC EXCHANGES:** 1 starch, 1 fat.

desserts | 151-250 CALORIES

bananas foster sundaes

Lisa Varner | CHARLESTON, SOUTH CAROLINA

I have wonderful memories of eating Bananas Foster in New Orleans, and as a dietitian, wanted to find a healthier version. I combined the best of two recipes and added my own tweaks to create this Southern treat.

classic

- 1 **tablespoon butter**
- 3 **tablespoons brown sugar**
- 1 **tablespoon orange juice**
- 1/4 **teaspoon ground cinnamon**
- 1/4 **teaspoon ground nutmeg**
- 3 **large firm bananas, sliced**
- 2 **tablespoons chopped pecans, toasted**
- 1/2 **teaspoon rum extract**
- 3 **cups reduced-fat vanilla ice cream**

- In a large nonstick skillet, melt butter over medium-low heat. Stir in the brown sugar, orange juice, cinnamon and nutmeg until blended. Add bananas and pecans;

BANANAS FOSTER SUNDAES

233 CALORIES

cook, stirring gently, for 2-3 minutes or until bananas are glazed and slightly softened. Remove from the heat; stir in extract. Serve with ice cream.

YIELD: 6 servings.

NUTRITION FACTS: 1/3 cup banana mixture with 1/2 cup ice cream equals 233 calories, 7 g fat (3 g saturated fat), 23 mg cholesterol, 66 mg sodium, 40 g carbohydrate, 2 g fiber, 4 g protein

187 CALORIES

CARAMEL APPLE BREAD PUDDING

caramel apple bread pudding

Michelle Borland | PEORIA, ILLINOIS

Tender, sweet pudding with delicious apple pieces, spices and a luscious low-fat caramel topping make this a rich tasting comfort dish without all the fat. Yum!

- 1 **cup unsweetened applesauce**
- 1 **cup fat-free milk**
- 1/2 **cup packed brown sugar**
- 1/2 **cup egg substitute**
- 1 **teaspoon vanilla extract**
- 1/2 **teaspoon ground cinnamon**
- 5 **cups cubed day-old bread**
- 1/2 **cup chopped peeled apple**
- 1/2 **cup fat-free whipped topping**
- 1/2 **cup fat-free caramel ice cream topping**

- In a large bowl, combine the applesauce, milk, brown sugar, egg substitute, vanilla and cinnamon. Fold in bread cubes and apple.

- Pour into an 8-in. square baking dish coated with cooking spray. Bake, uncovered, at 325° for 35-40 minutes or until a knife inserted near the center comes out clean. Serve warm with whipped topping and caramel topping. Refrigerate leftovers.

YIELD: 8 servings.

NUTRITION FACTS: 1 serving equals 187 calories, 1 g fat (trace saturated fat), 1 mg cholesterol, 201 mg sodium, 40 g carbohydrate, 1 g fiber, 4 g protein.

lemon angel cake roll

Tart and luscious, this pretty cake roll from our Test Kitchen will tickle any lemon lover's fancy. Its feathery, angel food texture enhances the guilt-free goodness. It's impressive enough for spring holidays.

> 9 egg whites
> 1-1/2 teaspoons vanilla extract
> 3/4 teaspoon cream of tartar
> 1 cup plus 2 tablespoons sugar
> 3/4 cup cake flour
> 1 tablespoon confectioners' sugar

FILLING:

> 1 cup sugar
> 3 tablespoons cornstarch
> 1 cup water
> 1 egg, lightly beaten
> 1/4 cup lemon juice
> 1 tablespoon grated lemon peel

Yellow food coloring, optional

Additional confectioners' sugar

- Place the egg whites in a large bowl; let stand at room temperature for 30 minutes. Meanwhile, line a 15-in. x 10-in. x 1-in. baking pan with waxed paper; lightly coat paper with cooking spray and set aside.

- Add vanilla and cream of tartar to egg whites; beat on medium speed until soft peaks form. Gradually beat in sugar, 2 tablespoons at a time, on high until stiff glossy peaks form and sugar is dissolved. Fold in flour, about 1/4 cup at a time.

- Carefully spread batter into prepared pan. Bake at 350° for 15-20 minutes or until cake springs back when lightly touched. Cool for 5 minutes.

- Turn cake onto a kitchen towel dusted with 1 tablespoon confectioners' sugar. Gently peel off waxed paper. Roll up cake in the towel jelly-roll style, starting with a short side. Cool completely on a wire rack.

- In a large saucepan, combine sugar and cornstarch; stir in water until smooth. Cook and stir over medium-high heat until thickened and bubbly. Reduce heat; cook and stir 2 minutes longer. Remove from the heat. Stir a small amount of hot mixture into egg; return all to the pan, stirring constantly. Bring to a gentle boil; cook and stir 2 minutes longer.

- Remove from the heat. Gently stir in lemon juice, peel and food coloring if desired. Cool to room temperature without stirring.

- Unroll cake; spread filling to within 1/2 in. of edges. Roll up again. Place seam side down on a serving plate; sprinkle with additional confectioners' sugar.

YIELD: 10 servings.

NUTRITION FACTS: 1 slice equals 243 calories, 1 g fat (trace saturated fat), 21 mg cholesterol, 57 mg sodium, 55 g carbohydrate, trace fiber, 5 g protein.

LEMON ANGEL CAKE ROLL

243 CALORIES

233 CALORIES

HOT BERRIES 'N' BROWNIE ICE CREAM CAKE

hot berries 'n' brownie ice cream cake

Allene Bary-Cooper | WICHITA FALLS, TEXAS

This decadent dessert is a taste of Heaven. The hot mixed berry topping seeps through the brownie layer into the cool vanilla ice cream for a zippy chilled cake.

- 1 **package fudge brownie mix (13-inch x 9-inch pan size)**
- 1/4 **cup water**
- 1/4 **cup unsweetened applesauce**
- 1/4 **cup canola oil**
- 2 **eggs**
- 1 **carton (1-3/4 quarts) reduced-fat no-sugar-added vanilla ice cream, softened**

BERRY SAUCE:

- 2 **tablespoons butter**
- 1/3 **cup sugar**
- 1/4 **cup honey**
- 2 **tablespoons lime juice**
- 1 **tablespoon balsamic vinegar**
- 1 **teaspoon ground cinnamon**
- 1/4 **to 1/2 teaspoon cayenne pepper**
- 1 **quart fresh strawberries, hulled and sliced**
- 2 **cups fresh blueberries**
- 2 **cups fresh raspberries**

- Prepare brownie mix using water, applesauce, oil and eggs. Bake according to the package directions; cool completely on a wire rack.

- Crumble brownies into 1-in. pieces; sprinkle half into a 13-in. x 9-in. dish coated with cooking spray. Spread evenly with ice cream. Press remaining brownie pieces into ice cream. Cover and freeze for 1 hour or until firm.

- Remove from the freezer 5 minutes before serving. For sauce, in a large skillet, melt butter over medium heat. Stir in the sugar, honey, lime juice, vinegar, cinnamon and cayenne. Add berries; cook for 3-5 minutes or until heated through, stirring occasionally. Cut cake into squares; top with hot berry sauce.

YIELD: 24 servings.

NUTRITION FACTS: 1 piece with 3 tablespoons berry sauce equals 233 calories, 9 g fat (3 g saturated fat), 27 mg cholesterol, 140 mg sodium, 36 g carbohydrate, 2 g fiber, 4 g protein. **DIABETIC EXCHANGES:** 2 starch, 1-1/2 fat, 1/2 fruit.

163 CALORIES # fresh raspberry pie

Patricia Staudt | MARBLE ROCK, IOWA

This flavorful and bright raspberry pie is the perfect ending to a heavy meal.

- 1/4 **cup sugar**
- 1 **tablespoon cornstarch**
- 1 **cup water**
- 1 **package (.3 ounce) sugar-free raspberry gelatin**
- 4 **cups fresh raspberries**
- 1 **reduced-fat graham cracker crust (8 inches)**

Reduced-fat whipped topping, optional

- In a small saucepan, combine the sugar, cornstarch and water until smooth. Bring to a boil, stirring constantly. Cook and stir for 2 minutes or until thickened. Remove from the heat; stir in gelatin until dissolved. Cool for 15 minutes.

- Place raspberries in the crust; slowly pour gelatin mixture over berries. Chill until set, about 3 hours. Garnish with whipped topping if desired.

YIELD: 8 servings.

NUTRITION FACTS: 1 piece equals 163 calories, 3 g fat (1 g saturated fat), 0 cholesterol, 124 mg sodium, 30 g carbohydrate, 4 g fiber, 2 g protein. **DIABETIC EXCHANGES:** 1-1/2 starch, 1/2 fruit.

makeover toffee crunch dessert

Kim Belcher | KINGSTON MINES, ILLINOIS

This is one of my favorite desserts. The original recipe had too much fat and too many calories, so I trimmed it down by using fat-free and sugar-free ingredients. Guests will never suspect this fluffy, layered treat is on the lighter side.

1-1/2 cups cold fat-free milk

   1 package (1 ounce) sugar-free instant vanilla pudding mix

   2 cartons (8 ounces *each*) frozen fat-free whipped topping, thawed

   1 prepared angel food cake (8 to 10 ounces), cut into 1-inch cubes

   4 Butterfinger candy bars (2.1 ounces *each*), crushed

- In a large bowl, whisk milk and pudding mix for 2 minutes. Let stand for 2 minutes or until soft-set. Stir in 2 cups whipped topping. Fold in the remaining whipped topping.

- In a 13-in. x 9-in. dish coated with cooking spray, layer half of the cake cubes, pudding mixture and crushed candy bars. Repeat layers. Cover and refrigerate for at least 2 hours before serving.

YIELD: 15 servings.

NUTRITION FACTS: 3/4 cup equals 177 calories, 3 g fat (2 g saturated fat), trace cholesterol, 255 mg sodium, 33 g carbohydrate, 1 g fiber, 3 g protein. **DIABETIC EXCHANGES:** 2 starch, 1/2 fat.

MAKEOVER TOFFEE CRUNCH DESSERT

177 CALORIES

175 CALORIES

TROPICAL AMBROSIA

tropical ambrosia

Marie Dietz | NORTH TROY, VERMONT

This invigorating dessert combines citrus fruit, coconut, dates and nuts for a real taste of the tropics. If you like, you can skip the sugar and add a little pineapple juice.

1/2 cup chopped pink grapefruit sections (about 1/2 medium grapefruit)

1/2 cup chopped orange segments

   1 snack-size cup (4 ounces) pineapple tidbits, drained

   2 tablespoons chopped walnuts

   2 tablespoons chopped dates

   2 tablespoons flaked coconut

1/2 teaspoon sugar, optional

classic

- In two small serving dishes, layer the first six ingredients in the order listed; sprinkle with sugar if desired. Let stand for 5-10 minutes before serving.

YIELD: 2 servings.

NUTRITION FACTS: 1 cup (calculated without sugar) equals 175 calories, 7 g fat (2 g saturated fat), 0 cholesterol, 20 mg sodium, 28 g carbohydrate, 4 g fiber, 4 g protein.

MERINGUES WITH FRESH BERRIES

meringues with fresh berries

Agnes Ward | STRATFORD, ONTARIO

Juicy ripe berries and a dollop of light cream fill these cloud-like meringue desserts. When I double this recipe to serve friends, they always rave about it.

- 2 egg whites
- 1/8 teaspoon cream of tartar

Dash salt

- 1/4 cup sugar
- 1/4 teaspoon vanilla extract
- 1 cup mixed fresh berries
- 1/2 teaspoon sugar, optional
- 1/3 cup sour cream
- 1/8 to 1/4 teaspoon rum extract

- Place egg whites in a small bowl; let stand at room temperature for 30 minutes. Add cream of tartar and salt; beat on medium speed until soft peaks form. Gradually beat in sugar, 1 tablespoon at a time, on high until stiff peaks form. Beat in vanilla.

- Drop meringue into two mounds on a parchment paper-lined baking sheet. Shape into 3-1/2-in. cups with the back of a spoon.

- Bake at 225° for 1 to 1-1/4 hours or until set and dry. Turn oven off; leave meringues in oven for 1 hour. Remove to wire racks to cool.

- In a small bowl, combine berries and sugar if desired; let stand for 5 minutes. Combine sour cream and extract; spoon into meringue shells. Top with berries.

YIELD: 2 servings.

NUTRITION FACTS: 1 serving (calculated without optional sugar) equals 222 calories, 7 g fat (5 g saturated fat), 27 mg cholesterol, 149 mg sodium, 33 g carbohydrate, 2 g fiber, 5 g protein. **DIABETIC EXCHANGES:** 2 starch, 1-1/2 fat, 1/2 fruit.

168 CALORIES — yummy s'more snack cake

Deborah Williams | PEORIA, ARIZONA

This cake tastes just like s'mores by the campfire!

- 2-1/2 cups reduced-fat graham cracker crumbs (about 15 whole crackers)
- 1/2 cup sugar
- 1/3 cup cake flour
- 1/3 cup whole wheat flour
- 2 teaspoons baking powder
- 1/4 teaspoon salt
- 3 egg whites
- 1 cup light soy milk
- 1/4 cup unsweetened applesauce
- 1/4 cup canola oil
- 2 cups miniature marshmallows
- 1 cup (6 ounces) semisweet chocolate chips

- In a large bowl, combine the first six ingredients. In a small bowl, whisk the egg whites, soy milk, applesauce and oil. Stir into dry ingredients just until moistened. Transfer to a 13-in. x 9-in. baking pan coated with cooking spray.

- Bake at 350° for 12-15 minutes or until a toothpick inserted near the center comes out clean. Sprinkle with marshmallows. Bake 4-6 minutes longer or until marshmallows are softened. Cool on a wire rack for 10 minutes.

- In a microwave, melt chocolate chips; stir until smooth. Drizzle over cake. Cool completely on a wire rack.

YIELD: 20 servings.

NUTRITION FACTS: 1 piece equals 168 calories, 6 g fat (2 g saturated fat), 0 cholesterol, 159 mg sodium, 28 g carbohydrate, 2 g fiber, 3 g protein. **DIABETIC EXCHANGES:** 2 starch, 1 fat.

ice cream sandwich dessert

Cathie Valentine | GRANITEVILLE, SOUTH CAROLINA

This chocolaty treat is perfect for summer days, and so easy to make! With store-bought ice cream sandwiches, you can whip it up in no time.

- 17 miniature ice cream sandwiches, *divided*
- 1 jar (12 ounces) caramel ice cream topping
- 1 carton (12 ounces) frozen reduced-fat whipped topping, thawed
- 1/4 cup chocolate syrup
- 2 Symphony candy bars with almonds and toffee (4-1/4 ounces *each*), chopped

- Arrange 14 ice cream sandwiches in an ungreased 13-in. x 9-in. dish. Cut remaining sandwiches in half lengthwise; fill in the spaces in the dish. Spread with caramel and whipped toppings. Drizzle with chocolate syrup. Sprinkle with chopped candy bar. Cover and freeze for at least 45 minutes. Cut into squares.

YIELD: 15-18 servings.

NUTRITION FACTS: 1 piece equals 244 calories, 10 g fat (6 g saturated fat), 13 mg cholesterol, 105 mg sodium, 39 g carbohydrate, 1 g fiber, 3 g protein.

ICE CREAM SANDWICH DESSERT

244 CALORIES

caramel cream crepes

209 CALORIES

Created by our Test Kitchen experts, these lovely, homemade crepes are a cinch to prepare. The creamy caramel filling is irresistible, and the end results are oh-so impressive.

- 2 tablespoons fat-free milk
- 2 tablespoons egg substitute
- 1/2 teaspoon butter, melted
- 1/4 teaspoon vanilla extract
- 2 tablespoons all-purpose flour
- 2 ounces fat-free cream cheese
- 1 tablespoon plus 2 teaspoons fat-free caramel ice cream topping, *divided*
- 3/4 cup reduced-fat whipped topping
- 1/2 cup fresh raspberries
- 2 tablespoons white wine *or* unsweetened apple juice
- 1 tablespoon sliced almonds, toasted

- In a small bowl, whisk the milk, egg substitute, butter and vanilla. Whisk in flour until blended. Cover and refrigerate for 1 hour.

- Lightly coat a 6-in. nonstick skillet with cooking spray; heat over medium heat. Pour about 2 tablespoons of batter into center of skillet; lift and tilt pan to evenly coat bottom. Cook until top appears dry and bottom is golden; turn and cook 15-20 seconds longer. Remove to a wire rack. Repeat with remaining batter.

- In a small bowl, beat cream cheese and 1 tablespoon caramel topping until smooth. Fold in whipped topping. Spoon down the center of each crepe. Drizzle with remaining caramel topping; roll up.

- In a small microwave-safe bowl, combine raspberries and wine. Microwave on high for 30-60 seconds or until warm. Using a slotted spoon, place berries over crepes. Sprinkle with almonds.

YIELD: 2 servings.

NUTRITION FACTS: 1 crepe equals 209 calories, 6 g fat (4 g saturated fat), 5 mg cholesterol, 223 mg sodium, 29 g carbohydrate, 3 g fiber, 8 g protein. **DIABETIC EXCHANGES:** 2 starch, 1 fat.

plum dumplings

Martha Voss | DICKINSON, NORTH DAKOTA

Special meals call for elegant desserts, but they don't have to be full of calories. My sweet black plums are halved then tucked inside a pretty pastry pocket.

1-1/2 cups all-purpose flour
  1/4 cup sugar
     1 teaspoon baking powder
  1/8 teaspoon salt
     6 tablespoons 2% milk
     1 egg, lightly beaten
     3 medium black plums, halved and pitted
     1 cup water
     3 tablespoons butter

Melted butter and cinnamon-sugar

- In a large bowl, combine the flour, sugar, baking powder and salt. Stir in milk and egg just until blended. Divide into six portions.

- On a lightly floured surface, pat each portion of dough into a 5-in. circle. Place a plum half on each circle. Gently bring up corners of dough to center; pinch edges to seal.

- In a Dutch oven, bring water and butter to a boil. Carefully add dumplings. Reduce heat; cover and simmer

PLUM DUMPLINGS

for 20-25 minutes or until a toothpick inserted into a dumpling comes out clean. Serve warm with pan juices, melted butter and cinnamon-sugar.

YIELD: 6 servings.

NUTRITION FACTS: 1 dumpling (calculated without melted butter and cinnamon-sugar) equals 235 calories, 8 g fat (4 g saturated fat), 52 mg cholesterol, 175 mg sodium, 37 g carbohydrate, 1 g fiber, 5 g protein.

SLOW COOKER BERRY COBBLER

slow cooker berry cobbler

Karen Jarocki | YUMA, ARIZONA

I adapted my mom's yummy cobbler recipe for slow cooking. With the hot summers here in Arizona, we can still enjoy this comforting treat without turning on the oven!

1-1/4 cups all-purpose flour, *divided*
     2 tablespoons plus 1 cup sugar, *divided*
     1 teaspoon baking powder
  1/4 teaspoon ground cinnamon
     1 egg, lightly beaten
  1/4 cup fat-free milk
     2 tablespoons canola oil

- In a large bowl, combine 1 cup flour, 2 tablespoons sugar, baking powder and cinnamon. In a small bowl, combine the egg, milk and oil; stir into dry ingredients just until moistened (batter will be thick). Spread batter evenly onto the bottom of a 5-qt. slow cooker coated with cooking spray.

- In a large bowl, combine the salt and remaining flour and sugar; add berries and toss to coat. Spread over batter.

- Cover and cook on high for 2 to 2-1/2 hours or until a toothpick inserted into the cobbler comes out without crumbs. Top individual servings with 1/4 cup frozen yogurt if desired.

YIELD: 8 servings.

NUTRITION FACTS: 1 piece (calculated without frozen yogurt) equals 250 calories, 4 g fat (trace saturated fat), 27 mg cholesterol, 142 mg sodium, 51 g carbohydrate, 4 g fiber, 3 g protein.

caramel apple pizza

Tari Ambler | SHOREWOOD, ILLINOIS

I made a favorite recipe lighter by making my own cookie crust. I used less fat and sugar, and part whole wheat pastry flour. I also used a combination of fat-free and low-fat cream cheese as well as fat-free caramel sauce. My family doesn't notice the difference.

- 1/4 cup butter, softened
- 1/4 cup sugar
- 1/4 cup packed brown sugar
- 1 egg
- 2 tablespoons canola oil
- 1 tablespoon light corn syrup
- 1 teaspoon vanilla extract
- 1 cup whole wheat pastry flour
- 3/4 cup all-purpose flour
- 1/2 teaspoon baking powder
- 1/4 teaspoon salt
- 1/4 teaspoon ground cinnamon

TOPPING:
- 1 package (8 ounces) fat-free cream cheese
- 1/4 cup packed brown sugar
- 1/2 teaspoon ground cinnamon
- 1/2 teaspoon vanilla extract
- 3 medium Granny Smith apples, thinly sliced
- 1/4 cup fat-free caramel ice cream topping
- 1/4 cup chopped unsalted dry roasted peanuts

- In a large bowl, cream butter and sugars until light and fluffy. Beat in the egg, oil, corn syrup and vanilla. Combine the flours, baking powder, salt and cinnamon; gradually add to creamed mixture and mix well.

- Press dough onto a 14-in. pizza pan coated with cooking spray. Bake at 350° for 12-15 minutes or until lightly browned. Cool on a wire rack.

- In a small bowl, beat the cream cheese, brown sugar, cinnamon and vanilla until smooth. Spread over crust. Arrange apples over the top. Drizzle with caramel topping; sprinkle with peanuts. Serve immediately.

YIELD: 12 slices.

NUTRITION FACTS: 1 slice equals 238 calories, 9 g fat (3 g saturated fat), 29 mg cholesterol, 228 mg sodium, 36 g carbohydrate, 2 g fiber, 6 g protein.

CARAMEL APPLE PIZZA

238 CALORIES

do-it-yourself
MEAL PLANNING
worksheet

date: _____

planned breakfast

_____ _____
_____ _____
_____ _____
_____ _____

PLANNED BREAKFAST TOTAL CALORIES: _____

actual breakfast

_____ _____
_____ _____
_____ _____
_____ _____

ACTUAL BREAKFAST TOTAL CALORIES: _____

planned lunch

_____ _____
_____ _____
_____ _____
_____ _____

PLANNED LUNCH TOTAL CALORIES: _____

actual lunch

_____ _____
_____ _____
_____ _____
_____ _____

ACTUAL LUNCH TOTAL CALORIES: _____

planned dinner

_____ _____
_____ _____
_____ _____
_____ _____

PLANNED DINNER TOTAL CALORIES: _____

actual dinner

_____ _____
_____ _____
_____ _____
_____ _____

ACTUAL DINNER TOTAL CALORIES: _____

planned snacks

_____ _____
_____ _____

PLANNED SNACKS TOTAL CALORIES: _____

actual snacks

_____ _____
_____ _____

ACTUAL SNACKS TOTAL CALORIES: _____

PLANNED TOTAL CALORIES: _____

ACTUAL TOTAL CALORIES: _____

more on the WEB

Log on to www.ComfortFoodDietCookbook.com for additional meal planning worksheets you can print for yourself. Remember to use the code MyDiet.

do-it-yourself
MEAL PLANNING
worksheet

date: _____

FOOD	CALORIES	FOOD	CALORIES
planned breakfast		**actual breakfast**	
_____	_____	_____	_____
_____	_____	_____	_____
_____	_____	_____	_____
_____	_____	_____	_____
PLANNED BREAKFAST TOTAL CALORIES:	_____	**ACTUAL BREAKFAST TOTAL CALORIES:**	_____
planned lunch		**actual lunch**	
_____	_____	_____	_____
_____	_____	_____	_____
_____	_____	_____	_____
_____	_____	_____	_____
PLANNED LUNCH TOTAL CALORIES:	_____	**ACTUAL LUNCH TOTAL CALORIES:**	_____
planned dinner		**actual dinner**	
_____	_____	_____	_____
_____	_____	_____	_____
_____	_____	_____	_____
_____	_____	_____	_____
PLANNED DINNER TOTAL CALORIES:	_____	**ACTUAL DINNER TOTAL CALORIES:**	_____
planned snacks		**actual snacks**	
_____	_____	_____	_____
_____	_____	_____	_____
PLANNED SNACKS TOTAL CALORIES:	_____	**ACTUAL SNACKS TOTAL CALORIES:**	_____
PLANNED TOTAL CALORIES:	_____	**ACTUAL TOTAL CALORIES:**	_____

exercise _____

_____

index by food category

To help you find the perfect dish for your family, we've created three different indexes.

The first is divided into food and meal categories as well as major ingredients. Use this index when you're looking for recipes that call for a specific item or when you want to find an ideal appetizer.

You'll also notice that major categories are broken down a bit. If you look up "Chicken" for instance, you'll notice that there are sub-categories for dinner options, lunch dishes and even breakfast items that call for chicken.

Best of all, every entry in every index offers the calorie count per serving of that item. Planning a healthy meal for your family has never been easier!

index | THE COMFORT FOOD DIET

index | THE COMFORT FOOD DIET

alphabetical index

With the *Comfort Food Diet Cookbook*, serving your family heart-smart meals is a breeze. This index (organized by recipe title) also offers the per-serving calorie count of every dish.

If you have a hard time remembering the names of all of those family favorites you've prepared from this book, simply begin to highlight those dishes that get thumbs-up approval from your gang. You could also set a blank sticky note on the back of this book and write down the titles of the recipes your family enjoys most.

ndex by calories

he Taste of Home Comfort Food Diet elies on the calories you consume ach day. To better help you plan our caloric intake and daily menus, his index categorizes recipes by type snacks, breakfast, dinner, etc.). The ems are then broken down into their pplicable calorie ranges.

Vhen looking for a dinner that's on he lighter side, see the 48 dishes sted under "Dinners: 250 Calories r Less." If you saved a few more alories for the end of the day, onsider the recipes found under Dinners: 251 to 350 Calories." here you'll find 71 recipes.

Vith a little help from this index, ou'll be amazed at how easy it is to eep within your goals and make the aste of Home Comfort Food Diet a ealthy…and delicious…part of our life.

DESSERTS

STOCK IMAGE CREDITS

tomato & mozzarella, page 8
barbaradudzinska/Shutterstock.com

couple preparing food, page 8
Yuri Arcurs/Shutterstock.com

bowl of fruit, page 9
picamaniac/Shutterstock.com

food diary, page 10
Graça Victoria/Shutterstock.com

watermelon, page 10
svariophoto/Shutterstock.com

kiwi, page 11
AntiGerasim/Shutterstock.com

salad, page 13
picamaniac/Shutterstock.com

apples on scale, page 14
Picsfive/Shutterstock.com

pasta piles, page 15
Olga Miltsova/Shutterstock.com

salt on spoon, page 15
maymak/Shutterstock.com

brown eggs, page 15
picamaniac/Shutterstock.com

pumpkin seeds, page 16
Susan Fox/Shutterstock.com

cheese triangles, page 16
Shesternina Polina/Shutterstock.com

steak, page 16
Paul Binet/Shutterstock.com

woman shopping for veggies, page 17
Yuri Arcurs/Shutterstock.com

sugar cubes, page 17
drfelice/Shutterstock.com

nutrition facts, page 19
XAOC/Shutterstock.com

shopping cart, page 20
Baevskiy Dmitry/Shutterstock.com

sweet cherries, page 21
Dallas Events Inc/Shutterstock.com

potatoes, page 21
Robert Stone/Shutterstock.com

grilled chicken, page 21
marco mayer/Shutterstock.com

stacked hamburger buns, page 22
Steve Cukrov/Shutterstock.com

glass of milk, page 22
Torsten Schon/Shutterstock.com

woman shopping, page 22
Monkey Business Images/Shutterstock.com

refrigerator, page 23
matka_Wariatka/Shutterstock.com

grocery list, page 23
blueking/Shutterstock.com

woman shopping for corn, page 24
Yuri Arcurs/Shutterstock.com

blueberries on a spoon, page 26
Pinkcandy/Shutterstock.com

bowl of broccoli, page 26
spfotocz/Shutterstock.com

walnuts, page 26
VASilyeV A.S./Shutterstock.com

bowl of cherry tomatoes, page 26
Olga Miltsova/Shutterstock.com

peppers, page 26
barbaradudzinska/Shutterstock.com

bowl of dry oatmeal, page 26
Nika Novak/Shutterstock.com

family preparring dinner, page 28
Monkey Business Images/Shutterstock.com

marinated chicken, page 28
a9photo/Shutterstock.com

bowl of rice, page 28
Noam Armonn/Shutterstock.com

tablespoons of sugar, page 29
Ambient Ideas/Shutterstock.com

cupcakes baking, page 29
Christopher Elwell/Shutterstock.com

mom and daugther baking, page 29
Sean Prior/Shutterstock.com

whisk, page 29
Kelly MacDonald/Shutterstock.com

chopping veggies, page 31
auremar/Shutterstock.com

salmon dinner, page 32
Paul Binet/Shutterstock.com

pretzels, page 32
LampLighterSDV/Shutterstock.com

topped crackers, page 33
Svetlana Lukienko/Shutterstock.com

popcorn, page 33
Stephen Mcsweeny/Shutterstock.com

hot dog, page 34
David P. Smith/Shutterstock.com

bran muffins, page 34
Branislav Senic/Shutterstock.com

family eating together, page 35
Monkey Business Images/Shutterstock.com

family walking, page 36
Losevsky Pavel/Shutterstock.com

women walking a dog, page 37
Brian Goodman/Shutterstock.com

two hikers, page 38
Jerry Horbert/Shutterstock.com

plate of veggies, page 41
picamaniac/Shutterstock.com

bunch of asparagus, page 42
AntiGerasim/Shutterstock.com

veggie platters, page 42
Konovalikov Andrey/Shutterstock.com

mom and daughter cooking, page 42
Sean Prior/Shutterstock.com

sliced and stacked fruit, page 43
Sven Hoppe/Shutterstock.com